THE IMM

ATATURK

THE IMMORTAL ATATÜRK

A Psychobiography

Man, as an individual, is condemned to death. To work, not for oneself but for those who will come after, is the first condition of happiness that any individual can reach in life. Each person has his own preferences. Some people like gardening and growing flowers. Others prefer to train men. Does the man who grows flowers expect anything from them? He who trains men ought to work like the man who grows flowers.

Atatürk
17 March 1937

VAMIK D. VOLKAN
and
NORMAN ITZKOWITZ

THE UNIVERSITY OF CHICAGO PRESS
Chicago and London

The University of Chicago Press, Chicago 60637
The University of Chicago Press, Ltd., London

Paperback edition 1986
Printed in the United States of America
95 94 93 92 91 90 6 5 4 3

Library of Congress Cataloging in Publication Data

Volkan, Vamık
The immortal Atatürk.

Bibliography: p.
Includes index.
1. Atatürk, Kemal, 1881–1938—Personality.
2. Presidents—Turkey—Biography. I. Itzkowitz, Norman.
II. Title.
DR592.K4V65 1984 956.1′024′0924 [B] 84-149
ISBN 0-226-86388-3 (cloth)
ISBN 0-226-86389-1 (paper)

For
Betty and Kevin, Susan, Alev, and Kurt;
Leonore and Jay and Karen;
Harry Starr;
and
Virginia Kennan

Contents

Illustrations

Acknowledgments

WE WISH TO THANK ALL THOSE PEOPLE WHO TALKED TO US ABOUT ATATÜRK, although some of them, for their own reasons, prefer to remain anonymous.

The late Edith Weigert, M.D., of Bethesda, Maryland, the first psychoanalyst to practice in Turkey, supplied many details about life in Ankara during the early days of Kemalist Turkey and about the association between her late husband, Professor Oscar Weigert, and Atatürk.

Another well-known woman psychiatrist, Ruth W. Lidz, M.D., of Yale University, kindly shared with us sections of her private memoirs of life in Turkey. Professor Wolfram Eberhard, of the University of California at Berkeley, allowed us to read some of the diary he kept while in Turkey, including his description of the reactions and feelings of the people on the day Atatürk died.

Dr. Volkan spent the 1974/75 academic year in Turkey supported by the University of Virginia and the University of Ankara with a travel grant from Mr. Frederick Scott, Jr., and Mrs. Susan Scott. Visiting many of the places where Atatürk lived, battled, drank, and made love, he talked with a number of people who had actually spent time with Atatürk and were willing to share their memories of him. Shortly before his death, Şevket Süreyya Aydemir, perhaps the leading biographer of Atatürk, shared his thoughts and feelings about Turkey's leader with Dr. Volkan and disclosed in conversation much that he felt would have been inappropriate for him to include in his formal writings. Dr. Fuat Göksel, professor of psychiatry and historian of medicine, proved to be a living history book, particularly since he had spent two months with Dr. Adnan Adıvar and his wife, Halide Edib, just before Dr. Adıvar's death. The Adıvars had both known Atatürk on an intensely personal level and had themselves played major roles in the struggle for independence. Dr. Göksel passed on to Dr. Volkan the many memories they had shared with him, thereby providing us with much material unattainable otherwise.

Ms. Sabiha Gökçen, one of Atatürk's adopted daughters, was most generous in describing to Dr. Volkan aspects of her life in the presidential palace at Çankaya, Ankara, which she still refers to as her home. She also introduced Dr. Volkan to Mr. Abdürrahim Tuncak, who was brought up by Atatürk's mother and considers himself Atatürk's adopted son. We are especially mindful of our debt to him, for he generously granted an extensive interview despite poor health.

Considerable light was shed on Atatürk's personality by Mrs. Kıymet Tesal, the daughter of Nuri Conker, one of Atatürk's closest companions. A highly intelligent and insightful person, Mrs. Tesal made an invaluable contribution. Thanks are also due Mrs. Lütfiye Gürsoy, Mrs. Adile Ayda, and Professor Perihan Çambel for their accounts of how their lives had been affected by Atatürk.

Professor Abdülkadir Özbek was most helpful in discussing with Dr. Volkan the psychological aspects of the Turkish life-style. As a young man he had seen Atatürk riding in an automobile with the visiting shah of Iran, Reza Shah. Although the shah is known to have been above average in height, Professor Özbek clings to his memory of Atatürk as an even more commanding figure. Some of the particulars of İsmet İnönü's character were filled in by Professor Cahit Örgen, Dr. Volkan's uncle, who was one of the physicians to Turkey's second president during his last years. We are also grateful to Mr. Rauf Raif Denktaş, president of the Turkish Republic of Northern Cyprus, for sharing the dream he had about Atatürk in the summer of 1974, when Turkey was sending troops into Cyprus to intervene in the Turkish-Greek confrontation there. That dream, and Mr. Denktaş's reaction to it, indicate that many present political leaders among the Turks are still under the spell of Atatürk more than forty years after his death.

We conferred in Charlottesville, Virginia, during the summer of 1975, reviewing the data then on hand and making our initial formulations about our subject. Those months of work were made possible in part by a grant to Professor Itzkowitz from the Lucius N. Littauer Foundation and Mr. Harry Starr, its president. At that time, Dr. Larry Merkel, then a fourth-year medical student at the Unversity of Virginia and now a psychiatrist, became our assistant, and we are grateful to him for his research on life in Salonika toward the end of the last century. After the first draft of this work was completed, Dr. Barbara J. Novak, another fourth-year medical student at the University of Virginia and also now a psychiatrist, became associated with our project as part of her psychiatric elective, carefully reviewing the manuscript, and helping us to enlarge upon and explain certain technical statements to make them more understandable to readers not knowledgeable about psychiatry or psychoanalysis. Her pleasant personality was greatly appreciated during our last-minute efforts to complete this book in 1981, the year declared by UNESCO to be the Year of Atatürk in celebration of his hundredth birthday (19 May 1981–18 May 1982).

Our special thanks go to Mrs. Virginia Kennan, Dr. Volkan's friend and editorial assistant for the past fifteen years. She was intimately involved in the project and not only helped with editorial matters but also served as a sounding board as different formulations about the life and times of our subject emerged.

We have both spoken about Atatürk before audiences of our professional colleagues and have benefited from their suggestions and criticisms. Their interest in the ongoing inquiry into the relationship between individual personality and the historical process and their encouragement of this project was always greatly appreciated. Professor Cyril E. Black of Princeton University read the manuscript and made valuable suggestions, for which, along with his encouragement, we are most grateful.

Turkish Names

Inasmuch as the general reader may be unfamiliar with either the old or the modern Turkish names that appear throughout this book, we list below those mentioned repeatedly, making no attempt to list any that appear but briefly. We hope this will help to orient the reader to names that might be difficult for an English-speaking person to recall from one appearance to the next.

It will be noted that we use the Roman alphabet—characters long familiar to the West but adopted in Turkey only in 1929. Turkish usage made small modifications in that alphabet necessary. They were introduced to make certain fine discriminations in Turkish pronunciation possible, while preserving the notion of one sound being represented by one character. For example, although the letter *i* is pronounced as a short vowel (it, bit), when it appears without the dot it is something between the customary *i* sound and the sound of *a* in the English word *along*. The diacritical mark used in German to indicate umlaut is used over *o* and *u* in Turkish with much the same effect. The presence of a cedilla under *c* and *s* in Turkish indicates that they are pronounced *ch* and *sh*, respectively. The upturned arc over *g* indicates pronunciation in a rough guttural that is hardly audible. A circumflex over an *a* or a *u* broadens the sound to a harsher note.

Not until 1934 did it become legally necessary in Turkey to have a surname. At that time surnames were adopted by people who had not previously used them. Thus, when we refer to certain people, we have placed the surname in parentheses if the reference concerns events that took place before 1934, that is, before the use of surnames became mandatory.

Kemal Atatürk's name changed as his self-perception changed. He was born Mustafa, but became Mustafa Kemal as a schoolboy. Later, he was known as Ghazi M. Kemal, or, more simply, as the Ghazi ("victorious warrior"). In his later years he became Kemal, and briefly Kamal (Atatürk). *Atatürk* means "Father Turk."

His mother was Zübeyde, his father, Ali Riza. His only sibling to survive into adult life was Makbule (Atadan). The names of three of his adopted daughters appear often in the text. They were Sabiha (Gökçen), an aviator; Afet (Afetinan), an historian; and Ülkü, the last to be adopted and the youngest. Brief but repeated reference is made to another adopted daughter, Zehra, a suicide victim. The name of his adopted son was Abdürrahim (Tuncak).

Şemsi, who taught him in his childhood, played a role in his identity formation.

The women involved in his life included Corinne, an Istanbul widow; Miti (or Dimitriana), his love in Sofia; the tragic Fikriye, whose real love for him was spurned; and Lâtife, whom he married and divorced. Other women who were important in his life but not romantically involved with him included the celebrated Halide Edib (Adıvar), who with her husband Adnan, stood by Atatürk during the Turkish war of independence, became one of the most famous novelists of modern Turkey, but was ultimately rejected by his circle; Kıymet (Tesal), the daughter of Atatürk's friend Nuri Conker; and Adile (Ayda), whose father's rift with Atatürk caused her considerable conflict in her adult life.

At the time of Atatürk's birth the Ottoman Sultan Abdülhamid II was on the throne. Later, Atatürk deposed Sultan Mehmed VI, who had been known as Vahideddin while still a prince. Enver, a leader of the Young Turks, was Atatürk's rival. Fethi (Okyar) was with him in Sofia. Four important figures in the initial phase of the struggle for independence were Kâzım (Karabekir), Ali Fuat (Cebesoy), Refet (Bele), and the naval hero Rauf (Orbay).

İsmet (İnönü) was the second president of modern Turkey and Fevzi (Çakmak) was for many years the Turkish chief of staff. Both men played significant roles in the fight for independence, as did Arif (Adana), who was subsequently hanged for his role in a plot against Atatürk's life.

Nuri Conker was Atatürk's lifelong friend. Kılıç Ali (Ali the Sword) was another friend. Atatürk's aide-de-camp was Salih (Bozok). Celâl (Bayar) was the Turkish prime minister at the time of Atatürk's death. He later became Turkey's third president. Journalists mentioned often in the text are Falih Rıfkı (Atay) and Yakup Kadri (Karaosmanoğlu).

Introduction

In May 1973 a group of scholars that included historians, sociologists, anthropologists, psychologists, linguists, psychiatrists, and psychoanalysts gathered at Princeton University to share ideas on the psychological dimensions of Near Eastern studies. Peoples of the Near East, such as Arabs, Armenians, Iranians, Israelis, and Turks, it was noted, are all too often perceived as stereotyped figures—oil-rich sheiks, revolutionaries, military opportunists, xenophobic religious fundamentalists, or freedom fighters. Members of this group were struck by the increasing importance of the psychological understanding of history in overcoming stereotypic thinking. Historians, however, were quickly polarized in their opinions on the application of psychological insights to the explanation of historical events. Nonetheless, the group agreed that the psychological approach to Near Eastern studies should not attempt to replace traditional disciplines but should supplement them.

Synthesis of the language and the concepts of diverse disciplines is not without its pitfalls. At this group's initial meetings, moreover, most of the members were strangers to one another and had to become accustomed to the modes of communication of their new associates and to their habits of mind if they were to transcend the competition inherent among individuals seeking the acceptance of wisdom to which they are committed professionally. The goal was to develop formulations that could condense the knowledge of several disciplines.[1] Interested readers can judge for themselves how effectively that goal was realized by turning to the published papers of that conference (Brown and Itzkowitz 1977).

The authors of this book met for the first time in the course of the Princeton conference. An historian and a psychoanalyst discovered that they shared a common interest in psychoanalysis and in the biography of Mustafa Kemal Atatürk. Also shared was an agreement with the view of another participant in the conference, Dr. John E. Mack, who held that

[1]Mary Catherine Bateson (1972) has given a personal account of a conference that brought together representatives of disciplines as diverse as psychology, cybernetics, anthropology, and neurology. Her informal narrative allows the reader to participate in a conference in which the integration of knowledge from seemingly disparate fields was gradually achieved, and her description might very well be applied to the meeting of the Princeton group.

psychoanalysis evolved "from a science of psychopathology to a general psychology concerned with an individual's total psychological existence and history"; that it enabled the biographer to "understand character, to provide psychological coherence to the pattern of a life, to fathom motivation, and to understand how intrapsychic conflicts are transformed and surmounted in the subject's life" (Mack 1978, p. 108); and that it could make the study of prominent men more holistic. Any psychoanalytic biography of an historical figure should take into account the intertwining of external historical events and the individual's inner psychic world.

Additional common ground was revealed in our acceptance of Peter Blos's (1979) notion that the core of individual personality begins to coalesce in childhood and then crystallizes in adolescence, which provides a second chance to complete the work of the earlier stages of psychosexual development. From adolescence on, the individual will relate to the world around him, and to his inner world, in his own idiosyncratic way. External events are perceived and felt differently by each of us, with differing effects upon our inner worlds. We also agreed that things "out there" not only symbolically represent for us some of our own unconscious impulses and notions but may also unconsciously represent aspects of our own self-images and our images of the important others in our lives.[2] For example, if one who has been hurt through the loss of some close person watches a play in which a character is faced with a similar loss, the viewer may experience identification, however transient, and may weep at what is seen. Sometimes, such identification occurs on a far grander scale and with greater stability and persistence. A phenomenon in the outside world can become the target for the externalization of an inner aspect of a leader's self so that he struggles to alter the outside world in an unconscious search for his own inner comfort.

Through an odd coincidence both of us had come to the meeting at Princeton with papers on Atatürk, and we both had chosen to speak on Atatürk's relationships with women, although neither had had prior knowledge of the other's topic. During the course of his political life, Atatürk used his enormous eloquence to effect the liberation of Turkish women from the heavy burden imposed upon them by the traditions of their Islamic society. Speaking out against their use of the veil, he elevated women to equality with men. But despite his public posture, he was never loyal to any one woman among the many he enjoyed. When asked what it was he valued most in women, he is said to have answered, "Their availability." How was it possible for a man to espouse the advancement of women but treat them in terms of service for his plea-

[2]For more on this theme, see Volkan 1979.

sure? We had both tried to find the answer to this paradox in the emotional interaction between him and his mother during his childhood. It was this common interest that brought the two of us together and led us, in the interdisciplinary atmosphere of the Princeton conference, to discuss collaboration on a biography of Atatürk.

Our interest in such a venture persisted beyond the conference and the publication of its papers. We were well aware that this was because both of us were, as Freud (1910) had said about certain biographers, "fixated on [our hero] in a quite special way" (p. 130). Freud had warned that:

> In many cases [biographers] have chosen their hero as the subject of their studies because—for reasons of their own emotional life—they have felt a special affection for him from the very first. They then devote their energies to a task of idealization, aimed at enrolling the great man among the class of their infantile models—at reviving in him, perhaps, the child's idea of his father. . . . They thus present us with what is in fact a cold, strange ideal figure, instead of a human being to whom we might feel ourselves distantly related. That they should do this is regrettable, for they thereby sacrifice truth to an illusion, and for the sake of their infantile phantasies abandon the opportunity of penetrating the most fascinating secrets of human nature. [1910, p. 130]

Freud's comments about the idealization of the hero and the intense need to write about him can also be applied to the devaluation of a hero. A wish to devalue an important figure from one's own childhood may lead one to write about some historical figure, if the wish is sufficiently persistent. Both of us were aware that Atatürk was an idealized figure for us. He represented a repository of some idealized aspects of ourselves, and to study him would be first of all to study ourselves. Each of us felt able to conduct this self-analysis, relying upon the strength gained in personal therapeutic psychoanalysis.

One of us (Dr. Volkan) was born of Turkish parents on the island of Cyprus and received his medical education in Turkey. He not only knew the effects within himself of Turkish culture but felt himself to be a typical product of Atatürk's design for Turkish youth. Volkan was only six years old when Atatürk died, but he grew up regarding Atatürk as a godlike figure.

Before Volkan was born, his father, a schoolteacher in a Cypriot Turkish village, had made a dramatic gesture in imitation of Atatürk. While pursuing the cultural revolution after the establishment of the Turkish republic, Atatürk had gone to a conservative Muslim area of Anatolia (İnebolu and Kastamonu) to introduce the hat as appropriate modern headgear for Turkish men. It was a daring move, for the hat had long been considered an emblem of the infidel. On this trip Atatürk appeared before the populace wearing a panama hat which he pointed to, saying, "Gentlemen, the name of this is *şapka* [hat]!" So great was Atatürk's charismatic hold over the people that they all removed their fezzes, turbans, and other Muslim headgear and rushed out to find hats, some even making their own approximations of European-style hats.

When he heard of this, Dr. Volkan's father went to a coffeehouse in his village, and, climbing up on a chair with a hat in his hand, he repeated Atatürk's message. He expected his audience to respond as Atatürk's had, but he soon found himself staring into the barrel of a gun. He was ordered to step down from the chair and to be quiet on the subject of headgear or face the consequences. The persistence of the story as a sort of family myth led Volkan to regard his father as a failure. Not until much later did he appreciate the raw courage his father had displayed and understand his extremely honest and obsessional, though apparently essentially peace-loving, nature. It was only after his personal analysis, as part of his training at the Washington Psychoanalytic Institute, that Dr. Volkan allowed his warm and appreciative feelings about his father to surface fully. He was never able to enter into the loving man-to-man friendship his father deserved, however, for the older man died on the distant and turbulent island of Cyprus after a long illness.

Because Atatürk had always been Dr. Volkan's idealized father, studying the hero's life necessarily meant studying himself first, including the somewhat unintegrated image he had of his father. Inevitably involved in this transference experience was the opportunity to integrate his perception of his father as "failure" and his new perception of him as a man of enormous personal courage. He had to "mend" his fragmented image of his father. While this process toppled Atatürk from the pedestal he had occupied in Volkan's mind, it established him as a human being with all the diversity, passion, inconsistency, and wrongheadedness that implies, along with compelling dignity and pride. The odyssey involved in the study was a stormy one. Volkan's regard for the Turkish leader swung from a defensive strengthening of his idealization to extreme devaluation. In the end, however, he gained a balanced view that fostered a genuine appreciation of how Atatürk accomplished what he did despite his lordly isolation and largely denied inner suffering. By the time the study was completed Dr. Volkan was greatly changed. He no longer saw Atatürk as a figure in fantasy, but rather as a man with faults and difficulties who nonetheless managed to perform magnificent deeds against overwhelming odds.

An equally complex concatenation of circumstances brought Professor Itzkowitz to this collaborative effort. Born in New York of Polish immigrant parents, he was not even remotely connected with anything Turkish or even Islamic. Nevertheless, he became a student of the Ottomans (Itzkowitz 1972) and resided in Turkey frequently. As an Ottoman historian he had been trained to read Ottoman Turkish, something Dr. Volkan is unable to do, for he began his education on Cyprus after Atatürk's reform of the Turkish alphabet.

From the time of his trip to Turkey in 1956 to do research in the Ottoman archives, Itzkowitz was captivated by the success of Atatürk's reforms. Closer acquaintance with Turkey and its people drew him to entertain the subject of Atatürk and the Turkish revolution as a viable research topic. Traditional historical research had not been able to answer many of the questions his own knowledge of Turkey had raised in his mind. Psychological history appeared to promise a better approach, but the fruits of research embodying that perspective were unsatisfactory. Historians did not know enough psychology, and psychologically-minded scholars lacked an adequate knowledge of history. Intent upon preparing himself to undertake a psychological study of Atatürk, Itzkowitz became a psychoanalytic candidate at the National Psychological Association for Psychoanalysis in New York, where he studied theory, underwent personal analysis, and worked with patients under close supervision. Examining his own life, Professor Itzkowitz became aware of the relationship between his interest in other cultures (and their languages) and his unconscious wish to understand the dynamics of his mother's personality. Just as Dr. Volkan's odyssey had led him to a deeper understanding of Atatürk through greater knowledge of his relationship with his father, Professor Itzkowitz's comprehension of aspects of the Turkish leader's personality was broadened by his inner voyage that focused on the mother-child dyad. By his own route each collaborator had prepared himself to embark upon a study of Atatürk, and each welcomed the opportunity to engage in a joint effort that would combine their individual contributions.

Much has been written about the difficulties involved in writing sophisticated psychoanalytic biographies of historical figures (Beres 1959, Bergmann 1973, Erikson 1958, 1969, Greenacre 1955, Klauber 1968, Kohut 1960, Kris 1952, Lifton 1972, Mack 1971, Niederland 1965). Early writing of this kind was motivated by the desire to clarify an artist's inner motivations for creative work. It focused first on interpreting the symbols used in works of art, but as the young science of psychoanalysis established itself, psychobiography based on the interpretation of symbols was questioned, for "Symbols are overdetermined and their meaning is less constant and less universal than Freud assumed" (Bergmann 1973, p. 835).

Knowledge gained through ego psychology and the study of human development led to a focus on the subject's actual life history, the interaction that had taken place between the subject as a child and his early environment. Cultural and social influences were also plumbed. Later, Erik Erikson introduced his concept of the psychosocial stages of development with the adolescent crisis as a central notion. Subsequently, attention was also called to midlife crises, but difficulties in the psychological approach to biography remain.[3]

In his clinical practice the psychoanalyst learns about his patient's inner psychic structure chiefly from his "transference neurosis" rather than from his collection of memories, however important those may be. A transference neurosis is the patient's displacement during analysis of his representations of important figures of his childhood onto his analyst, along with the way in which he then expects the analyst to reproduce their behaviors. In this relationship a peculiar continued "story" unfolds, and by bringing the patient's childhood experiences into the "here and now," this unfolding discloses the particulars of his early life and the ways in which the core of his psychic system was established during childhood.

When an analyst writes about someone who has *never been on his couch*, one questions what data can substitute for the transference reactions, and free associations, of an actual analysand—and how valid any such data can be.[4] Nevertheless, psychogenetic factors that contributed to that person's personality can be inferred with some confidence when autobiographical information, along with records made available by others, establishes the existence of certain *consistent* behavioral patterns in the life of the subject. Thousands of books and articles have been written in many languages about Atatürk, and he left a considerable body of his own writing, including his "Great Speech" (Atatürk 1927). Their disclosures constitute a reassuring amount of material. Moreover, we have had the opportunity to supplement that information with insights and anecdotes from people who knew him. When Dr. Volkan spent the 1974/1975 academic year as visiting professor of psychiatry at the University of Ankara, he was able to interview a number of people who had been close to Atatürk or whose lives had been significantly touched by his

[3]See Erikson 1958 on Luther; Bergmann 1973, p. 835. Bergmann states that with Erikson we came to recognize that the first years of life cannot by themselves entirely account for adult character. The shift of emphasis in Erikson's work, according to Bergmann, is one that "from the construction of infantile history to a crisis in early adulthood transforms psychoanalytic biography into psychohistory. While the life space of the infant and child is restricted to the family, the historical situation is significant in the life of a young adult" (p. 843).

[4]Most psychoanalytic biographers have been optimistic about the availability of such substitutes as surveyed by Bergmann (1973, p. 847). See also Greenacre 1955, p. 13. Niederland (1965) found Schliemann's "language exercises," in which he revealed unconscious wishes and dreams in sentences written to master a new language, similar to free associations.

even in brief encounters. We consider the material obtained from these three different sources sufficient to give reliable insight into his actions and belief systems. We feel that we have found a clear window into his self-system and have grasped how he interacted with the environment to maintain his self-esteem during his later life in the historical arena. Recent developments in psychoanalysis that give new insights into the self and its interactions with others guided us in formulating our ideas about Atatürk.[5] We have been able to reconstruct his early life and to compare his character and behavior as an adult with our knowledge of both his early experiences and the changing historical circumstances in the world around him.

We came early to the conclusion that Atatürk had an inflated and grandiose self-concept,[6] basing this on the way others described him, but also—and more significantly—on his own delineation of his personality organization.[7] He believed he was a unique man above all others and endowed with the right to assert his will. He saw others in two categories—those who were his admirers and followers and those who were not and who therefore had no existence at all as far as he was concerned. Our clinical studies indicate that people with this kind of orientation toward others may have what is technically known as a narcissistic personality organization. This is a pathological response to psychological deprivation

[5]The term *self* is a layman's term referring to one's own person—the bodily and psychic attributes exhibited to the external world. Psychoanalysts use terms such as self-image, self-representation, object image, and object representation. The self-image is a construct of a person's ego for experiences, sensations, emotions, and conscious and unconscious thoughts and perceptions of body and mind seen as an object at one particular time or in a specific situation; and self-representation refers to dynamically and affectively organized self-images leading to an intrapsychic structure that reflects the person's conscious and unconscious and stable and long-standing perception of himself. Parallel to the concept of self-representation is that of an object representation, which is an intrapsychic structure from a multitude of images, impressions, affective experiences (real and fantasied) with objects other than the self. Jacobson (1964) and Kernberg (1966, 1975, 1976, 1980) have systematized the development and maturation of such representations in persons. See also Volkan 1976.

[6]*Grandiose self* is a technical term first introduced by Kohut (1971). Others, including Kernberg and Volkan, use the same term (in spite of major theoretical differences from Kohut's formulations as to its establishment) to refer to a self-representation that is associated with excessive self-absorption, intense ambition, the wish to be unsurpassed in power, beauty, and brilliance. Kohut (1977) sees the grandiose self as exhibited by adults as a representation of a deficit in normal development of the libidinal (loving) investment in the self. Following Kernberg, Volkan sees it as arising from an early formation of pathological narcissism to protect against the conflicts and early rage and envy that a child experiences.

[7]*Personality organization* refers to how a person inwardly clings chiefly to certain self-representations and object representations which are invested with instinctual drives and unconscious fantasies. It roughly corresponds to the individual's character.

and trauma suffered when a child prematurely builds a sense of identity, and it involves a precocious and exaggerated sense of autonomy and omnipotence.

As we reconstructed Atatürk's childhood, we saw the development of a self-concept of this sort. We were keenly aware of the danger of viewing him as a patient and unconsciously deprecating the role of such personality organization in the fulfillment of this remarkable man's military, political, and creative urges. The clinical practice of psychiatry can point to few, if any, *patients* who have actualized an aberrant concept of the self and have thereby become acknowledged leaders. People whose unique endowments coincide with unique opportunities seldom come to the couch, whereas those whose self-concepts are poorly substantiated by their gifts and situation often do.

It will be seen that Atatürk had certain difficulties in relating to others in his personal life and that he demanded the honor due a nonpareil, but nothing eroded his loyalty to the Turkish nation. It is true that he was frustrated over and over in his efforts to assume the role of a savior before his nation's needs coincided with his aspirations. A match was then accomplished between a passionate intent and a vacuum that needed filling. Although Lloyd George disliked Atatürk intensely, having lost his leadership in Britain largely on account of Atatürk's successes, he said of him that only in a hundred years does a man with Atatürk's abilities appear and that in this century it had been Turkey's turn to entertain one.

We do not know much about the "constitutional factors" that determine why one person with a given personality organization operates more or less successfully but another with the same organization does not. We can, however, point to our subject's extraordinary ability to draw realistic borders or limits around his narcissistic aspirations. Although he strove for accomplishment on a grand scale, he was able to achieve it largely through his intuitive wisdom about where to stop as he took each step toward a goal. One might call this moderation, but the term is odd for one so flamboyant.

Clinical research (Kernberg 1975, Volkan 1976, 1981, 1982*b*) indicates that the adult with a grandiose self-concept had a special kind of early relationship with his mother. It often becomes clear that the mother was cold and nongiving toward her child and left him emotionally hungry and inclined to develop a self-concept that made him rise above hurts by being grandiose. At the same time she perceived him somehow as being "special," perhaps seeing him as an ornamental plaything or the savior of the family's name, and she regarded him as valuable to her in ways that she took pains to reinforce. This paradoxical situation is likely to give a child the sense of being unique, which he will further amplify by collecting other idealized images and putting aside (splitting off) anything about himself or others that he devalues.[8] He will then deny that devalued part. Our theme in this work is that Atatürk's relationship with his mother was of such a character.

Those who in childhood develop an inflated self-concept (grandiose self) grow up to be excessively self-engrossed, with grandiose fantasies accompanied by an overdependence upon acclaim and an insatiable need to attain brilliance, power, and beauty. They may simply seem intensely ambitious, but deeper scrutiny will reveal that they strive toward their goal without the ability to understand and love other people and without any consideration for others. This description fits Atatürk's personality, with the important reservation that he was capable in his own way of a kind of grand love, caring for his homeland as passionately as a man might love another human being.

It is necessary for the person with a grandiose self to protect it in order to avoid the influence of his rejected (devalued) aspect and to maintain his self-esteem.[9] Throughout this book we show Atatürk struggling to maintain his grand self-esteem in the midst of defeats and victories. Lloyd Etheredge (1979), of the Massachusetts Institute of Technology, has described what he calls "hardball politics" as a "subculture of the domestic and international political culture, a subculture constructed and sustained by a particular personality type, men with what is known clinically as a narcissistic personality disorder" (p. 3). Atatürk may have belonged to such a subculture, but unlike most he would become a mighty, godlike, and immortal leader, reflecting the defensive adaptation of his childhood in the world of public affairs.

During the seven years it took us to write this book we both lived closely with images of Atatürk. By the time we had completed it, we saw him as having worked his way out of the cocoon he had spun to live in, alone with his illusion of grandeur. The more we learned about him, the more love, anger, pity, jealousy—and more significantly—empathy, we could feel for him. We are both now able to let him rest in peace.

[8]Splitting of early images of one's self and others is a normal developmental occurrence. Under the influence of pleasurable and unpleasurable experiences, the self-system (and corresponding systems of internalized objects) develop in a bipolar fashion. The person with a narcissistic organization from childhood on uses already existing splitting in a *defensive* way in order to avoid acknowledging the hurtful and painful aspects of himself.

[9]Although we do not agree with the metapsychological assumptions of Kohut (1971, 1977) as to how the grandiose self develops, we know that he has described typical ways (for example, narcissistic transferences) of protecting the cohesiveness of the grandiose self. See also Volkan 1981 for other ways.

1
Atatürk's Ottoman Background in Perspective

MUSTAFA KEMAL, LATER TO BE KNOWN AS ATATÜRK, WAS BORN A QUARTER of a century after the end of the Crimean War into a world still affected by the highly disruptive consequences of that war. One of its dislocations was in the pattern of diplomatic relations that had governed European international affairs since the end of the Napoleonic era. Gone was the Concert of Europe idea with its commitment to the map of Europe established at the Congress of Vienna in 1815. Exercise of self-control and cooperation had governed relations among the major European powers from 1815 to 1854. There had been crises during those years, but they had been managed. For almost four decades Europe had known no major war. The Crimean War, blundered into by both sides through misperceptions and miscalculations, ended an era of diplomacy characterized by cooperation between Russia and Britain in the interests of peace and the containment of France and French political ideas. Post-Crimean dynamics were far different.

Two major European states emerged from the Crimean War as revisionist powers. Russia would seek to render the Black Sea clauses of the treaty, which had neutralized the Black Sea and demilitarized its shores, null and void. Neither the Ottoman Empire nor Russia could maintain any warships on the Black Sea except for the few light vessels allowed to each by separate agreement between the sultan and the czar. The sultan also maintained the "ancient rule" of his empire that kept foreign ships of war from entering the Dardanelles and the Bosporus as long as the Ottoman Empire was at peace.

Maladroit diplomatic maneuvering had contributed to Russia's blundering into the Crimean War. No such clumsiness marked Russia's attempts to rid herself of the restrictive and galling clauses of the Treaty of Paris, which Czar Alexander II considered a lasting nightmare. Patience exercised over a decade and a half enabled Russia to achieve nullification. When Europe's attention was absorbed by the Franco-Prussian War of 1870, Russia unilaterally abrogated those mortifying clauses on 31 October 1870. The original signatories to the Treaty of Paris then met in London early in 1871 and embodied their acceptance of Russia's action in the Treaty of London (March 1871).

Under its provisions Russia and the Ottoman Empire could maintain naval forces on the Black Sea and establish arsenals on its shores wherever they saw fit. As before, the Dardanelles and the Bosporus were closed to foreign warships, but the sultan could now open the straits in time of peace to warships of friendly and allied powers.

Russia was only one of the two powers committed to the overthrow of the 1856 settlement. France was the other. Drawn into the Crimean War by Napoleon III's inept attempt to curry favor with French Catholics by championing the claims of the Latin Church in the Near East, France emerged from the war bent on redrawing the map of Europe along national lines. Napoleon I had spread revolution. Under Napoleon III, France's exportable commodity would become nationalism.

Embracing the doctrine of nationalities, Napoleon III had visions of a Europe reorganized along national and federated lines. The first arena in which his ideas were to be tested seriously was Italy. He hoped that under his aegis Italy could become free and federated. Nationalism was a sleeping dog whose full fury he had underestimated entirely.

Nowhere more than in the Near East would nationalism demonstrate its corrosive power. The Ottoman Empire was a multiracial, multireligious, and multilinguistic congeries, but above all else it was multinational. The Ottoman Empire had already begun to lose territory on its periphery prior to the Crimean War, but in the second half of the nineteenth century nationalism became a festering sore of disintegration for which the empire could find no ready remedy.

Napoleon III's doctrine of nationalities found its first fertile Balkan soil in the dual principalities of Moldavia and Walachia, which, when united, would form Rumania. From the beginning of the eighteenth century, in the reign of Peter the Great, Russia relentlessly exerted pressure on the periphery of the Ottoman Empire, slowly advancing into the area bordering the Black Sea. In less then a hundred years after the death of Peter the Great in 1725, the Russian advance reached Moldavia. In the series of treaties that regulated Russian-Ottoman relations from 1774 to 1829 the Russians sought to legitimize their meddling in the affairs of the principalities. Powerless to resist Russia's demands, the Ottomans promised them everything but delivered as little as possible.

Ottoman procrastination was assisted by the mutually distrustful attitudes of the great powers. The principalities were made to order for the mixture of romanticism and political opportunism in Napoleon III's mind. Already committed to the principle of nationality with regard to Italy, Poland, and even Prussia, Napoleon embraced the concept of union for Moldavia and Walachia. He unleashed a doctrine for the principalities that would soon undermine the essence of the Ottoman

Empire and transform the Balkans and the Near East beyond recognition.

Eventually, the principalities were united under a foreign prince, Charles of Hohenzollern-Sigmaringen. When offered the throne, Charles had to consult an atlas to locate his new home. Formal independence was granted at the Congress of Berlin (1878), and Charles became king of Rumania in 1881.

Rumanian nationhood, although not achieved until after Napoleon III's death, was an outstanding victory for his doctrine of nationality, which took firm root in the Balkans as Bulgaria quickly succumbed to the blandishments of nationalism. Religion complicated the issue, and the Ottomans sought to placate the Bulgars by granting them permission to form their own "national" church. While the religious issue was being resolved in Bulgaria's favor, the political problem moved closer to a military confrontation when the Bulgarians revolted in May 1876. Local Turkish militia forces, never noted for restraint, met violence with violence. Thousands of Bulgarians died in what anti-Ottoman Europeans called the "Bulgarian Atrocities," and outcries against the Ottomans spread across Europe from St. Petersburg to London.

Mutual suspicions kept the cauldron of Balkan nationalism from boiling over into a general war. Austria viewed the preservation of the Ottoman Empire as a bulwark against the extension of Russian influence in the Balkans. Russia could neither generate a coherent policy nor attract an ally. France was less troubled. Still recovering from her defeat in the Franco-Prussian War, she had no stomach for distant adventures. Bismarck was unwilling to choose between Austria and Russia. Gingerly, he walked the tightrope of neutrality, maintaining good relations with both in order to keep revenge-minded France isolated diplomatically. Britain alone remained constant, adhering to her policy of support for the sultan and the preservation of the territorial integrity of the Ottoman Empire.

Britain sought to contain the crisis by means of a conference of the great powers in Constantinople to discuss reforms designed to ameliorate the conditions under which Christians lived in the Ottoman Empire. The conference met under the threat of Russian intervention if the powers failed to achieve results. Discussed were the possible union of Bosnia and Herzegovina under a Christian governor appointed by the sultan, the enlargement of Serbia and Montenegro, and the creation of a rather large state of Bulgaria with a western and an eastern half. This amounted to the dismantlement of the Ottoman Empire in Europe.

Centuries of success precluded the Ottomans from merely folding up their tents and quietly stealing away. Instead, they attempted to blunt

SERBIA
RUMANIA
Danube
Niş
HUNGARY
Sofia
Burgas
Black Sea
BULGARIA
Philippopolis
OTTOMAN EMPIRE
Edirne
Struma
THRACE
Istanbul
Tirana
Monastir
Serrai
Vardar
Meriç
Sea of Marmara
MACEDONIA
Salonika
Gallipoli
Bursa
ALBANIA
ANATOLIA
Aegean Sea
Balikesir
Larisa
THESSALY
GREECE
Ottoman Empire c. 1881
100 Km.

the demands of the powers by promulgating a constitution that guaranteed full civil liberties to all subjects of the sultan. As far as the Ottomans were concerned, the Constantinople conference was now superfluous. Banking on British support and Austro-Russian rivalry, they rejected all demands. When diplomatic pressure on the Ottoman Empire failed, Russia secured Austrian neutrality by the promise of Bosnia and Herzegovina. Then, on 24 April 1877, Russia delared war on the Ottoman Empire.

This latest in a long series of Russian-Ottoman wars confirmed the inability of either side to win speedily or thoroughly. The Ottomans gave a good account of themselves for a time, but eventually the Russians broke through the Ottoman defenses and pushed all the way to the outskirts of Istanbul. Russia dictated a harsh peace in the Treaty of San Stefano, one of the principal provisions of which was the establishment of a huge autonomous state of Bulgaria. San Stefano would have made Russia the dominant power in the Balkans, and it presented the real possibility of a Russian occupation of Istanbul itself. Austria and Britain could not tolerate such a revision of the power relationships in the Near East. Together they pressured Russia into agreeing to a revision of the treaty by a general European congress.

Presided over by Bismarck, the Congress of Berlin rewrote the unacceptable Treaty of San Stefano. There would be a self-governing principality of Bulgaria, but it would be significantly reduced in size. For her labors, Austria was allowed to "occupy and administer" Bosnia and Herzegovina. By separate treaty with the sultan, Britain was ceded the island of Cyprus.

Bulgaria's rise to the status of a fully independent nation (1909) was symptomatic of two trends. One was the steady advance of nationalism among the subject peoples of the Ottoman Empire, and the other was the increasing inability of the Ottomans to find in the European diplomatic community consistently staunch supporters of their territorial integrity. Britain alone bore the burden of propping up the "sick man" of Europe.

Neither altruism nor love of the Turks dictated British policy. Britain's stance was determined by the need to protect her own vital interests, including the lifeline to India. British policy in the Near East from the time of Palmerston (prime minister, 1855–58, 1859–65) called for the creation of a truly viable Ottoman Empire that would be rejuvenated by internal reforms of its own. Reform would eventuate in an efficient army, a productive bureaucracy, fiscal soundness, and the amelioration of the conditions under which the Christians of the empire lived, eliminating pretexts for interference in the internal affairs of the Ottoman Empire.

Reform in the Ottoman Empire was nothing new. It had a long, if not glorious, history. When Ottoman armies experienced defeat in the seventeenth century, the sultan was urged to engage in a series of reforms, but little was done until the crisis of 1656. In that year Istanbul was thrown into a panic when the islands of Lemnos and Tenedos at the entrance to the Dardanelles were seized by Venice, which was then in a position to blockade the sultan's capital city. At this moment of maximum danger, Mehmed Köprülü was made grand vizier. He was an octogenarian whose long but undistinguished career gave no evidence that he would be able to restore Ottoman fortunes. Years of service in the retinues of leading Ottoman statesmen had been a good training ground, however, and he knew from considerable experience exactly what ills beset the empire. Remedies for them had occupied his thoughts, and therefore he was not unprepared when his opportunity suddenly arrived.

His program was deceptively simple. Corruption and graft in the empire must cease. He wanted to restore Turkish institutions to the pristine glory they had known in the sixteenth century during the reign of Suleiman the Magnificent. With its institutions purged of innovations and its regulations once again respected, the state would be restored to its past greatness.

Köprülü's reform program was suprisingly successful. Internal disorder that had manifested itself in a series of provincial rebellions against the sultan's authority was put down, and the war against Venice was prosecuted with energy. Lemnos and Tenedos were retaken, and the Ottomans launched a campaign against Crete that was crowned with success in 1669 under Ahmed Köprülü, who had followed his father into the grand vizierate in 1661.

Under Ahmed Köprülü the Ottomans renewed the attack against Europe, making their deepest penetration into Poland. Not even the death of Ahmed in 1676 slowed the Ottoman recovery. Ahmed was succeeded by his brother-in-law, Kara Mustafa Pasha. Dreaming of becoming one of the greatest Muslim warriors for the faith of Islam (a *ghazi*), Kara Mustafa Pasha conceived of an attack on a grand scale against Vienna, the prime objective that had just narrowly eluded Suleiman's grasp in 1529. The conquest of Vienna would be a fitting climax to an era of reform modeled on Suleiman's reign.

Kara Mustafa Pasha's fantasies of grandeur disintegrated in the woods around Vienna. There his forces failed to halt the Christian counterattack and had to retreat all the way back to Belgrade, where Kara Mustafa Pasha paid the ultimate price for his failure. On 25 December 1683, he was strangled on the sultan's orders. The fruits of the Köprülü reform era were squandered in one histrionic gesture.

Victory at Vienna whetted Christian appetites. They pressed their advantage, forming the Holy League against the Ottomans in 1684. Not even the accession to the throne of a more vigorous sultan, Mustafa II, in

1695 could reverse the downward spiral in Ottoman fortunes. Personally leading his troops, Mustafa II counterattacked in 1697. While crossing the Theiss River at Zenta, north of Belgrade, the Ottoman army was practically annihilated by Hapsburg troops before the sultan's very eyes.

With the army seriously mauled and the empire badly in need of tranquility, a peace party emerged to negotiate a settlement with the enemy. On 26 January 1699, the Treaty of Karlowitz, calling for the Ottoman evacuation of Hungary, was signed. The task of making the treaty palatable to Ottoman public opinion was entrusted to the historian Naima. Following a long line of Ottoman statesmen-writers who had pondered the causes of Ottoman decline and proposed remedies to halt it, Naima offered a diagnosis and prescription of his own.

A bureaucrat by training and an historian by inclination, Naima was familiar with both the historical reality of the empire's situation and the fund of ideas in the Islamic intellectual arsenal. He drew upon a variety of Islamic ideas to demonstrate that the peace policy was the only workable one for the empire to adopt.

Moving from diagnosis to prescription, Naima postulated five principles that would save the state: income and expenditures had to be balanced; salaries should be paid on time; abuses in the military establishments should be eradicated; the provinces should be administered with justice so as to restore the peasantry to prosperity; and the sultan should be as optimistic as possible in order to inspire both love and fear in his subjects.

Simple as Naima's recommendations were, they worked. Following the respite provided by the Treaty of Karlowitz, Ottoman armies were again highly successful. In 1711 Ottoman forces defeated the army of Peter the Great on the banks of the Pruth River. After that victory the Ottomans retook the Morea from the Venetians in 1715. Naima personally participated in that campaign. From 1736 to 1739 the Ottomans fought the Russians and the Austrians again and managed to recover the city of Belgrade.

Naima's analysis of what ailed the Ottomans and what needed to be done was strictly within the Islamic frame of reference. Thoughtful Ottomans looked back to the reign of Suleiman the Magnificent, measuring their own performance against his accomplishments as the ideal, concluding that all that was required was to do things as they had been done during his reign. Eighteenth-century Ottomans like Naima were convinced that once morality was restored to society and the state machinery, and strong viziers punished offenders harshly, justice would reign. Through justice the empire would again know great victories.

Naima died in 1730 without seeing the results of the success he had predicted. After 1739 the Ottomans experienced an unusually long period of peace on their frontier with a Europe which was preoccupied with the Seven Years' War. Lulled into tranquility, they became less watchful and permitted the army and navy to languish—just how much they realized in 1768 when they were once again embroiled in war with the Russians.

Neither side had been anxious for war, but it dragged on for six years. Finally, in July 1774, peace was arranged with a treaty that shattered the Ottoman self-image of being a restored and revitalized empire. Failure now demonstrated that Ottoman achievement since 1699 had been merely a short-lived rally. The empire's continued existence would depend upon a deeper understanding of its problems and on institutional reform that looked not to the past of Suleiman's golden era, but to Europe and the future.

Sultan Selim III, who came to the throne in 1789, realized the need to carry out institutional reforms based on western models. The need was most acute in the military sphere, for without the ability to resist the empire's enemies in the field, other reforms would be unavailing. New military and naval schools were opened, with advice and instructors from France. The French and the Ottomans had had a close working relationship since the early sixteenth century, and now they cooperated in a new program of reform.

In an effort to bring the Ottoman Empire into closer contact with Europe, the source of technological knowledge, Selim III established the first permanent Ottoman embassies in London, Vienna, Berlin, and Paris. A new generation of young Ottoman officials trained in western languages who would be important to the continuing reform process received their first exposure to the West in those embassies.

Selim III's reign coincided with the era of the French Revolution and Napoleon I. The French invasion of Egypt in 1798 put a severe strain on Ottoman-French relations, and Selim's reform program soon ran into serious opposition. His opponents were appalled by the secularism evident in the French Revolution, and in 1807 Selim was driven from his throne.

Quickly, the forces of decentralization and localism came to the fore, and reform was shelved for the time being. With decentralization threatening the very existence of the Ottoman Empire, Sultan Mahmud II set about restoring the authority of the central government. Like Selim III before him, Mahmud II recognized the need to update the military and in 1826 succeeded in abolishing the centuries-old Janissary corps. Mahmud II then launched a series of military, bureaucratic, and educational reforms designed to restore the sultan's authority and the government's ability to cope with its enemies and its problems. He was aided in this enterprise by a new ally, Britain.

Mahmud II died in 1839. His successor, aware that it would be easier for Britain to support an Ottoman Empire committed to reform, issued the famous imperial rescript of November 1839. This document spoke of many principles hitherto foreign to Ottoman thought, including the security of life, honor, and the property of the sultan's subjects. Also mentioned was the radical notion that all religions would be equal in the application of new laws.

Under the guidance of Britain, the Ottoman Empire embarked upon a series of reforms intended to give substance to the pious promises embodied in the rescript of 1839. The Turkish-Arabic term *tanzimat*, meaning "reorganization," has been applied to this period of reform. From the outset, progress was slow. There was no strong consensus in favor of reform among the ruling elite, and the responsibility for bringing the empire into the modern age fell upon a few men, most of whom had served in Ottoman embassies in Europe.

Ottoman statesmen were particularly vulnerable to demands made by European states on behalf of the Ottoman minorities. It was just such a situation that initiated the chain of events which led to the outbreak of the Crimean War. Russia championed the claims of the Orthodox Greeks, and the French those of the Ottoman Latins, with regard to certain rights in the Church of the Holy Sepulchre in Jerusalem. Interference in the internal affairs of the Ottoman Empire carried with it the potential for war, for the interests of any one European power might come into competition with those of another. Diplomacy failed in the face of the intricacies of minority rights, national pride, and national interest; and Europe found itself embroiled in the Crimean War.

In that conflagration the Ottoman Empire was allied with Britain and France against Russia. Remembered more perhaps for Tennyson's poem commemorating the charge of the Light Brigade than for anything else, the war drew to a close in 1855 with the Ottomans and their allies victorious. As preparations were being made for peace deliberations in Paris, the Ottomans issued another imperial rescript. This rescript was intended to reassure the European powers of Ottoman intentions to carry out the reforms alluded to in 1839. In order to be accepted into the European diplomatic community as a signatory to the Treaty of Paris, the Ottomans again declared their intention to treat all their subjects as equal. The rescript of 1856 reaffirmed the earlier principles and stressed the equality of all Ottoman subjects before the law, regardless of religion.

By 1859, the reform movement in the Ottoman Empire was in the hands of men who can be considered the second generation of reformers. They had been the pupils of Reşid Pasha, the father of the 1839 rescript, and his circle. It was now their turn to take up the reins. Leading this new group of reformers were Ali Pasha and Fuat Pasha. Ali Pasha had gotten his start in the translation bureau. He served abroad and rose to the rank of ambassador. In 1840 he was ambassador to London, and in 1852 he succeeded Reşid Pasha as grand vizier. In addition, he was head of the High Council for Reform. By the time the imperial rescript of 1856 was issued, Ali Pasha was entrenched as grand vizier.

Ali Pasha was assisted by Fuat Pasha, who had been trained in the new medical school established by Sultan Mahmud II. After serving in the Army Medical Corps, he entered the translation bureau and in 1840 was posted to London to serve on Ali Pasha's staff there. A close friendship developed between the two men and their careers progressed in tandem. Their knowledge of French contributed to their rapid rise in the bureaucracy.

Under Ali and Fuat reform moved ahead in the familiar grooves. The main paths had been set out in 1839 and 1856. Now the pace was quickened somewhat. Legal reform was undertaken and included new maritime and commercial codes, as well as a new empirewide penal code. All these codes were inspired primarily by French models, and the western imprint was clear.

Education vied with law as a major interest of Ottoman reformers. A thoroughly westernized secondary school was opened in 1868, the Imperial Ottoman Lycée at Galatasary in Istanbul. The language of instruction there was French, and its graduates, Muslim and non-Muslim alike, went on to play significant roles in many areas of Ottoman life.

Reform was arduous work, and it took its toll. Fuat Pasha died in 1869 at the age of 54, and Ali Pasha, born in the same year as Fuat, died in 1871. With their deaths the *tanzimat* lost its impetus. Conditions within the empire deteriorated, and the sultan's extravagance resulted in heavy borrowing from Europe, which threw the empire into debt. Bankruptcy was an imminent threat, and in October 1875 the empire suspended interest payments on the Ottoman debt.

Financial woes were soon dwarfed by internal disruption in the form of the Bulgarian atrocities mentioned earlier. Four decades of reform notwithstanding, the empire was at low ebb. It appeared that Europe was about to drive the Turks out of the Balkans "bag and baggage." The Ottomans, who had made their first incursions into Europe early in the fourteenth century, were merely hanging on in the last quarter of the nineteenth.

As the Ottomans dug in their heels, a new sultan came to the throne. Abdülhamid II was installed as sultan on 1 September 1876, in the midst of a severe international crisis centered around the powder keg of the Balkans, which Britain attempted to defuse by calling the Constantinople conference. Sultan Abdülhamid II tried to undermine the conference by issuing the first Ottoman constitution, which provided for a parliament of two houses. A Chamber of Notables was to be appointed by the sultan, and a lower house, the Chamber of Deputies, consisting of 120 members, was to be elected and to include representation from the religious minorities. The old issue of equality for all subjects was laid to rest in Article 17, which stated that all subjects were equal in the eyes of the law. Once again, the Ottoman Empire had responded to pressure from Europe by issuing a document.

Constitutional concessions failed to halt Russian ambitions. War with Russia in 1877 resulted in terrific territorial losses, modified by the Congress of Berlin in 1878. As Bismarck and Disraeli contained Russia's advance, Abdülhamid II moved against the reformers who had shifted the reform movement from concern over the revitalization of the state to attempts at limiting the absolute power of the sultan.

On 14 February 1878, Sultan Abdülhamid II dissolved the Ottoman parliament, ending the experiment in constitutional government which had lasted less than two years. Centralizing power in his own hands, and exercising it through a small group of trusted intimates, he ushered in an era of absolutism. This did not mean, however, that Abdülhamid II and his government would shut the door on reform and endorse xenophobic rejection of the West and westernization. On the contrary, matters had gone too far; the Ottoman Empire was too entangled in the European balance of power to permit a policy of splendid isolation. Abdülhamid II's recognition of the need for economic development and the continued modernization of the military led to the establishment of a new military school system with elementary and secondary schools, with a military academy for the ablest students. The best Western-style education available in the Ottoman Empire was offered in its military schools. Paradoxically, as Ottoman society grew more repressive under Abdülhamid II, the military elite was being educated in a more liberal atmosphere and being exposed willy-nilly to ideas from the West that opposed such despotism as the sultan exercised. It was into this atmosphere of a return to centralized rule, continuing westernization, and corrosive nationalism, that Mustafa Kemal was born.

2

Mustafa: Born into a House of Mourning

MUSTAFA KEMAL ATATÜRK, FOUNDER OF THE MODERN REPUBLIC OF TURKEY and one of the architects of the twentieth century, was born in Salonika. Today that city is an important port of Greece, but at the time of his birth it was a leading provincial center of the Ottoman Empire. Despite the fact that Mustafa Kemal Atatürk became a figure of worldwide historical significance, many details of his birth are obscure. Everything about the date of his birth—the day, the month, and even the year—is still unresolved. Bureaucratic as the Ottoman Empire was, it did not keep systematic records of such particulars. No official notice of the date of his birth has come to light, nor has an unofficial record of his birth been found, even though Muslim Turks in the late nineteenth century still tended to note the essential events of the human cycle from birth to death in the family copy of the Koran or in some other cherished volume. Late in her life Atatürk's mother stated that his birth had indeed been recorded in one of the family's two Korans, but the copy with the notation had been given away (Cebesoy 1967, p. 3).

Atatürk's career has been minutely documented by a people who have made the record of his life a national preoccupation. At this juncture, then, it is highly unlikely that any new documentation on the date of his birth will surface. As accurately as can be determined, the year of his birth was 1881. An identity card issued to Atatürk later in life indicated the year of his birth as 1296 in the Rumi calendar, one of the several dating systems in use in the Ottoman Empire, corresponding to the period from 13 March 1880 to 12 March 1881. It is likely that he was born during the winter of 1880/81, for one of his mother's memories recorded close to the end of her life was to the effect that she had given birth to her son Mustafa during the stretch of days known locally in Salonika as the "freezing forty," the forty coldest days of winter.[1]

Atatürk himself did not know the exact date of his birth. After he had become president of the Turkish republic, he was asked to supply the date of his birth for a biography that was to appear in a foreign encyclo-

[1]Toward the end of her life Zübeyde gave an interview to a Turkish historian, Enver Behnan Şapolyo, and told him that Mustafa was born during the "freezing forty" (Şapolyo 1959, p. 17).

paedia. He chose as his birthday 19 May—the day he had landed at the port of Samsun on the Black Sea coast of Anatolia, where he launched the Turkish struggle for independence.[2]

Similar uncertainty remains about the exact place of his birth, although it is generally accepted that his birthplace is a three-storied pink house in one of the Turkish quarters of Salonika. Atatürk's younger sister has claimed that although Atatürk grew up in that pink house, he was actually born in a house in a nearby quarter occupied by his father's family (Aydemir 1969, vol. 1, p. 27). There, Atatürk's mother would have been attended during her labor by the women of the extended family. In any case, based on things he had heard from his mother, Atatürk considered the pink house his birthplace. Today, that house, purchased partly by funds contributed by Atatürk himself, is a museum maintained by the Turkish government.

Salonika had come under Ottoman Turkish control in 1430. The city was taken as the result of combat and was, therefore, available as booty. Sultan Murad II, who ruled at that time, turned over much of the devastated city, including churches and houses, to the invading Ottomans.[3] Most of the Turks settled in the upper part of the city in and around the acropolis, although Turkish holdings were scattered throughout the city. Many churches were converted into mosques. Only four were left to the Greeks. The majority of the Greek population was concentrated around the monastery of Vlatades (Tachaous Monastery). Murad II's successors, especially Sultan Selim I (1512–20), opened Salonika to the Sephardic Jews after their expulsion from Spain and Portugal. Other Jews arrived from Sicily, southern Italy, and Provence. The bulk of this Jewish immigration flowed in from the late 1480s to the 1520s, and in such magnitude that the new arrivals not only absorbed the older, Hellenized, Romanite Jews, but also established themselves as the major ethnic group in the city of Salonika. By the mid-seventeenth century there were 56 Jewish districts, most of them close to the waterfront, 48 Muslim districts, and 16 Christian districts inhabited by Greeks, Armenians, and other Balkan Christians.

Fully half the city's 70,000 inhabitants at the time of Atatürk's birth were Jews. Turks, numbering about 15,000, made up the second largest group, with the Greeks in third place. The Jews, with their distinctive and

[2]This information comes from Afet Afetinan, one of Atatürk's adopted daughters. Afetinan also reports that, according to his mother's recollections, Mustafa was born in the springtime (Afetinan 1959, p. 3).

[3]Murad II ascended to the throne in 1421 at seventeen years of age. Having stabilized the state, he abdicated in 1444, but returned when the empire was threatened by a European crusade. He died in 1451 and was succeeded by his son, Mehmed II, who captured Constantinople in 1453 and became known to history as Mehmed the Conqueror.

colorful clothes, their facility with European languages, and international contacts through trade which brought Salonika its prosperity, were primarily responsible for the city's evident European flavor. Despite its reputation as one of the most Westernized cities of the Ottoman Empire, Salonika still preserved its Turkish-Muslim character.

Seaborne trade had made Salonika's fortune. Fittingly, the docks and warehouses dominated the lower city. From there the city rose up the foothills and the slopes of Mount Khortiatis. The higher up the hill, the more Turkish, in the Ottoman style, the area became. Ramshackle wooden houses with their typically jutting windows gave way to houses made of stone and decorated handsomely with wrought iron. Gardens became larger and better tended. Some of the more lavish houses had vineyards and fountains. The Turkish homes had red tile roofs, enclosed balconies, outhouses, and pavilions. Bathhouses (*hamams*), about eleven public and three hundred private, adorned the Turkish quarters. Bey Hamam was the most famous of the baths, which were beautifully domed structures, like mosques though without minarets. H.G. Dwight, an American essayist and short-story writer born in Istanbul in 1875, visited the Turkish quarters of Salonika and wrote about them in romantic terms: "you keep discovering little squares where a plane tree or two make shadows, where water is sure to trickle, and where grave persons sit on rush-bottomed stools, sipping coffee, smoking water-pipes, and listening maybe to a naturalized gramophone" (Dwight 1915, p. 229). He was charmed by the costume of the Turks. Upper-class Turks wore satin coats with multicolored linings and sable fur, while Turks of the middle class wore coats of fabric from Drama and topcoats of English cotton; women wore veils.

In that colorful setting, close to the arch of Galerius in what was known as the Ahmed Subaşı quarter, stands Atatürk's pink house. It is not very far up the hill. Ahmed Subaşı was one of the poorer Turkish sections, populated by small businessmen who traded in agricultural goods and other products. Such tradesmen, known as *esnaf*, tended to stick together and live in tight-knit neighborhoods. In the traditional manner such a neighborhood had its mosque at the center, with a market nearby, a fountain, a school for the children, and a graveyard. Made cohesive by long-standing family and ethnic bonds, it was a rather self-sufficient and closed community.

Turkish life in Salonika honored the traditions of the patriarchal, patrilineal, and patrilocal extended family. More than just the nuclear family itself lived under one roof, which often sheltered many relatives and several generations at the same time. Members of such traditional extended families shared a group self-concept.[4] Each member was to some extent the psychological extension of the others, and all depended on the same interpersonal web for support and emotional nourishment, sharing emotional, social, and economic problems and presenting a unified front to the world. The need of the individual to assert himself was secondary to the mutual identification within the family. Each shared the success of any member as well as his or her misfortunes. To a great extent, emotionally the members lived as Siamese twins. Nevertheless, efforts at psychological assertion of one's identity were required and surfaced in constant low-key bickering, nagging, sulking, and bargaining. The group members required some testing of and collision with the boundaries of other personalities in the family in order to test the integrity of their own personality structure. Within what was generally a closed social system as far as the outside world was concerned, families had conflicts with and gossiped about each other even as they honored strong intrafamily allegiance.

Dominant though the male was in such a family, it was the mother (or oldest female member) who set its emotional tone. A Turkish proverb holds that "hell and heaven are found at the feet of the mother." Great influence, subtle and unspoken as it might be, was exerted by the chief female figure in the family over her male counterpart. It was she who persuaded him to end a family feud or to approve a daughter's marriage. Often lying beneath the surface, her power was nonetheless effective. A young bride joining her husband's extended family might be passive and fearful at first, but over the years she was likely to exercise power in her turn over the next generation of young brides. Domineering and witch-like old women, wielding powers that bordered on being magical, abound in Turkish folklore (Sümer 1970).

The "togetherness" of the extended family, and the inability of its members to individuate fully, foster the belief that each family is in some way unique. Disparagement of other groups, who are viewed as "bad" when they disagree with or oppose the extended family in question and "good" when they agree, is encouraged by the atmosphere of enclosed solidarity. Each family regards outsiders paradoxically either as appropriate targets for family hostility or disapproval or as a source of rescue and help. All perceptions of other people are colored by the habits of a domestic life exclusively and exquisitely shared. Turkish culture is "other-directed" and more given to polarizations than to merging toward the middle ground on issues. People "out there" who influence one's daily life are envisioned as either "all good" or "all bad."

[4]For more information on the traditional Turkish extended family, see Volkan 1979 and also Özbek and Volkan 1976.

A grateful nation pays homage to Atatürk's mother. An unidentified Turk kisses Zübeyde Hanım's hand.

This "other-directedness" perhaps had its origins in the ready availability to the Turkish child of more than one mothering figure within the extended family (Volkan 1979), in which the upbringing of a child is not the exclusive prerogative of the natural mother. Other women in the household, a grandmother, an aunt, an older sister, or perhaps a wet nurse, feel entitled to mother the child in their own way. Although this holds true for children of either sex, it is especially important for males. The child-mother unit must actually be extended to include multiple mothers. The necessary frustrations and their resolution with regard to a child in such circumstances who is struggling with psychological separation from others in order to find his own identity are unlike those of the child constantly in a one-to-one encounter with the same woman. Thus, the child, when frustrated by one "mother" whom he consequently sees as "bad," can easily find a more amenable "mother" to oblige and soothe him. He can then consider that "mother" as "good." Indeed, he might have to carry his case to as many as three or four women until his wish is ultimately gratified. Satisfied, he can readily let bygones be bygones with respect to the frustrations inflicted by those who had refused him. He is spared the necessity of having to accommodate himself to the frustrating "bad" behavior of a principal figure in his life whom he alternately recognizes as pleasing and "good" when she gratifies his needs or wishes. In healthy psychological development, if a child is to learn to appreciate the independent and realistic identity of another important person, that person must be perceived as being sometimes well disposed to one's self and one's enterprises, but at other times antagonistic.

Being raised in a home with multiple mothers makes it difficult to blend the contradictory frustrating and pleasing images of important others. This psychological phenomenon may appear later in life as a tendency to see people in terms of black and white, as all good or all bad, and to have difficulty in appreciating grey areas.

Obviously psychological makeup differs from person to person for a variety of reasons. It is safe, however, to assume that in their cultural and social interactions the Turks in Salonika shared the behavior patterns summed up under "other-directedness." Greeks and Jews also had multiple mothers in their family structures, and it is possible that they, too, were "other-directed." Furthermore, the "other-directedness" of these different communities may have played a role in keeping the various ethnic groups living side by side in the same city emotionally distant from each other.

Although noted for its cosmopolitan atmosphere and its unrivaled ethnic diversity, Salonika's various communities remained separate within their own languages, habits, ideals, and customs. There was little, if any, intermarriage. Business relations, however, were carried on among the communities, and a complex network of economic ties developed. Despite being second in population, the Turks maintained strict control over Salonika, holding administrative offices, living off their incomes as landowners, and lending money at high rates of interest. The Greeks and Jews were dedicated to trade. Because of their numerical superiority and their long-term presence in Salonika, the Jews enjoyed a special relationship with the city's Turks. By learning to conceal their wealth and never to offend the Turks, the Jews often fared much better economically than the Turks themselves (Moore 1906).

In addition to economics, the relationship between the Turks and the Greeks in Salonika was influenced by the rising tide of Greek nationalism during the early nineteenth century. The Hellenic revolution of 1821 had brought Turkish might down upon the Greeks of Salonika, taking a heavy toll of the population and bringing commerce to a halt. With the reforms of Sultan Mahmud II in 1826 the city began a rapid recovery, but nationalism among the Greeks continued to affect their relations with the Turks.[5]

Atatürk's father, Ali Riza, was at home in this environment of extended families and close-knit neighborhoods. His was an old Salonika family, but the prosperity manifest in his new pink house was a recent triumph for him.[6] Ali Riza's family, although it boasted of men who could read and write, no mean accomplishment in that time and place, was a modest one. An uncle of his taught school in one of the quarters of the city and enjoyed some local notoriety because of a flaming red beard from which his sobriquet "Red" was derived. Ali Riza's father had gained notoriety of a more ominous nature.[7]

Somehow or other he had become embroiled in the momentous events of early May 1876. On the fifth day of that month a young Bulgarian Christian girl had arrived in Salonika by train. She was accompanied by the Muslim religious leader (*imam*) of her village. The purpose of her trip was to see the proper authorities before whom she would declare her conversion to Islam. Her mother, who had been on the same train, appealed to fellow Christians at the station to help her rescue her daugh-

[5]Those reforms were chiefly military and bureaucratic. Mahmud II formed a new army, the uniforms for which were manufactured at first in Salonika.

[6]Ali Riza's family originally came from near Söke in Turkey's Aydın district (Atay 1980, p. 17). Söke is directly south of Izmir.

[7]Ali Riza's father's name was Ahmed. Apparently he had a red beard, and at least one source (Atay 1980, p. 17) refers to him as Kırmızı (Red) Hafız. "Hafız" is an honorific term applied to a person who knows the text of the Koran by heart. Since Ahmed's brother Mehmed was also referred to as Red Hafız (Aydemir 1969, vol. 1, p. 31), it is possible that some sources may confuse the two brothers. Most likely, both of them were known by the same nickname. In any case, Atatürk's grandfather also had another nickname, Kaçak (Fugitive) (Aydemir 1969, vol. 1, p. 31).

ter from taking such a fateful step. Even as she sought assistance, a group of Muslim Turks were escorting the girl to the governor's office. A band of Greeks seized the girl and spirited her off to the American consulate, where she was secluded for the night.

Angry Turkish crowds roamed the streets in the vicinity of the American consulate on the morning of 6 May. The German and French consuls, seeking to avoid irate protestors, took refuge in a mosque, but they were discovered and killed (B. Lewis 1968, p. 56). Communal discord, more volatile since the recent rise of nationalism in the Balkans, thus claimed two more victims. The violence of the Turks was directed as much against their own feelings of impotence engendered by foreign intervention in the internal affairs of the Ottoman Empire (in favor of the minorities) as it was against those local Christians who had abducted the young Bulgarian girl.

Reacting swiftly to this wanton attack on their official representatives, the foreign powers dispatched warships to Salonika and demanded the arrest and punishment of those responsible for the murders. Some accounts indicate that six people were ultimately seized and hanged. Other accounts say some forty people died on the hastily constructed gallows. Obviously, it was a dangerous time for anyone who had taken part in the demonstrations or murders. Ali Riza's father, who may have had some connection with the military, had been among the demonstrators. Fearing for his life, he escaped to the Macedonian mountains, where he lived as a fugitive for seven years, until death claimed him. In this manner the path of Ali Riza's family had crossed with the emerging lines of larger historical events. That intersection was without effect in the larger historical arena, but within Ali Riza's family the excitement, fear, and anxiety touched off by such a brush with destiny, combined with certain other events that left their intrapsychic marks, produced a psychological impact that would be transmitted to Atatürk's generation.

Instrumental in that transmission was the fugitive's son, Ali Riza. While his father endured self-imposed exile in the mountains of Macedonia, Ali Riza entered military service in late 1876. As war between Russia and the Ottoman Empire approached, a national guard unit of volunteers was organized in Salonika. Ali Riza had been employed as a clerk in the administration of pious endowments and then in the customs service. His ability to read and write brought him an appointment as a lieutenant in this militia unit. Once again, the family's history became intertwined with the larger, more exciting, and dangerous outside world of pressures and forces whose nature was only dimly perceived.

Late in 1877 or early in 1878 Ali Riza left the military. As with practically everything else in Ali Riza's life, it is difficult to pinpoint the exact date. The war with Russia had been halted by the Treaty of San

Stefano signed on 3 March 1878 (see chap. 1). That treaty was modified at the Congress of Berlin, which opened on 13 June 1878. Sometime in this interim Ali Riza returned to Salonika, where his wife was waiting for him.

Ali Riza's marriage must have taken place in the mid-1870s. Marriages in that part of the world were still arranged affairs. His older sister had undertaken the role of matchmaker, no simple task in this instance since Ali Riza could not afford a large dowry payment. In addition, he had his heart set on marrying a fair-haired woman. Such a woman would be for him literally a dream come true. A dream of Ali Riza's has been preserved (Aydemir 1969, vol. 1, p. 26) in which he saw a white-bearded holy man with a young blonde girl at his side. The holy man told the dreamer, "This girl is your destiny." It is impossible to tell whether this was a real sleeping dream or only the expression of an intense longing. Such a longing would not have been unique to Ali Riza, inasmuch as many Turkish men, even today, regard blonde women as particularly desirable.

Whether it was through resourcefulness or pertinacity, we do not know, but Ali Riza's sister found the desired mate for her brother. Zübeyde was the girl's name. Her family came from the region west of Salonika near Albania,[8] where the Ottoman government had relocated a number of nomadic Yürük Turks from the region of the Taurus Mountains in southeastern Anatolia. Relocation, forcible or otherwise, was an old Ottoman practice by which the government managed either to remove dissident elements from a region or bring desired groups into an area. In this instance a staunchly Muslim group of Turks had been introduced into a threatened border region to bolster its Turkish Muslim character. Zübeyde's dark blond hair, deep blue eyes, and fair skin conveyed her Anatolian origins. Ali Riza's sister had found his dream girl for him. Negotiations for the marriage almost foundered on the question of the dowry. In the end Zübeyde's step-brother intervened on Ali Riza's behalf. The match was arranged and the couple married.

Zübeyde must have been in her early teens at the time of her marriage, some twenty years younger than her husband. A young adolescent, she had hardly had time to explore her feelings and know her own mind. Like any youngster, her head was perhaps more filled with fantasies than with reality-tempered notions of the world. Yet, such a marriage of a girl to a man two decades her senior was common in that part of the world. Inherent in such "age-split" marriages are unusual stresses and strains, some of which precipitate internal conflicts, whereas others find external "solutions."

[8]Zübeyde's family was known as Hacısofular. Hacı in Turkish refers to those Muslims who had made the pilgrimage to Mecca. *Sofular* is the plural of *sofu*, which means a religious devotee. Thus, we assume that some important person or persons in Zübeyde's background had made the pilgrimage to Mecca and that her family had deep religious roots.

Just how these forces worked in the case of Zübeyde and Ali Riza is crucial for their ultimate effect upon the child who was to become Atatürk. Conforming to the partrilocal traditions of the extended family, Zübeyde took up residence within the bosom of Ali Riza's family in the Yenikapı district of Salonika. The status of a young bride in the extended Turkish family depends on her bearing children, especially sons. Zübeyde soon established her identity as a fruitful wife, and, still in her teens, she had three children in rapid succession, a daughter, Fatma, and two sons, Ömer and Ahmed, apparently all born in the extended family's home in the Yenikapı district.

Zübeyde, engaged in having and raising their children, was parted from her husband a great deal of the time. Ali Riza was employed in the Ottoman customs service and assigned to a bleak checkpoint in the wooded foothills of Mount Olympus on the border between the Ottoman domains and Greece. That checkpoint, called Paşaköprüsü, while only 80 miles from Salonika, was so remote that direct road communications between the two places did not exist. It could be reached only by sea and then overland. The distance and the difficulty of access meant that Zübeyde and Ali Riza had to endure long separations. Those were difficult years, especially for the young and inexperienced Zübeyde. Her daughter Fatma died in infancy during this period. When Ali Riza returned from military service and was reassigned to Paşaköprüsü, he found the loneliness and strain of continued separations a hardship. He determined that the family should leave Salonika and join him at his post. Reunited with the girl of his dreams, whom he was fond of calling "the rose garden of his paradise" (Aydemir 1969, vol. 1, p. 26), Ali Riza could not have foreseen what a fateful chain of events he had set in motion.

Paşaköprüsü was not a hospitable environment at that time. With hardly more than a few buildings in addition to the command post, only a vivid imagination could consider the establishment civilized. It was certainly no place for a young mother and her two young children. Life on the border was both desolate and dangerous. In addition, Zübeyde was deprived of the support of the extended family she had known in Salonika. In Paşaköprüsü there were no doctors or medications and no amenities of any sort. In the surrounding primeval forest, once the habitat of the gods of Greek mythology, now roamed smugglers, poachers, and Greek bandits bent on ruining the prosperous Turkish timber trade. Those predators set fires, robbed, hijacked loads of timber in transit, and generally kept the region in a state of agitation. Boundary demarcation and maintenance between the Ottoman Empire and Greece was and continued to be a most sensitive and painful issue, which the spread of nationalism into the Balkans served only to exacerbate. Anxiety levels were high, especially for the Muslim Turks harassed by the armed and determined Greeks. Attack was always possible and usually feared as being imminent. One story preserved in Atatürk's family concerned the expectation of just such an attack by Greek bandits whose object was to kidnap Zübeyde. Although the attack never materialized, the emotions that its anticipation engendered reverberated in the family's shared memory.[9]

Fear of bandits was neither the only, nor the most harrowing hardship endured by Ali Riza and his family. Freud would one day write what a monstrous thing it was to have a child predecease its parents.[10] It was the lot of Zübeyde and Ali Riza to have that calamity befall them three times before the birth of Atatürk. Their first child, Fatma, had died before the family moved to Paşaköprüsü. There the two boys, Ömer and Ahmed, died, each, as far as can be determined, at the age of three. A family story about the death of Ahmed is horrible in the extreme, and one can only imagine its impact upon the child's parents. Upon his death the young boy was buried in a sandy grave on the seashore, but during the night the waves exposed the corpse, which was seized upon by jackals and ripped apart (Aydemir 1969, vol. 1, pp. 35–36). Whether this story, which was repeated at home and recalled by Atatürk's younger sister in her adulthood, is accurate in all its grim detail is unimportant; it provides a poignant reflection of parental anguish. What had been a happy home for Ali Riza and Zübeyde was transformed into a house of mourning.

Having lived through such experiences, it is not surprising that Ali Riza should, with his wife's concurrence, seek some way to renounce the life of a customs official. His work had brought him in contact with the timber merchants of Salonika who conducted the trade in the Mount Olympus forest. They knew him to be thoroughly familiar with the details of the trade, its dangers, and its rewards. One of the merchants, Cafer Efendi, agreed to go into partnership with Ali Riza. Cafer contributed the capital and Ali Riza brought his knowledge and expertise to the joint enterprise. They would share the profits.

Initially, there were profits. Ali Riza's experience made him an excellent field man. He directed the cutting of the timber in the forest and its shipment to Salonika or Greece. He moved Zübeyde back to Salonika and was able to spend more time with her in spite of having to supervise operations in the forest. The pink house in Salonika attests to his newfound prosperity and would come to be considered the birthplace of Mustafa, a blond boy, the fourth child of Ali Riza and Zübeyde, who would grow up as Mustafa Kemal and later achieve fame as Atatürk.

[9]In an interview with Şapolyo (1959), Atatürk's sister Makbule referred to this incident. Also see Aydemir 1969, vol. 1, p. 36.

[10]This reference by Freud can be found in a letter he wrote to Ludwig Binswanger soon after the death of Freud's daughter, Sophie (Schur 1972, p. 329).

3

From Mustafa to Mustafa Kemal

A birth in an extended Turkish Muslim family was an occasion for the women involved to get together, for childbirth was the province of the women. As the time for delivery approached, the midwife, a most respected person, would bring her walnut birthchair to the house of the pregnant woman. This was a signal for the menfolk to leave the house. The birthchair was a horseshoe-shaped seat on which the pregnant woman would sit and grip the arms while the midwife helped her deliver. Throughout the process the midwife would offer incantations and recite, "God is most great." After the delivery, the new mother would be put on mattresses covered with special rich shawls and quilts with matching bolsters to prop her up (R. Lewis, 1971). The birth of a boy was especially welcome. But, whatever the sex of the newborn infant, the child and the mother would be considered vulnerable to the harm contained in the glances of "bad others," especially during the first forty days after the delivery. Therefore, the child and the mother had to be protected against the "evil eye" by the offering of prayers and the wearing of amulets. Certainly Mustafa would have come into the world properly protected against such "bad others." Like any Turkish Muslim father, Ali Riza would have been familiar with those practices that would ward off the evil eye, but Ali Riza also had his military sword hung alongside Mustafa's crib to invoke divine assistance in furthering a career in the military for his young son.[1]

It was the custom that in the days following the delivery the father or an older man in the extended family would say prayers and speak the name of the baby into the baby's ear. We do not know who it was who called, "Mustafa, Mustafa," to this future leader. If the great uncle, Red-bearded Hafiz, was still alive and present, he might have had that honor. The choice of the name Mustafa appears to have had emotional overtones, for Ali Riza is said to have caused the death of his own infant brother, named Mustafa, by accidentally overturning the baby's crib (Kinross 1965, p. 10). Now the name was being bestowed upon Ali Riza's

[1]Aydemir 1969, vol. 1, p. 55. In his interview with Dr. Volkan on 13 December 1974, Aydemir reported that the sword was kept as a memento in Zübeyde's home after Ali Riza died when Mustafa was seven years old. According to his sister Makbule, Atatürk used to play with his father's sword as a child.

son. We can only surmise that Ali Riza's sense of guilt over having accidentally caused the death of his infant brother found an echo in naming his son after him.

Infant death could not have been far from Zübeyde's mind either as she settled in the new pink house. She was only twenty, and the shadows of her three dead children must have been ever present with her. She would surely try to protect the new child from the fate that had befallen the others, but she might also have been psychologically prepared for a similar fate for her newborn son. This may account partly for what has been described as her acid disposition and rather callous responses at the time. She has been remembered as having a character almost dual in nature, bright and merry in her attire and socially independent, but severe in her religious devotion and the honoring of traditional Muslim customs. She dressed herself rather gaily, wearing blouses trimmed with lace, colorful long skirts, and jewels in her curly hair. The Turkish housewife of that time usually remained at home except when visiting other women in the neighborhood. Zübeyde's house was always open to other women of the extended family. Men were not included in such visits, but prepubertal male children could accompany older women. Mustafa's mother had the habit of abruptly terminating her visits to the homes of her friends, neglecting the ceremonious and protracted farewells demanded by custom. Her brusqueness led others to regard her as decidedly unconventional in her personal relationships, but in other areas of her life she was very much bound by convention. In certain practices she remained a peasant woman. Unaccustomed to sleeping in a Western-style bed, she spread her mattresses on the floor. Away from home, she hid her face with a veil in the traditional manner of Muslim women. During the time the family lived in the pink house, Zübeyde was called "Molla," a term applied only to the deeply religious. Her resort to religion is not surprising in view of the deaths of her children.

While we cannot be sure of what Zübeyde's thoughts about her newborn son were, one thing is certain; she did not have a sufficient supply of milk for nursing him. A black wetnurse was hired to assist Zübeyde with the feeding of the infant.[2] Though it can be assumed that Mustafa did not face physical hunger, we think he may have experienced early frustrations by having a grieving mother who could not give him the full satisfaction of abundant milk.

While Zübeyde busied herself with raising Mustafa, her husband left behind him the role of humble civil servant and became an aspiring businessman in the timber trade. He was responsible for securing permis-

[2]Kinross 1965, p. 10. Blacks were not especially numerous in the Ottoman Empire. Generally, they were brought in as household slaves from Egypt and the Sudan.

sion from the appropriate Ottoman government officials to cut trees in specified areas in timberlands, for supervising the cutting, sale, and shipment of the harvest, and for completing the paperwork involved. Those responsibilities still made it necessary for him to leave Salonika to visit the bandit-infested border where he had been isolated as a customs official and where the weakened Ottoman government was having difficulty maintaining order. Problems with the Greek bandits continued. They interfered with the shipments and, on occasion, detained and threatened Ali Riza as he sought to trace stolen timber. When at home in Salonika he talked about his job, his adventures, and his trials and tribulations at the border. Mustafa's early perceptions of life must have included awareness, both reality-based and fantasized, of his father's struggles at the border and of his parents' continuing anguish over the loss of their other children. Such awareness might, in fact, have been superimposed on his earliest perceptions of frustrating experiences, especially that of his mother's having an insufficient milk supply.

Mustafa's first memory of life, to which reference will be made later, is from the age of six or seven. His perceptions of the issues of his earlier childhood can only be inferred from one of his own writings. His essay on freedom, written on 27 January 1930, when he was nearly fifty, which can be seen today in his own handwriting, opens with a discussion of the relationship between man and nature. "Man does not decide whether to be born or not. At the moment of birth he is at the mercy of nature and a host of creatures other than himself. He needs to be protected, to be fed, to be looked after, to be helped to grow" (Afetinan 1971, pp. 77–78). Reference to the deprivation at his mother's breast, as well as to his dead siblings and to the concern that both he and his mother felt about safety can be seen. He saw "men born at the mercy of nature and . . . [its] creatures" and then continued in his essay to refer to "primitive people." Those "primitive people," whom he went on to describe as living "in fear of thunder, the darkness of night, floods, wild animals, and even one another" (Afetinan 1971, p. 78), are probably representative images from his childhood. One catches an echo of jackals tearing at a child's body.

Before the newfound prosperity and the relative security inherent in the move to Salonika could cover over the memories of previous hardships and heartbreaking events, new tragedies overtook the family. Ali Riza was unable to obtain assistance from the Ottoman authorities in Salonika against the Greek bandits, some of whom were themselves fugitives from the oppression of local Turkish officials. On occasion, he was captured by the bandits and had to give his timber to them. Once they threatened to cut his throat, but each time he managed to negotiate with them and save himself. We suspect that each time he returned to Salonika he had new stories to tell his family, probably inducing in his little son's mind images of an adventurous, idealized man able to survive against great odds.

At least one Ottoman official is said to have suggested to Ali Riza that he burn down the forests in which he cut his timber with the idea, no doubt, that the bandits would disappear (Aydemir 1969, vol. 1, pp. 39–40). It was the bandits, however, who did in fact burn the timberland on which Ali Riza depended for his livelihood. He soon found himself without employment. There is no record to indicate whether his partner, who had supplied the capital, dissolved the venture, but it is clear that Ali Riza had failed despite having risked death at the border in his effort to succeed. Ali Riza next tried his hand at the salt business, but again, he met with defeat, for this business, too, failed.

Ali Riza died when Mustafa was seven years old. Many years after his death, Zübeyde spoke of the depression that overtook her husband during the last three years of his life. In that period he drank heavily and suffered from what was said to be intestinal tuberculosis. Mustafa's perception of this "degraded" image of his father, we believe, could not be integrated with the idealized images he held of this man as the courageous adventurer.

Ali Riza's death left Zübeyde a widow at the age of twenty-seven. She had only a small pension with which to look after her son and the two daughters she bore after Mustafa. One daughter, however, soon followed her father in death. The house into which Mustafa had been born continued to be a house of death. Of the six children born to Ali Riza and Zübeyde, only two reached adulthood.

In the human cycle, times of birth and death are fraught with possibilities for psychological impact. Anthropologists and psychiatrists, following the lead of novelists, have demonstrated the propensity for the human mind to link the occurrence of two separate and disparate events in some causal pattern or relationship. Mustafa's birth coincided with the initiation of the family's relatively brief period of prosperity symbolized by the move into the pink house. His birth was amalgamated with the family's hopes and their expectations for a brighter future.

At the same time that these good feelings were being engendered by Mustafa's birth, the psychological environment encompassing the mother and her infant was stressful. Zübeyde had already lost three children. She had been uprooted from her own family at a young age, had endured long periods of separation from her husband, and had undergone hardships while living with him in the bandit-infested forest. Her milk had been insufficient to meet her infant's needs. Such are the materials out of which traumas in the relationship between mother and child can originate. D. W. Winnicott, the British psychoanalytic theorist who has most sensitively explored the world of interaction between mother and child, would probably have observed that Mustafa grew up without the benefit of what he termed "good enough" mothering (Winnicott 1965) at the time he was building his sense of self, and defensively Mustafa established a precocious and vulnerable sense of autonomy that was supported by fantasies of omnipotence.[3] The effects of this type of development on his personality structure would be seen in his later behavior patterns. The death of Mustafa's father, at the height of the boy's oedipal period, provided him with the sense of another trauma to bear. During the oedipal phase, approximately between the ages of three and six, the child has incestuous strivings for the parent of the opposite sex while he wishes the disappearance or death of the parent of the same sex. If the parent of the same sex actually becomes weak or dies during this time, the child feels triumphant, but guilty. Ali Riza was ill at the peak of Mustafa's oedipal period and died when the child was seven. The normal resolution of the conflicts of the oedipal period through the identification with rather realistic aspects of the father cannot take place since exaggerated guilt interferes with this process. The child expects punishment and has retaliatory fears with which to deal. Obviously, different children who have traumas due to the loss of the father in their oedipal period deal with such traumas in different ways according to what is available to them internally—their already developed psychic structure—and what is available to them externally—people who can absorb the children's fears.

Mustafa had come to the oedipal age, we believe, with two durable images (representations) of his mother: the one in which she was *not* a "good enough" mother, and the other in which she saw her little boy as something special and nurtured this specialness. This specialness was due to Zübeyde's perception that little Mustafa embodied the family's new life-style of prosperity and, more important, by replacing his dead siblings, he was the savior of the grieving mother. The blond boy, in turn, developed two basic senses of self; on the one hand, he was deprived, dependent, and emotionally hungry; on the other hand, he was omnipotently self-sufficient and special.[4] He dealt with the loss of his father in a similar fashion by keeping two images of him. The first father image was

[3]Modell (1976) describes how, in certain circumstances when the mothering is not "good enough," the child prematurely uses his own resources to deal with the shortcomings of the mother. This leads to the development of an inflated self-concept in the child. Kohut (1971, 1977), using a different theoretical frame of reference, also suggests the same process.

[4]This formulation about little Mustafa is more in line with Kernberg's (1975) and Volkan's (1976, 1981, 1982*a*, 1982*b*) findings regarding children who develop an inflated self-concept. (Such persons are generally known as having narcissistic personality organizations.) Dissociated from the omnipotent self-concept, one finds an opposing and devalued representation of the self as well as important others. Such nonintegration of inflated good and devalued bad parts of one's self or images of others is referred to as "primitive splitting" in psychoanalytic literature.

that of an idealized, adventurous man on the Ottoman border; the other one was the degraded, drinking, and depressed man. Mustafa attempted to identify with the idealized father while constantly trying to distance himself from the "bad" image of the father. His father's death further increased, defensively, his belief that he was above hurts (he had, after all, psychologically effected the death of his rivaling parent) and that he could, by identification with the selected (idealized) part of his father, chart his own destiny alone and without dependence.

Given the little that is known about Ali Riza in general, and specifically about his relationship with Mustafa, his impact on Mustafa's life has generally been written off as negligible. That view is decidedly shortsighted. Just prior to his death Ali Riza bestowed a "gift" upon his son that had a profound psychological impact upon Mustafa and was of immense historical significance for the Turkish nation. The psychological value of that "gift" is underscored by the fact that it constituted Atatürk's first memory of life. Zübeyde wanted Mustafa to receive his education in a religious school. His father, who was partial to the reform movement that sought to introduce secular education, found an "artful" solution to the problem.

Education in the Ottoman Empire was primarily the responsibility of the religious communities. It was also an area of life in which the impact of the West was felt earliest and most deeply. As the relationship between technology and warfare became more evident to the Ottomans toward the end of the eighteenth century, a naval and a military engineering school were established in 1773 and 1793, followed by a medical school in 1827, all along Western models. Some westernized secondary schools were in operation by mid-century. These new schools had their own curricula and teachers outside the purview of the religious establishment. Gradually, secular education seeped down to the elementary or primary school level and spread to other major cities besides Istanbul.

Salonika was one of the cities where secular primary school education was available when Mustafa came of school age. Zübeyde, whose nickname "Molla" reflected her religious bent, wanted Mustafa to attend the traditional neighborhood religious school. Such religious schools continued to exist side by side with the newer westernized schools and still attracted by far the larger number of students, those whose parents were not sympathetic to westernization, which was viewed as an attack upon the comfortable Muslim way of life. Despite the central government's interest in westernization, with its accompanying changes in almost every aspect of society, religion and popular semireligious beliefs and superstitions were still the dominant influence in everyday Turkish Muslim life. It would have been natural for Zübeyde, given her predilections, to indulge herself even more in the magic of religion after having lost three children to the fate dictated by Allah.

Not only had Zübeyde picked out the type of school she wanted Mustafa to attend, but she had also set her heart on his becoming either a *hoca* (a teacher in a religious school) or a *hafiz* (a memorizer and reciter of the Koran). On the other hand, perhaps because of the experience he gained through his brief military career, as an Ottoman government official, and finally as a businessman, Ali Riza opposed Zübeyde's educational plans for their child. He wanted Mustafa to be educated along Western, secular lines that would prepare him for a future in the rapidly westernizing Ottoman Empire.

Atatürk revealed his memory of how the dispute between Zübeyde and Ali Riza was resolved in an interview he gave to the Turkish journalist Ahmed Emin (Yalman), which was published in the daily *Vakit* on 10 January 1922.

> The first thing I remember from my childhood is about entering school. There was a deep struggle between my mother and father concerning this. My mother wished that I commence my education by enrolling in the quarter's religious school with chanting of the appropriate religious hymns. But, my father, who was a clerk at the customs office, was in favor of sending me to the newly opened school of Şemsi Efendi and of my getting the new type of education. In the end, my father artfully found a solution. First, with the usual ceremony, I entered the clerical school. Thus, my mother was satisfied. After a few days I left the clerical school and enrolled in the school of Şemsi Efendi. Soon afterwards, my father died. [Yalman 1922]

Atatürk is reported to have spoken rarely of his father, but often of his mother when he was the president of Turkey. This is not to be taken as a measure of his father's limited importance in the molding of Atatürk's psychological makeup. It was his father's artful solution that enabled him to get a Western education. Moreover, it not only gave direction to his life, but provided him with a way to extricate himself from the possessive relationship with his mother. This theme of satisfying the religious mother first, before following the route provided by the idealized father would appear again in his adult life.

In Atatürk's first memory of life, his father appears in idealized form. He refers to his father as an official of the customs service. In other words, the father is remembered as a person who held a job we now know he had given up years before Mustafa was of school age. It is possible that until his death Ali Riza himself held onto his identity as an official working on the Ottoman frontier. We know that Ali Riza, according to his wife's recollections, was having a difficult time with depression and alcohol about the time he gave his son this "gift." Atatürk's ability psychologically to reiterate the theme of this "gift" and his identification with the idealized father (as the surname Atatürk, "father Turk," implies) made him, to a great extent, what he was. His first memory of life, although containing elements of the truth, inasmuch as he did attend the secular school run by Şemsi Efendi, is pregnant with possibilities. In the psychoanalytic sense it could be called a "screen memory," that is, a story, usually both true and false, that includes condensation of important psychological constellations, and attempts to understand them, that the child faces and assimilates.[5] Furthermore, the secular school Mustafa eventually attended was associated in his mind with a man, Şemsi Efendi, while the religious school, which he entered dressed in a white robe with a gold threaded scarf wound about his head like a turban, but which he left in a few days, was associated with a woman, Fatma Molla Kadın.

The Şemsi Efendi school, and Şemsi Efendi himself, are also important from another psychological perspective. Both the school and its founder were the center of controversy and struggle, rather similar to the atmosphere faced by Ali Riza in the forest, but this time all the protagonists were Muslims. Offering instruction in a Western manner, the school and its driving force, Şemsi Efendi, were the object of attacks by conservative elements among Salonika's Turkish Muslim population. Insight into that situation was offered in an interview given to the newspaper *Akşam* in 1938 by an old Turkish general, Korgeneral Galip Pasinler, reminiscing about his early education in Salonika during the 1870s. He and his brothers had been attending a traditional school where learning was primarily by rote. When Şemsi Efendi opened his school, with its reputation for discipline and military salutations between teacher and students, the old general's father, an Ottoman officer living in Salonika, sent his sons there.

In a delightful manner the general recounted his own introduction to the Şemsi Efendi school and his adventures there:

> Upon entering the school from the street, one came upon a small courtyard. On the left there was a staircase of four or five steps leading to a landing where the door to the classroom was. Twenty or thirty boys were playing in the courtyard. A young man who was walking among the children saw us come in and turned his attention to us. He took the note our father had written and given to the servant. Welcoming us, he had us go and play with the other children. This was our teacher, Şemseddin Efendi. We played for a little while and began to

[5]The child forgets (represses) most of the memories of his experiences during the first five years of his life. In other words, he has what psychoanalysts call "infantile amnesia." Screen memory refers to those fragments of memory of this period of infantile amnesia. Such fragments of memory, when they surface to consciousness, are associated with other forgotten memories.

get acquainted with the other youngsters. At that moment there was a command—"Children, go to the classroom." His command struck our ears, and we lined up in two rows, and we went up the steps with the teacher in front. Upon entering the classroom, there was a delicious odor coming from the brand new pine benches arranged in rows with an aisle between them. At the left of the door stood Şemsi Efendi and behind him there was a beautiful raised chair mounted by two steps, and hung on the wall was a blackboard with an eraser and chalk. Our teacher arranged us in two rows. When we had entered the room, he told us to sit down. We sat up straight, and in front of us there were tall, fitted desks. How beautiful it was! This was the school's opening day. The teacher [Şemsi Efendi] questioned us from his chair and separated us into those who had already been and those who had not yet been to school. He taught us the alphabet, each letter in association with the vowels. He wrote them on the board and then had us write them. Then we had a break. We played in the courtyard under supervision, and we were made to do some gymnastics. At the same time, the doors and windows of the classroom were opened and fresh air let in. While we were playing, they were careful to see that we did not argue with each other or use bad language.

A month or two later a crowd appeared and an uproar broke out on the street one day. Unfriendly words and curses were shouted, the hall door was broken, and the interior of the building was stormed. Upon seeing this state of affairs, our teacher, who apparently had been on the alert, fled by way of a window that opened onto the neighbor's garden.

The troublemakers consisted of a group of forty or fifty men from a large collection of rogues. They entered the classroom and reduced it to ruins, breaking the benches, the teacher's chair, the blackboard, the windows, and the doors, after having thrown us out amidst curses. We all ran home. Why did they do it? Şemsi Efendi was teaching children by the methods of the infidels. He was making the children play games and having them do gymnastics!

Up to that day the number of students had been diminishing a bit every day. About twenty of us, the children of officers and officials, remained.

A few days passed. Our servant took us to the school that Şemsi Efendi opened anew. This school was in a large room above the teacher's own house. Our teacher worked and made us work. Not one iota of damage had been done to his tenacity and zeal, or more correctly, to his love of pedagogy. On the contrary, it had increased.

Meanwhile, one day another similar attack took place here.

> They threw the children into the street amidst threats and curses. Şemsi Efendi hid himself and escaped danger. Again, the benches and the blackboard were broken, that blackboard which was the symbol of heathenism. They were unable to do anything to the house.
>
> Many years later, according to what I heard from the teacher's own mouth, they had caught him on the street and beat him up. They insulted him and threatened his life with knives. Şemsi Efendi should either leave Salonika or give up his school and teaching, or else!
>
> Şemsi Efendi did not pay any attention to this. He tried again for a third time. He began to come to our homes in the evening and give us lessons. In this way he visited his last twenty students every night, and he would teach us for five or ten minutes or supervise us.
>
> One day, Şemsi Efendi took a group of five or six of his students (I was among them) to the *rüşdiye* located adjacent to the Alacaminare mosque, which was the only high school in Salonika. We entered the classroom of the *rüşdiye*'s leading teacher. There were a number of people there, members of the provincial administrative council and some city notables.
>
> They brought in five or six of the *rüşdiye*'s students. They had us read the newspaper. The *rüşdiye* children could not read as well as we did. They had us do some arithmetic, calculations, and writing. The *rüşdiye* children were unable to do as well. They hung a map on the wall. The *rüşdiye* students could not read the map as well as we could. In short, we beat them out, and they were chosen from the senior class!
>
> This procedure was entered into for the sake of comparison. By demonstrating the results of his extraordinary will, courage, and determination, Şemsi Efendi gained the people's favor and confidence. After this, Şemsi Efendi's school was reopened under the government's protection.[6]

This was the school to which Ali Riza sent his son Mustafa. It had survived several attempts to close it. Only the tenacity and heroism of its founder had enabled it to remain in existence. The new educational methods had been vindicated, but only by determination and a strong act of will. The story of Şemsi Efendi reminds us of the story of Ali Riza, who had kept going to the forest to face bandits. When Mustafa's father died, he may have perceived Şemsi Efendi as an idealized father and attempted to identify with him. The idealized father continued to live in the person of Şemsi Efendi.

[6]This material by General Pasinler is from *Akşam* (13 December 1938) and is quoted in Ergin 1939–43, vol. 2, pp. 395–96.

A similar theme distinguishes another early memory of Atatürk's, perhaps also a screen memory, which may or may not be altogether true to the facts, and it, too, deals with the triumph of the will over tradition. In the religious schools the students sat half-kneeling to do their calligraphy lessons in much the same manner that a Muslim sits to recite the Koran. Mustafa's refusal to do this led to a confrontation with his teacher on this matter. Apparently the teacher gave in, for the other children copied Mustafa's example. This memory suggests the way in which an identification with Zübeyde's stubborn unconventionality, evident, for example, when she abruptly took her leave after visiting friends, was used by her son to oppose another of her characteristics, her devotion to traditional religious usage.

Ali Riza died while Mustafa was attending the Şemsi Efendi school. Economic necessity led to his family's removal to a farm some twenty miles outside of Salonika. There they lived under the sponsorship of an "uncle," Zübeyde's stepbrother, the man who had intervened on Ali Riza's behalf and relieved him of the burdensome dowry payment. Perhaps this uncle felt responsible for the family in light of his role in promoting the marriage.

Many years later Atatürk and his sister reminisced about their life on the farm. They recalled what any child might remember about farm living and brother-sister relationships, such things as chasing and frightening the crows, making a shed, and the boy thrusting his sister's face into a bowl of yogurt. The period must have represented an unwelcome decline in the family's fortunes, for the uncle was only the caretaker of an estate whose owners feared the Greek and Bulgarian bandits too much to live there themselves. Mustafa was sent to a nearby Christian church for his education, but he disliked it. At length, his mother sent him back to Salonika to stay with an "aunt" whose exact relationship to the family is unclear. In his interview with Ahmed Emin (Yalman 1922), Atatürk referred to her as his aunt on his mother's side. Although she may have been Zübeyde's sister, this is far from certain.

Back in Salonika again, Mustafa enrolled in a secular secondary school. At this point in the reform of education in the Ottoman Empire there were three main educational avenues open to Muslims. Onc was still the traditional system of local religious schools followed by advanced training in the main mosques of the principal cities, especially Istanbul. This type of training led to careers in the religious establishment either as a teacher or as a *kadı*, a judge in the Ottoman administrative system. Another avenue was represented by the military schools from primary school through the military academy. Those who chose this route usually went on to careers in the Ottoman military. The third main school system involved the secular or civil schools where training could lead to a variety of careers, including government administration. Those interested in the bureaucracy would go on to study at the Mülkiye, the higher educational facility organized in 1859 and reorganized and expanded in 1877 as a training ground for civil servants. Students generally entered one educational avenue and pursued those opportunities with little, if any, crossing over from one system to another. If one wished to switch, it was better to do so as early as possible.[7]

Mustafa was rather unhappy in the civil school in which he had been enrolled, and that unhappiness played a significant role in his decision to leave that school. The teacher, Kaymak Hafız, appears to have been of a sadistic nature. Atatürk recalled in his interview with Ahmed Emin that the teacher one day caught him quarreling with another student. Kaymak Hafız, who had already administered corporal punishment to Mustafa on other occasions, beat him severely this time and left him bloodied. Mustafa refused to return to the school. It is not clear if Zübeyde still lived at the farm when he left the school. Ultimately, Zübeyde, too, returned to Salonika with the rest of the family; by then there may have been but one daughter, but the date of the other daughter's death is not known.

It appears that even in those early years Mustafa was markedly different from his peers, not only because of his blond hair, blue eyes, and fair skin, but also in his demeanor. It is safe to assume from what evidence is available that Mustafa was already a "loner" and suspicious of others. As a boy he had few friends and was largely a bystander in their play. Once Mustafa was asked to participate in a game of leapfrog, but he refused because he was "too proud" to bend over and allow the other boys to vault over his back. Instead, he asked the boys to jump over him while he stood up straight (Atay 1980, p. 21; Parushev 1973, p. 30).

What little is known about Mustafa's actual behavior as a child goes along with the idea that he had to be self-sufficient, special, different, and above the other children. His own self-concept was rather inflated as a defense against the deprivations and traumas that he had experienced and that had left their mark on his psyche. There was a certain Major Kadri who lived in Mustafa's neighborhood (Yalman 1922). The major's son was a student in a military secondary school and wore a military uniform. Atatürk described his jealousy of this youngster and of the lieutenants he used to see on the streets wearing their neat uniforms. He developed a wish to wear one too, desiring the best available. He knew that, in order to realize his wish, the only road to follow was to enroll in a

[7]There are, however, a few outstanding examples of Ottomans who changed careers in mid-stream, so to speak. The most notable was Cevdet Pasha, who went from a religious to a bureaucratic career. He then became a leading statesman of the reform era in the Ottoman Empire and an outstanding historian.

military secondary school. Whatever other reasons might have been present, Atatürk's own admission that his desire to wear a uniform led him to choose a military career indicates that his inflated self-concept was involved. Typically, such a trait goes along with an interest in personal appearance and the illusion of being handsome. On that score, however, Mustafa had no need of illusions, for he was, in fact, a rather strikingly handsome youngster.

Mustafa's decision to embark upon a military career flew in the face of his neighbors' basic values. The neighborhood was staunchly Muslim, yet somewhat paradoxically the people were what is called in Turkish, *atak*, that is, active and extroverted. During Mustafa's childhood each block in the district had its own strong man. Some of them, genuinely protective of their own people and mutually respectful, were thieves in the Robin Hood mold. Such a strong man might remove his traditional sash and stake out his domain with it, daring anyone to challenge him by crossing the boundary line. Although the neighborhood residents were accustomed to this type of cockiness and tolerated such display among locals, they disliked members of the military proper whom they regarded as snobbish.

Zübeyde was unhappy about Mustafa's desire to enter the military. It meant separation between mother and son, and it was also a dangerous profession. Atatürk described his mother's feeling on this issue. "She strongly objected to my becoming a soldier. Without letting her know, I took the entrance examination for the military secondary school on my own. Thus, I achieved a fait accompli against my mother" (Yalman 1922). With his inflated self-concept he alone knew what was best for him. He chose his own destiny. We do not know if he followed his father's practice of offering his mother some form of satisfaction before charting a different future for himself against her wishes. We do know that he was about twelve years old at the time. Most Turkish Muslim boys in that period were circumcised at the age of seven, eight, or nine in a ceremony for which their culture prepared them and in which the knife that cut the skin around the glans penis castrated them symbolically even as it initiated them into manhood.[8]

It was around the age of puberty that Mustafa made a definite commitment to obtain a modern military education. This was in part an implementation of his desire, which one might call a narcissistic desire, to wear a uniform. In part, it was also an attempt at identification with the idealized father, the same father who had dedicated Mustafa to the military by hanging his sword alongside his crib. It was also an act as well

[8]For more information on the psychological effects of circumcision on Turkish boys, see Öztürk (1963, 1973), Öztürk and Volkan (1971), and Volkan (1979).

that put him in touch once again with his father's "gift"—a way to separate himself from his religious mother. At the same time he was rejecting the influence of his religious Muslim neighborhood, an extension of the "bad" mother images, which regarded the military as arrogant. On another level it also won him approval, for in the Ottoman world the military attracted the best society had to offer and rewarded its members not only materially, but with respect as well.

Military school brought out the best in Mustafa. By that time, we believe, his self-concept, which demanded from him that he be "number one," had probably crystallized. Modern psychoanalysts would say that such an inflated self-concept reflects a narcissistic personality organization. Just as his good looks provided a "fit," if you will, between the demands of his defensively inflated self-concept and reality, his native intelligence provided a similar solution for the demands of being superior to his peers and even his elders. Mustafa developed an interest in mathematics and was good at it. Later, when Atatürk discussed his relationship with his mathematics teacher, his description of it reflected that glorified and inflated self-concept we have seen developing in the young Mustafa. "In a short time," he said, "I had knowledge [in mathematics] as much as the teacher who taught us, even perhaps more than he had." He recalled being interested in issues above and beyond the class lessons. He wrote questions to and received written answers from his mathematics teacher.

Atatürk recalled the teacher as being a "stern man," and he also had the name Mustafa. "The teacher," Atatürk said, "in class did not call on anyone first or second. One day he said to us, 'Those of you who are confident that you know the work should stand up. I'll let you ask the questions!' At first I hesitated. Such outstanding people stood up that I preferred not to stand. I was cross-examined by one of them. At the end of it my patience had reached its limit. I jumped up and said, 'I can do better than that.' Thereupon, the teacher made me the questioner and I asked them of the other students" (Yalman 1922).

In the same interview Atatürk also remembered that it was from this mathematics teacher that he received his nickname Kemal, "perfection," or by extension, "the perfect one." "One day the teacher said to me, 'My son, your name is Mustafa and mine is too. This can't be. We have to find some difference. From now on your name should be Mustafa Kemal.' From that time on my name in fact did remain Mustafa Kemal."

Atatürk's Turkish biographer, the late Şevket Süreyya Aydemir, in an interview with Vamık Volkan in 1974 reported that he had unearthed a different version of how Atatürk came by the name of Kemal. It seems that there was another student in the class named Mustafa who in his adulthood lived in Istanbul and had become a prosperous shipowner. By giving Atatürk the name Kemal, that teacher was actually differentiating him from the other student, not from himself. It is not surprising, if this version is correct, for Atatürk to have remembered the story the other way around. His grandiosity and inflated self-concept would be responsible for his recalling the incident in a manner that compared him in a favorable light with his teacher. The name Kemal "fit" well with Mustafa's inflated self-concept. He accepted it and set out to pursue a military career as a "perfect" person and opened the way for his own history to converge with that of his motherland.

4

Mustafa Kemal: The Making of an Ottoman Officer

At twelve years of age Mustafa Kemal was a student in the military secondary (preparatory) school in Salonika. Against the wishes of his mother, he had entered the world of those fellow adolescents who stood out from among their peers by the attractiveness of the uniforms they wore, the seriousness of their purpose—the future of the Ottoman Empire would be in their hands—and the respect and envy they aroused. On their way to becoming officers by virtue of their education, they were among that small elite who could read and write. Their young lives quickly became regimented as they were trained to take and to give orders. For the most part their teachers were army officers, and the world in which they circulated was almost totally a male world.

Mustafa Kemal's relationship with his mother at this point was characterized by a slight estrangement. She was angry with him for choosing a career that placed the life of her only surviving male offspring in jeopardy, but she secretly took great pride in seeing her handsome son in his military school uniform. It is not surprising that during this period Mustafa quickly became infatuated with a young girl. For a long time she was identified by Atatürk's biographers only as "E," and she was said to have been the daughter of a high military official. In 1964, Y. Çetiner, a reporter on the staff of *Cumhuriyet*, one of Istanbul's largest daily newspapers, located her in old age and was granted an interview. Her name was Emine and in her youth she had been a neighbor of Mustafa Kemal's. She recalled that she was four years younger than Mustafa Kemal, and she gave her age at the time of the interview as seventy-seven.[1] There are some inaccuracies in her recollection, for according to her stated age, she would have been about six years younger than he was.

Emine recalled how impressed she had been with Mustafa Kemal's difference from other boys his age and how fastidious he had been about his appearance.[2] In her childish fantasies she expected him to become the

[1]Çetiner (1964). According to Emine, her father, Şevki, was a pasha (general) then stationed in Salonika. Also see Borak 1970, pp. 7–17.

[2]Atay (1980) heard from Mustafa Kemal's childhood friends that Mustafa Kemal had started to pay a great deal of attention to the way he dressed when he fell in love at this time of his life (p. 19). Atay does not identify the girl by name, but he speaks of another girl named Müjgan, a lieutenant major's daughter whom Mustafa Kemal wished to marry, most

sultan. Although what each felt to be love for the other began when she was eight and he was twelve, Turkish Muslim customs made it quite difficult for them to meet as they approached adolescence. She could only peer at him from behind her window as he passed her house dressed in uniform with his fellow students from the military school.

In his adult life Atatürk expressed great fondness for a popular song which declared love for "My Emine," saying, "There is an Emine in the heart of every man!" It is likely that his relationship with young Emine was but a youthful, platonic, and idealized idyll. It seems, however, to have done very little to ease the pain he experienced when his widowed mother remarried. He was then about thirteen years old.

In addition to all the reasons why a still young and handsome widow would want to remarry, Zübeyde's second marriage was also an economic necessity. Ali Riza's death had left her with only a most modest pension on which to manage. Prospects were not good for a poor widow with two young children. She most likely took the first suitor who came along, a man named Ragıp, who was thirty-two or thirty-three years old and a newcomer to Salonika. He worked as a civil servant in the tobacco monopoly. His first wife had died and left him with two or perhaps three children (Atay 1980, p. 19). He became what the Turks call an *iç güveyisi*, a groom who, contrary to the usual custom, moves into the bride's or her family's home.

Zübeyde's remarriage enraged Mustafa Kemal. The event occurred during his first or second postpubertal year. During postpubertal years, youngsters go through a process of relinquishing their inner attachments to representations of important figures of their childhood. This leads to a psychological disorganization that is followed by a new inner organization which includes newly evaluated aspects of the parents and important others. The youngster, then freed to a great extent from tight connection with the images of his childhood, turns to new attachments and new values in the world. Mustafa Kemal's early childhood environment had been seriously traumatic, and the representations of the important people of his childhood not fully integrated. The second process of individuation of his childhood attachments during puberty was not only difficult, but was an extremely important task for him since it gave him another chance to individuate in a more integrated manner.[3] Thus, his mother's

---

likely a little later in life. However, since he was very shy and afraid of rejection, he did not formally press the marriage (p. 22). We found no other information on Müjgan.

[3]The second individuation process referred to in the text deals with the disengagement of loving (libidinal) and aggressive investment from the mental representations of important loved and hated people of childhood in adolescence. During this period there occurs an obligatory regression which is in the service of development since it brings the more advanced ego of adolescence into contact with infantile drive positions and earlier con-

remarriage, we believe, was an extra burden for him. Not only did it reawaken in him aspects of his original oedipal struggles, but also his feeling of being "number one" was shaken. He could not accept her renunciation of their "special" relationship which the remarriage represented despite the fact that, paradoxically, he wished to be free of her religious side, which was intertwined with the side of her that was the grieving, smothering mother.

In his anger about the marriage, Mustafa Kemal searched for a gun with which to frighten his mother and her new husband. Fortunately, by the time he found one, they were out of reach.[4] Later in life, Atatürk described to one of his adopted daughters how he packed his books in a bag and left his mother's house (Gökçen 1974). She was no longer the source of satisfaction for his narcissistic needs—the single-minded adoration that gratified even as it chafed. He moved in with a distant relative, a woman whose husband was a *clerk in the customs office*. Thus, on one level the boy was making his escape from home, but on another, which must have been repressed or dissociated, he was returning to the symbolic early home provided by his father when he was a customs clerk.

Estranged from his mother, Mustafa Kemal did not even visit her when he finished his studies at the military school. In 1895 he was ready to move on to a military training school. Some of his teachers, including his mathematics teacher Mustafa, encouraged him to apply for the school at Monastir instead of Istanbul. He took the examination and was accepted. At the age of fourteen he left Salonika for Monastir, where he would be a boarding student, lodging and taking his meals in the military school.

Today, Monastir (Bitola), like Salonika, lies outside the borders of Turkey, in Yugoslavia. When Mustafa entered school in Monastir in 1895, the city was the strategically important Ottoman provincial center of Macedonia. Situated in a broad plain between mountain ranges, Macedonia monitored the Ottoman frontier with Greece and Albania. Whenever there was trouble in Serbia or Bulgaria, Monastir played an important military role in that as well. Macedonia itself was a weathervane for the winds of nationalism that were blowing through the domains of the Ottoman Empire, especially in the Balkans. Complaints and demands from Greeks and Slavs in Macedonia created a tense environment that must have been exciting and stimulating for a fourteen-year-old away from his hometown for the first time. Prior to Mustafa

---

flictual constellations as well as earlier object relations. In other words, psychologically speaking, the youngster visits his childhood psychological makeup, loosens his investment in it, and thus becomes ready to consolidate his personality on a different and higher level (Blos 1967, 1979).

[4]This incident was told to Dr. Volkan by the late Şevket Süreyya Aydemir (1974), who had heard it from Celâl Bayar.

Kemal's departure, one of Ragıp's sons gave him a pocket knife with which to protect himself from the aggressive interests of other men.[5] In those days when Turkish women lived behind their veils and in the protective surroundings of their homes and were denied the company of suitors, there was a possibility that some men might satisfy their sexual interests with youngsters of the same sex.

Mustafa Kemal threw himself into the swirling world of Monastir and thrived on it. He did not, however, sever his ties with Salonika. His relationship with his mother after her remarriage continued to be a chilly one, despite the fact that respect for one's elders is required in Turkish culture, which has an endless list of courtesies expected of the young toward their seniors. Mustafa Kemal spent his vacations in Salonika, but there was a considerable time during which he did not see his mother. Some of the time he spent visiting Emine and tutoring her in her studies. Atatürk's sister later recalled that he considered marrying Emine at this time, but nothing came of it.

Zübeyde tried to patch things up with her son. Troubled by Mustafa Kemal's dislike of her second husband, she tried to make peace between them. Whenever he visited her, she maneuvered a role reversal in which her husband carefully paid his respects to the younger man. She would, for example, ask her husband to stand up whenever Mustafa Kemal entered the room. All this ran counter to accepted Turkish standards of behavior. Zübeyde explained this as an effort to make Mustafa Kemal feel more kindly toward his stepfather, but it seems more like an unconscious support of her son's defensive use of his inflated self-concept. This sycophantic behavior appeared to have had the desired result, for Mustafa Kemal is said to have begun to accept his stepfather. Yet he never again lived under the same roof with his stepfather, except perhaps during brief periods of leave when he did stay in his mother's house.

Reconciliation with his mother and stepfather coincided with the period when Mustafa Kemal was cementing the friendships with some of his Monastir schoolmates that would become lifelong relationships. He had already met these people in Salonika, and they became close through the shared experiences of Monastir. Among his friends were Nuri (Conker) and Salih (Bozok).[6]

[5]The name of the stepbrother who gave the pocket knife to Mustafa Kemal was Süreyya (Toyran). As an adult he committed suicide. Another of his stepbrothers was named Hakkı (Atay 1980, p. 20).

[6]Other people from his Salonika and Monastir days who remained friends throughout his lifetime include Fuat (Bulca) and Ismail Hakkı (Kavalalı). It is known that as the president of Turkey he was closer to his schoolmates than to his relatives. One informant whose family lived next door to Ali Riza's house in Salonika told Dr. Volkan in 1975 that he personally had known some of Atatürk's relatives who continued to sell milk in the streets of Istanbul

All of his close friends from this period have shared their memories of Mustafa Kemal in print. In adulthood, most of them became satellites of Atatürk. We know that as an adult Atatürk took the center of any stage and regarded his followers as extensions of himself, and it would appear that he had this proclivity even as a youngster. Profound indifference for anything beyond his own concerns, narcissistically considering it unworthy of his attention, marked his demeanor. He felt himself above the preoccupations of the average person.

Among his schoolmates at Monastir was an excitable young man named Ömer Naci, who subsequently became an important spokesman for the Young Turks (see chap. 6). At Monastir young Ömer busied himself writing poetry, and he would often recite his verses to Mustafa Kemal. One day he asked Mustafa Kemal to loan him something to read, but he did not care for any of the books offered to him. That disturbed Mustafa Kemal greatly, a feeling he divulged in the interview with Ahmet Emin. It seems that he could not tolerate being second to another man in any field. He set about studying literature and tried his hand at becoming a poet himself. Later, he recalled that one of his teachers deterred his interest in writing poetry. "The wish, however, to write well stayed with me," he commented (Yalman 1922). His interest in poetry soon gave way to the more absorbing discussion of political issues and experimentation with oratorical style. Nothing remains of the poetry he wrote.[7]

There is in existence a paraphrase he wrote of some lines by Namık Kemal. As the poet of incipient Turkish nationalism, Namık Kemal had a great vogue among Mustafa's contemporaries, especially the young military officers and students who sought guidance for curing the ills of the Ottoman Empire. They found in the poetry, plays, and essays of Namık Kemal a voice that sought to harmonize traditional Islamic values with the new ideas about society, government, and culture that were penetrating the empire from the West. Born in Rhodosto in 1840 of an aristocratic Ottoman family, Namık Kemal had served in the Ottoman bureaucracy. In addition to his traditional education centered on the knowledge of Turkish, Arabic, and Persian, he had learned French and had spent time in Europe. During some of that time he was in exile, having incurred the wrath of the sultan for some of the ideas in his writings. The patriotism that infused his work struck a responsive chord in Mustafa Kemal. One of Namık Kemal's best known verses conjures up a desperate scene:

---

while Atatürk was president. Supposedly these relatives asked no favor of the president, nor did he seek them out.

[7]One wonders if he destroyed his poems. According to his personality organization they may have been "too good" to be shared with others or "too bad" and therefore had to be disowned. We know that later in life he would order the destruction of some of the "bad" pictures taken by his photographers.

The enemy put his knife at the throat of the country,
There is no one to save the ill-fated mother.

Mustafa Kemal was to paraphrase this last line, substituting:

There is someone to save the ill-fated mother.

This line refers not only to the threatened Ottoman Empire, but to Mustafa Kemal's relationship with his own mother now displaced onto the country, which he saw in need of rescue as well.

While Mustafa Kemal gave up his interest in becoming a poet at the suggestion of one of his teachers, the broadening of his educational background continued under the tutelage of another friend, Ali Fethi (Okyar), usually called Fethi. It was he who introduced the future leader to political ideology.[8] Ali Fethi was proficient in French, a subject with which Mustafa Kemal was experiencing difficulties. His French teacher reproached him several times for his inability to master the language, and, offended by this treatment, Mustafa Kemal redoubled his efforts to learn French. During vacations in Salonika he took private lessons in order to overcome his deficiencies. Improvement made it possible for Fethi to introduce him to the works of Rousseau, Comte, Voltaire, Desmoulins, and Montesquieu.

Mustafa Kemal's physical development kept pace with his intellectual growth. While at Monastir he grew into a handsome young man. He dressed impeccably in well-pressed uniforms and sported a fine moustache. In the Near East, facial hair was intimately associated with masculinity. Only eunuchs had no beards or moustaches. Mustafa Kemal and his friends frequented the European section of Salonika while on vacation. The European quarter by the waterfront was renowned for its cafes and bistros run mostly by Greeks. The atmosphere was much more permissive than anything Mustafa Kemal had known in his native Turkish Muslim quarters of the city. Unveiled women sang and danced and sat at tables with men.

Enjoying himself, Mustafa Kemal joined in the fun and in the drinking.[9] The women who frequented the nightspots found him irresistible. He responded to their overtures without becoming emotionally involved with any of them. His platonic attachment to Emine seems to have kept his many sexual encounters from touching him in a meaningful way. He was the pursued one rather than the pursuer, getting rather than

[8]Parushev 1973, p. 38. Ali Fethi was born in 1880 and thus was slightly older than Mustafa Kemal.

[9]One unsubstantiated rumor speaks of his having become accustomed to alcohol while still a child. Another story relates that he was introduced to rakı, the Turkish national drink, while attending the War College in Istanbul and became a habitual drinker of it then.

The Grey Wolf. Mustafa Kemal stares into the future shortly after his victory at Gallipoli.

giving. Such a situation could only have served to reaffirm his inflated self-concept.

Life as a military cadet, with its periods of intense study and equally intense vacation breaks, was not out of touch with the real world. Movements of national liberation that inflamed the Greeks, the Serbs, and the Bulgars threatened to break out into armed rebellion at any moment. In 1896 Macedonia was thrown into turmoil as the result of a confrontation between the Greeks and the Ottomans. A Greek war of liberation was initiated on the island of Crete, then under the Ottomans. The Greek islanders were supported militarily and diplomatically by the Greek government in Athens. The situation on Crete smoldered all through the year as the Great Powers sought some way out of the diplomatic crisis by pressing Sultan Abdülhamid to agree to a reform program for the island and by keeping the Greek government from openly supporting the insurgents on Crete. Trouble in Crete was also a signal for the Greeks in Macedonia to organize against both the Ottomans and the Bulgarians, whose expansionist dreams they found equally disconcerting.

Matters degenerated on Crete early in February 1897. Muslims and Christians began slaughtering each other in earnest, and the Greek consul on the island telegraphed for support from Athens, where intense public demonstrations in favor of intervention forced the government to respond favorably. A Greek force landed on Crete on 13 February, but for the Greek officer corps Crete was only a sideshow. Most of the officers belonged to Ethnike Hetairia, a secret organization dedicated to galvanizing national forces and strengthening Hellenism. Their sphere of action included Thessaly, Epirus, and Macedonia, and their program was to drive out the Ottomans and to replace them with Greeks and a Greek government. Ethnike Hetairia had its own "volunteer" force, which it equipped at government expense and massed on the frontier with the Ottoman Empire. The organization also pressured the government to put its regular forces in Thessaly on a war footing and to move against the Turks. Complete mobilization of the Greek army was ordered on 15 March. War was imminent.

Faced with this growing Greek threat, the Ottoman government, which had been trying to reach a settlement of the Crete insurrection through negotiations with the Great Powers, was compelled to place itself on a war footing as well. Excitement ran high throughout the European domains of the Ottoman sultan, but nowhere more than in Monastir. An important military center, Monastir was abuzz with mobilization, recruitment, organization, and the dispatch of troops. Mustafa Kemal and a friend tried to join the fighting forces but were discovered and returned to school. His own personal history, like that of his grandfather's, had become enmeshed with the strands of the larger historical web. He was still not in a position to be a significant actor in the unfolding drama, but he was coming closer to that moment when his own personal destiny and that of his times would intermingle.

Greek regulars poured across the Ottoman frontier on 17 April, forcing the Ottoman government to break off relations and to declare war. The Greek initiative was foolhardy from the start. They could not match the Ottomans either in manpower or in equipment. Recently trained and re-equipped by the Germans, the Ottomans soon drove the Greeks back, and they themselves pushed into Greek territory. Within two weeks the Greek army was thoroughly demoralized and on the point of complete collapse. A thoroughgoing defeat of Greece would alter the diplomatic status quo in the Near East, something the Great Powers were not prepared to countenance. Diplomatic maneuvers were set in motion which ultimately resulted in an armistice on 19 May 1897. Peace negotiations dragged on through the summer and only reached a conclusion in September with the peace treaty being signed in December. Germany and Russia put pressure on the sultan to accept a great deal less than he had hoped for or had won on the battlefield. Greece had embarked upon the war with visions of aggrandizement, but only the support of the European powers enabled her to emerge practically unscathed. No matter what the rivalries were among the Great Powers, they would not allow territory that had been liberated from Muslim control to slip from their grasp and revert to the infidel Ottoman Turks.[10]

Sultan Abdülhamid II, who embodied the empire for most of its subjects, found himself in a most precarious position. In order to defend the empire against both its internal and external enemies, he had to embark upon a wide-ranging program of reform and modernization that touched almost every aspect of Ottoman society and its institutions. Perhaps most involved in the reform process was the military establishment. Its educational system was overhauled, foreign instructors, especially Germans, were introduced, and many young Ottoman officers were sent abroad to expand their background. At the same time that some of the Great Powers assisted the Ottomans in their reform efforts, they also maintained steady pressure on Abdülhamid to ameliorate the conditions under which the empire's minorities lived. Moreover, the empire was treated merely as a spectator at the international diplomatic game known as the Eastern Question that involved the very existence of the Ottoman state.

[10]An autonomous regime was established in Crete. The island remained under the sultan's suzerainty, but with a Christian governor approved by the sultan with the concurrence of the Greek government. Greece annexed the island in 1912.

Seeking to preserve as much of his empire as possible, Sultan Abdülhamid II became increasingly despotic in his management of both the modernization process and the empire's internal affairs.[11] His despotism soon embroiled him in a confrontation with the young officer class and the students in the military education system, the very people he relied upon to hold the empire together. This new emerging military elite, having studied the development of Western constitutional history and having seen Western, especially British, political institutions at work firsthand, came to resent their sultan's heavy-handed political repression.

Given Abdülhamid's tight control over most aspects of Ottoman society, there were not many avenues open to the dissidents. Some went into voluntary exile in the capital cities of Europe where they mingled with others who had been driven into exile by the sultan. Some stayed in the sultan's domains and created clandestine groups for the discussion and organization of political action. Those in the military carried out their meetings and discussions in the barracks and dormitories, always fearful of having their group infiltrated by Abdülhamid's spies. It was a difficult time for most Ottomans who had been brought up to respect the person of the sultan and to revere him almost as a father.

Mustafa Kemal was not untouched by all this political activity. While he was still a student at Monastir, there had been an attempt to overthrow the sultan. The movement was spearheaded by the students of the Imperial Military Medical School in Istanbul. They had formed the first revolutionary society in the Ottoman Empire in 1889 and tried to effect their coup d'etat in 1896, without success. Mustafa Kemal and his friends were not directly involved at this time, but talk about the event must certainly have swept through the school.

In March 1899 Mustafa Kemal completed his training at Monastir and was sent to join the entering class at the War College in Istanbul. Revolutionary influences from the medical school reached into the War College, but Mustafa Kemal seems to have remained aloof from the fervor. In recalling his years at the War College he commented:

> During the years at the War College political ideas emerged. We were still unable to gain real insight into the situation. It was the period of Abdülhamid. We were reading the books of Namık Kemal. Surveillance was tight. Most of the time we found the chance to read only in the barracks after going to bed. There seemed to be something wrong in the

[11]Abdülhamid II was extremely suspicious, almost to the point of paranoia. It is said that he built a new palace in Istanbul, further inland, so as to be more distant from any possible shelling by warships. Politically reactionary, he was, nonetheless, an active reformer and westernizer. See Shaw and Shaw 1977, pp. 197–271, and B. Lewis 1968, pp. 171–205.

> state of affairs if those who read such patriotic works were under surveillance. But, we could not completely grasp the essence of it. [Yalman 1922]

Aware that there was "something wrong," Mustafa Kemal did not, however, invest much of his energy at this time in trying to understand the political scene. He was, after all, a lusty and sexually active young man in a city where the promiscuity and pleasures he enjoyed were readily available to him. Although in the long run he compiled a fine record at the War College, ranking twentieth in a class of 460 in his second year and eighth among 459 in his third, Mustafa Kemal claims to have passed the first year in a life of youthful fantasy (Yalman 1922) in the capital of the Ottoman Empire, a city that offered something for every taste.

What Mustafa Kemal described as youthful fantasy also involved depressionlike episodes, including difficulty falling asleep at night. It is likely that initially his inflated self-concept could not find durable means to maintain itself in the capital. Istanbul was a new place for him and he hardly knew anyone there. His inflated self-concept needed adoration and narcissistic supplies. They were not readily forthcoming, and their absence was a blow to his self-esteem.

Seeking to protect himself from the onslaught of depressive feelings and a sense of low self-esteem, Mustafa Kemal frantically sought the admiration of many loose women.[12] This type of "sexually promiscuous narcissistic behavior" (Kernberg 1975, p. 288) was an effort on his part to reestablish the cohesiveness of his inflated self-concept. One function of this promiscuity was to hold out to him the hope of better relationships with new people. The other function was to protect the objects of his sexual impulses from destruction.

One story that has come to light suggests very strongly that at this time of his life Mustafa Kemal suffered from premature ejaculation (Aydemir 1974). This would not be surprising. On one level he used women as his adoring subjects, but on another, he also had split-off images of them as his "bad" mother. This made them targets for his hostility. Thus, premature ejaculation was a form of "hit and run" behavior that allowed him to protect himself from women who at first appeared desirable but would turn sour, that is, "bad." It is clear that he wished to be "number one" among his loose women.[13]

[12]Kinross (1965) states that Mustafa Kemal at this point in his life sampled women without inhibition.

[13]Evidence of this is embodied in a story told about a visit he made to Istanbul when he was president of the country. At that time, he fell into discussion with his drinking companions concerning which of the group was the most virile. Challenged to prove his prowess, he had the city's red-light district blocked off from its usual traffic and went there with his challengers to look for a certain Madame Katrina, whom he had known in his

These frantic sexual encounters nearly caused Mustafa Kemal to fail in his first year at the War College. He saved himself by forming a friendship with Ali Fuat (Cebesoy), the son of a retired general. He introduced Mustafa Kemal to his father who was pleased with his son's new friend. Ali Fuat made the transplanted provincial from Salonika welcome in his own home and took him around to the showplaces of Istanbul. He is the one who is said to have introduced Mustafa Kemal to the pleasures of rakı.

Once more Mustafa Kemal seems to have become rather well organized. Possibly his discovery of an ideal father who paid attention to him provided the psychological incentive. He began to read widely again and developed a lively, but not uncritical interest in Napoleon. He began to resent the tyranny of the sultan, the "bad" father, and managed to come to the forefront of a group of young political thinkers who put out an underground newspaper. Mustafa Kemal often wrote the editorials. On one occasion school officials entered the room in which this paper was being prepared, but apparently they chose to ignore the presence of incriminating evidence. Mustafa Kemal was permitted to complete the program at the War College. He graduated as a second lieutenant at the age of twenty-one. Upon graduation he had a photograph taken in his full-dress uniform and sent it to his mother for her to admire.

Having done well at the War College, Mustafa Kemal was permitted to go on to the Staff College, also located in Istanbul. He was now considered outstanding, but he was not yet *the best*. He was just a student among other students, all of whom had been chosen from the best of the crop. Those depressive episodes he had experienced during his first year at the War College returned now and again. He had spells of low self-esteem and sulky behavior. In later life he claimed that he could not understand why this was so. He was able to recall rebellious feelings, but could not account for them. Sleep eluded him at the Staff College, and mornings often found him deep in the sleep of exhaustion. Atatürk recalled how often in this period of his life his head and body felt tired when he awakened, and he jealously described his classmates as having been "more clean-minded and happy" than he in the classroom (Aydemir 1969, vol. 1, p. 77).

Such depressive episodes occurred simultaneously or alternately with his grandiose feelings.[14] In his fantasies he was the reigning figure. He was

---

younger years. She testified to the group that he was the best man she had ever known (Aydemir 1974).

[14]Such alterations of mood in persons with narcissistic personality organization are typical. Bach (1977) differentiates these mood swings from the classical cyclothymia insofar as these are "characterized by limited duration and rapid vacillations, with relative maintenance of insight and the general integrity of the personality" (p. 224).

the hero of adventures to come and a savior of the troubled country. In reality, he gathered others around him who appeared to be his admirers and to be his extensions. Once when he and his friends were discussing a future they envisioned for the government, Mustafa Kemal handed out various cabinet posts and positions of leadership in this future government. He was questioned as to his own role. In reply, he said grandly, "It is I who will give you these positions." His eloquence and presence were beginning to be commanding.

In 1905 Mustafa Kemal graduated from the Staff College fifth in a class of fifty-seven. He was twenty-four years old and a captain.

As a staff captain he settled in a house in the Beyazit section of Istanbul. Additionally, he and his friends rented an apartment in a nearby house in which they could meet, read, and discuss books forbidden by the sultan's government and talk about their ideals. Such activities did not escape notice. One day a young man who had been expelled from the military school approached them with a story of having fallen on hard times. The group took him in, but he turned out to be a spy and an informant for the government. Mustafa Kemal, Ali Fuat, and others were caught, questioned, and imprisoned. This episode jeopardized their military careers, but instead of being cashiered, they were given assignments to remote areas of the empire. Mustafa Kemal longed at this point to visit Salonika, where all his mother had left of him was a new photograph showing her son in his dress uniform with his face almost concealed behind a dashing, up-curled moustache. Salonika was now out of the question. He was posted, along with Ali Fuat, to the Fifth Army stationed in Syria, which was then still under Ottoman control.

5
The Exile

Banished to Damascus for his political activities, Mustafa Kemal felt devastated. He had expected to be posted to the Balkans and had written his mother to prepare her for his imminent return. It would now be some time before they would see each other. The only consolation was that his friend Ali Fuat was being sent to Damascus with him. After hearing their fate, Mustafa Kemal and Ali Fuat bought a bottle of scotch and some soda water and retired to the home of Ali Fuat's parents. There they proceeded to drink their sorrows away (Cebesoy 1967, p. 80).

Together with another of their group who had also been assigned a similar fate of duty in Damascus, Mustafa Kemal and Ali Fuat set out for Syria. They went first by boat to Beirut, which even then was known for its westernized atmosphere. With its large Christian Arab population that had strong ties to Europe, Beirut resembled Salonika in many respects, especially with its waterfront cafes and entertainment spots. Mustafa Kemal and Ali Fuat had already decided to spend a few days there before going on to Damascus.

The voyage to Beirut was uneventful. They traveled first class, ate well, and in general enjoyed themselves. Although the feeling that they might be watched or spied upon never left them, the three young officers made the best of the situation. Mustafa Kemal was moved to remark that life was beginning anew for them.

Upon their arrival in Beirut they were greeted by two classmates who had preceded them to Syria and had managed to get themselves assigned to Beirut rather than Damascus. Their brother officers showed them the town and put them up in a good hotel, encouraging them to seek assignment to Beirut, where readily available pleasures would soon make them forget Istanbul.

From Beirut Mustafa Kemal and his comrades proceeded to Damascus by train. Since Ali Fuat's father was a well-known military figure, a pasha of distinction, the commanding officer in Damascus received his new subordinates cordially, inquiring after the health of Ali Fuat's father. He wished them well in their new duties, but even these raw officers could tell that the Fifth Army was far from being an effective fighting force. The scruffiness of the soldiers they had met on the streets was enough to convince them of that.

Damascus was not the best environment for Mustafa Kemal. Trained in the most modern military schools the empire had to offer, Mustafa Kemal was prepared to convey what he had learned to others, but in Damascus they had little interest in what he had to impart. Moreover, he was regarded as an exile working out his punishment. He was received as a nobody in this strange land. He suffered another blow when after three days Ali Fuat was reassigned to Beirut to serve with the special cavalry force that acted as the provincial governor's guard.

Deprived of his favorite companion, Mustafa Kemal tried to make the best of a bad situation. He joined forces with the remaining member of their original trio, Müfit (Özdeş). Together they rented a small house and settled in. Damascus was an historic Arab city, but the changes that had swept through Istanbul and Salonika had not yet begun to touch Damascus. There was no cosmopolitan population with its eyes open to the Western world. The leadership of the Turkish Fifth Army paid scant attention to Mustafa Kemal who, along with his friend, was still under suspicion. They were given no duties to perform.

One of the principal preoccupations of the cavalry in this area was to put down local uprisings. These occasions were viewed as opportunities not only for military action, but for plunder as well. At this time the Druzes of Havran were causing problems. A military action against them was ordered, but Mustafa Kemal and his fellow exile were not included in the party being sent out. They tried to get assigned to their units, but were unsuccessful. Sensing that something was afoot, Kemal and his friend took their horses and joined the force on their own. Their superiors were upset, but allowed them to participate in the raid on promise that they would keep quiet about it. Mustafa Kemal was shocked at his close-up glimpse of corruption within the Ottoman army. When Müfit was offered a share in the booty, he refused it. This pleased Mustafa Kemal greatly and led him to idealize his comrade. He considered himself and his friend to be men of the future rather than the corrupt present.

This and similar experiences turned Mustafa Kemal's mind once again to projects for reform and involved him anew in clandestine activities. In the Hamidiye bazaar of Damascus Mustafa Kemal had come across an interesting shopkeeper who turned out to be a former medical school student who had been expelled and banished to Damascus for revolutionary activities. His name was Mustafa Efendi, and later, in the days of the Turkish republic, he would take the name Mustafa Cantekin. Mustafa Kemal and his brother officer struck up a friendship with this Mustafa Efendi, who urged them to think about working for the overthrow of the sultan's government. Inspired by these conversations, Mustafa Kemal founded an organization called the *Vatan ve Hürriyet Cemiyeti* (Society for the Motherland and Freedom). He, Müfit, and Mustafa Efendi were the founding members.

Moving about on military assignment to some of the main cities of the area, including Beirut, Jerusalem, and Jaffa, Mustafa Kemal sought to establish branches of his society. Ali Fuat and some friends founded a branch in Beirut, but the society's expansion went no further. In spite of the diversion provided him by these activities on behalf of the society, Mustafa Kemal continued to be plagued by depressive moods and insomnia, which by now had become habitual. He came to see Damascus as "all bad," totally Arab and Muslim, with an overwhelming atmosphere from which he needed to be rescued. The events of his life that we will review here are minor episodes in the historical sense, but they contributed significantly in the psychological realm to much that followed.

When as a child Mustafa had to surrender to the religious mother and enter a religious school, it was his father who rescued him from the domination of his mother and gave him a new direction. Mustafa Kemal was now being smothered by Damascus, with its old-fashioned Muslim religiosity. Once again he needed a father to rescue him and, by necessity, that man would be an idealized father figure. Ali Fuat's father had played that role when Mustafa Kemal was in Istanbul.

In time, as Atatürk (Father Turk), Mustafa Kemal would come to rely fully on the idealized father image that dwelt within his own psyche. This was not yet possible for him, so he was obliged to create an idealized father image in fantasy and outside of himself.[1] At this juncture Mustafa Kemal thought of a general in Salonika, the head of the artillery there, who was known to hold progressive political views. Mustafa Kemal wrote him a letter, explaining his ideas, describing his background, and expressing the wish to be transferred to Salonika. The general replied simply that if and when Mustafa Kemal returned to Salonika it might be possible to help him in some way. Mustafa Kemal seized upon this meager and indifferent reply. He idealized that distant pasha and pinned extravagant hopes on a perfectly perfunctory promise.

Obsessed with the notion of escaping from Syria in order to come under the protection of his idealized pasha in Salonika, Mustafa Kemal began to plot his return to Macedonia. A model of the fugitive had long ago been present for him in the form of his grandfather who had had to flee Salonika. Getting back to his home would not be simple, for when he had been assigned to the Fifth Army his orders stipulated that he was not to leave the region under its command. Such a stipulation could only have meant that he was still under suspicion.

[1]Heinz Kohut (1971) would call such a phenomenon the idealizing transference.

Despite the hazards, Mustafa Kemal resolved to undertake the journey. With his military friends covering for him in Syria and with others alerted along the route to assist him, he went first to Egypt, where he boarded a ship headed for Piraeus. There he boarded a Greek ship calling at Salonika. He wired ahead for a friend to meet him who would get him through customs without being discovered.

Safely ashore in Salonika, Mustafa Kemal immediately went to see his mother. Much of the reunion's joy was undermined when she questioned the propriety of her son's acting against the sultan's wishes. Astonished to see him, she was also concerned for his safety. He calmed her fears and told her that he had had to return to Salonika, and one day he would be able to explain it all to her, but not at that moment.

Mustafa Kemal was upset by his mother's demeanor and her anxiety. His main concern was to see Şükrü Pasha, the man whom he had established in his fantasies as his protector and idealized father. He had rehearsed this anticipated meeting with his "protector" many times in his mind. In his fantasies he was welcomed warmly by Şükrü Pasha and given every assistance one could expect from a father. We can only imagine the degree of his disillusionment when he made his way to the pasha's home and was denied an audience by the man whom he had thought of as his champion, but who could not, in fact, recall ever having heard of him. Şükrü Pasha replied through an aide that there was nothing he could do for him.

Although he was devastated by this reply, Mustafa Kemal would not allow himself to be put off so cavalierly. He insisted to the general's aide that he had written to the pasha and that he had to see him. His pertinacity prevailed, and he was ushered in to see the general. Obviously annoyed and put out with Mustafa Kemal, Şükrü Pasha did not even ask him to be seated. All of Mustafa Kemal's fantasies evaporated as the pasha coldly and precisely told him that there was nothing he could do for him. As Mustafa Kemal left the room the pasha told him not to bother him again.

Rebuffed in this manner, Mustafa Kemal would have found it no comfort to consider that Şükrü Pasha could scarcely have been expected to jeopardize his career by helping a fugitive who was under governmental suspicion. His dreams shattered, Mustafa Kemal had to confine himself to his mother's house, where she nagged him constantly. Finally, through the intercession of a staff colonel whom he had known while at the military preparatory school, Mustafa Kemal applied for and received a sick leave of four months' duration. He was then, at least, able to circulate freely without fear of being arrested. His superiors in Syria and Istanbul knew nothing of this at the time.

Mustafa Kemal put this time to use, organizing a chapter of the Society for the Motherland and Freedom. The founders of this branch included his old friend from Monastir days, Ömer Naci, and Bursalı Tahir, who would go on to become one of Turkey's leading intellectuals and literary historians. At the ceremony launching the chapter Mustafa Kemal wrote down on a card the several charter articles that bound the group together. He read them aloud, placed the card on a table, and took up a revolver, which he kissed and placed on top of the card. The rest of the group followed suit, and they all took an oath on the Koran. Mustafa Kemal instructed his comrades to keep the sacred revolver in trust for him until the day he needed it. As nearly as can be determined, the chapter was founded some time in April or May 1906.

While Mustafa Kemal engaged in these activities, the military authorities in Istanbul became aware of the fact that he was not present at his assigned duties. Inquiries were made as to his whereabouts. Through the network of his friends and classmates stationed in Syria, Istanbul, and Salonika, Mustafa Kemal received word of that investigation. He had no choice but to return to Syria as quickly as possible. Some of his objectives had already been achieved, including a respite from the tedium of life in Damascus, a short reunion with his mother, a confrontation with the image of the idealized father and its quick devaluation, and playing a leading role in the establishment of a branch of the Society for the Motherland and Freedom.

Upon his return to Syria, Mustafa Kemal went directly to Beersheba to join a Turkish force that was protecting Ottoman interests in a dispute with the Anglo-Egyptian government over the port of Akaba. When official inquiries were made about Mustafa Kemal, it was made to appear that he had been with the troops in Beersheba all the time. Through administrative inefficiency and with the collusion of his classmates and friends, that story prevailed. Mustafa Kemal was finally removed from the limbo he had been cast into for his political activities at school. He was declared to be a loyal officer and transferred to the General Staff in Salonika in September 1907. His "exile" had endured for some three years.

6

The Young Turks

UPON HIS RETURN TO SALONIKA, MUSTAFA KEMAL FOUND THE ENVIRONMENT startingly changed. This was most obvious in respect to underground activities directed against the dictatorial regime of Sultan Abdülhamid II. Coming to the throne at the end of August, 1875 at a moment of great danger for the Ottoman Empire, which was threatened with the loss of a substantial part of its remaining European territory, if not with extinction itself, Abdülhamid embarked upon a wide-ranging program of modernization aimed at rejuvenating the empire's military establishment.[1]

His accession had also coincided with the culmination of the movement for an Ottoman constitution by which some of its framers hoped to convert the sultan into a British-style constitutional monarch. Promulgated in December 1876, the Ottoman constitution called for a parliament of two chambers,[2] a Senate consisting of 25 members nominated by the sultan and a lower chamber of 120 members elected in such a manner as to insure representation for and from the empire's minorities. Elections were dutifully held, although there were claims of undue political pressure having been exercised by the sultan. The first Ottoman parliament met on 19 March 1877.

Proceedings of the Ottoman parliament and descriptions of it at work indicate that the Ottomans were not yet ready for this leap into modernity. The parliament deputies quickly settled down to making accusations of incompetence and corruption directed against the government's ministers who formed the cabinet under the grand vizier, and against the ruling class. They then asked that three particular ministers come before them to defend themselves against these charges of corruption. With the outbreak of the war with Russia, the deputies also took to criticizing the conduct of the grand vizier and the war minister. In an attempt to appease them and thus gain their loyalty, Abdülhamid II sought to involve the

[1]The sultan viewed modernization as necessary for the Ottoman Empire's survival in the face of the rising technology of the West and the pressure of European states sympathetic to Christian minorities in the empire. Traditionalists in the empire would view the process of modernization, which extended to education and religion as well, as responsible for the state's demise.

[2]The deputies for the two chambers of parliament, the Senate and a lower chamber, were elected; however, the sultan appointed his own grand vizier (prime minister) as well as his own ministers who then would form the cabinet.

parliament in the decision to invite the British navy into the Sea of Marmara. He was rebuffed by deputies who told him that he was consulting them much too late. Thereupon, the sultan dismissed the parliament on 14 February 1878 and sent the deputies home. The Ottoman Empire had had a parliament for only eleven months; it would not have another for three decades.

Abdülhamid's prorogation of the parliament did not, however, spell the end of his attempts to modernize. That process continued unabated, especially in the military and education spheres. Increasing numbers of students were being educated in westernized schools and being exposed to European ideas on state and society. Classroom discussions were continued in the dormitories and led to like-minded people attempting to band together to effect changes in the sultan's despotic rule. The model of Mazzini and Young Italy, with its secret organization and interlocking networks, was constantly before them.

As far as the sultan was concerned, westernization or modernization was a process that had to be engaged in, but it had also to be carried out by an elite few acting under the direction of the sultan, and it had to be imposed on Ottoman society from the top. Control over the society would be maintained by censorship, police powers, and systematic surveillance by a spying apparatus. Those who dared to speak against Abdülhamid II would be rooted out, made to see the error of their ways, or sent into exile, either abroad or to the distant reaches of the empire.

Despite the sultan's ability to bring the full weight of the government to bear on dissidents, many people raised their voices. It is not surprising that the first society organized against the sultan's repressive regime was founded by four medical students in 1889 in the garden of the Istanbul military medical college which was one of the most westernized educational institutions in the Ottoman state.

From this modest beginning the opposition movement spread to other schools and other branches of the military. Societies cropped up under various names, most of which included such words as motherland, freedom, Ottoman, union, and progress in their titles. Many had their own journals, newsletters, and newspapers. The sultan increased his surveillance of these clandestine groups, employing paid informants and planting agents in their midsts. Communities of exiled Ottomans grew up in the leading cities of Europe. In various ways they smuggled their journals back into the Ottoman Empire and kept up the pressure for the deposition of the sultan. At times Abdülhamid offered these exiled leaders amnesty and tried to coax them back home. Some returned to take lucrative governmental positions and were roundly criticized by their fellow conspirators for doing so, some refused to return, and others made their way back only to continue their opposition.

This opposition is known collectively as the Young Turk movement, but at this early stage it is perhaps best to consider it as a "Young Ottoman" movement. Most of its members were from the ruling Ottoman elite and had been officeholders. Their roots were deep in the traditional Ottoman society. As the sultan tightened his hold on society he drove the Young Turks into planning and taking more drastic actions. A coup d'etat was prepared to depose Abdülhamid, but it was revealed to the police who arrested the conspirators in August 1896. Challenged and threatened by the subversive activities of the cadet corps, the sultan instituted a special court martial in June 1897 to weed out dissidents. As a result of this process, nearly one hundred officers and cadets were exiled to Tripoli.

Abdülhamid's resoluteness had the desired effect. The opposition movement lost a good deal of its momentum, and only the defection of a member of the royal family managed to instill new life into the Young Turk movement. In 1901 Damad Mahmud Pasha, the grandson of Sultan Mahmud II and brother-in-law to Abdülhamid II, defected and fled to Europe with his two sons. One of them, Prince Sabahüddin, soon emerged as the leader of one of the major opposition factions in Europe. Under his leadership a congress was convened in Paris in 1902.

Prince Sabahüddin envisioned an Ottoman Empire organized along federal lines with a constitutional monarch. His ideas met with the hostility of the minorities, who looked to the European powers for their salvation which they hoped would come in the form of the establishment of separate, sovereign states. In the face of nationalist strivings on the part of the minorities, federalism appeared to the Turkish army as a threat to the very existence of the Ottoman Empire. They would have to find a solution to the despotism of Abdülhamid other than Prince Sabahüddin and his federal ideas. This realization led to a revitalization of the anti-Abdülhamid movement among the military.

Mustafa Kemal's efforts on behalf of the Society for the Motherland and Freedom were part of this renewal campaign. The movement had now left the dormitories and the classrooms and was centered in the barracks and the officers' quarters. Mustafa Kemal set up the first group in Damascus and then, when he slipped away to Salonika, he organized a branch there. Upon his return to Salonika late in 1907 he found a very different state of affairs.

What had changed was the rapid development of the Committee of Union and Progress. This secret organization that committed its members to fight against the corruption in the sultan's government had now spilled over from the military into the professional schools of Salonika and Macedonia, including the law faculty. High-ranking officers of the Third Army were now involved all the way up to the command level. New personalities had emerged and were firmly in control when Mustafa Kemal returned. He had to be content with a minor and subordinate position, for his organization was overshadowed by the Committee of Union and Progress.

Despite the fact that it was rather difficult for Mustafa Kemal, with his inflated self-image, to accept a minor role, he had no choice. On 29 October 1907, he joined the Committee of Union and Progress. At this time Mustafa Kemal's military assignment involved the inspection of the railroad line between Salonika and Üsküp (Skopje, which is now Yugoslavia). He spent his time maintaining that vital rail link, carrying out his staff assignments at headquarters in Salonika, and participating in the secret activities of the Committee of Union and Progress.

Although it was better organized than before, the Committee of Union and Progress had no immediate plans for an overthrow of the sultan's government. Its major concerns at that moment were to counteract the terrorist activities of the minorities in Macedonia, to inform the sultan's government of the threat posed to the integrity of the empire by the separatist movements in the Balkans supported by the Greek and Bulgarian churches, and to make its existence known officially to the major European powers in an effort to force them to cease discussions about reforms which the committee saw only as weakening the Ottoman Empire and leading to its disintegration. The committee wanted the Great Powers to know that it was prepared to defend the empire, and it wanted the sultan to know that only the restoration of the constitution of 1876 could save the situation.

This information was conveyed to the powers by a manifesto in May 1908 which they promptly ignored. Sultan Abdülhamid II's response to the rumored existence of a widespread network of disaffection throughout the Third Army under the guidance of the Committee of Union and Progress was to dispatch an inspection committee under the direction of a loyal general to uncover the truth. The sultan's agents fanned out into Macedonia to track down this network throughout June and July of 1908. There were denunciations of committee members and assassinations of the sultan's agents and officials. Acts of terror perpetrated by both sides inflamed the situation. Both the Committee of Union and Progress and the sultan's government sought the support of the minorities, thus further weakening the united Ottoman front and control over those groups.

In June 1908 an adjutant-major named Ahmed Niyazi was denounced as a committee member by a Muslim army hoca (chaplain). On 28 June the chaplain was shot dead. At this point, surrounded by inspectors sent out from Istanbul at the sultan's orders and constantly fearful of exposure, the Committee of Union and Progress, led by Adjutant-Major Niyazi, came out in the open in an effort at self-preservation.

Niyazi looted the military base at Resne (Ohrid) of rifles and ammunition while most of the garrison was at prayers on Friday, 3 July 1908. With some two hundred followers, he took to the hills. Others joined him, including a young staff major named Enver who would eventually come to power and then, as a pasha, lead the Ottoman Empire into World War I on the side of Germany and the Central Powers.

Abdülhamid II had no choice but to try to suppress this uprising. He sent Şemsi Pasha to Macedonia to take charge of the government's troops and to put down the insurrection. On 7 July Şemsi Pasha was assassinated in Monastir. The Committee of Union and Progress was now clearly acknowledged as the leadership behind the movement that had as its major rallying cry the reinstatement of the constitution. In an attempt to discredit the Committee of Union and Progress the sultan sought to unleash a propaganda campaign against it, branding the committee anti-Christian and anti-Islam. He also moved troops from Anatolia to Macedonia to deal with the situation, but the Anatolian troops soon went over to the rebels.

Quickly, the situation in Macedonia worsened for the sultan as city after city declared for the Committee of Union and Progress. So rapidly did events move that Salonika, the city that had been the committee's cradle, did not have time to rise in support of the movement before the sultan bowed to the essential demand. Sultan Abdülhamid II restored the constitution on 24 July in an effort to appear as the defender of the constitution rather than its suppressor, issuing a call for the parliament, which he had prorogued in 1876, to reconvene. In this manner he could maintain that the constitution had never been suspended and that he had ruled under its provisions all the time. His rationale was that he had suspended the parliament in order to get on with the task of modernizing the empire, but that he had now completed that effort and the parliament should reconvene to help him save the empire from its enemies.

Coming out of lower echelons of the ruling Ottoman elite than their predecessors in the opposition movement, the Young Turks were now in control, but as yet they had no firm idea of what to do with their power. They could not envision the empire without the sultan at its head, and they lacked the experience of high administrative office. Therefore, they agreed to cooperate with the sultan and his government.

Initially, the Young Turk victory ushered in an era of good feelings. Enver catapulted into the role of hero of the hour, was greeted tumultuously in Salonika, and the brotherhood of all Ottomans, regardless of race or religion, was proclaimed. The city's Muslim holy men, Christian priests, and Jewish rabbis paraded arm in arm in a joyous mood. Calls from the minarets mingled with the sounds of church bells, celebrating the dawn of the Young Turk millennium.

In Istanbul, which had been spared the fighting that took place in Macedonia, similar scenes were enacted. Halide Edib (Adıvar),[3] who would become a leading figure in Atatürk's Turkey, was a young woman at the time, and she has left in her memoirs an animated picture of events as they transpired in the capital. On the day the sultan issued his rescript there was much confusion and suspicion, followed by great joy on the next day:

> The people gathered at street corners and tried to talk in undertones, but there was a feeling of uncertainty, even of distrust, a vague questioning as to the meaning of this sudden change; some went so far as to take it for a trap in which to catch the people of Istamboul. [Adıvar 1926, p. 256]
>
> [The next day] there was a sea of men and women all cockaded in red and white, flowing like a vast human tide from one side to the other. The tradition of centuries seemed to have lost its effect. There was no such thing as sex or personal feeling. Men and women in a common wave of enthusiasm moved on, radiating something extraordinary, laughing, weeping in such intense emotion that human deficiency and ugliness were for the time completely obliterated. Thousands swayed and moved on. Before each official building there was an enormous crowd calling to the minister to come out and take the oath of allegiance to the new regime. [Adıvar 1926, p. 258]

What Halide Edib was describing was a group process, that is, a number of people sharing the same emotions. Obviously, the population was highly charged and held common hopes of a coming change, the change from oppression to freedom that probably meant different things to different people, but which was shared as a concept by the whole group. The members of a group surrender their own will in the service of the will of the leader and, in turn, identify with each other (Freud 1921). At this point, however, there seemed to be no one leader in the middle of the ecstasy of these people. There was confusion as to whom to turn to as a leader, and Halide Edib's description of those days in Istanbul reflects this search for a leader. She says, for example, "the news of the change had come from Saloniki through several young officers whose names were shouted as its symbol" (Adıvar 1926, p. 258). At one street corner she observed a man with a long beard who attempted to glorify the change while continuing to glorify the sultan. He addressed a crowd,

[3]Halide Edib (Adıvar) was born in 1884 and died in 1964. She became one of Turkey's greatest writers. Her memoirs (Adıvar 1926) give a colorful description of everyday life in the Ottoman Empire's capital, Istanbul, and of the new political movements developing there. In a later publication she described the Turkish struggle for independence (Adıvar 1928).

saying, "I have a beloved wife and five children. I swear that I am ready to cut them to pieces for the sacred cause as I would have done for his Majesty" (Adıvar 1926, p. 259). Halide Edib wondered why this man did not cut himself rather than his wife and children, and why he felt such deep love for "His Majesty" at that particular moment. She believed sheer hysteria made him speak in this way at that time. There were other figures, better known and more easily recognizable, who paraded on horseback and spoke to the mobs that followed them. Everyone was swept up in emotion. A crowd of Kurdish porters asked one of the well-known speakers, "Tell us what constitution means." He answered, "Constitution is such a great thing that those who do not know it are donkeys." Thereupon the porters shouted, "We are donkeys." The speaker continued his banter with them, saying, "Your fathers also did not know it. Say that you are the sons of donkeys." The Kurdish porters roared back, "We are the sons of donkeys" (Adıvar 1926, p. 260).

When the uproar diminished one man caught the fancy of the people of the empire. It was Enver who emerged as the charismatic leader. His picture appeared everywhere and babies were named after him.

Besides being bright and a good organizer, Enver was also an excellent equestrian and a brave man. Psychologically speaking, he had an obsessional narcissistic character. Attention to detail was one of his strong points, and he could work long hours without experiencing fatigue. Like Mustafa Kemal, he was intensely vain, given to preening himself before mirrors, and meticulous in dress. Enver was a romantic figure enormously appealing to young women, but in one major respect he differed from Mustafa Kemal. Enver was religious and carried a copy of the Koran in his breast pocket when he went into battle. In addition, he neither drank nor smoked. His private life was impeccable. To Enver the life that Mustafa Kemal led and enjoyed immensely must have seemed grossly immoral. It was Enver who was responsible in large part for Mustafa Kemal's relegation to an insignificant position within the Committee of Union and Progress. These two men of enormous drive and character, thrown together by fate in the same time and place, had come to know and thoroughly dislike each other.

Throughout the events that forced Sultan Abdülhamid II to restore the constitution and that brought Enver to the fore, Mustafa Kemal played only a minor role, if any at all. Both his rivalry with Enver and the fact that he had no power base from which to thrust himself into a leadership position capable of sustaining his inflated self-image, served to keep Mustafa Kemal far in the background. Meanwhile, the Young Turk revolution captured the heart of Europe, at least for the time being. The European powers relaxed their pressure on the Ottoman Empire for reforms. Seeing the Young Turk revolution as but a continuation of a process they had initiated in 1789, the French were prepared to cooperate with the new Ottoman government, and the British ordered their ambassador in Istanbul to assist the Young Turks as much as possible.

Despite (or perhaps because of) Enver's success, Mustafa Kemal believed that in the final analysis Enver would harm the empire. He viewed him as a good enough soldier, but an indifferent reformer. There were not many forums in which Mustafa Kemal could present his opinions. Continuing to frequent Salonika's nightspots and sidewalk cafes, Mustafa Kemal talked openly of his views as he drank. Meeting with his friends and drinking with them, he continued to tell them what he would do if he were in power and to what offices he would assign them. They asked him what position he had reserved for himself, the job of sultan? He replied that he would be greater than the sultan.

Such talk and behavior did not sit well with the leadership of the Salonika branch of the Committee of Union and Progress. Mustafa Kemal was making a nuisance of himself and they began to feel that it would be best if he were to leave Salonika. Üsküp was not far enough away. An opportunity arose to send Mustafa Kemal to Libya as the representative of the Committee of Union and Progress. While absent from a meeting, the Salonika group voted to send him to that remote corner of the Ottoman Empire, a place of exile that the sultan himself might have chosen for him.

Mustafa Kemal was informed of the decision to send him to Libya by a letter from the committee's headquarters in Istanbul, but it did not take much imagination to realize that Libya had been chosen for him by his Salonika colleagues. It was a place of political exile where he might easily meet some significant setback to his career, or even his death. In Libya the Ottoman government was having difficulties with the local Arab population led by the Sanusi family, who combined political leadership with the religious aura that clung to them as the heads of a dervish order. Ostensibly, Mustafa Kemal was being sent to Libya to investigate the situation there and to establish the committee's authority, but he realized that he was being gotten rid of, doubtless at the urging of Enver.

After consulting with a leader of the Committee of Union and Progress, Mustafa Kemal understood the nature of his predicament. Refusal to undertake the assignment would cause him to lose face. He accepted the large sum of money given him for expenses and, without sending word to his mother, set out for Libya. Traveling as a civilian, he went by ship to Izmir and Iskenderun, and then to Tripoli in Libya. His personality makeup caused him to perceive his mission as the representative of the Young Turks in Libya as a crucial test. Letters written to a childhood friend during the voyage reveal how he struggled to see himself as a secretive and powerful man bent on clandestine goals.[4] He experienced all the excitement of a youngster caught up in mysterious enterprises. As luck would have it, his fantasies and reality came together. In Tripoli he did find a testing ground for his ability as a soldier, a diplomat, and as a forceful, charismatic person.

No one welcomed him to Tripoli upon his arrival. Tripoli lacked port facilities, and Mustafa Kemal was brought from the ship to the shore by a local boatman who dropped him on the beach with his luggage and personal effects. He had put on his best staff officer's uniform, but to no purpose, since no one had come out to greet him. Mustafa Kemal wandered about trying to find suitable lodging. None could be found in that dirty, medieval town. Tired, disillusioned, and unrecognized, he went to the beach. Almost fainting with fatigue, he stretched himself out on the sand and placed his bag beneath his head as a pillow. He was discovered there by a Turkish lieutenant, who, seeing that the newcomer outranked him, saluted and offered him shelter in his own billet.

Mustafa Kemal accepted this hospitality and spent the night in his colleague's shabby quarters. The next morning he sought out and presented himself to the local commander. Claiming only to be a military officer who knew nothing about politics, the commander reacted cautiously. Mustafa Kemal soon made the commander recognize the validity of his mission, and he took over the quarters reserved for the pasha of Tripoli. Thereupon, he asked the lieutenant who had assisted him to share these sumptuous quarters.

Having asserted his authority over the Turkish forces on the scene, Mustafa Kemal set out to test himself against the local Arabs, who were attempting to rid themselves of Turkish domination. Courageously, he faced them in the courtyard of the mosque which was the center of their activities. In spite of the great danger in which he found himself, Mustafa Kemal managed with words to win the dissidents back to submissiveness. He even forced the respected religious leader of Bengazi, Shaykh Mansur, to recognize the authority of Sultan Abdülhamid and the Committee of Union and Progress. Against great odds Mustafa Kemal met the challenge and proved his gifts of leadership. Singlehandedly, he transformed an assignment to political exile into a deeply significant personal triumph. On the wings of this success, he returned to Salonika. Establishment of the committee's authority in Libya did not win any new friends for Mustafa Kemal in Salonika, where the hostility toward him still filled the air.

[4]These letters were written to his childhood friend, Salih (Bozok). Salih later was to serve as his first aide-de-camp. See Aydemir 1969, vol. 1, p. 135.

Reforms the Committee of Union and Progress had pressed upon Sultan Abdülhamid II touched off a conservative counterrevolution in Istanbul on 13 April 1909 (known in Turkish as the event of 31 March due to the difference in the calendars in use). Theorists of modernization, especially Marion J. Levy, Jr. (1966, vol. 2, p. 773; see also Levy 1972), have noted that one reaction against stepped-up modernization is often a religiously imbued counterstroke. When students from the religious schools, with support from the lowest echelons of the military and the artisan and laboring classes, began to agitate against the "irreligious" actions of the Committee of Union and Progress, several leaders of fundamentalist religious groups such as various dervish orders gave voice to the discontent, demanding a government that would uphold the holy law of Islam and keep the minorities in their place. A group called the Society of Islamic Unity was formed to promote these ideas. On the evening of 12 April the students held a mass meeting at the Mosque of Sultan Ahmed, where they were joined by the troops of the First Army. Demands were formulated for the resignation of the government, banishment of certain deputies, enforcement of the Sharia (Islamic law), and an end to the influence of the Committee of Union and Progress in the army. Demonstrators flooded into the parliament building, where two deputies were killed. In the ensuing chaos the cabinet offered its resignation to the sultan, who accepted it along with all the demands made by the leaders of what was now a revolt. The mob then vented its anger on the Committee of Union and Progress by sacking its newspaper offices and headquarters. Quick to sense his opportunity, Sultan Abdülhamid II appointed a new cabinet of his own supporters and took control of the fighting forces. The sultan was through with sharing power with the Committee of Union and Progress. He would again both reign and rule.

Once more all eyes focused on Macedonia and the Third Army, which had engineered the successful rising against Abdülhamid. The commander of the Third Army, Mahmud Şevket Pasha, rose to the occasion, assisted by his chief of staff, Mustafa Kemal. Moving rapidly, Mustafa Kemal organized a strike force, dubbed the Army of Action, to be sent against Istanbul. He was responsible for its morale, discipline, staff work, and the speed of its movement. The army advanced against the rebellious city and met with little resistance. It took up positions at Yeşilköy (formerly San Stefano), the present site of Istanbul's international airport. Enver, who had been assigned to Berlin as military attaché, returned to Macedonia to take part in the action. He played an important role, once again overshadowing Mustafa Kemal, in the negotiations with members of parliament who sought to restore order and constitutional government in the wake of the revolt. The Army of Action entered Istanbul on 24 April, and after some sporadic resistance occupied the capital. Under orders from Mahmud Şevket martial law was established and summary courts were set up. On 27 April the rump parliament met and, acting under the authority of a religious decree (*fetva*), deposed Sultan Abdülhamid II for his role in the counterrevolution and for financial chicanery. After having ruled the Ottoman Empire for thirty-three years, Abdülhamid was packed off to Salonika at the age of 66.

Abdülhamid was replaced by his brother Mehmed V. As the sultan's younger brother, he had been mewed up in the imperial palace for the past thirty years, and had not seen his older brother for nineteen years. Upon his ascendancy to the throne it was clear that the Ottoman Empire, which had once been the scourge of Europe, was in its death throes. The Ottoman sultan whose predecessors had twice led the ever-victorious Ottoman troops to the very gates of Vienna, once in 1529 and again in 1683, would now be a figurehead. Real power would eventually be in the hands of the leaders of the Committee of Union and Progress, including Mustafa Kemal's arch rival, Enver, aided by Cemal and Talât.[5]

Having been instrumental in organizing the resistance to the counter-revolution, Mustafa Kemal returned to Salonika, where he pondered, along with others, the dependency of the Committee of Union and Progress on military might rather than on any hoped-for, freely elected parliament. In the early days of Mehmed V's reign there was a good deal of discussion on the future structure of the state. Mahmud Şevket tried to hold the middle ground in an attempt to keep the military out of politics and the Committee of Union and Progress out of the government. Late in the summer of 1909 the Committee of Union and Progress held its second annual congress in Salonika. Mustafa Kemal participated as the representative of Tripoli. A small group of like-minded men began drawing together under the influence of Mustafa Kemal, including some of Mustafa Kemal's classmates and friends from the War College and men he had come to know recently, Ali Fuat (Cebesoy), Fethi (Okyar), Kâzım (Karabekir), Rauf (Orbay), a naval officer, Tevfik Rüştü (Aras), and İsmet (İnönü), an artillery officer who would become his second in command in the establishment of the new Turkish republic.

In the course of this congress Mustafa Kemal put forward several notions that aroused the ire of the leading members of the Committee of Union and Progress. He urged that the military play no role in politics and that those in the military who wished to take an active part in politics

[5]Cemal (Ahmed) Pasha (1872–1922), one of the leaders of the Committee of Union and Progress, was minister of the navy and governor of Syria during World War I. In 1922 he was assassinated. Talât Pasha (1874–1921) was the grand vizier in 1917–18. He was also a leader of the Committee of Union and Progress. Joined by Enver Pasha (1881–1922), they were the dominant figures in the Ottoman Empire between 1913 and the end of World War I. In 1921, Talât was assassinated.

should resign their commissions. He even wanted the committee to pass a regulation to that effect. As for himself, he elected to withdraw from the political scene and devote himself to his military career.

Mustafa Kemal's reputation as a military tactician grew when he voiced considerable criticism of outdated Turkish military techniques. He also translated military training manuals from German into Ottoman Turkish. Throwing himself into the task of improving the training of Turkish military recruits, he amazed his fellow officers with his ability to work during the day, stay up late drinking and arguing, and still report for duty earlier than anyone else, ready for whatever the day would bring.

When military maneuvers resumed in Macedonia, Mustafa Kemal became an outspoken staff officer who pushed his views with officers who were much senior to him. The fact that he was often right did not endear him to them. They managed to get him reassigned from staff work to field command, but here, too, he demonstrated the correctness of his military notions. He was especially effective in putting down a minor uprising of Albanians. His rivals had to endure his boasts after that action, and their only revenge was to deny him his promotion. He hardly missed an opportunity to lecture his colleagues. Although he was becoming a nuisance, he was named to the army mission that observed the French maneuvers in Picardy.

Despite some obvious signs of recognition, Mustafa Kemal was plagued by bouts of depressive moods. Promotion was still being denied him while Enver's star continued to rise. He drank heavily in the cafes and casinos of Salonika and harangued his friends on the true nature of greatness. His frame of mind is disclosed in one story from this period which has him defining greatness as the recognition of oneself as small and weak, and aware that help will not come from any quarter. Knowing that, he said, one must head straight for the goal and overcome all obstacles.

As despondency settled over Mustafa Kemal, the honeymoon between the Young Turks and the European powers soon came to an end. Italy decided to occupy some Ottoman territories in North Africa, and the situation in the Balkans became more explosive. In the fall of 1911 the Italians attacked Bengazi, Tripoli, and other strongholds in Libya.[6] A number of officers and their followers volunteered to go to North Africa to direct the struggle there. Enver saw the situation as one in which he might win glory for himself. Mustafa Kemal thought that the situation in the Balkans was more threatening to the continued existence of the empire, but he could not afford to absent himself from this military

[6]The scene of the conflict was, in the geographical terminology of the time, Tripolitania in the west and Cyrenaica in the east. These made up modern Libya.

engagement. Following in the footsteps of Enver, he set out for the front in Cyrenaica.

In order to get to his comrades Mustafa Kemal had to pass through Egypt, which was under British control. He fell ill with malaria in Alexandria and had to interrupt his journey for a while. In Arab dress he managed to reach the front near Derna, but only after talking some Egyptian officers, who had orders to arrest a number of Turkish officers heading for Libya, into letting him go. He did this by appealing to their Islamic sentiments, asking to be allowed to get to his destination to take up the struggle against the invading Christians. He was not above using religious sentiment to achieve his objectives.

When Mustafa Kemal reached Derna, the struggle was already lost. The Italians had initiated the conflict on 29 September 1911. By 4 October they had landed at Tobruk, and by 13 October they were in Derna. Mustafa Kemal took command of the Derna front, but there was little he could do. He fell ill again. The malaria he had contracted in Egypt would continue to plague him off and on for some time to come. In addition, he was having a great deal of difficulty with his eyes. On doctor's orders he was evacuated to a field hospital, and then, ahead of his fellow officers, he would have to leave North Africa for more medical treatment in Vienna.

The situation in Libya deteriorated steadily. The Italians officially annexed Tripoli and Bengazi on 4 November 1911, having driven the Ottomans out, and had only to contend with guerrilla resistance led by Sanusi tribesmen. Moreover, the Ottoman government found itself faced with other difficulties in the Balkans and at home. Italy began to arm the Montenegrins and the Albanians in the expectation that the Balkan cauldron would bubble over into full-scale war. On the home front the debacle in Libya undermined the reputation of the Committee of Union and Progress. Wrangling between the cabinet and the parliament forced the sultan to dissolve the parliament on 13 January 1912. In the new elections the Committee of Union and Progress, the only real organized party, won an overwhelming victory, but a group of army officers who feared the establishment of an autocracy by the committee threatened a coup. The sultan sought to resolve the crisis by appointing a cabinet that would be above politics and thus able to deal with the gathering crisis in the Balkans.

Nationalism had done its work well in the Balkans, corroding the cohesiveness the Ottomans had been able to establish in an area characterized by a jumble of religions, tongues, ethnic ties, and competing territorial claims. International rivalry found this decaying region fertile soil. Russia and Austria-Hungary each sought to stalemate the other in the drive for dominance in the Balkans. At the same time, Serbia, Bulgaria, and Greece tried to take advantage of Ottoman preoccupations to enlarge their own national states. Italy's attack on the Ottoman Empire following Austria's annexation of Bosnia and Herzegovina in 1908 stimulated a series of political moves that prepared the way for a full-scale campaign against the Ottoman Empire by her Balkan neighbors.

On 13 March 1912 Serbia and Bulgaria made an alliance, dividing certain territories among themselves should they be victorious against the Ottomans. This was followed by an alliance between Greece and Bulgaria 29 May 1912 and understandings among Montenegro and Bulgaria and Serbia, which were concluded on 27 September and 6 October. These moves convinced the shaky Ottoman government that it must settle its disputes with Albania and Italy in order to meet the growing Balkan threat. On 4 September 1912, a settlement was reached with Albania, and on 15 October an accord was reached with Italy, calling for the Ottomans to pull all their forces out of Tripolitania and Cyrenaica.

As expected, war broke out in the Balkans. It was initiated by Montenegro's move into northern Albania, which brought the negotiated alliances into operation. The Greeks, Bulgarians, and Serbians soon joined in and pressed the attack against Ottoman strongholds in the Balkans. Greece formally annexed Crete. By the last week of October the Bulgarians had Edirne under siege, and early in November they reached the outskirts of Istanbul itself. The Serbs quickly spread over much of Macedonia, and on 8 November they took Salonika, the city of Mustafa Kemal's birth.

By the time Mustafa Kemal returned to Istanbul, the First Balkan War—an action whose swiftness would be matched only by the German blitzkriegs of World War II—was all but over. The loss of Salonika and Monastir, two cities full of fond memories for Mustafa Kemal, must have shocked him greatly. He is reported to have asked fellow officers how they could allow such a thing to happen. Those who knew him later, when he was president of the Turkish republic, note the longing he kept in his heart for his birthplace and his nostalgia for the days spent in a land no longer Turkish.

Refugees poured into Istanbul. Among them were Mustafa Kemal's mother, his sister and her husband. Mustafa Kemal located them and settled his family in a house he managed to rent. Ragıp's nieces, an adolescent girl named Fikriye and her younger sister Julide, came to Istanbul at about the same time and apparently lived nearby. Also among the refugees was Abdülhamid II, whom the Germans got out of Salonika and brought by ship to Istanbul. He was housed in the palace called Beylerbeyi on the Asiatic side of the Bosporus. There he would die on 10 February 1918.

With the enemy at its doorstep, the Ottoman army began to prepare for the defense of Istanbul. As a member of the General Staff, Mustafa Kemal was assigned to the Gallipoli Peninsula, which borders on the Dardanelles, the straits that connect the Aegean Sea with the Sea of Marmara. Its defense was crucial, for any enemy warship that got through the straits could easily attack Istanbul.

While Mustafa Kemal was still in Istanbul, Enver, who had returned from North Africa, led a successful coup d'etat. On 23 January 1913, a mob burst in upon a cabinet session, shot the war minister to death, and forced the grand vizier to resign. The coup was in large measure a response to the plans to cede Edirne to Bulgaria as part of the peace settlement to end the war. Edirne was the first significant Ottoman conquest in Europe, captured in 1361, nearly a century before the fall of Constantinople itself. A flood of emotions was released by its imminent loss. Enver personified the popular reaction. Arriving at the scene on a white charger, he dramatically led the rush into the cabinet room. Ömer Naci, the poet and public orator of the Committee of Union and Progress, and an old friend of Mustafa Kemal's, voiced his feverish praise of the action to the crowd that had gathered.

This coup d'etat was not to Mustafa Kemal's liking. He was particularly critical of the manner in which it had been carried out. Not only was political assassination abhorrent to him, but the coup brought Enver and his friends back into the good graces of the populace, which was a blow to Mustafa Kemal's fortunes. Once again, Mustafa Kemal was pushed aside, and his criticism of Enver and the leadership of the Committee of Union and Progress made it certain that events would pass him by.

Initially, the general public was pleased with the coup because it had saved Edirne and the slim Ottoman foothold in Europe. The city had deep emotional power as a symbol of Ottoman military greatness, and it was also the site of the Selimiye Mosque, Sinan's architectural masterpiece, completed in 1574.[7]

The coup failed, however, in its expressed aim of retaining Edirne. Military pressure was stepped up by the Bulgarians, who starved the city into submission. Edirne surrendered on 28 March amidst atrocities committed against the local Muslim population. The Ottoman government, led by Grand Vizier Mahmud Şevket, had to enter discussions aimed at restoring peace. Negotiations led to the Treaty of London early in June 1913. Political violence again broke out in Istanbul, where Mahmud Şevket was assassinated. He was gunned down by a group of army officers who opposed the Committee of Union and Progress, but they themselves were rounded up and sentenced to death by a court-martial. In the wake

[7]Sinan, one of the greatest architects in the world, was born in 1489 and lived almost a century (until 1588) during the golden age of the Ottoman Empire. See Stratton 1972.

of these events the Committee of Union and Progress instituted a dictatorship that would ultimately lead the Ottoman Empire into World War I as an ally of Germany.

Enver, Talât, and Cemal emerged as the triumvirate that ruled the Ottoman state. The Balkan states were unable to agree among themselves on the division of the spoils of war, and their squabbles led to a resumption of the war with the Ottomans. In this Second Balkan War Enver led his troops in the recovery of Edirne, becoming the most powerful man in the Ottoman state. Between 1913 and 1915 he promoted himself again and again, attaining the rank of lieutenant general and holding the office of minister of war. He married an Ottoman princess and became virtually a military dictator. The modernization movement in the Ottoman Empire had now come full circle.

Enver was thirty-three years old, one year older than Mustafa Kemal. He was the hero of the day and could do no wrong. Few chose to speak out against him. Mustafa Kemal continued to do so. With peace restored at the end of the Second Balkan War, relations with Bulgaria were normalized. Mustafa Kemal's friend Fethi (Okyar) was selected as ambassador to Sofia. Shortly thereafter, Mustafa Kemal was offered the post of military attaché for the Balkans with his headquarters in Sofia. Once again, he was faced with the acceptance of a position that amounted to political exile. Having no alternative, he accepted and set out for Sofia.

7

Women and Mustafa Kemal: A Gay Blade in Istanbul and Sofia

Assignment to Sofia had more than political implications for Mustafa Kemal. It meant another separation from his mother and an interruption in a significant relationship he had established with a woman named Corinne. Failure to accept the assignment would have left resignation from the army as the only alternative. His friends cautioned against this, warning him that he had no independent political base from which to attack Enver's policies. Since Enver was so powerful, it would be prudent not to arouse his enmity further.

While stationed in Salonika, Mustafa Kemal had seen his mother quite regularly, and he had been reconciled with his stepfather. When actual warfare broke out in Macedonia, Mustafa Kemal's mother joined the thousands of others who fled to the safety of Istanbul and other places in the Ottoman heartland. Zübeyde's husband stayed behind and later died in Salonika. People who knew Zübeyde during this period recall that although her husband's name was mentioned occasionally, he was never referred to as Zübeyde's husband or as Mustafa Kemal's stepfather (Aydemir 1974). The union that had aroused young Mustafa Kemal's narcissistic rage was over, and an extended family was reestablished in a three-story house in the Beşiktaş district of Istanbul. Mustafa Kemal's sister Makbule and her husband occupied the first floor. He reserved the second floor for his own use whenever he was in the city, and the third floor, with its three rooms, was his mother's domain. Mustafa Kemal preferred to live in Western style, but his mother was accustomed to her peasant ways and continued to sleep on the floor on a mattress rather than use a bed.

Another member of this extended household was a small boy named Abdürrahim, who later took the surname Tuncak. He was born about 1910 and, when interviewed by Dr. Volkan in 1974 (Tuncak 1974), he was a retired engineer, having been trained in Germany. He stated in the course of the interview that although he had no definite knowledge of his origins, gossip had it that when his widowed mother had died and left him an orphan in 1913, Mustafa Kemal adopted him and presented him to Zübeyde as an *emanet*, or "trust," for them to protect. In the dining room of his apartment in the Bahçelievler section of Ankara hung an enlarged photograph of Mustafa Kemal with the small boy Abdürrahim. It had been taken when the boy accompanied Zübeyde on a visit to Mustafa Kemal in Aleppo in 1917. The child was wearing an Arab headdress. Although he did not have blue eyes and blond hair like Mustafa Kemal, there was a remarkable likeness between the facial contours of the Turkish hero and those of the elderly engineer, and the eyebrows of both men swept upward at the temples.

Regardless of where he came from, Abdürrahim's presence in the house in Beşiktaş has historical and psychological significance. He remains a living witness not only to historical events, but also to the quality of Zübeyde's mothering. She referred to Abdürrahim as her "son." Mustafa Kemal himself addressed the child as "my son," but this is open to interpretation as he called his friends and members of his military staff his "children," and it is usual even today for Turkish men to call the children of friends or relatives "sons." What is psychologically important is that Zübeyde and Mustafa Kemal, mother and son, shared a "son" in what represented an oedipal triumph for Mustafa Kemal. The stepfather was no longer in his mother's life. Mustafa Kemal was now reunited with her, and Abdürrahim was the symbol of the link between them.[1]

Abdürrahim accompanied Zübeyde everywhere. During the interview with Dr. Volkan, Mr. Tuncak remarked that he had been her "walking stick." He remembered her as having been very authoritarian and overprotective and as having an intense relationship with Mustafa Kemal. Zübeyde often spoke, he said, of having made her second husband pay obeisance to her son. When Mustafa Kemal greeted his mother upon arrival or took his leave of her, he kissed her on the cheek, although it was customary for a son to kiss only the hand of his mother upon such occasions. His behavior may have raised some eyebrows, but within the family circle it was written off as simply being a reflection of the intense love he felt for her. His mother addressed him as "Mustafam" (my

[1]It is remarkable that although Atatürk's practice of adopting daughters, which he engaged in after he became president of Turkey, is common knowledge in the country, hardly anyone appears to know of the existence of this adopted son. Surprised when he found out about Abdürrahim Tuncak, Dr. Volkan questioned Şevket Süreyya Aydemir, Atatürk's Turkish biographer, about him. He had no knowledge of an adopted son, but did allow the possibility that Mustafa Kemal had adopted an orphan Armenian boy and suggested that this might account for Mr. Abdürrahim Tuncak. If this is the case, his being Armenian might explain why the boy was never publicly identified as a member of the household.

On 5 December 1974, Mr. Tuncak kindly granted Dr. Volkan a long interview concerning his earliest memories of life with Zübeyde right up to the time of her death. It was especially generous of Mr. Tuncak to grant this interview, for he was experiencing considerable pain at that time in his knee. His account of his early life was vivid, although he refrained from any reference to his origins. He agreed to a second interview, but could not undertake it, citing ill health and out-of-town visitors.

Mustafa) and later, after he became a general, called him "Paşam" (my Pasha).

At the same time, Mustafa Kemal's relations with other women indicated a split in his loyalties. Although he grew extremely close to his mother after her separation from his stepfather, he centered his social life on westernized Turkish women and on women from Europe. While he had as his base his old-fashioned Muslim home with its prescribed daily routine, he was also a regular guest at the home of a woman called Madame Corinne, who lived in Pera, the westernized district of Istanbul. There people lived in the European style and followed Western ways. He was a different person in this relaxed environment.

Corinne had been born in Genoa and was the widow of Captain Ömer Lüfti, an Ottoman military officer whom Mustafa Kemal had known before the man's death in the Balkan War. It is believed that her father, a physician, was an interpreter in the Department of the Navy.[2] Her uncle, who assumed a Turkish name, became a pasha in the Ottoman army. Corinne was a graduate of the Paris Conservatory of Music and an accomplished pianist; she spoke Italian, French, and Turkish. She was the hostess of a European-style salon at which chamber music and singing were the attractions. Someone took Mustafa Kemal to one of these gatherings, and he made an immediate impression upon the hostess. They were to become fast friends, and the letters exchanged between them from the time he went to Sofia as the military attaché have been published (Borak 1970, pp. 43–65). Mustafa Kemal sometimes wrote to Corinne in French, with which he had spelling difficulties, but occasionally he also wrote in Turkish. Interestingly, when he wrote in his own language he substituted Latin script for the Arabic then in use, foreshadowing his later demand that all Turks use the Latin script.

Mustafa Kemal wrote to Corinne from Sofia in 1913, from the Dardanelles in 1915, and from a position somewhere near the present Turkish-Syrian border in 1916 and 1917. Although their correspondence was to dwindle, the early letters indicate a relationship more fervent than mere friendship. It is also obvious that his interest in her was more than as a student of Western mores. When Mustafa Kemal was assigned to Sofia, he left behind both his mother and his growing relationship with Corinne.

Through his correspondence Mustafa Kemal kept Corinne informed of his adjustment to Bulgarian society. She, in turn, praised the progress he was making in his command of French, having undertaken to be his tutor in the language. She remarked that she thought of him every day. Mustafa Kemal was pleased and hastened to reassure her on the lack of

[2]Dr. Luigi had worked for the Turkish government for some time and had become a Turkish citizen. Borak 1970, p. 43.

beautiful women in Sofia. "No, no, Corinne," he wrote, "it isn't possible to see even one beautiful woman in Sofia." He told her of meeting a Parisienne who was a noted hostess in the city, but added, "Let me tell you that I did not find this Parisian lady beautiful." Corinne was also informed of his meeting two Hungarian women at a nightspot in Sofia called the Novia Amerika. From his description of them they were obviously singers in the floor show who then circulated among the guests to stimulate the sale of drinks. One of the women spoke German, but the other, who was younger, could speak only Hungarian. Mustafa Kemal did not enjoy himself in the situation. Feeling bored, he and his friends departed, leaving the women to their own devices. He ended his letter with, "Always give me news of yourself. With all my Heart," and signed it M. Kemal. In the closing sentence he reminded her to give his greetings to her mother and sister.[3]

Mustafa Kemal's letters to Corinne reflect both the fact that he was kept busy by his official duties and that he quickly found social acceptance in Bulgaria's capital city. Handsome and striking in his military uniform with its kalpak, the distinctive brownish curly lamb fur headgear, Mustafa Kemal cut a dashing figure. He was soon seen at all the best parties, for making the rounds and getting acquainted socially was also part of his mission as military attaché. Although it had not been long since the Bulgarians had faced the Turks in battle, they were now trying to make friends. People in that part of the world, having been for so long under Ottoman domination, were now trying to assimilate their mixed feelings about their former conquerors. For generations they had thought that all roads led to Istanbul and that the Ottoman ruling elite set the pattern for acceptable social interaction. Now, Sofia and the Bulgarian governing class were looking westward, taking their cues from Europe. Sofia was taking on the appearance of a modern, Western city. The Bulgarians spared no effort to change the city's appearance, putting in wide boulevards, parks, and other amenities. Mustafa Kemal was deeply impressed with this westernization and talked about doing the same for Ottoman cities. Another reform he was concerned with at this time was the unveiling of Turkish women, which had already been adopted by some Turkish women in Bulgaria.

Material published for the first time in 1962 gives further insight into Mustafa Kemal's relationship with his idealized, European women. Early in 1962 a young Turkish man, Edip Erenler, injured in an accident in Germany was taken to St. Joseph's Hospital in Aachen. There he came to the attention of a German nurse, who, as a small child had lived with her parents in Sofia. Mustafa Kemal had taken a room in their house and

[3]This letter was written on 3 November 1913.

entered into an intense relationship with the entire family, but especially with the mother. The encounter of the Turkish youth with that nurse in Germany led to the discovery of three letters Mustafa Kemal had written to the nurse's mother and one he had addressed to her husband. The mother, Hildegard Christianus, had taught her boarder German and French. We shall return to these letters written from the battlefield at Gallipoli and compare them with those Mustafa Kemal wrote to Corinne. The similarity in the manner in which he related to the two women in his correspondence is striking.[4]

Atatürk's Bulgarian biographer Parushev (1973) gives a vivid description of Mustafa Kemal's life in Bulgaria, but his Turkish biographer, Aydemir (1969, vol. 1) passes over this period of his hero's life as merely a time of waiting for better things, since he was, during that interval, practically a political exile. Enver did not want him in Istanbul, and the Committee of Union and Progress had had enough of his constant criticism. Mustafa Kemal's refusal to hold his tongue had resulted in his being packed off to Sofia. While in Sofia he continued to be critical of the committee and the approach of its leaders to Germany. Enver was beginning to align the Ottoman Empire with Germany, and German officers were appearing everywhere in the Ottoman high command. General Otto Liman von Sanders already had executive authority over Turkish troops.[5] Mustafa Kemal was unsure of Germany's capacity to win the coming war, an opinion he had formed when observing the maneuvers in France. If Germany did win, then the Ottoman Empire would fall completely under the domination of Germany; if she did not win, then everything would be lost.

Mustafa Kemal's criticism reached its peak in a letter he wrote to a friend in Istanbul in September 1914.[6] In it he took exception to the rash attitude of "others in Istanbul," by which he probably meant Enver, and talked about the personal hurt of being away from the center of political and military ferment. He did not, however, experience much loneliness

[4]Some of Mustafa Kemal's letters to Hildegard Christianus first appeared in the first and second issues of a journal called *Tarihin Sesi* (1962). Soon this journal ceased publication, and the remaining letters were delayed. All of the letters appeared later in book form. See Terzioğlu 1964, pp. 112–25. Also see Borak 1970, pp. 66–77.

[5]Liman von Sanders was born in 1855 and died in 1929. He was first appointed commander of the Ottoman First Army with authority over all other German officers in Ottoman service. Because other nations, for example, England and France, feared that Germany would take control of the Ottoman army, Liman von Sanders became an "inspector general," an advisor. From 1913 to 1918 he was advisor to the Ottoman army, and indeed he commanded Ottoman armies at Gallipoli in 1915 and in Syria and Palestine in 1918. See Liman von Sanders 1927.

[6]This letter was written to Dr. Tevfik Rüştü (Aras), who was later interviewed by Aydemir. See Aydemir 1969, vol. 1, p. 194.

during his stay in Bulgaria between 14 October 1913, and 7 November 1914. He devoted himself to winning the admiration of a number of Western women, which greatly improved his self-esteem. Even King Ferdinand of Bulgaria yielded him homage in an encounter that took place two weeks after Mustafa Kemal's arrival in Sofia. The opera *Carmen* was being presented at the opera house at the time, and he went to a performance. It was the second such production he had ever attended.[7] During the intermission King Ferdinand summoned the handsome young Turkish military attaché to his box and asked his opinion of the opera. Mustafa Kemal replied that he thought it was extraordinary. That gala evening left a deep impression on him and would be reflected in the one operatic extravaganza he would sponsor as the president of Turkey.

Another encounter with King Ferdinand also left Mustafa Kemal deeply affected. He had become a favorite of Sofia's leading hostess, Sultane Rasha Petroff. She invited him to a masked ball at the palace. Mustafa Kemal sent to Istanbul for a Janissary costume complete with its distinctive headdress and sword. The Janissaries were the Ottoman elite troops organized in the reign of Sultan Murad I (1362–89) and not disbanded until 1826, when the reforming Sultan Mahmud II did away with them almost five centuries later. Dazzling as their uniforms were, and Mustafa Kemal could hardly have made a better choice of costume, it is significant that the Janissaries were originally recruited from Christian war captives and then on a regular basis by levy from among the Christian population of the Ottoman empire, primarily in the Balkans. The photograph of Mustafa Kemal in that uniform is striking. When the revellers unmasked at midnight, King Ferdinand sent for Mustafa Kemal to congratulate him on his costume and stunning appearance. King Ferdinand presented him with a silver cigarette case in honor of the occasion.[8]

While Mustafa Kemal was in Sofia, his name was connected with that of the youngest daughter of the Bulgarian minister of war, but no hint of that relationship found its way into his letters to Corinne. As military attaché, it was natural that Mustafa Kemal should meet General Kovachev, and he also came to know the general's wife, who, like himself, was a Macedonian. Mustafa Kemal was also introduced to the general's daughters, and he became a regular visitor in the Kovachev home, where Turkish was often spoken. The eldest daughter was married, but the youngest, Dimitriana, who was called Miti, was not. Mustafa Kemal became greatly interested in her. Although already well

[7]According to Parushev 1973, p. 79, Mustafa Kemal had attended the performance of an opera when he was in Paris.

[8]Mustafa Kemal never forgot King Ferdinand's gesture. Years later, when the king was in exile, Atatürk sent him a gold cigarette case; Kinross 1965, p. 74.

launched in society, she gladly found time for the exciting young military attaché. They obtained the permission of her parents to go out together. This was a rather western mode of behavior for Mustafa Kemal, for even in Istanbul young Muslim men were not seen about town with unattached women of good families. Mustafa Kemal adopted other Western ways at the same time. For example, he began to wear a European style hat in Sofia in preference to the Ottoman kalpak even when he was not with Miti. This foreshadowed another of his reforms in Turkey, the introduction of the hat.

Miti and Mustafa Kemal were often seen in each other's company, at dances or strolling in the park. Mustafa Kemal wanted to marry her, and she in turn was greatly taken by his charm and confident manner, but the match was frowned upon by her parents. Their opposition was signalled by their refusal to attend a ball at the Ottoman embassy. It would have been out of the question for a Christian girl to marry a Muslim in any case. Mustafa Kemal's friend Fethi, the ambassador to Bulgaria, experienced the same rejection. He had fallen in love with the daughter of General Petroff, who refused to entertain the match, saying, "I would sooner cut off my head than have my daughter marry a Turk."

Rejection as a suitor sharply lowered Mustafa Kemal's self-esteem, but he had little opportunity to brood about it, because the outbreak of World War I necessitated his return to Istanbul. This romance was to have a bittersweet reprise, however, when he went back to Sofia after his heroism at Gallipoli had been acclaimed.[9] The pair met again, and although it appears that they were still in love, they bowed to the inevitable and separated forever. There is some evidence that Dimitriana tried to go to Istanbul four years later, but the collapse of the Bulgarian front prevented her visit. She later married a Bulgarian deputy and was living in Sofia as a widow in 1965. For years she followed Atatürk's career and hoarded photographs of him cut from newspapers and magazines, and felt great sadness at his relatively early death (Parushev 1973, p. 91).

[9]This time Mustafa Kemal stayed in Sofia for only six weeks; Parushev 1973, p. 91.

8
The Crystallization of Immortality

While Mustafa Kemal was enduring his exile in Sofia, Enver rose meteorically, promotion after promotion, to become a pasha and minister of war. Accumulating all the trappings of power and authority, he became the central figure in the empire and set about to restructure the army. He was confident in his fantasies of glories to come that would salve the wounded pride of the Ottomans.

Enormously envious of Enver, Mustafa Kemal nevertheless wrote him a letter in which he congratulated the war minister on his work with army reform. Although the two men were roughly the same age, thirty-four, Mustafa Kemal was agonizingly aware of the fact that the gap between them had widened. Enver was a pasha and a royal son-in-law while Mustafa Kemal, finally promoted, was but a lieutenant colonel. It is said that at this point the disheartened Mustafa Kemal thought of leaving the army for a career as a teacher or to enter trade. He could then seek consolation by becoming the idol of adoring women and, symbolically at least, turn his back on his consuming jealousy of Enver. Nothing came of those idle schemes, and he remained in the army. Mustafa Kemal continued to nurse his hopes of somehow becoming the savior of the Ottoman Empire. He was open in stating his belief that involvement in any widespread and prolonged war would adversely affect the Ottomans. Enver's friendliness toward and fascination with the Germans continued to be objects of Mustafa Kemal's scorn and criticism.

Enver's position as war minister was not an enviable one. The Ottoman army had suffered serious setbacks in the Balkan wars and had emerged from them in a considerably weakened condition. A rebuilding effort had to be undertaken, and in this he had only the support of Germany. England and France had already rejected any idea of an alliance with the Ottoman Empire.[1] That left the Ottomans to face a substantially increasing threat from Russia on their own. Enver reasoned that Germany had demonstrated no expansionist tendencies in the direction of the Near

[1]Since its occupation of Egypt in 1882, Great Britain had decided to base its Near Eastern policy on Egypt rather than on the straits. France had effected a rapprochement with Russia out of fear of Germany. Britain would be drawn into the Franco-Russian alliance, forming the Triple Entente.

East. Germany could be relied upon to hold Russia in check in the Balkans, leaving the Ottomans to devote themselves more assiduously to the defense of their eastern frontier against the Russians. An alliance with Germany also offered hope for restraining further Austrian ambitions in the Balkans.

Russia protested vigorously against the authority granted to General Liman von Sanders with respect to Ottoman troops. Viewing any revitalization of the Ottoman army and deeper involvement of Germany in the affairs of the Ottoman Empire as a threat to her own security, Russia was drawn closer to Britain and France in the search for allies to offset any disturbance in the balance of power. So intense were Russia's feelings of insecurity that by June 1914 she was willing to offer Britain the neutral zone in Persia, established by the agreement reached with the British in 1907, in return for support against a German attack.

Great Power rivalries poisoned the international environment, but as is so often the case in relations among large, powerful states, the actions of lesser entities can determine the course of events. Serbia's intensifying hatred for Austria is illustrative of this phenomenon. Austria's annexation of Bosnia and Herzegovina in 1908 led to the foundation of several Balkan organizations, official and semiofficial, as well as clandestine.[2] The Union or Death Society had a large number of military officers among its members, dedicated extremists who trained many terrorists and then planned and carried out the assassination of Archduke Francis Ferdinand in Sarajevo on 28 June 1914.[3] As heir to the throne of the Hapsburgs, the archduke's support for the Croats as a counterbalance against the Magyars in the complex relations among the Austro-Hungarian Empire's ethnic minorities was considered a threat to Serbia and to the hopes for a united South Slav state.

Serbia's connections with the assassination plot were too close. The man who concocted the plan was head of the Serbian General Staff's intelligence department, and Serbian customs officials helped the group of assassins cross the frontier into Bosnia. Once the plot was set in motion the Serbian government could not control these extremists. Archduke Francis Ferdinand's murder started a chain of events that culminated in an Austrian ultimatum to Serbia on 23 July.[4] Russia would not allow Serbia to be crushed, and Germany moved to support Austria. Serbia's

[2]The annexation was denounced by Serbs and South Slavs who wished to fulfill their own nationalist objectives rather than become part of the Austro-Hungarian Empire.

[3]The Union or Death Society, known also as the Black Hand, was founded in May 1911 and by 1914 had 2500 members, mostly Serbs and South Slavs.

[4]The Serbian government was asked to disavow pan-Serbian agitation. There were ten specific demands dealing with the suppression of anti–Austro-Hungarian agitation, dismissal and arrest of certain officials, dissolution of secret societies, and Austria-Hungary's right to take part in the investigations aimed at rooting out the conspiracy.

response to the ultimatum was conciliatory. Austria, however, rejected it and declared war on Serbia on 28 July.

With the outbreak of hostilities, it was difficult to limit the war to one between Austria and Serbia alone. Russia entered into a partial mobilization on 25 July, and the czar ordered full mobilization one week later. That was followed by a German declaration of war on Russia the next day. German war plans called for a simultaneous war against Russia and France. On 3 August, Germany went to war with France, which necessitated an invasion of Belgium. Germany's violation of Belgium's neutrality brought Britain into the conflict on 4 August.

With war brewing in their own backyard, the Ottomans were still unprepared for its outbreak. The Ottoman cabinet was not of one mind on the best policy to pursue. Cemal was in favor of an alliance with Britain and France, but he had been rebuffed. Enver took the lead in orchestrating an agreement with Germany. Initially, only Enver and a few others, including Grand Vizier Said Halim and Talât, were aware of the discussions that culminated in the signing of a secret agreement with Germany on 2 August 1914. Enver viewed the alliance as a matter of self-interest for the Ottomans because it provided them with support against Russia. He persuaded Cemal and the others to go along with the agreement once it was signed.

Unenthusiastically undertaken by the Ottomans, the alliance called for the Ottomans to intervene in support of Germany only if war should break out between Germany and Russia as a result of German aid to Austria. While the agreement was kept secret, the Ottomans proceeded to order full mobilization on 3 August. On that same day the British seized control of two warships that were being built for the Ottoman navy in a British shipyard, fearing that they might come under German control.

Relations with the British were further embittered when the Ottomans gave sanctuary to two German war vessels, the *Goeben* and the *Breslau*. Those two ships, under the command of Admiral Souchon, were cruising in the Mediterranean and had bombarded ports in North Africa. Pursued by a superior combined British and French force, the German ships made for Turkish waters. They were permitted to enter the straits, an act that violated both Ottoman neutrality and the international treaties that governed access to the straits when the Ottoman Empire was at peace. The Ottomans got around the sticky issue of adherence to international treaties by "purchasing" the *Goeben* and the *Breslau* on 11 August. Renaming the ships the *Yavuz Sultan Selim* and the *Midilli*, the Ottomans commissioned them, together with their crews, into the Ottoman navy on 16 August, and Admiral Souchon was given command of the Ottoman fleet.

Despite the existence of the secret Ottoman-German alliance and the presence of German warships in Ottoman waters, Enver was not yet able to win the cabinet over to a declaration of war on Germany's side. Acting unilaterally, he gave orders to Souchon to cruise the Black Sea and to engage Russian warships if possible, but on 19 September the cabinet, aghast at the implication of those orders, forced Enver to rescind them. Liman von Sanders and Souchon increased their pressure on Enver to bring the Ottoman Empire into the war. The German ambassador in Istanbul, Wangenheim, was of the opinion that the Ottomans were not ready for war, and in this he echoed the sentiments of several cabinet members. War material, men, and advisers were sent from Germany to bolster the defenses of the straits, and financial support was arranged as well. Upon Souchon's insistence that he had not come to Istanbul to play the comedian, the cabinet gave its permission for him to take a portion of the fleet into the Black Sea for maneuvers. On 25 October, Enver, on his own initiative, gave Souchon written instructions to conduct maneuvers in the Black Sea with the "entire fleet," and to attack Russian ships if a "suitable opportunity" presented itself (Trumpener 1968, p. 54).

Armed with this written authorization, Souchon's squadron steamed into the Black Sea two days later. On the morning of 29 October, Odessa and other Russian ports were bombarded. Four days later Russia declared war on the Ottoman Empire. Sir Edward Grey, the British foreign secretary, felt that by their own actions the Ottomans had given the signal for their own destruction, and "richly deserved whatever consequences might follow" (Grey 1925, vol. 2, p. 190).

Unfolding events gave Mustafa Kemal confirmation of his worst misgivings about Enver's capacity for leadership. Prior to the outbreak of war, Mustafa Kemal had made known his deep distrust of the Germans, but now that war had been declared he was prepared to cooperate with them and to play any role that was expected of him. As a lieutenant colonel, he would be entitled to command a division, but Enver refused to allow him to leave his post in Sofia and come to the capital. He performed the small assignments given to him, such as the procurement of arms and supplies from the Bulgarians, with deftness, but he kept up the pressure for a military command.

Impatient for orders to report for active military duty, Mustafa Kemal gave up his lodgings and moved into the embassy compound in order to be ready to leave on an instant's notice. Despair characterized his mood as the leadership in Istanbul put him off with one excuse or another about how important it was for him to remain at his post in Sofia. Adding to his depressed mood was the recognition that the real mover of events was his archrival, Enver, the man who would have the most to say about his future destiny with respect to any military command. Driven to despair, he wrote to Enver, "If in your opinion I am devoid of the qualifications to be an officer of the first rank, please say so plainly" (Aydemir 1969, vol. 1, p. 216). Enver did not reply.

Enver's own self-importance focused for the moment on more weighty matters. His grandiosity was perhaps no more marked than Mustafa Kemal's, but it was considerably more unbridled. Mustafa Kemal had a realistic bent that led to shrewd assessments of possibilities. He was able to work out appropriate compromises between his passion for extraordinary achievements and the realities of the moment. His capacity to do this was related, we believe, in a complex fashion to his earliest relationship with his father. His mother's prolonged and intense posture of grief, by which she managed to keep alive the images of her dead infant children, promoted in Mustafa Kemal a premature sense of autonomy. Evidence of that can be seen in his decision to take the entrance examination for military school without informing his mother and the cavalier manner in which he left his post in Syria to return to Salonika.

Along with this premature sense of autonomy went a tendency to hold on to idealized images of himself and significant others in his life, including an idealized image of his father. Ali Riza was perceived as a man who guarded the frontiers of his country, an image that had its origin in the years Ali Riza spent in the forest at odds with the Greek bandits who infested it and in family stories that recalled those years of hardship. Those experiences gave Mustafa Kemal a respect for boundaries and limits on the individual level so that he could contain the impetuous thrusts of his grandiose nature. Enver, on the other hand, sought to emulate Napoleon. Mustafa Kemal believed that it was Napoleon's failure to plan adequately prior to taking action that led to his downfall and ultimate exile. Enver's dreams were global in their boundlessness. After defeating the Russians, he would enter Persia and then India, where he would stir up a Muslim revolt against the British. He would, he felt, become another Alexander the Great!

World conquerors, whether in the Napoleonic or Alexandrine mold, first have to make conquests. Enver saw his opportunity arise in a projected campaign against the Russians in Transcaucasia.[5] On 6 December 1914 he left Istanbul for the east, bent on bringing internal fantasies and external realities into alignment. Initially, impressive inroads were made against the Russians in the mountainous terrain of Transcaucasia. Then, in January 1915, the winter's snows and freezing temperatures slowed the Ottoman advance, turning victory into defeat and finally into full-scale rout and disaster. Enemy action and winter's toll reduced Enver's force from 90,000 men to about 12,000. The disaster was not

[5]Transcaucasia is the region south of the Caucasus Mountains stretching between the Black and Caspian seas to the borders of Turkey and Iran.

unlike Napoleon's defeat in Russia one century earlier in the ravaging winter of 1812.

Abandoning the fantasies that had been smashed in the craggy mountains of Transcaucasia, Enver turned over command of the Ottoman Third Army to an aide and scurried back to Istanbul. News of the disaster was kept from the public, and Enver sought to brazen it out by claiming that he had "given a strong beating to the enemy," but censorship could not long keep the truth from surfacing. Eventually, the dimensions of the debacle became known. Süleyman Nazif, an Ottoman poet, offered the laconic comment, "Enver Pasha has killed Enver Pasha." It was only too clear that Enver was no longer the empire's hero, nor the idol of the leading women in Ottoman society. He responded to this deep narcissistic blow by becoming more dictatorial in style and substance. The Young Turks had lost their bloom.

It was under these circumstances of Enver returning from a disastrous military campaign and Mustafa Kemal turning away from his preoccupation with Western or westernized women and standing ready for an opportunity to lead that these two rivals met in Istanbul. After having been forced to wait out the time in Sofia, Mustafa Kemal was finally recalled to Istanbul to take command of the Nineteenth Division. Encountering Enver one day, Mustafa Kemal commiserated with him and remarked upon his fatigue, which Enver denied. When questioned about what had happened, Enver replied, "We fought, that's all." His response to Mustafa Kemal's inquiry about the current status of things in the east was a simple, "Very good" (Aydemir 1969, vol. 1, p. 224). Mustafa Kemal then changed the subject out of consideration for Enver's discomfort, but one is obliged to believe that he enjoyed seeing his rival brought low.

In that same conversation with Enver, Mustafa Kemal inquired about his division. He had already learned that Enver himself had given the order to place him in command of the Nineteenth. No one seemed to know anything at all about this phantom division, however, and Mustafa Kemal was beginning to feel like an impostor every time he sought information about it. He asked Enver where he might find his division and to which army corps it was attached. Enver told him to consult with General Liman von Sanders at General Headquarters.

At headquarters Mustafa Kemal met the same blank stares. The Nineteenth Division did not appear to exist. He was finally ushered in to see Liman von Sanders, who was not very helpful either. He took the occasion to talk to Mustafa Kemal about Bulgaria and whether the Bulgarians would enter the war. With characteristic candor, Mustafa Kemal told the German general that the Bulgarians did not believe the

Germans would be successful in the war. When Mustafa Kemal added that he shared that opinion, the interview was quickly brought to a close.

Perseverance bore fruit when Mustafa Kemal managed to locate a Nineteenth Division that was being organized in the area of Tekirdağ.[6] When the division was assembled, its headquarters was established at Maydos on the Gallipoli Peninsula in February 1915. There was a great deal of conflicting opinion about where the Allies would eventually launch an attack on the Ottoman Empire. Gallipoli, which forms the western shore of the straits,[7] was not an unlikely target.

Not content to sit and wait for the Allies' advance, Enver had meanwhile given his blessings to a combined Ottoman and German attack upon Egypt by way of the Sinai, the traditional invasion route since pharaonic times. Led by Cemal Pasha, the Turkish forces took the British by surprise, but only a few Turkish soldiers were able to cross the Suez before they were pushed back by British reinforcements. Enver's second great military gamble had failed.

Initiative in the Near East now went over to the Allies. Pressure had been mounting on the Allies to open a second front to relieve the Russians of the tremendous burden they were bearing in all sectors. Something had to be done to shore up the Russians. An attack somewhere against Turkey seemed to be the answer. Lord Kitchener, secretary of state for war, and Churchill, first lord of the admiralty, discussed the matter late in December 1914, and on 2 January 1915, Kitchener suggested the Dardanelles as the appropriate target. Once the Dardanelles were forced, troops could be landed to march against Istanbul with an eye to opening up direct communication with Russia through the Black Sea and knocking the Ottoman Empire out of the war. The job could be done by several British battleships that were too old to be used against the German navy, but were deemed adequate for this assignment. It was also felt that the Gallipoli Peninsula was poorly defended by only one division.

Discussions ultimately led to an agreement that the admiralty should devise a plan for a naval expedition to take place in February 1915 to bombard and then take the Gallipoli Peninsula, with the city of Istanbul as its ultimate objective. This audacious plan was predicated on the view of the Ottoman Empire as weak and inefficient, poorly led, and on the verge of collapse. The view gathered adherents and momentum. Only Admiral Fisher questioned the idea of attacking the Dardanelles without

[6]Tekirdağ, on the shores of the Sea of Marmara, is about equidistant between Istanbul and the Dardanelles.

[7]The Turkish straits include both the Bosporus and the Dardanelles.

military support, but he too was won over to the operation in late January 1915.

Assembling the greatest concentration of naval strength seen in the Mediterranean up to that time, the Allies opened their attack on the morning of 19 February 1915. The plan called for a long-range naval bombardment followed by a further shelling at close range. Minesweepers would then clear the way for the attack vessels to steam up the straits. The original shelling was not a complete success, but a serious change in the weather forced a halt to the attack. When resumed on 25 February, the bombardment still did not knock out all the Turkish guns. After more bad weather and indecision, the attack was renewed on 18 March. For the first time the Allied fleet suffered serious casualties, with a number of ships sunk or severely damaged. Observing the operation was General Sir Ian Hamilton, who had just been named commander in chief of an Allied army that would now take part in a combined sea and land attack. He and his staff had been hastily rushed to the battle scene. All the elements were being assembled in one place for the decisive battle that would thrust Mustafa Kemal onto the world stage.

Failure on the part of the Allies to press the attack against the Turkish fortifications on the following day left little doubt that there would then be a combined naval and land forces attack. Enver Pasha called in General Liman von Sanders and offered him command of the forces defending the Dardanelles. His first concern was to strengthen his forces on the Gallipoli Peninsula. He had six divisions grouped together as the Fifth Army at his disposal. One of those, the Nineteenth, was under the command of Mustafa Kemal. He assigned this division to the pivotal role of floating unit, ready to move from its base at Maydos south or north as the need arose. Liman von Sanders was of the opinion that the major Allied thrust would come on the Asiatic side of the straits. Mustafa Kemal was certain that "if the enemy were to attempt a disembarkation, he would attempt it at two points [on the Gallipoli Peninsula], one at Seddülbahir and the other near Kabatepe" (Ünaydın 1930, pp. 14–15).

Events soon proved the accuracy of Mustafa Kemal's military insight and intuition. The Allied attack was launched at dawn on 25 April against five points, four of them on the Gallipoli Peninsula and one on the Asiatic side of the straits. Seddülbahir and Kabatepe, or more precisely, Arıburnu, were the focal points of the Allied landings. As the battle developed, Mustafa Kemal realized, whereas Liman von Sanders had not, that the key to holding the southern half of the Gallipoli Peninsula was Conkbayırı and the Kocaçimen Plateau. Without waiting for orders from headquarters, he committed his men to the battle, marching in the direction of Conkbayırı to halt the advance of the British forces. Mustafa Kemal derived the confidence to act in this manner, without hesitation and with authority, from his own grandiose self. This action was his alone and based on his own assessment of the situation. The risk was enormous. Had he been in error and had the enemy launched a major attack at some other point at which the reserve division was needed, the Turks would have met with disaster. But he was right, and his conviction led him to move amongst his soldiers, exhorting them never to retreat. As Mustafa Kemal marched his men into position to oppose the enemy, he came upon a company of Turkish soldiers in full flight, having exhausted their ammunition. Mustafa Kemal himself described the scene in which he halted their retreat:

> "Why are you running away?" I said. "The enemy, sir," they said. "Where?" "There," they said, indicating the hill altitude 261. Actually, a skirmishing party of the enemy had approached Hill 261 and was advancing freely. Imagine the situation now. I had left my troops, to let the men have ten minutes' rest. . . . The enemy had reached this hill. . . . This meant that the enemy was nearer to me than my own men, and if the enemy should come where I was, my forces would be faced with a very bad situation. Then, whether by logic or instinct I do not know, I turned to the soldiers who were running away, "You cannot run away from the enemy," I said.

When the men told him they had no more ammunition, Mustafa Kemal replied:

> "If you have no ammunition, you have your bayonets." And I shouted the command to fix bayonets. I made them lie on the ground. At the same time I sent an officer hurriedly back to tell the infantry regiment that was marching toward Conkbayırı . . . to come to the place where I was, on the double." [Ünaydın 1930, pp. 24–25]

Seeing the Turks throw themselves upon the ground, the British troops hesitated, and then they, too, took up positions by lying on the ground. This crucial moment of hesitation allowed Mustafa Kemal to gain the upper hand. While the British delayed pressing their attack and advantage, reinforcements reached Mustafa Kemal, who threw all his available men into the counterattack. The battle raged through the night. Unfamiliar with the terrain, the Turks were only able to push the British back to the last ridges of the coastline instead of into the sea, as was Mustafa Kemal's intention. Nevertheless, he prevented the Allied forces from dominating the peninsula in their initial thrust. Exhorting his men to give their all in the ensuing close combat, Mustafa Kemal issued eloquent commands: "I am not ordering you to attack, I am ordering you to die. In the time it takes us to die, other forces can come and take our place" (Ünaydın 1930, pp. 30–31).

So fierce was the hand-to-hand fighting that Sir Ian Hamilton could not find words to describe it in his diary (Hamilton 1920). It continued from 25 April to 1 May. Anzacs, Gurkhas, Britons, and Turks lay dead side by side in great numbers. On 30 April Mustafa Kemal sent his men a ringing message: "I am of the opinion that we must push the enemy before us back to the sea. . . . I cannot accept the idea that there is anyone among us in the troops I have commanded who would not die rather than repeat the shame inflicted upon us during the Balkan wars. If you know anyone who thinks otherwise, let us kill him now with our own hands" (Ünaydın 1930, p. 41).

Mustafa Kemal fought like a man possessed. He was everywhere, indefatigable despite flare-ups of the malaria he had contracted while in Egypt en route to Libya. Masterful in his diagnoses, rapid in making decisions, and energetic in carrying them out, Mustafa Kemal's performance in this campaign claimed for him the status of military genius. Experts agree that here he was even more brilliant than in his later achievements in the Turkish struggle for independence, holding that at Gallipoli he was alone and obliged to improvise rather than to execute carefully conceived maneuvers.[8] A mere divisional commander, he took independent action at times without the benefit of consultation with the General Staff, relying on his own internal, grandiose, but keenly knowing, self. It was his uncanny ability to be at the right place at the right time that won the battle for the Turks.

In recognition of Mustafa Kemal's enormous contribution to halting the enemy advance after their initial landing, he was promoted to full colonel on 1 June. A stalemate settled over the front as both sides dug in, the Allies holding their slim beachhead and trying to move inland. A breakthrough would be possible by taking the key town of Anafartalar. During the night of 6/7 August the Allies landed some 20,000 reinforcements in an attempt to take Anafartalar. This attack came right at the sector held by Mustafa Kemal's Nineteenth Division.

Numerically superior, the Allies pressed the attack. Mustafa Kemal realized that the situation was dangerously delicate. He told Liman von Sanders that, "there is one moment more. If we lose this moment it is very probable that we shall be faced with a general disaster." His remedy was to put all the forces in the area under a single command. There was no other alternative, he suggested, than to put them under his command.

[8]We are indebted to the late Demir Uğur (1975), who had made a hobby of studying Mustafa Kemal at Gallipoli, for showing his pictorial exhibit on this topic to Dr. Volkan. The exhibit was shown publicly in 1973 and was sponsored by the Turkish Historical Society.

The chief of staff asked sarcastically, "Won't that be too many?" Unruffled, Mustafa Kemal responded, "It will be too few" (İğdemir 1962, p. 26). His self-confidence was undiminished.

At the outset of their association, Liman von Sanders had been dismayed at Mustafa Kemal's self-righteousness, tactlessness, and self-assurance. The events of Gallipoli, however, made him admire Mustafa Kemal's military competence. Therefore, he allowed all the available troops to be assigned to him as he had asked. The division doctor was assigned to accompany Mustafa Kemal, who was showing signs of exhaustion due to the recurring malaria. In accepting this assignment, Mustafa Kemal was well aware of the risks, and he acknowledged that "to assume such responsibility was no simple affair, but because I had decided not to live after the ruin of my country I accepted the responsibility with all due pride." At a later date, recalling Gallipoli, he would remark that "responsibility is heavier than death" (Aydemir 1969, vol. 1, p. 242).

Assuming his new command, Mustafa Kemal quickly set about organizing an offensive against the British forces. On 10 August he personally led a bayonet charge against the enemy. During this prolonged battle an event took place that would serve to solidify Mustafa Kemal's unconscious belief in his own immortality. As he stood on a hill under enemy fire, he was seen to jump convulsively and clutch at the left side of his chest. Lieutenant Colonel Servet (Yurdatapan) witnessed this and was horrified to see his commander hit (Aydemir 1969, vol. 1, pp. 248–49). To his surprise, Mustafa Kemal calmly turned to him and gestured for silence by putting a finger to his lips. Years later Mustafa Kemal himself recalled the incident in a different manner. According to him, a young officer at his side had blurted out, "Sir, you are hit." Mustafa Kemal then put his hand over the man's mouth and said, "Silence" (Ünaydın 1930, pp. 74–75). He did not want to risk undermining the confidence of his troops by letting them know that the man they looked to for leadership had been wounded.

Physically, the wound Mustafa Kemal had sustained was negligible, but its psychological consequences appear to have been profound. It was true that a bit of shrapnel had hit him over the heart, but a pocket watch he carried in his breast pocket absorbed most of the blow. Beneath the shattered watch there was, he claimed, a "rather big pool of blood," but whatever injury he sustained was superficial. That night, while reporting to Liman von Sanders how his men had fought the enemy with bayonets, he admitted that he had been hit and offered the damaged watch to his commander as a souvenir. Haydar Mehmet (Alganer), who saw this gesture, recalled later that the German general had tears in his eyes when he accepted the gift and impulsively pressed his own timepiece on Mustafa Kemal as a replacement. The shattered watch, which was in effect "evidence" of Mustafa Kemal's immortality, later found its way to Liman von Sanders's home in Munich. It disappeared years later when the general's house was entered by thieves (Aydemir 1969, vol. 1, p. 249). There is no reason to believe that the robbers were aware of its "magical" properties.

Gallipoli changed Mustafa Kemal, both in the real world and in the world of his inner self. The British official historian wrote, "Seldom in history can the exertions of a single divisional commander have exercised, on three different occasions, so profound an influence not only on the course of a battle, but perhaps on the fate of a campaign, even the destiny of a nation" (Kinross 1965, p. 111). The coming together of reality and Mustafa Kemal's fantasies during the course of the Gallipoli campaign had a tremendous effect upon him and once again provided a "fit" of reality-based glorification with his own grandiose self-concept. Fortunately, insight into that process is available from several letters Mustafa Kemal wrote to two women who were important in his life, Corinne and Hildegard.

In both Corinne and Hildegard he created his ideal woman, so much so that in his letters these two actually quite different women seem virtually interchangeable in his mind. Through idealizing them and then having their attention centered on him, he could maintain the cohesiveness of his grandiose self. What he wrote was often full of feeling, but he addressed himself very much alike to each. This is particularly true of the letters he wrote to them from Gallipoli. Two brief letters to Hildegard are dated 17 January 1915 and 13 April 1915. Written after his departure from Sofia, he simply told her that he thought of her always. On 6 June, after the engagement at Gallipoli, he wrote to her at greater length. In this letter his perception of her as the idealized woman is clear:

> Yesterday I received your letter which was written one and a half months ago. It has been five months since I left you. I have been completely busy since then. But I never forget the German lessons you gave me. You can rest assured that during the war, even under the noise of cannon blast and the rain of bullets, the best memories of my life were those beautiful and friendly hours during lessons. I never doubted that you would not forget me. But, not to hear from you made me very sad. . . . Your letter of 28 April 1915 made me pleased beyond anything you can imagine. . . . It is a psychological truth that man has to work hard and make sacrifices in order to obtain certain friendships. For example, when you asked me, "When are you going to be promoted to the rank of colonel?" My answer was that "such promotion could be won on a battlefield," to which you responded, "Prove it."

> By obliging your desire, I have been a colonel for five days. Besides this, exalted people have given me silver and gold war medals, and the Bulgarian King Ferdinand bestowed upon me the decoration of St. Alexander, command rank.
>
> Emperor Wilhelm (the greatest commander of our time), whom I value, honored me with the Iron Cross. *I owe all of my gains to your noble inspiration.* [Italics added; Borak 1970, pp. 73–74]

Corinne, his other correspondent, whom he also treated as an idealized woman, was the recipient of letters in the same vein. On 14 June 1915, he wrote to her:

> I am afraid that you will say, "Look, there is no news from you (for a century). . . ." Here is the news: We are fighting with great success always. I hope that you heard of my being given a silver medal for distinguished service, a gold medal for efficiency, and the Iron Cross; also, that I have been made a colonel. Greetings to the whole family. Mademoiselle Edith [Corinne's younger sister, who was later to become a Muslim and change her name to Edibe]—is she still caring for the wounded? If I return to Istanbul wounded, which one of you will have the kindness to look after me? [Borak 1970, p. 58]

Having achieved a reputation as a hero and superb military strategist, Mustafa Kemal returned to making himself the object of adoration among Western women, seeking enhanced self-esteem and recognition from the leaders he regarded as idealized fathers. He even managed to elicit a friendly letter of congratulation from Enver upon his promotion to the rank of colonel.

Failure at Gallipoli cost Winston Churchill his position as first lord of the admiralty. He left the admiralty on 26 May as the stalemate continued at Gallipoli. The cost to the Allies in lives and war matériel was enormous, as they spared little in their all-out effort to dislodge the Turks. Mustafa Kemal described the scene for Corinne in a letter written on 20 July, saying, "Life here is not calm. Shrapnel and other shells explode above our heads night and day. The whistle of bullets mingles with the roar of the cannon. Really, we are living in hell" (Borak 1970, pp. 58–59).

War, with its enforced intimate association with death, wrung from Mustafa Kemal the disclosure of a side of him seldom seen. In that same letter to Corinne of 20 July he revealed a subtle deference to religious feelings he ordinarily denied since they were split off from his dominant self, the part of him that in general preferred to have nothing to do with religion. He wrote:

> Thank God, my soldiers are brave and resist more fiercely than the enemy. Besides, their personal beliefs make it easier for them to obey my orders driving them to their deaths, since they see only two consequences of obedience—either they will become victorious Ghazis [revered Muslim warriors for the Faith] or martyrs. Do you know what is involved in the latter case? To go directly to heaven, where God's most beautiful women, the houris, will meet them and be at their disposal forever. Supreme happiness! [Borak 1970, p. 59]

In this letter, in addition to the mild flirtatious sexual innuendo and bravado, there is an echo of his mother's view of the world and the life hereafter, as well as a view of idealized womanhood. As a westernized man, Mustafa Kemal was usually unable, on the conscious level, to permit himself to recognize that he, too, held the same beliefs. Instead, he had to displace his notions onto the men who were more open about their adherence to Islam. As an immortal infant, a man balanced between life and death through whom his mother maintained contact with her dead offspring, Mustafa Kemal had two paths available to him—he could become the hero-savior of his mother (and, by extension, of the nation) so that she in turn would be able to devote herself to his care, or he could become a martyr in heaven where he would live forever with idealized mothers.

At this point in his life Mustafa Kemal felt deeply the need for someone who would care for and soothe him, as well as soften his harsh edges. He tried to convert Corinne into a "good," nongrieving mother who would help him handle the derivatives of aggression that were being stimulated by war and welling up within him. The letter continues:

> While I am waiting for your logical advice I have decided to read novels which will soften my harsh character which developed so because of present events; thus I hope I will come to feel the pleasant and good aspects of life. If it were not impossible for me to have the pleasure of your agreeable and witty conversation, which seduces everyone, I would have no need to read novels that only inspire feelings of love and convey the view of life of a man whose opinions very seldom fit my own.[9]

Mustafa Kemal then asked Corinne to make a list of novels for him to read and to give her selections to someone who could buy them for him.

Where Mustafa Kemal would find the time to read those novels is a mystery. The battle for Gallipoli continued to be hotly contested on both

[9]Borak 1970, p. 59. We know that on the night before the great offensive against the Greeks, he attempted to relax by reading a novel.

sides, and there were ghazis and martyrs aplenty. In spite of the stubbornly fought battles in which he had engaged so brilliantly, Mustafa Kemal had few illusions about an ultimate Ottoman victory. The losses at Gallipoli were heavy. Estimated Allied casualties numbered 214,000 men. Turkish dead, wounded, missing, and ill were set at 120,000 (Shaw and Shaw 1977, vol. 2, p. 318). Naval superiority had failed to win the day for the Allies. On 9 January 1916 the Allies evacuated their last man from Gallipoli, 259 days after the initial landing in April 1915. Mustafa Kemal received the news of the evacuation in Istanbul, where he had been assigned on sick leave ten days earlier.

Until Gallipoli Mustafa Kemal's psychological makeup had often led him to seek out people he could idealize, those who, in turn, would admire him so greatly that the cohesiveness of his inflated self-concept could remain intact. People not inclined to offer him instant acclaim found themselves faced with an extremely irritated man. Prior to being swept into military exploits at the age of thirty-four, he had consistently beaten on any door in the hope that its opening would provide the adulation he so desperately needed and sought. The following he had succeeded in attracting was limited mostly to women. In return for their compliance with his need for their admiration, he endowed them with impossible virtues. From time to time he did attract the attention and support of some men, but both he and they were very much at the periphery of power. Gallipoli had made Mustafa Kemal a hero at last, and his conviction of immortality had been confirmed, but he was mistaken if he thought he had arrived at the center of the stage. The appropriateness of his grandiosity had not yet been established once and for all. Others still remained to be convinced of the superiority that was so evident to him. Enver, for example, was not particularly impressed.

Enver and the Committee of Union and Progress people continued to head the government and continued to disregard Mustafa Kemal. Enver had always snubbed him. While visiting Gallipoli and talking with the ranking military men there, Enver avoided seeing Mustafa Kemal. That slight drove him to write a letter of resignation, but Liman von Sanders did not pass the letter on to the appropriate authorities. After the Allies had been stymied at Gallipoli, *The War Magazine*, published in Istanbul by the ministry of war, planned to have a picture of Mustafa Kemal on its cover, but Enver intervened, ordering the publisher not to use the photograph. Despite the fact that his return to Istanbul had failed to attract welcoming crowds in the streets of the city, Mustafa Kemal's reputation was spreading. Aware that the Allied landing at Gallipoli had panicked the people of Istanbul and that there was talk of moving the seat of government inland to Eskişehir on the Anatolian Plateau, Mustafa Kemal enjoyed referring to himself as "the savior of Istanbul."

Uncelebrated by the masses, the hero's return to Istanbul did not go unnoticed by his "split" women who were elated to have him back. He stayed with his mother, who had by then learned that her second husband had died in Salonika. That arrangement lasted only for a short time. Mustafa Kemal tired of the nagging and fuss of the women in the household, and he decided to move into a place of his own. It is not clear when Fikriye, his stepfather's young Muslim kinswoman from Salonika, became his mistress, but we do know that he began to take notice of her at this time.

Zübeyde had reestablished contact with Fikriye and her sister Julide sometime after coming to Istanbul. The sisters were living with friends or relatives. In a land where the extended family was the norm, orphans or lonely relatives, even friends, had little difficulty finding households that would unofficially "adopt" them. Abdürrahim Tuncak (Tuncak 1974), who would later recall how the two young women had visited his family in the Beşiktaş district of Istanbul, remembered that Zübeyde warned him that Julide was tubercular and that he should avoid kissing her. Apparently, Fikriye was well disposed toward Abdürrahim, who, as a child, was very fond of her.

Fikriye and Julide had an older brother, oddly enough named Enver, with whom they had no close contact. Zübeyde behaved toward them rather like an adoptive mother. An Egyptian husband was found for Fikriye. At that time solitary women or daughters for whom it was not easy to find a husband were married off to "traveling Arabs," and hers may have been such a match. In any case, it did not last long, and it is assumed that Fikriye and Mustafa Kemal became lovers when he settled in the house in the Şişli district of Istanbul.

Fikriye was an extension of his old life in Salonika, but in his characteristically split fashion he also sought the company of Corinne. A little later he went to Sofia on a holiday and visited both Hildegard and Miti, his beloved but forbidden Bulgarian girl. He brought gifts to Hildegard and her family—rugs and a handmade picture frame (Borak 1970, p. 75). During his six-week stay in Sofia, Hildegard and her family left the city. Seeing them off at the railroad station, he gave her a last message, *Von Herz zu Herz geht ein weg* (Borak 1970, p. 75). They never saw each other again.

9
The Peregrinations of a Frustrated Hero

DISAPPOINTED BY THE ABSENCE OF OFFICIAL FANFARE OR PUBLICITY WHEN he returned to Istanbul after demonstrating his military prowess at Gallipoli, Mustafa Kemal had to make do with enthusiastic greetings from his mother, his sister, and Fikriye. Corinne's assessment of him was prophetic and brimming with praise. At one of her soirees attended by Mustafa Kemal, she was at the piano when he happened to leave the room. To the surprise of the gathering, she stopped playing and turned to her guests, asking them if they recognized the man who had just left. "He is Mustafa Kemal," she announced. "He will become a great man, and one renowned not only in Turkey, but throughout the world" (Borak 1970, p. 45). Such awed devotion, which he had seen in the eyes of Hildegard and Miti upon his recent visit to Sofia, could not satisfy his hunger for general acclaim.[1]

An opportunity to satisfy his appetite for recognition was presented to Mustafa Kemal when he was placed in command of the Sixteenth Army Corps, which, after its service in Gallipoli, had been transferred to Edirne.[2] It is uncertain to what extent Mustafa Kemal engineered his own triumphal entrance into Edirne, but a ceremonial event it certainly was. Mustafa Kemal set out from Sofia, where he was vacationing, to his new assignment by rail, a prosaic enough means of transportation. Somehow, he managed to enter the city on 15 January on horseback at the head of ranks of infantry. School children helped to swell the crowds that cheered his arrival, and they placed a yoke of flowers around the neck of his mount. For Mustafa Kemal this was real acclaim, recognition that was not limited to a few admirers in some private place. Not since the night when he had caught the eye of King Ferdinand at the costume party in Sofia because of his splendid appearance in the Janissary uniform had he been so grandly in the limelight. His acclaim at the masked ball owed much to his costume and its adornments, but now it was his prowess on the battlefield that had brought him glory. This acknowledgment that he had risen to the rank of national hero brought confirmation of his unique identity, which he had been aware of for a long time.

[1]Corinne may have been realistically anticipating his ambitious potential.

[2]Edirne (formerly Adrianople) is in Turkish Thrace, close to the present-day border with Greece.

Glorious as his entry into Edirne had been, his stay there was cut short when, after a month, the Sixteenth Army Corps, along with the rest of the Ottoman Second Army, was assigned to the Russian front. Enver had already encountered disaster there, and Mustafa Kemal was determined that he would not be next to do so. In order to prepare for the conduct of his corps on the Russian front, Mustafa Kemal returned to Istanbul for a month. There he again made a nuisance of himself, demanding audiences with those in charge and offering to one and all unsolicited criticism. He was rebuffed and experienced deep disillusionment. In 1926, in an interview Mustafa Kemal gave to two newsmen, Falih Rıfkı (Atay) and Mahmud (Saydam), he recalled his state of mind at that juncture. Arguing that it was he who had been responsible for the success at Gallipoli, he added:

> it was I who saved the capital city. Since I thought that their natural human response to me would involve pleasure over my modest service, I went to see the top Ottoman statesmen. I had pressing matters to talk to them about—matters of national importance seen from the standpoint of my grasp of science, art, and contemporary events—issues of life and death for our people. I wanted to share these with those at the top. [Saydam and Atay 1926]

One can imagine his indignation when the foreign minister kept Mustafa Kemal waiting, and the humiliation he suffered upon seeing others admitted to the inner sanctum while he waited in the anteroom. In the same interview, he recalled that in view of his superior importance to those being admitted, he asked the assistant undersecretary if the minister had forgotten that he was waiting. He was given no consideration and told to wait his turn. Thereupon, Mustafa Kemal apparently harangued the undersecretary about the minister's wasting time with such inconsequential visitors as those who were being admitted. Finally, when told that he could enter the minister's office, Mustafa Kemal held back and in a loud voice replied that the minister could now wait for him. In spite of his inappropriate behavior, he was given a polite welcome. Mustafa Kemal began to berate the minister for the condition the empire was in and then asked him for help in getting rid of the German officers. The minister was unable to conceal his irritation, and later he complained to Enver about Mustafa Kemal's demeanor.

Enver did not much appreciate Mustafa Kemal's presence in Istanbul and his assignment to the Russian front no doubt brought him satisfaction. While en route to the east, Mustafa Kemal received word that he had been promoted to general on 1 April 1916. He was thirty-five years old. Enver and his Committee of Union and Progress cohorts had postponed this promotion as long as they could, bestowing it only after Mustafa Kemal's departure for the Russian front in the east, where he would be too far away to be a threat to them. It is reported that in Istanbul Enver remarked that Mustafa Kemal would never be satisfied. From general he would aspire to rise to the rank of lieutenant general and, finally, to become the sultan. When, much later, Enver's comment was reported to him, Mustafa Kemal smiled and said, "I didn't know how clever Enver was—how much he could see into the future" (Aydemir 1969, vol. 1, p. 279)!

The year 1916 was a trying one for the Ottomans. They were hard pressed to maintain a military presence on a number of fronts simultaneously. From the eastern shores of the Black Sea to Lake Van, they had to contend with the Russians. Revolts in Iraq and Syria, in the Arab Muslim heartland of the empire, were disconcerting, and troops were required in Macedonia, Rumania, and elsewhere as well. The Ottoman economy had collapsed, foodstuffs and other necessities for daily living were rapidly being depleted and morale was low.

Conditions were also poor for the Turks on the eastern front where Enver's dreams of glory had already been shattered and Mustafa Kemal's were threatened. Invading Russian forces had already taken the Black Sea port of Trabzon (Trebizond) and had penetrated inland to capture the important communications center of Erzurum. Mustafa Kemal's men, starving and wearing rags for boots, fought a number of engagements with the Russians, including one hand-to-hand fight. Mustafa Kemal was able to raise the morale of his men. Troops under his direct command were the only ones to score a victory over the Russians. Other divisions fell back, but he and his troops captured Bitlis and Muş.

Hectic as his days must have been, Mustafa Kemal still found time to write to Corinne. On 6 May he gave her some insight into his frame of mind, complaining, "Wouldn't you think that after a tiresome travail moving from west to east over a period of two months there would come a moment of peace? But alas! It seems that such a moment must await death. But I will not easily accept the necessity of entering Allah's heaven before finding comfort—and that imaginary." He told her he was planning to see his friend Nuri (Conker), who had been with him at Gallipoli, within three days, and he was anticipating their talking together about those good and charming memories created by her "dear existence." His letter concluded with a line from Chateaubriand: "I would rather never have been born than to be forgotten forever" (Borak 1970, pp. 60–61).

On 17 September 1916 Mustafa Kemal wrote again to Corinne, who apparently had reported to him that she had been ill for some forty days. He wrote of being sorry to learn of her malady, but added, "Your letter comforted my mind. Although you wrote it while still in bed, I took it as evidence of your returning health." He told her that Nuri had been gone for some fifteen days, but they had been together during the time that Mustafa Kemal was in command of the battle. "What pleasure it is to expose one's breast to fire and death at the side of those whom one values." He reported that the general who was his superior in the chain of command had been hit by a bullet in the forehead, and had died "at the place of honor," adding, "It was something to see how Nuri Bey wanted to follow that example of heroism. . . . But thank God, he listened to my advice until the villa that awaits him in heaven is completed" (Borak 1970, pp. 61–63).

Winter brought a stalemate to the easten front as both the Russians and the Turks were immobilized by winter's woes. The plight of the Turkish army was horrifying, but Mustafa Kemal insisted that the officers, at least, keep up appearances in the officers' mess. Always fastidious in matters of his own dress, he ordered his officers to attend meals on time and to keep their tunics buttoned. He took to sitting at the head of the table and engaging his fellow officers in spirited discussions. Mustafa Kemal continued this pattern of dinner-table conversation with his cronies throughout his later life.

Having distinguished himself in the battle for the city of Muş, Mustafa Kemal was awarded a distinguished decoration, the medal of the Golden Sword. In addition, he was assigned to Second Army Headquarters, which was under the command of İzzet Pasha. When İzzet took over responsibility for both the Second and the Third armies, Mustafa Kemal replaced him as the head of the Second Army. He then set about planning an offensive against the Russians for the spring. At this time Mustafa Kemal came in contact again with İsmet (İnönü), who had been one of his supporters at the second congress of the Union and Progress coalition held in Salonika, where he had urged military men to separate themselves from politics.

At this point in his career İsmet was a colonel, acting as Mustafa Kemal's chief of staff. İsmet had chosen a military life for himself in preference to the religious career followed by his father. If it is true that opposites attract, İsmet was the perfect south to Mustafa Kemal's north. His slow and plodding nature complemented Mustafa Kemal's unorthodox brilliance. İsmet had married the woman picked out for him by his father and was a loyal and faithful husband. Mustafa Kemal was promiscuous, and balanced İsmet's abstemiousness with his own hard drinking. Slightly younger than Mustafa Kemal, İsmet was obsessional, cautious, serious, dependent on the ideas of others, and better read than his commander. Mustafa Kemal, on the other hand, had such a strong belief in his own destiny that he did not depend on the thinking of other men, but took action based on his own conclusions. Taken together, the two made a perfect pair. Their close relationship was cemented at a headquarters dinner soon after Mustafa Kemal's arrival. Mustafa Kemal gave a speech in which he praised his new chief of staff, İsmet, and indicated his pride in having such a competent colleague. İsmet responded, indicating the confidence he had in his commander and welcoming the hero of Gallipoli to the Second Army.

Whatever plans these two had developed for an offensive against the Russians were shelved when the revolution that broke out in March 1917 effectively took Russia out of the war. On the Caucasian front, as in Europe, the Russian army voted for the revolution by deserting. The eastern front disintegrated as the demoralized troops, purged of their officers, fell back to Tiflis.

Russia's collapse freed Mustafa Kemal and İsmet for service in the Fertile Crescent. The British, launching their attack from Egypt, were mounting strong pressure against the Ottoman forces guarding the Islamic holy cities of Mecca and Medina and the vast areas of Syria and Mesopotamia. Mustafa Kemal had already spoken to Enver Pasha about the declining Ottoman position in the Hejaz, saying that he favored evacuating all Ottoman forces from the Arabian heartland and concentrating on the defense of Syria, which formed a barrier to the British advance into Anatolia itself.[3] Enver disregarded his advice as usual, but did forsake his plan to mount an Ottoman expeditionary force to defend the Hejaz.

Disaster quickly overtook the Ottoman forces in Arabia. Compounding the problems presented by the invading British forces was the uprising of the Arabs under Sharif Husayn of Mecca and his son, Emir Feisal. The uprising was declared in June 1916 and has become known as the Arab Revolt. Mecca was taken from the Turks by the Sharif's forces and the main Turkish garrison finally surrendered on 9 July. Arab forces quickly overran the rest of the Hejaz, and only Medina held out.

Although Enver had abandoned his plans for an expeditionary force to reconquer the Hejaz, when Baghdad fell to the British in March 1917, he felt compelled to respond. Public opinion at home once more turned against Enver. He tried to recoup the situation by organizing a special strike force to be called the Lightning Armies Group, harking back to Sultan Bayezid I (1389–1402), whose swiftness in shunting between Europe and Anatolia had earned him the sobriquet "Yıldırım," the Thunderbolt. Enver's fantasy was to have this army, which was being assembled in Aleppo, traverse the desert with lightning speed and retake Baghdad. The operation would be under the command of another Ger-

[3]The Hejaz is the region of the Arabian Peninsula where the holy cities Mecca and Medina are located.

man, General von Falkenhayn,[4] but the manpower would be supplied largely by the Turkish Seventh Army. Command of the Seventh Army was offered to Mustafa Kemal, who accepted with one aim in mind—to prevent von Falkenhayn from attacking Baghdad and destroying the Seventh Army in a grandiose gesture.

After he arrived in Aleppo, Mustafa Kemal resisted von Falkenhayn's plans openly in staff meetings and in official communications. He had the support of Cemal Pasha, one of the original Committee of Union and Progress triumvirate, who was in command of Syria. He too wanted to defend the Aleppo-Damascus region against a possible breakthrough that would threaten the Turks' own Anatolian heartland. Enver pushed aside all resistance to his plan, and only General von Falkenhayn's own disillusionment with the project brought on by his personal inspection of the front in Syria prevented the debacle from materializing.

Mustafa Kemal's days in Syria were crucial ones for him as he tested himself against the will of Enver Pasha and his German coterie. It was in this period of his life that he was visited by his mother, who was accompanied by little Abdürrahim and a maid-companion. Perhaps drawing strength from his renewed contact with his mother, Mustafa Kemal kept up his criticism of Enver Pasha's plans. With General von Falkenhayn losing interest in the Baghdad campaign, Enver suggested another scheme. This would be an attack against the British designed to oust them from Egypt. The attack would be launched through the Sinai by the Eighth Army supported by the Seventh Army hitting the British flank at Beersheba. Mustafa Kemal was offered command of the Seventh Army in this operation as well, the most critical assignment, but recognizing that the British were in a better position with respect to numbers, matériel, and disposition of their forces, he wanted no part of this project.

Never reluctant to criticize higher-ranking officers, Mustafa Kemal wrote a detailed report 20 September 1917 to Enver who was the acting commander in chief and to the war ministry sharply faulting von Falkenhayn's plan. He was assisted in drafting this document by İsmet, who also had been transferred to Syria and was now serving as head of the Third Army Corps. Neither Mustafa Kemal nor İsmet had any burning religious zeal for pan-Islamic conquest, which they regarded in any case as a lost cause. Their mutual concern was the safety of Turkey proper.

He also sent a copy of his statement to Talât,[5] to whom he had often had recourse. Mustafa Kemal claimed that the bonds between the Ottoman

[4]Erich Georg von Falkenhayn was born in 1891. He commanded Ottoman forces in Palestine in 1917 but was soon replaced by Liman von Sanders. He died in 1922.

[5]Another of the original Committee of Union and Progress triumvirate who was serving as grand vizier at the time.

government of the day and the Turkish people had been severed. He described the corruption of government officials, accusing them all of accepting bribes, and he detailed the breakdown of the administrative machinery, the courts of justice, and the economy. Due to the recent turbulence, the Turkish public, he maintained, was now largely composed of women, children, and the disabled, and they were weary of war. Mustafa Kemal warned that "If the war continues, the greatest danger we face is the possibility that the great dynasty of the sultans, rotten in all its parts, may collapse suddenly from within" (Atatürk 1964, vol. 4, p. 2).

This incredible letter could only have been written by someone with a personality makeup such as Mustafa Kemal's. An officer of the Ottoman army was boldly telling his government in a written and signed communication that its policies were wrong and its personnel corrupt. Mustafa Kemal went on to state that the government's goals should be to save every Turkish soldier possible and to avoid prolonging the war until Turkey became virtually a German colony.

Mustafa Kemal could hardly have been surprised when he learned that the high command did not receive his memorandum with pleasure, nor did they share his views. Reacting in characteristic fashion, Mustafa Kemal relieved himself of his command and installed his deputy in his place. This was an unheard of action, especially from a commander on an active front during wartime. The authorities in Istanbul attempted to get Mustafa Kemal to withdraw his resignation, but to no avail. Thereupon, they appointed him to the command of his old army, the Second Army on the eastern front. This, too, he refused to accept.

With his remedies exhausted, Mustafa Kemal decided to return to Istanbul. Short of funds, with the help of Cemal Pasha he sold his own horses for a good sum that would enable him to make his way back to the capital. He returned as a self-styled "rebellious commander." The government sought to put a good face on the situation by placing him on sick leave for three months. At this point, rather than move in with his mother, he took up residence in the Pera Palas Hotel, located in the European quarter of Istanbul.

Intermediaries tried to reconcile Mustafa Kemal with Enver Pasha, and a luncheon at the Pera Palas Hotel was planned with this in mind. It is said to have been a rather formal affair at which both men behaved properly. When Enver invited Mustafa Kemal to leave the army and enter politics, it was clear to Mustafa Kemal that the military was the real seat of power.

During this period, General Allenby's forces passed to the attack on the Sinai front, bearing out all of Mustafa Kemal's objections to General von Falkenhayn's plans and to Enver's dreams for his Lightning Army

Group.[6] The British deftly took targets with their superior forces, meeting with little resistance from the depleted Ottoman army. Lloyd George had asked General Allenby for a Christmas gift for the British people, the capture of Jerusalem.[7] This was accomplished, validating Mustafa Kemal's prescience.

While Mustafa Kemal was in Istanbul, he was assigned to accompany a royal Ottoman group that was making an official visit to Germany. Kaiser Wilhelm had invited the sultan to Germany in return for his own earlier visit to the Ottoman lands. The sultan was unable to accept the invitation personally, but appointed his brother, Crown Prince Vahideddin, to make the trip in his stead.[8] By assigning Mustafa Kemal to Vahideddin's entourage, Enver Pasha eased him out of Istanbul. Not only would he have his rival in friendly exile, but Enver Pasha could also hope that Mustafa Kemal might become as infatuated with Germany as he was himself and that as a result he would stop criticizing Enver's conduct of the government and the preponderant influence of Germany in it.

Prior to the departure of the Ottoman party for Germany, Mustafa Kemal was granted an audience with the heir apparent, who was then in his fifties. During this, their first meeting, Vahideddin, a somnolent man with sloping shoulders, did little more than raise his eyelids to acknowledge the introduction. The contrast of this occasion with his meeting with King Ferdinand in Sofia's glittering opera house must have struck Mustafa Kemal forcibly. He concluded that Vahideddin was a stupid man, and with such a man destined to become sultan the empire's prospects were bleak.

Increasing Mustafa Kemal's displeasure with the prince was the fact that he refused to travel in military uniform as Mustafa Kemal had suggested. Once the two were in the train together en route to Germany, things took a turn for the better. Prince Vahideddin told Mustafa Kemal that he had heard about his military career and his successes at Gallipoli. He was honored to have Mustafa Kemal as his traveling companion and considered himself to be one of his greatest admirers. Thereupon, Mustafa Kemal reversed his judgment of Vahideddin. He could readily overlook any deficiency in a declared admirer, and he devoted himself to awakening whatever latent leadership ability there might be in Va-

[6]Sir Edmund Allenby (1861–1936), a British cavalry general in World War I, commanded the occupation of Syria and Palestine. From 1919 to 1925 he was high commissioner for Egypt.

[7]David Lloyd George was born in 1863 and lived until 1945. He was the British prime minister from 1916 until 1922.

[8]Vahideddin (1861–1926) later would become Sultan Mehmed VI and reign from 1918 to 1922.

hideddin. He wanted to be able to idealize the future sultan and be an extension of him.

Although even at this point in his life Mustafa Kemal saw himself as an omnipotent savior, he sometimes resorted to the idealization of another person in order to enhance his own self-esteem through a relationship with someone he could perceive as being of impressive stature and unique endowment. His idealization of Corinne and Hildegard exemplifies this process. It also appeared occasionally in connection with a man in whose reflection he was able to feel greater self-confidence. At the War College in Istanbul, for example, he had a bewildering time until the father of a friend took a liking to him. That relationship had given Mustafa Kemal the opportunity to reorganize himself. Similarly, he had idealized a general in Salonika with whom his relationship was largely one of fantasy, and King Ferdinand of Bulgaria served him in the same way.[9] While Mustafa Kemal was in Germany with the Ottoman crown prince, the two visited the kaiser and other high German officials, including von Hindenburg and von Ludendorff. Despite their preeminence, Mustafa Kemal apparently did not find any of them a suitable candidate for idealization.

Perhaps partly responsible for Mustafa Kemal's failure to find among the Germans someone to whom he could attach himself was the fact that his tour of the front served to convince him even more firmly than before that the Germans would not win the war. In the course of the visit he made many remarks calculated to cast doubt upon the kaiser's talk of the future success that the Germans and Turks could expect. Mustafa Kemal put his faith in Vahideddin and tried to get him to take a more active role in the conduct of state affairs, urging the crown prince to ask for command of the Fifth Army upon their return to Istanbul and offering to serve as his chief of staff.

On his return to Istanbul, whatever fantasies Mustafa Kemal might have had in his head were pushed aside so he could attend to his personal health. The kidney trouble that had plagued him for some time began to torment him again. It was related, perhaps, to a poorly treated case of gonorrhea he is said to have contracted in his youth. Since he was obviously in considerable pain, his doctors sent him to Vienna for medical consultation. After a month he was sent to Carlsbad to recuperate, and he spent June and July of 1918 there. Until that time Mustafa Kemal

[9]The narcissistic person in need of securing a narcissistic balance may turn from attempts at confirming his grandiosity to finding idealized images with which he merges. Kohut (1971) calls this an idealizing transference when it occurs in patients in analysis. We know that the idealization can alternate with devaluation of the other. In this period of his life, in fact, Mustafa Kemal alternated between devaluing the prince and idealizing him (Kernberg 1975; Volkan 1976).

had not been in the habit of keeping a systematic diary, but the quiet atmosphere of Carlsbad and his enforced detachment from any regular responsibilities led him to write his thoughts down daily. The statement that follows, written on 6 June 1918, reflects his narcissistic personality organization, condensed with his passion for repairing and lifting up other people:

> If I obtain great authority and power, I think I will bring about by a coup—suddenly in one moment—the desired revolution in our social life. Because, unlike others, I don't believe that this deed can be achieved by raising the intelligence of others slowly to the level of my own. My soul rebels against such a course. Why, after my years of education, after studying civilization and the socialization processes, after spending my life and my time to gain pleasure from freedom, should I descend to the level of common people? I will make them rise to my level. *Let me not resemble them: they should resemble me.*[10] [Italics added; Aydemir 1969, vol. 3, p. 482]

While Mustafa Kemal was still in Carlsbad, Sultan Mehmed V died. He was succeeded by Vahideddin, who took the regnal name of Mehmed VI. Informed of these events, Mustafa Kemal could not decide upon a course of action for himself—should he return to Istanbul or continue with his convalescence until recalled? He congratulated the new sultan by telegram and wrestled with his own decision. The matter was taken out of his hands when he received a telegram from his aide-de-camp that his presence was desired in Istanbul.

Leaving Carlsbad by train on 27 June 1918, Mustafa Kemal headed back to Istanbul, but had to interrupt his journey at Vienna. The Spanish influenza that was spreading all over Europe had struck him. When he had recovered from the virus and returned to Istanbul, he settled once again at the Pera Palas Hotel and began to consult with his friends on the best course of action.

Prior contact with the new sultan during their trip to Germany led Mustafa Kemal to hope for great things,[11] but he was not absolutely certain where Mehmed VI stood on the important military issues facing the empire. From the sultan's new aide, İzzet Pasha, Mustafa Kemal learned that the sultan wished to see him, but for what reason was

[10]Aydemir states that he took this piece from Mustafa Kemal's unpublished diary, which is in the possession of Afet Afetinan.

It is interesting that after Mustafa Kemal attempted to idealize the prince and failed, he once more returned to confirmation of his own grandiose self, as is very clear in his statement here.

[11]Once more Mustafa Kemal was ready to idealize the sultan by putting his grandiose self into the sultan, so to speak, and becoming an extension of the latter.

unclear. İzzet was of the opinion that the situation looked promising, since one of the men recently appointed as aide had accompanied him on the trip to Germany.

An audience with Mehmed VI was arranged for Mustafa Kemal. The sultan greeted him cordially and even offered him a cigarette, extending to him the match with which he had just lit his own. Encouraged by this reception, Mustafa Kemal put forth his views to the sultan again and urged him to take command of the army and to appoint a chief of staff. The sultan asked him if there were others who thought as Mustafa Kemal did. Receiving a positive answer, he replied that he would think about it.

Several days later, Mustafa Kemal was again received by the sultan. Nothing of significance was discussed in this audience. Mustafa Kemal began to despair as it became obvious that his cause was hopeless. He gave up his attempt to create a sultan he could idealize out of this weak ruler who could not free himself from Enver's orbit. Bringing the audience to an end, the sultan remarked, "I have discussed with their Excellencies Talât and Enver Pasha what needs to be done" (Aydemir 1969, vol. 1, p. 303).

Despondent, Mustafa Kemal nevertheless continued to attend the formal Friday prayers held in Yıldız Palace. This ceremony of the *selâmlık*,[12] where leading generals and statesmen put in an appearance, resembled the levee of the French kings. One Friday Mustafa Kemal was informed that the sultan wished to see him after the prayer session. Hoping for a private audience, he was disappointed to find two German generals with the sultan. Mehmed VI announced that he was appointing Mustafa Kemal army commander in Syria, and urged him not to allow the region to fall into enemy hands. Mustafa Kemal realized as the sultan signed the order that this was the work of Enver Pasha. Indeed, Enver was waiting in a nearby anteroom when Mustafa Kemal left the sultan's presence. Encountering the gloating Enver Pasha, Mustafa Kemal did not disguise his feelings. Enver had done an extraordinary thing in getting the sultan to issue a direct order to Mustafa Kemal to take over the moribund command in Syria.

Greeting Enver, Mustafa Kemal said, "Bravo, I congratulate you. You have succeeded" (Aydemir 1969, vol. 1, p. 305). He let Enver Pasha know that his action had breached military custom and that he was aware of the fact that the Syrian command really existed in name only. Whatever Mustafa Kemal's feelings were at that moment, he could only content himself with the knowledge that once before Enver Pasha had assigned him to the command of a nonexistent unit, and he had emerged as the hero of Gallipoli.

[12]The word *selâmlık* itself refers to the men's apartments in an old-style Ottoman house.

10
The Defeat of the Ottoman Empire

Appointed, or rather exiled, to Syria on 7 August 1918, Mustafa Kemal departed almost immediately to take up his new assignment. He left Istanbul, which was teeming with starving refugees, by train on a journey that took him across Anatolia. There the scene was hardly more encouraging since the high Anatolian Plateau had been depleted of its young male population. Only old people, children, and women were visible in the run-down railroad stations and nearly deserted towns and villages through which his train passed. As the empire was collapsing, the new sultan in Istanbul fell more and more under the sway of the Committee of Union and Progress, and particularly under the domination of Enver Pasha.

It could not have been an enjoyable trip for Mustafa Kemal, but it served to prepare him for the chaos he found upon his arrival in Syria. Multitudes of sick, wounded, and hungry soldiers were in disarray as Ottoman armies had collapsed and were in need of reorganization. Von Falkenhayn had been transferred and replaced as chief of staff by Liman von Sanders, who at least had an appreciation of Mustafa Kemal's strength as a strategist. Another bright spot in the otherwise bleak scene was the presence in Syria of his old friends and associates, İsmet and Ali Fuat, who were serving as army corps commanders in his own Seventh Army.

Even a cursory tour of Turkish positions convinced Mustafa Kemal that the upcoming battle was already lost. The best he could hope for was to save as many Turkish lives as possible. Opposing Mustafa Kemal and the Turks were the forces of General Sir Edmund Allenby, who enjoyed an overall manpower superiority of two to one. But in addition to an overwhelming advantage in cavalry, General Allenby also had air support, which the Turks lacked altogether. Buoyed by his military preponderance, General Allenby devised a simple scheme for the absolute annihilation of the three Ottoman armies, the Fourth, Seventh, and Eight, that were facing him. His plan was to thrust head on at the enemy while sending his cavalry to swoop in from behind in order to cut off their avenues of retreat.

Plans called for the initial breakthrough to come along the coast against the Eighth Army. An elaborate charade was entered into by the British, including the construction of bridges across the Jordan River, to make the Turks believe that the main attack would be made inland. Allenby's attempt at deception almost went awry when an Indian trooper deserted from the British forces and went over to the Turks. He revealed to them the time and place of the projected British onslaught, but only Mustafa Kemal believed him. Rising from the sickbed where his kidney ailment had confined him, Mustafa Kemal gave orders to İsmet and Ali Fuat to expect the attack on the 19 September, that is, the next morning. No sooner had he put his army on alert than the British bombardment began.

Quickly it became obvious that the real attack was being launched against the Eighth Army along the coast, just as the Indian had detailed. Unprepared, the Eighth Army was soon put to rout. According to plan, Allenby's cavalry wheeled eastward to cut off the retreat and hem the Turks in. Mustafa Kemal was in serious danger of having his Seventh Army destroyed. Recognizing that his only hope was to cross the Jordan, he ordered a retreat in the direction of the river. With his troops harassed by air strikes and the hostile local Arab population anxious to join the Arab Revolt, only Mustafa Kemal's infectious determination enabled the surviving remnant of his Seventh Army to cross the Jordan. İsmet, who had the task of fighting the rearguard action, also managed to get across, as did Ali Fuat. A general retreat in the direction of Damascus ensued. On 30 September Mustafa Kemal assembled what remained of the Seventh Army at Kiswe, south of Damascus. At this point, Liman von Sanders ordered him to turn the command of the Seventh Army over to the Fourth Army and to proceed to Rayak, where he was to organize whatever units had been salvaged into a fighting force.

Syria was collapsing rapidly. As Mustafa Kemal headed for Rayak, Damascus fell to Lawrence of Arabia and the forces of Emir Feisal. At Rayak only scattered units existed, and stories abounded of commanders deserting their posts and heading northward. Taking matters into his own hands, Mustafa Kemal ordered İsmet and Ali Fuat to retreat northward. Linking up with Liman von Sanders, Mustafa Kemal confronted the chief of staff who agreed to his plan of withdrawing all forces to Aleppo in the northwest corner of Syria. The Fourth, Seventh, and Eighth armies would now take their orders from Mustafa Kemal, which is what he had proposed, and had been denied, when the sultan reassigned him to Syria.

Now that Mustafa Kemal had what he wanted, it was too late. All of Syria was on the verge of falling into British hands. Collecting his forces at Aleppo, he left their reorganization to İsmet and Ali Fuat while he devoted his energies to planning the defense of the region. His kidney ailment began giving him trouble again, and he was treated in the Armenian hospital, where he set up his command post. Liman von Sanders withdrew from Syria, leaving Mustafa Kemal in command of the battle scene.

British armored units pressed on Aleppo, forcing Mustafa Kemal to abandon the city and take up positions in the hills. In effect, Mustafa Kemal was now fighting on Turkish soil, for those hills and mountains behind them formed the natural boundary between Anatolia, the Turkish heartland, and the Arab provinces of the empire. İsmet was recalled to Istanbul to serve in the war ministry, leaving Mustafa Kemal with Ali Fuat as his confidant. Recognizing not only that Syria was lost but that the Ottoman Empire would have to sue for peace, Mustafa Kemal revealed his thoughts to Ali Fuat that out of this debacle might come the birth of a new nation comprising those regions of the empire populated by Turks.[1]

On 25 and 26 October, Mustafa Kemal and his troops fought their last important skirmishes with the enemy, forcing the British to halt their advance a few kilometers north of Aleppo. On 30 October negotiations that had begun several days earlier between representatives of the Ottomans and the British resulted in the signing of the Mudros Armistice.[2] Mustafa Kemal received his orders to cease fire while leading the resistance to the British advance in the Aleppine hills. After four years of fighting, Mustafa Kemal's record showed that he was the Ottoman military's only field commander who had not suffered a single defeat.

Undefeated in war, Mustafa Kemal looked forward to being called to a high office in the new government that would have to be organized to deal with the issues of peacetime. He had his heart set on becoming minister of war. Not only did he consider himself the man best qualified for the position, but the gratification he would receive from replacing Enver Pasha would be exquisite.

On every reasonable ground he could look forward to that appointment. Two weeks before the signing of the armistice, his former commanding officer and friend, İzzet Pasha, had been appointed grand vizier. Eventually, Talât, Enver, and Cemal, the ruling triumvirate of the Committee of Union and Progress, fled the Ottoman Empire by way of the Black Sea in a German ship. The new cabinet was staffed with several men who knew and admired Mustafa Kemal. Included in that group were Rauf (Orbay), who led the Ottoman navy and was the empire's other authentic military hero, and Fethi, who had been the ambassador in Sofia under whom Mustafa Kemal had served as military attaché.

[1]Ali Fuat (Cebesoy) wrote his own recollections of the national struggle. See Cebesoy 1953.

[2]Rauf (Orbay) was the head of the Turkish delegation that signed this armistice for the Ottomans.

Despite all positive indications, Mustafa Kemal was not named minister of war. İzzet Pasha put him off, telling him he looked forward to working with him in the future. Keeping the war ministry in his own hands, İzzet had already recalled İsmet to Istanbul to be his undersecretary. Mustafa Kemal was put in command of all Turkish troops in the south, replacing Liman von Sanders, who returned to Germany. At a farewell party given for the departing German officers, Mustafa Kemal responded to a German officer's speech to the effect that for them the war was over. He declared that while the war against the Allies might be over, the war for Turkish independence was beginning at that very moment.

Grandiose does not begin to describe Mustafa Kemal's declaration. He was among the very few whose eyes were on the future. His attempts to distribute arms to small groups who would act as guerrilla forces and his efforts at organizing the men under his command into a firm line of defense for the southern border of Anatolia indicate that he anticipated the invasion of the Turkish heartland by foreign forces.

Release of the Mudros Armistice text galvanized Mustafa Kemal into additional action. By a barrage of telegrams he protested to İzzet Pasha that the vagueness of some terms employed in several clauses endangered the territorial integrity of Turkey. The armistice called for the evacuation of all Turkish troops from Syria. What constituted Syria, he asked. Were the hills behind Aleppo to constitute its northern limit, or did Syria include the port of Alexandretta? Mustafa Kemal sought to stiffen the resolve of the cabinet against further foreign demands for crippling concessions: "It is my sincere and frank opinion that if we demobilize our troops and give in to everything the British want, without taking steps to end misunderstandings and false interpretations of the armistice, it will be impossible for us to put any sort of brake on Britain's covetous designs" (Kinross 1965, p. 153). He also conveyed to the grand vizier his fear that unless a firm stand were taken, the Allies would soon be nominating the cabinet itself.

Keeping the telegraph lines humming, Mustafa Kemal got himself into a steaming squabble with İzzet Pasha over the disposition of the port city of Alexandretta (present-day Iskenderun). There was a verbal agreement to the effect that the British would be able to use Alexandretta and the road to Aleppo to evacuate the wounded and receive supplies. Mustafa Kemal objected to this, as he did to any encroachment upon the bit of sovereignty left to the Ottoman state. He attempted to stiffen İzzet Pasha's resolve by acknowledging the difficulty of the Ottoman position, "I know very well just how weak and powerless we are. That does not alter my conviction that we must decide upon a limit to the sacrifices which the state is obliged to accept" (Kinross 1965, p. 155).

As with so many of Mustafa Kemal's attempts to get others to see events through his eyes, this too failed. İzzet Pasha, under unrelenting pressure from the British, could not accept Mustafa Kemal's definition of the Syrian frontier as that area being actively defended by Turkish bayonets. On 7 November he communicated to Mustafa Kemal that the Lightning Armies Group and the Seventh Army Headquarters were abolished, rendering Mustafa Kemal a general without an army. İzzet Pasha then ordered him to return to Istanbul.

Uncharacteristically obeying his orders, Mustafa Kemal arrived at Haydarpaşa, the Istanbul railhead on the Anatolian side of the city, on 13 November. His arrival coincided with that of the British and Allied fleet that had sailed through the Dardanelles and was making its way into the Bosporus. Angered by this spectacle, Mustafa Kemal told his aide-de-camp, "They will go as they have come" (Aydemir 1969, vol. 1, p. 331; Kinross 1965, p. 159).

Street scenes in the rest of the city, especially in the European district of Beyoğlu, could not have done much for his frame of mind either. Greeks had hung out their national flag to the annoyance of the Turks, thieves roamed the streets, and the city's lights were dark. Turkish currency was nearly worthless, and even everyday staples were in short supply, if available at all. Life in Istanbul was grim.

When the French general Franchet d'Esperey made his triumphal entry into the city astride a white horse, he rode without benefit of reins, as Mehmed the Conqueror had done when he took the city from the Byzantines in 1453. In this one act General d'Esperey sought symbolically to negate Turkish claims to the city. Although French, British, and Italian military personnel flooded into the Ottoman capital, their presence was not considered an "official" occupation since political and administrative control still rested with the Ottoman government. The triumphant foreign presence, however, made itself felt, especially to the likes of Mustafa Kemal.

Settling in again at the Pera Palas Hotel, Mustafa Kemal wanted to see the grand vizier as soon as possible. In his preoccupation he did not even have time for his mother, who lived in a nearby, modest section of the city. The political situation was in turmoil. The Union and Progress triumvirate had fled the country. İzzet Pasha was under enormous pressure from the sultan to find scapegoats for the Ottoman defeat in order to deflect dissatisfaction against the sultanate. The sultan fixed on three members of İzzet Pasha's cabinet and demanded their resignation.[3] İzzet viewed this as unconstitutional meddling in state affairs by the sultan. Rauf, who was responsible for naval affairs in the cabinet, supported

[3]On the Ottoman governmental structure, see Shaw 1976, vol. 1, pp. 22–27.

İzzet Pasha. In an interview with the sultan, Rauf reminded him of the misfortunes that had overtaken other rulers in the area, such as King Ferdinand of Bulgaria. Bent on reasserting his personal power, the sultan made his position clear when he replied to him "Sir, we have a nation here that is a herd of sheep. It has to have a shepherd. I am that shepherd" (Kinross 1965, p. 159).

On the following day Rauf reported to the cabinet on his audience with the sultan. İzzet Pasha, whose health was failing, was not inclined to continue the confrontation with the sultan. He decided that he and his cabinet should resign in protest against the unconstitutional actions of the sultan. The cabinet had no choice but to agree.

İzzet Pasha's resignation was a severe blow to Mustafa Kemal. He had been ordered back to Istanbul by the grand vizier because of his insistent and stinging criticism of government policies, but İzzet had softened the recall by saying, "I see some benefit from your being in Istanbul at this juncture. I have need of you" (Aydemir 1969, vol. 1, p. 334). For someone who had continually sought a connection with a figure in authority, such an invitation could not fail to arouse a flurry of fantasies. Now, just as he had arrived, the grand vizier was no longer the grand vizier. As he was about to set his foot upon the threshold of advancement, the door was again slammed in his face.

Diminished somewhat by this turn in his fortunes, Mustafa Kemal, nevertheless, resolved to try to salvage the situation. With Rauf he called on the ailing former grand vizier. Their plan was to forestall the confirmation of a cabinet under Tevfik Pasha and to talk İzzet Pasha into forming a new cabinet with a more nationalist character. Mustafa Kemal, who had previously argued against the military involving itself in politics, now committed himself to his first major political role. He got Fethi and İzzet Pasha to go along with his scheme. His next step was to lobby among the members of the Ottoman parliament and try to get them to deny a vote of confidence to the cabinet formed by Tevfik Pasha.

Donning civilian dress, Mustafa Kemal went to the parliament building. There he met with many deputies whom he knew and with many others to whom he was introduced. They were all anxious to hear his views and his presence caused quite a stir. In response to many who feared that a failure to confirm the cabinet would only lead the sultan to prorogue the parliament, Mustafa Kemal replied that he agreed with that assessment. He further warned, however, that the first act of Tevfik Pasha's new cabinet would be to dissolve parliament! He offered them the idea of a new cabinet under İzzet Pasha as a way to buy time. Burning with conviction, Mustafa Kemal put forward his views to a large group of deputies who gathered in one of the meeting rooms. Many of those present assured him that they would vote as he had counseled. They were then called away to hear Tevfik Pasha present his cabinet for confirmation.

Watching the proceedings from one of the visitors' boxes, Mustafa Kemal, flushed with the excitement of having been the center of attention, was confident of victory. His sense of optimism turned to deep chagrin as the deputies abandoned the resolve they had expressed to him and gave Tevfik Pasha a resounding vote of confidence. Reflecting on this event at a later date, Mustafa Kemal stated:

> What lie should I tell! I was stupefied. The number of deputies who said that they accepted my proposals could not be considered insignificant. Moreover, among them were those who gave the impression that their words and their positions were influential. At any rate, a soldier like myself, who was rather unaware how within an instant deputies could change their feelings and take on a thousand different colors, could not help marvelling at it. [Bayur 1963, p. 233; Aydemir 1969, vol. 1, p. 336]

Immediately after his defeat, Mustafa Kemal left the parliament building. He returned to his hotel where, without hesitation, he called the royal palace and demanded an audience with the sultan. His grandiose self encouraged him to believe that the sultan would see him at once because he was in the right and the need to put the Turks straight was imperative. Needless to say, the sultan did not see it that way and put him off until the general audience after the coming Friday noontime prayer.

One wonders why Mustafa Kemal once more sought out Mehmed VI in view of his intellectual awareness of the sultan's inability to be effective. Mehmed VI was the only sultan the Ottomans had, and, as is the case of a child, there is only one father, good or bad. Apparently, Mustafa Kemal was trying to "create" in him strength enough to lead his defeated nation, to protect the democratic parliament and, perhaps above all else, to offer Mustafa Kemal himself the opportunity to repair the nation.

In the days of Sultan Abdülhamid II, before the Young Turks forced him to permit parliament to function again, Mustafa Kemal, like many others, had talked and fantasized about, and even planned, ways in which to oppose the sultan's power. On one occasion Mustafa Kemal had conspired against Abdülhamid II while visiting in the pink house in Salonika. That discussion had been overheard by a maid who reported it to Mustafa Kemal's mother. She became alarmed. Mustafa Kemal recalled later that she had told him that the sultan was "the one with the strength of seven dragons" and that it was folly to rebel against anyone with such power.[4] Having been given such perceptions of a potent ruler by important others from childhood, it is not surprising that he turned to Mehmed VI—who might only have the strength of one dragon—in frustration over the failure of his first political project.

As might have been anticipated, Mustafa Kemal's meeting with Mehmed VI was a disappointment. He was only interested in pumping Mustafa Kemal for any information he might have about possible military plots against his throne. He wanted to pledge Mustafa Kemal to give warning should any plot come to his ears. The audience lasted for about an hour and only served to convince Mustafa Kemal that the sultan was not to be trusted.

Confirmation of the fact that the sultan was only thinking of his own position came within a few days, when he dissolved the parliament. Mustafa Kemal railed against the dissolution of parliament in the pages of the newspaper *Mimber*, which was put out by Fethi. He saw that without the presence of parliament the sultan would have a free hand in negotiating the final peace terms with the Allies. Faced with the choice of active opposition to the sultan or quiet dispersal, the deputies took the latter course.

What Mustafa Kemal had experienced as a blow to his self-image was in reality a blessing. The sultan continued to work with an appointed cabinet which functioned without a parliament. If Mustafa Kemal had been appointed minister of war in that cabinet, the Allies would have had to work with him officially. As it turned out, the Allies would later intern leading government officials on Malta, and Mustafa Kemal would have been among them. As an unofficial person he was considered harmless and had considerably more freedom of movement and action. Having been denied the office that Enver had occupied, it is doubtful that Mustafa Kemal appreciated the benefit at that moment.

With parliament dissolved, the scene in Istanbul was one of great confusion. Mustafa Kemal remained there from mid-November 1918 until the following May. The city was in effect an "occupied" city. British, French, and Italian soldiers crowded the streets of Istanbul's European quarters. Drunk and disorderly, they harassed the local population. The sections of the city in which wealthy non-Muslims had congregated attracted not only fraternizing foreign officers, but also Turks who were willing to compromise their morality and their patriotism for a share in

[4]See Mustafa Kemal's interview with Saydam and Atay (1926). See also Baydar 1967, p. 104. In this interview Mustafa Kemal tells that he explained to his mother that he would continue to attempt to save the country from the bad sultan. She advised him that what counted in the end was to be successful.

the high life. A young Turkish novelist, Yakup Kadri (Karaosmanoğlu) described the climate of the city in a novel titled *Sodom and Gomorrah*, in which he compared Istanbul's degeneracy with that of the biblical cities destroyed by an outraged God (Karaosmanoğlu 1966).

Life in the Muslim quarters of the city was bleak. Returning servicemen went about in tatters, and hunger was widespread. Anxiously, the women continued to wait for husbands and sons to return home, though many would never come back from the war. Grief was so pervasive that its sounds echoed day and night with the keening of the women.

Istanbul was in effect two cities, the Muslim city and the Europeanized city. Allowed to go about his business freely, Mustafa Kemal continued to live in the Pera Palas Hotel. His mother and sister continued to live in a house in a Turkish quarter called Beşiktaş. It must have been particularly humiliating for Mustafa Kemal to have to rub elbows with the Allied officers who frequented the Pera Palas Hotel. He was a much reduced person in his own surroundings, and there were constant, daily reminders of his diminished status. One story, perhaps apocryphal, persists: Some British officers, including General Harrington, noticed Mustafa Kemal in the Pera Palas lounge and inquired about him. Learning that he was Mustafa Kemal of Gallipoli fame, they sent someone to invite him to their table. He is said to have replied, "We are the hosts here. They are the guests. It is fitting for them to come to (my) table" (Aydemir 1969, vol. 1, p. 347).

Seeking some outsider who could reflect his sense of self-worth, Mustafa Kemal took up again with Corinne. It was in her home that he gradually prepared some of his plans for the future as it became clearer to him that the Allies were preparing to obliterate Turkey's sovereignty. He suffered one severe humiliation on an evening when he visited his mother and sister in Beşiktaş. An Italian military patrol forced its way in to search her house. Mustafa Kemal was furious. He declared that he was a general and they had no right to enter and search the house. When it became obvious that he was making no impression on the patrol, he rushed to a neighbor's house where he telephoned the Italian command and had to plead with the head of the search patrol to come to the phone and speak with his commanding officer. The man who had successfully commanded armies in the field and had been the hero of Gallipoli was obliged to deal with the head of an Italian patrol for the peace and security of his mother's home. By the time the Italians had departed, Zübeyde had fainted and his sister Makbule was hysterical. The two women were put into the same state a few days later when British troops, led by a lieutenant, searched the house again. Finding nothing of interest, they left. Mustafa Kemal was not present on that occasion.

Abdürrahim (Tuncak), Zübeyde's foster child, who was living in that house in Beşiktaş, was eight years old at the time of the search. In his interview with Dr. Volkan he was unable to recall those two incidents specifically, but he did remember well the general atmosphere of fear that pervaded the household (Tuncak 1974). In addition, he recalled one occasion when the family learned that the British planned to raid their house and search it for anything politically incriminating. Elaborate precautions were taken to defeat the anticipated incursion. The family hid away the many weapons belonging to Mustafa Kemal, some of which he had acquired as souvenirs and some of which had been given to him as presents. If weapons were found in the house, the British would have damning evidence against Mustafa Kemal and his family.

Zübeyde's house was made of stone and had a courtyard paved in stone. At the right of the courtyard, after one entered from the street door, was a room with a wooden floor. The weapons were hidden under the floorboards of that room. Little Abdürrahim was small enough to creep into a narrow space under the floor and deposit them there. Not only were the floorboards replaced, but a cow was brought in and hay was strewn around to make it seem that the place had always been a cowbarn. The family also burned some papers they felt the British might be able to use against them.

Another search, this one of Corinne's house, probably took place after Mustafa Kemal left Istanbul to initiate the war for independence in Anatolia. The Allied patrol ordered her to take down a picture of Mustafa Kemal that hung on her wall, but she refused. The men were too courteous to press her further about its removal, warning her instead to have no further communication with Mustafa Kemal. Some time later, Corinne left for Italy, but her sister, Edith, remained. Corinne never saw Mustafa Kemal again, but there may have been some communication between them. She returned to Turkey in 1941, after Mustafa Kemal's death.[5]

Encounters with the Allied officers who frequented the Pera Palas Hotel, while a humiliating experience for Mustafa Kemal, also offered him some gratification. He enjoyed being considered a Western man among Westerners, and in his fantasies, at least, he saw himself as

[5]The Turkish government may have advised Corinne against returning to Turkey during Atatürk's lifetime since he had become virtually a god figure in Turkey and the knowledge of an old relationship might prove embarrassing. Furthermore, during the time of his relationship with Corinne he was externalizing on her an idealized image so that, in turn, he would be loved and admired by an idealized person in order to maintain the cohesiveness of his own self-worth. As Atatürk, his idealization was within his own bosom, so he did not need someone like Corinne around him.

superior to them. The incident with General Harrington confirms that aspect of his personality.

However gratifying life in the Pera Palas Hotel might have been, it was also expensive. When Mustafa Kemal could no longer afford it, he accepted the invitation of an acquaintance to move in with him and his wife in their home in Beyoğlu. These friends were Salih Fansa and his wife Selma, whom Mustafa Kemal had known in Aleppo. While Mustafa Kemal was living with them, Selma Fansa became the intermediary for a possible marriage between Mustafa Kemal and Sabiha Sultan, the daughter of Sultan Mehmed VI.

Selma Fansa, it appears, was approached by an emissary from the palace to pass on the information that Mehmed VI was in favor of accepting Mustafa Kemal into the royal house as a son-in-law (*damad*). This would have raised him to a status equal with that of Enver Pasha, who had married an Ottoman princess in 1914. Mustafa Kemal enjoyed a reputation among the women of the imperial palace as a great ladies' man and was often referred to by the nickname "the yellow rose" (Aydemir 1969, vol. 1, pp. 348–49).

Delicacy was necessary in such matters, for the palace did not wish to be embarrassed, should anything go wrong in the negotiations. Selma Fansa broached the matter with Mustafa Kemal. His mother heard about it and applauded the prospect of her son's becoming a *damad*, but he discounted her enthusiasm simply as an expression of her interest in living in the palace. He, on the other hand, was not sympathetic to the scheme. Reacting to what he viewed as the sultan's attempt to get him allied with the palace clique, Mustafa Kemal declined an invitation to the palace, saying that he would see the princess only in his own home. Taken aback at the impropriety of such a suggestion, the palace emissary tried to get Mustafa Kemal to change his mind, but it was to no avail and there the matter died.

Shortly thereafter, Mustafa Kemal decided that, as comfortable as he felt with the Fansas, he needed his own living quarters. With their help he found a house in the Şişli district. That house still stands on what is the main avenue of Şişli beyond the Hilton Hotel. It is now the Atatürk Museum of the city of Istanbul, ironically enough, across the street from the old Italian headquarters. After moving in, Mustafa Kemal eventually brought his family to live with him. He occupied the middle floor, his mother and sister took the top floor, and his aide was billeted in the attic. Here Mustafa Kemal gathered his friends and comrades for discussions centered on the future of the country. He still dreamed of becoming war minister as a way of solving the nation's problems.

One of his visitors was Ali Fuat, his old friend from military school with whom he had been exiled to Syria for political activities against the sultan. Ali Fuat was stationed in Anatolia at this time and knew the situation there intimately.

He came to Istanbul in February 1919 and met with Mustafa Kemal several times. Sometimes Rauf joined their discussions along with others. The major topic was the general situation in the country, and slowly a plan for a national struggle against the enemies of Turkey materialized, including the establishment of a new seat of government in Anatolia, away from occupied Istanbul. This notion of a new Anatolian national movement was primarily the work of Mustafa Kemal and Ali Fuat.[6]

At the end of February 1919, Ali Fuat returned to Anatolia. Rauf resigned from the navy at about this time and remained in Istanbul as Mustafa Kemal's closest collaborator. Mustafa Kemal continued to see many other people in his home in Şişli to avoid giving the impression that he was organizing anything of consequence. Most of the men who would play important roles in the Turkish war of independence were in Istanbul then. Among them was İsmet, who had served for some time as undersecretary of war. All were in some danger, for the sultan wanted to be rid of anyone who had any connection with the old Committee of Union and Progress. Mustafa Kemal's outspoken criticism of the committee forestalled harassment at the hands of the sultan's men, but he was vulnerable to pressure from the Allies.

Opinions among the Allies on the future disposition of Turkey were, at best, mixed. Secret treaties concluded during the course of the war looked forward to a division of the spoils in the form of the dismantlement of the Ottoman Empire (see Anderson 1966, esp. chap. 11). The Russian Revolution had knocked one of the participants out of the game, and the rest were anxious to claim their due. Count Sforza, the Italian high commissioner in Istanbul, although a party to the plans to partition the Ottoman Empire among the victorious Allies, foresaw difficulties arising, especially from Lloyd George's support of the Greeks. He sought, therefore, to initiate some contact with the nationalist-minded opposition to the sultan.

Working through emissaries, Count Sforza arranged a meeting with Mustafa Kemal (Kinross 1965, p. 167). In the course of their conversation the count assured him that he could rely on the assistance of the Italian embassy. This assurance was especially important to Mustafa Kemal, for the sultan's government was arresting as many of its opponents as it could, and the British were cooperating in that process. By appearing to

[6]Cebesoy 1953, vol. 1, p. 37. Cebesoy later wrote a letter, dated 27 April 1960, to Şevket Süreyya Ademir and stated that it was he who had planned the initial strategy for the national struggle during his meetings with Mustafa Kemal at his house in Şişli. He claimed that initially they did not say much about the details to others. See Aydemir 1969, vol. 1, p. 363.

be under the "protection" of the Italian government, Mustafa Kemal might be able to avoid arrest.

Italian protection was needed by Mustafa Kemal sooner than he expected. The gentlemanly spirit that had been evident when the British and Turks signed the Mudros Armistice had rapidly disintegrated. Admiral Calthorpe, who had signed the armistice with Rauf himself, forbade all social interchange with the Turks, who were now seen in Allied propaganda as the slaughterers of millions of Christians (Aydemir 1969, vol. 1, p. 371). In an effort to save the Christian remnant within the empire, Christian missionaries were put in charge of major orphanages which were full as a consequence of the turmoil. They declared that each institutionalized child was a Christian unless proof to the contrary was demonstrated. The search for Christian children was extended beyond the walls of the orphanages. In that atmosphere an Armenian, accompanied by an Italian soldier, went to Mustafa Kemal's house in Şişli and accused him of hiding an Armenian boy. At that moment Mustafa Kemal was in conference with Rauf, and the situation—holding a political discussion—could have been embarrassing for them. Mustafa Kemal told the soldier that he would get in touch with the Italian ambassador, and this ended the matter, but it was evident that the times were out of joint and anything could happen. (It is not clear whether the young boy Abdürrahim was the object of the search.)

News from other parts of the empire drifting into Istanbul was equally depressing. The Arab lands had been taken by the British and the French. Parts of eastern Antolia were being seized by bands of Armenians. In the spring of 1919 the Aegean and Mediterranean coastal lands of Turkey were claimed by the Greeks and Italians, while the Allies were experiencing difficulties in reconciling their conflicting claims at the peace conference that opened in Paris in January 1919. Various agreements had been entered into among the Allies during the course of the war, both to encourage certain nations to enter the conflict and to keep others out of it. The Ottoman Empire was divided up to satisfy the selfish motivations of the Allied countries. While Russia, Great Britain, and France negotiated the prospective spoils of war in March 1915, in the following month these same three powers entered into agreement with Italy, giving her some heavy concessions in order to obtain her support.[7] Italy honored the agreement by declaring war on the Ottoman Empire on 20 August 1915.

[7]On 18 March 1915, Russia, Great Britain, and France had agreed to certain arrangements: Russia would get "Constantinople, the western coast of the Bosporus, the Sea of Marmara, and the Dardanelles, southern Thrace as far as the Enos-Midia line, the coast of Asia Minor between the Bosporus and the river Sakaria and a point on the Gulf of Ismid to be defined later, the islands in the Sea of Marmara, and the islands of Imbros and Tenedos" (see Cocks 1918, p. 19). In return, Constantinople would become a free port for the Allies

On 16 May 1916 a wide-ranging agreement known as the Sykes-Picot agreement was entered into by Russia, France, and Great Britain. Russia would get the provinces of Erzurum, Trabzon (Trebizond), Van, and Bitlis, and territory in the northern part of Kurdistan, some 60,000 square miles rich in copper, salt, and silver. France would get the coastal part of the vilayet of Adana as well as the vast territory in southeastern Anatolia known as Cilicia. Great Britain would come into possession of the whole of southern Mesopotamia (Iraq), including Baghdad. In Palestine the British would get the port cities of Haifa and Acre. One or several Arab states would be formed between the British and French territories and the area would be divided into a French and a British zone of influence.

Secrets were poorly kept. When Italy found out about the Sykes-Picot agreement, a new agreement had to be entered into that spelled out the Italian sector of Anatolia more precisely. It came to include the city and vilayet of Izmir and a large part of the vilayet of Konya. Signed on 17 April 1917, this agreement was supposed to receive the assent of the Russians, but the revolution precluded that from happening. There were other designs, such as the promise to the Zionists of a "homeland" and the conflicting promises to the sharif of Mecca, but these formed the principal arrangements for the final interment of the "sick man" of Europe.

In Paris it quickly became apparent that the secret agreements were in conflict with the aspirations of the indigenous populations in whom nationalist sentiments had been aroused and that the Allies were on the verge of falling out among themselves over the spoils. Britain wanted revisions in the Sykes-Picot agreement, but France refused. Both powers had already moved into many of the areas assigned to them by the treaties. Greece, having entered the war late on the Allied side, now wished to secure a foothold in Anatolia in anticipation of a restoration of Greek dominion over the old lands of Byzantium.[8] Greece's claims

---

and there would be freedom of commercial navigation in the straits. Russia also agreed to recognize the special rights of Britain and France in "Asiatic" Turkey. For secret agreements, also see Cummings 1938.

In the 26 April 1915 agreement Italy was given full sovereignty over the strategically important Dodecanese Islands off the Turkish coast, which the Italians had occupied in 1912. All the sultan's rights in Libya given him by the Treaty of Lausanne (1912) were transferred to Italy. It was also agreed that if Asiatic Turkey was partitioned, Italy would get a just share of the Mediterranean region adjacent to the province of Adalia. That zone would be more precisely defined at a later time. Other articles of the treaty set out a timetable by which Italy might come into possession of the agreed-upon territories. See Cocks 1918, pp. 27–42.

[8]Greece had tried to remain neutral, but internal dissidents against the king headed by Venizelos led the Allies to intervene. King Constantine abdicated in June 1917. Venizelos formed a ministry, and Greece entered the war on the Allied side on 2 July 1917.

clearly conflicted with the promises made to Italy, but Lloyd George came to the support of the Greeks.

As the Allies wrangled in Paris, it became increasingly clear to Mustafa Kemal and his comrades that the future of Turkey was being decided by others, to the detriment of the Turks. Something needed to be done, and the best place to begin was Anatolia, where some Turkish army units were still intact and armed. There were a few well-placed officers there, including Ali Fuat, who were waiting for leadership to assert itself. Testing the waters, Mustafa Kemal called İsmet to his house in Şişli. He spread the map of Turkey out before him and asked his advice as to the best sector in which to initiate a resistance movement. İsmet inquired whether he had already a choice. Mustafa Kemal replied that he was unready to point one out. He insisted that he wanted İsmet's advice since Ismet knew the terrain, the army's situation there, and the people. At this point İsmet, too, refused to commit himself. He simply indicated that Anatolia presented plenty of opportunities.

Another visitor to the house in Şişli at this time was Kâzım (Karabekir) Pasha who was being transferred from Thrace to the command of the demoralized Fifteenth Army Corps in eastern Anatolia.[9] Kâzım had served with Mustafa Kemal on the Caucasian front early in the war. He was well liked by the people in the east and had troops upon whom he could rely. Less cautious than İsmet, he urged Mustafa Kemal to supply the leadership that was necessary and sketched a plan that prepared the ground for Mustafa Kemal's arrival. Once they had established a national movement centered in Erzurum, Mustafa Kemal would then be able to return to the western part of Turkey to arouse the national cause there.

Decision time was approaching rapidly. At the end of 1918 local groups of Turks, feeling threatened either by the ill will of indigenous non-Muslims or by the possibility of foreign invasion, were organizing themselves into paramilitary outfits and calling themselves Defense of Rights associations. Under that banner they hoped to be able to defend their lives and their homes. This Anatolian ferment represented the best opportunity for Mustafa Kemal. His inner longings were coming into closer contact with descriptive reality. Anatolia could be the mechanism to bring the inner and outer worlds together for him.

[9]Kâzım (Karabekir) (1882–1948), the son of a pasha, was a career army officer. Mustafa Kemal's other friend, Fethi (Okyar), was in jail at this time. Fethi was arrested by the government of Grand Vizier Ferid Pasha and unjustly accused of allowing Enver, Talât, and Cemal to escape on 2 November 1918. Kinross 1965, p. 168.

11

Passage to Samsun

Earlier in his military career, Mustafa Kemal had often wanted to remain in Istanbul, but had been sent elsewhere, usually on Enver's orders. Now, he greatly desired to be ordered to Anatolia, but, as a general who had been effectively shelved, there seemed to be little hope that such an assignment would come his way.

Events in Anatolia itself unexpectedly provided the mechanism for the dissolution of Mustafa Kemal's despair. Trouble had developed in the hinterland of the Black Sea port of Samsun. The collapse of the Ottoman Empire had encouraged the Greeks who lived in the area to dream of the establishment of an independent state of the Pontus that would eventually relate in some manner to Greece. Such a notion fit in well with the stirrings of empire being reawakened in Greece itself. The Turks, through their Defense of Rights associations, were getting into battles with the Christian populace along the Black Sea littoral. Anarchy threatened. News of the situation reached the Allied high command in Istanbul. Fearing intercommunal strife of mammoth proportions, the Allies began to press the Ottoman government for restoration of central authority in Anatolia. The new grand vizier who had assumed office on 3 March was Damad Ferid Pasha. He was the sultan's handpicked choice for the position, his main qualification being the fact that he was the sultan's brother-in-law (*damad*). Growing ever more anxious about the situation in Anatolia, the British made their concerns known to Damad Ferid Pasha. If the Ottoman government could not bring tranquility to the area around Samsun, and if they failed to stop the local Turks from "harassing innocent Greeks," the British themselves would take requisite action.

Frightened by the prospect of unilateral British action to pacify the port of Samsun, Damad Ferid Pasha sought the counsel of his acting minister of the interior, Mehmed Ali, a man with whom Mustafa Kemal had discussed his views and who was in sympathy with them. Here was the opportunity Mustafa Kemal had been seeking. Mehmed Ali recommended to the hard-pressed grand vizier that he send a reliable and competent officer to Samsun with the authority to restore law and order. Such a move would forestall the British and reassure them that the

Ottoman government was capable of dealing with the problem. Furthermore, he recommended Mustafa Kemal for the task and vouched for his trustworthiness.

Reliability at this stage meant being untainted by connections with the Committee of Union and Progress. Here Mustafa Kemal's rivalry with Enver Pasha stood him, for once, in good stead. Damad Ferid, however, still hesitated, recognizing Mustafa Kemal to be a dangerous choice. In the end, he decided he had more to gain from getting Mustafa Kemal out of Istanbul. He recommended to the sultan that he appoint Mustafa Kemal inspector general of the Third Army for the purpose of investigating the situation in and around Samsun.

Empowered by the sultan to proceed with the appointment, Damad Ferid Pasha passed the matter along to Şakir Pasha, the minister of war. Mustafa Kemal had made a giant stride forward in his advance to Anatolia. Meeting with Şakir Pasha to iron out the details of his assignment, Mustafa Kemal realized that he could take advantage of bureaucratic malaise to broaden his authority without unduly arousing anyone's suspicions about his ultimate intentions which were still somewhat inchoate. He told Şakir Pasha that he thought his appointment should be given a proper format and asked whether he should take that up with the General Staff. Şakir Pasha readily agreed.

Arriving at the General Staff offices, Mustafa Kemal again had good fortune on his side. He was directed to see the deputy chief of the General Staff who turned out to be a friend. Filling his friend in on his activities to date, they worked out a statement that would give Mustafa Kemal the widest possible latitude in his actions. As an army inspector he was to have authority to issue orders throughout Anatolia and to command obedience from the provincial governors, all in the interest of carrying out his mission, which was to punish Turks who were harassing the local Greek population and to disband all local nationalist organizations. The document they produced was far-ranging and doubtless exceeded anything the grand vizier would have sanctioned.

Fortunately, Mustafa Kemal had already sidestepped the grand vizier. All that was needed was for the minister of war to accept the document. When the deputy chief brought the matter to the minister, he found him somewhat indisposed. The minister merely asked him to read the document to him. Perceptively, the minister realized that what had been concocted was not simply authorization for an army inspector for Samsun, but for one that would cover all of Anatolia. The deputy chief noted that such authorization was nothing new. Hesitating, the minister smiled at his colleague, for he had found a way out of his dilemma. He did not wish to be responsible for giving authorization for such wide-ranging power, but the grand vizier had already given his sanction to the project. Picking up his seal, he threw it to his deputy chief. "My signature is unnecessary. Take this and seal it yourself," he said.

Seal affixed, the document vested awesome authority in Mustafa Kemal. He was empowered to restore law and order and ferret out the causes of the disquieting disturbances. Also, he could confiscate and store weapons and ammunition. Two army corps and five provinces were under his command, and five other provinces were ordered to give careful consideration to his commands.

Leaving the ministry of war, Mustafa Kemal was ecstatic. Later on he recorded his delight:

> What a wonderful thing! Fortune smiled on me, and when I found myself basking in her smile it is hard to describe how happy I was. I recall biting my lips with excitement as I left the office. The cage had opened; the whole universe lay before me. I was like a bird about to soar with the first movement of its wings. [Aydemir 1969, vol. 1, p. 392]

One more hurdle had to be negotiated before Mustafa Kemal could embark upon his mission. His orders required cabinet approval. Here again Mehmed Ali stepped in. Spending an evening over the card table with Damad Ferid Pasha at a club, Mehmed Ali got him to sign the document. It was now signed and sealed, a fact that compelled the cabinet to offer little resistance. On 30 April, with the document in order, the sultan approved Mustafa Kemal's appointment as inspector general. A combination of astute machinations, the willingness of a number of people to take risks, and good fortune had brought Mustafa Kemal to the threshold of greatness. At a number of points the entire project could have been sidetracked, and Mustafa Kemal might have been immobilized. Instead, everything clicked into place, adding force to Schiller's observation, "How narrow is the boundary between life's two paths."

One final piece of the historical tableau fell into place on 15 May, when the Greeks landed twenty thousand troops at Izmir and began their invasion of Anatolia. The Greek landing was carried out under the auspiccs of the Allies. Lloyd George, out of a mixture of motives that included pro-Christian, pro-Hellenic, and anti-Turkish sentiments, as well as political considerations that saw Greece as a possible pro-British bastion in the Mediterranean, backed the claim of the Greek premier, Eleutherios Venizelos that Greece had the right to occupy Izmir. Convincing Woodrow Wilson and Georges Clemenceau that support for Greece was the best policy, Lloyd George garnered the approval necessary to launch Venizelos's grand scheme for the resurrection of a Greek empire. Self-determination, one of Wilson's Fourteen Points, was going to be denied the Turks.

While the ships filled with the grim Greek troops were making their way toward Izmir, Mustafa Kemal was busy assembling his staff, making his farewells, and consulting with his superiors for the last time. İsmet decided to stay behind in Istanbul where he could observe the situation at the highest levels. Rauf would travel to Ankara as a civilian and meet with Mustafa Kemal later. News of the Greek invasion and the horrible massacres that accompanied it reached Mustafa Kemal while he was at the Sublime Porte, the offices of the grand vizier and leading ministers. Others expressed shock at this final outrage, but Mustafa Kemal was not surprised. What he could not know at the moment was that this event would convert national humiliation into national rage. As Mustafa Kemal was preparing to embark upon a voyage toward the leadership of his people, the people themselves would be ready to receive a savior and follow him toward a shared goal.

On the day following the Greek landings at Izmir, Mustafa Kemal was received by the sultan after the formal Friday prayers. The sultan was unusually gracious toward him on this occasion. Thumbing through a history book in the course of this farewell audience, the sultan said to Mustafa Kemal, "Pasha, Pasha, up to now you have rendered a number of services to the nation. All of it is part of the historical record. It has become part of history. Forget all that. The service you will perform now may be more important than all of those. Pasha, Pasha, you may be able to save the nation" (Atay 1965, p. 122). Mustafa Kemal was shaken by this remark and managed only to mumble some polite reply. It has been suggested that Sultan Mehmed VI, who wept openly when he heard of the Greek invasion of Izmir, was attempting to aid Mustafa Kemal in the realization of his objective. Given the sultan's weak character and his past actions, it seems unlikely that this could have been his conscious intention. In any case, it is still not known what the sultan meant by his comments. At the conclusion of the audience Mustafa Kemal was presented with a gold pocket watch that bore the imperial insignia as a gift from the sultan.

One final formality remained before Mustafa Kemal and his staff could leave for Samsun. Visas had to be obtained from the British for himself and his staff. A junior British officer's suspicions had been aroused when he looked over the list of officers for whom visas had been requested. It was a formidable collection of high-ranking and talented soldiers Mustafa Kemal had assembled,[1] more suited for making war than peace, he

[1]Eighteen people accompanied Mustafa Kemal on the boat from Istanbul to Samsun. Two of them were military physicians. One of these doctors, Dr. Refik (later Refik

thought. In the end, the officer was assured by his superiors that Mustafa Kemal had the confidence of the sultan and should be given the visas. They were granted and everything was in order for departure late in the evening of 16 May.

Departure and separation are practically synonomous terms. Separation from his mother always presented Mustafa Kemal with difficulties. It was clouded with ambivalence, being both devoutly desired and resolutely resisted. The separation involved in his leaving Istanbul for the unknown that awaited him in Anatolia stirred enormous feelings within Mustafa Kemal. A dinner was arranged with his mother and sister for the evening of 15 May, his last night in Istanbul. They dined at his house in Şişli.[2] They ate in the traditional manner, as they had eaten during his childhood days in Salonika, sitting on floor cushions with their legs tucked in under them, taking food from trays on the floor beside them. Mustafa Kemal is reported to have worn an aba, the traditional Near Eastern long gown. His behavior that night reflected in many ways his earliest memory—the assuaging of his mother's broken heart before leaving her to follow his father's suggestion that he enroll in a westernized, modern school. Paradoxically, what he wanted to do as a man was to repair the grieving mother, now associated with his grieving nation.

He told his mother of his plan to leave Istanbul the next evening, but did not elaborate the future. His mother prayed for him, but did not go to the dock to see him off. Abdürrahim, then nine years old, went to the Galata bridge at the harbor to bid his farewell (Tuncak 1974). Rauf had said his farewell earlier.[3] Mustafa Kemal had also recruited another officer, Colonel Refet (Bele) at the last minute. He had no exit visa but managed to get on board the ship, the *Bandırma*, on the pretext that he was loading some horses. He stayed with the horses until the ship cleared the harbor.

Saydam), functioned as Mustafa Kemal's private physician throughout the war of independence. Later, he served in Atatürk's cabinet and became the prime minister of Turkey in 1939 (after Atatürk's death). He died in 1942. He was the same age as Atatürk. Tevetoğlu (1971) wrote the life stories of all these 18 people and what happened to them later on.

[2]Kinross (1965, p. 184) states that his last evening was spent at Beşiktaş, at his mother's house, and not at Şişli. However, our understanding is that his mother and sister had moved with him to Şişli. See Atay 1965, p. 124. Visitors to the present-day museum are shown his mother's room, where this farewell meal took place.

[3]Mustafa Kemal later recalled how Rauf warned him about a possible danger ahead. He stated: "Rauf Bey came to me just as I was getting into my motor-car when I left Constantinople. He had heard from a confidential source that the ship in which I was going would be followed and that it was very likely that she would be sunk in the Black Sea, if I could not have been detained in Constantinople. This is what he came to tell me. I preferred to risk being drowned rather than being made prisoner in Constantinople" (Atatürk 1927, pp. 32–33).

Another man who accompanied Mustafa Kemal was one of his classmates, Staff Lieutenant Mehmed Arif (Adana), better known as Ayıcı Arif, a nickname that can be translated loosely as "someone who likes bears." Indeed, Arif had a pet bear with which he used to wrestle.[4] In the coming years Mehmed Arif would play an important role in Mustafa Kemal's life. We know from Ali Fuat's recollections (Cebesoy 1967) that Arif used to imitate Mustafa Kemal while they were in school together at the War College. In the second year at the school Mustafa Kemal had learned to waltz and tried to teach Arif how to dance. It was at about this time that Arif started to copy Mustafa Kemal's dress and speech. A type of "twinning" appeared between the two. Ali Fuat also remembers that Arif actually did look very much life Mustafa Kemal, recalling them as physical doubles. Some thought the two were brothers.

Famous for transporting Mustafa Kemal to Samsun, the *Bandırma*, a British-built cargo ship purchased from a Greek, hardly appeared capable of fulfilling its fateful mission on the evening of 16 May. Its top speed was only seven knots, and the compass was broken. Once the ship cleared the Bosporus and entered the Black Sea, Mustafa Kemal feared that the British might realize their mistake and come after him. He ordered the captain to sail closer to shore so that if anything happened he might be able to get ashore and escape. A typical Black Sea squall caught them and almost everyone was seasick. The captain of the *Bandırma*, Hakkı Dursun, recalled later that Mustafa Kemal spent much of the voyage sitting and brooding over his thoughts (see Aydemir 1969, vol. 1, p. 400). Neither the captain nor the British could have been aware that this one man was the savior awaited by an injured nation. None could have anticipated the surge of power that would be evoked from a war-weary country by this man and his friends.

Fateful for the nation, this passage to Samsun would also be psychologically fateful for Mustafa Kemal as well. His undying, unconscious, selfish childhood wish was to rescue his mother, to be her savior. It was a selfish wish because underneath it represented his desire to have a repaired mother who would be able to be a more nurturing mother to him. That wish to be the repairer of his mother became the altruistic wish to save his country; the two goals were linked in his unconscious mind.

Samsun was an unassuming little Black Sea port when Mustafa Kemal landed there on 19 May 1919, ferried by rowboat from the *Bandırma* to the rickety wooden jetty that served as a dock. The landing lacked the

[4]Arif had caught a three-month-old bear in a forest near İnegöl, where the Eleventh Division, which Arif commanded, was stationed. He carried this pet bear wherever he went. The bear would wrestle with the peasant boys, smoke cigarettes, and, it was said, even fall in love with girls. See Apak 1957.

grandiloquent statements that have marked other significant historical landings, but history would later record it as significant. Mustafa Kemal himself took the date as marking a crucial point, if not *the* crucial point, in his career. In 1927, during the congress of the People's party when he launched into the public defense of his policies that was to become his famous six-day speech, he began, "Gentlemen, I landed at Samson [Samsun] on the 19th of May, 1919" (Atatürk 1927, p. 9). Not only was this a turning point in Turkish history, but it was also psychologically significant for Mustafa Kemal. In his fantasy he saw it as his birthday, since it marked the beginning of his life as a savior. He offered 19 May as his birthdate to a writer composing a biography for a foreign encyclopedia (Afetinan 1971, p. 3). In 1936 he had his birthdate officially changed to 19 May to make his feelings and history congruent. Birth is often represented in dreams as emergence from the sea (Freud 1900), and it was indeed a new Mustafa Kemal who disembarked at Samsun from the sea. He arrived in Anatolia (the Turkish word *Anadolu* may be translated literally as "full of mother") completely true to the meaning of the word, with the mission of saving and repairing her. Thus, he could have a relationship with his mother unlike the one he had had during his infancy.

When under stress in the past, he had looked to others, in real life as well as in fantasy, to restore his grandiose image of himself. Now his grandiose self was newly made cohesive. There was no superior being from whom glory could be expected—he must look for it in himself. He was, in fact, to become a savior, and his destiny as such would bring into complete congruence his own concept of himself and the perception others would have of him.

12
"The Mist Has Fallen on Top of the Mountain"

It was seven o'clock in the morning when the thirty-eight-year-old Mustafa Kemal set foot on Anatolian soil. His landing came almost a week after the arrival of an Allied fleet in the harbor of Izmir. Admiral Calthrope, the English fleet commander who had negotiated the Mudros Armistice, informed the Turkish governor of Izmir that Allied troops were about to land. Actually only Greek troops landed on 15 May to initiate what they expected to be the first step in the Greek repossession of their ancestral rights in Asia Minor. In reality it became the opening phase of the Turkish war of independence.

News of the Greek landing flashed across what remained of the once redoubtable Ottoman Empire. It produced a shock wave of resentment among the Turks, who shrugged off their war weariness and girded themselves for battle with an ancient adversary.

From the first landing it seemed that there was little the Turks could do to keep from being engulfed. The native Greeks of Izmir jubilantly welcomed the Greek soldiers. Blessings were heaped upon them by the metropolitan of Izmir amidst shouts of *Zito Venizelos*, "Long Live Venizelos," from the city's populace. The Greeks celebrated as though their "great idea," the dream of restoring the Greek Empire, had been accomplished.[1]

[1]The "great idea" was also the primary psychological motivating factor in uniting Cyprus with mainland Greece; attempts at this union led to the Turkish occupation of the northern part of the island (Volkan 1979). A Cypriot-born Greek sociologist, K. C. Markides (1977, p. 10), who wrote on the "rise and fall" of the Cyprus Republic, describes the "great idea" as "a dream shared by Greeks that someday the Byzantine Empire would be restored and all the Greek lands would once again be united into a Great Greece." This Pan-Hellenic ideology arose in 1453, when Constantinople fell to the Turks. Markides continues, "The 'Great Idea' found expression in . . . parts of the Greek world, such as Crete and the Ionian islands. One could argue that the 'Great Idea' had an internal logic, pressing for realization in every part of the Greek world which continued to be under foreign rule . . . being the most central and powerful of institutions, the church [the Greek Orthodox Church] contributed immensely to its development. The church embraced the movement and for all practical purposes its guiding nucleus" (Markides 1977, pp. 10–11).

The essence of the "great idea" can be found in a speech delivered in 1884 by Premier John Kolettis, who was a leading spokesman of it.

"The Kingdom of Greece is not Greece; it is only a part, the smallest and poorest, of

Izmir, or Smyrna, was a natural choice for the entering wedge of Greek efforts at redemption. Next to Athens itself, it is perhaps the most important city in the Aegean area. Its beginnings are shrouded in legend, but it is known that it was settled about 1000 B.C. by Aeolian Greeks, who were followed by many other peoples, including the Romans and the Arabs. In the eleventh century it was captured by the Seljuk Turks of Konya and in the fifteenth century was incorporated into the Ottoman state. Izmir was seen by the Turks as a centuries-old Turkish stronghold, but the Greeks had never lost their attachment to the city, and now it appeared that their opportunity had come to repossess it.

Only in hindsight do some historians feel that the landing of Greek troops was a political as well as a military blunder. Other Allied occupation troops were already present in Anatolia, and while technically not under occupation, Istanbul itself was teeming with foreign troops. The French and British were present in large numbers near the present-day Syrian border, with Adana as their large base. Antalya was occupied by Italians, and when Mustafa Kemal landed at Samsun, a small detachment of British troops was situated there. There can be no doubt that the psychological response of the Turks would have been different had the Allies landed any troops other than Greeks at Izmir. The landing of Greeks undermined whatever trust might have existed between the Turks and the Allies. By using Greeks, the Allied leaders at Paris had neglected the psychological factor, in the estimation of Dagobert von Mikusch, who wrote:

> The members of the Peace Council no doubt believed, from the statistics submitted to them, that the Greeks had a claim to Smyrna. This slight mistake had incalculable results.
>
> This blunder had a rather humorous sequel in the English House of Commons. On May 26, 1919, Lieutenant-Colonel Herbert, a Member of Parliament, put the question whether the Allies had occupied Smyrna on the grounds of self-determination or simply from selfish interest.
>
> Harmsworth replied for the government: "The occupation of Smyrna followed on the express instruction of the Supreme Council of the Peace Commission, according to Article 7 of the Armistice Agreement of Mudros."
>
> Lieutenant-Colonel Herbert: "Following upon this answer, may I ask if it is true that rabies has broken out in Paris?" [von Mikusch, 1931, p. 195]

Greece. A Greek is not only he who lives in the kingdom but also he who lives in Yannina, or Thessalonika [Salonika], or Serroes, or Adrianople [Edirne], or Constantinople [Istanbul], or Trebizond [Trabzon], or Crete, or Samos, or in whatever country is historically Greek, or whoever is of the Greek race" (Xydis 1971, p. 237).

Madness bred in Paris of impatience and imperialist greed claimed its first victim as soon as the vanguard Greek regiment started to advance along the shoreline. A young Turkish journalist named Hasan Tahsin fired his pistol at them. Reprisal was immediate, and he fell as the first Turkish martyr in the struggle for independence. Another Turk shot the Greek flagbearer, triggering panic. Greek soldiers and local Greek inhabitants began to attack Turks indiscriminately and then marched on the city's fortress. The Turkish garrison had already surrendered its arms in accordance with the armistice terms. It was no match for the invading Greeks. Many Turkish officers fled inland where they would later join the national struggle against the invader, a fierce and prolonged encounter that would be marked by atrocities committed by both sides.

News of the Greek landing spread quickly over Anatolia's excellent telegraphic service, a by-product of Sultan Abdülhamid II's program of military modernization and his paranoid need to keep track of all that went on in even the most remote corner of his realm. It was through this system that Mustafa Kemal was able to learn about what had happened in Izmir while he was en route to Samsun.

On that misty morning of 19 May no fanfare welcomed Mustafa Kemal to Samsun, where there was considerable tension. A British presence was maintained through some two hundred officers and men. It was rumored that Greek soldiers might also arrive, for Samsun and its environs contained a large number of Greeks who were seeking to establish their autonomy in the region. Marauding bandits made the streets of the port town unsafe. Mustafa Kemal came to Samsun as an inspector general, a representative of the sultan, officially ordered to sort out the relations between the Greeks and the Turks, calm the people, and report back to Istanbul on his progress. His own agenda was to initiate resistance to foreign aggression, thereby launching the independence struggle.

Upon his arrival he sensed no particular encouragement from those with whom he tried to communicate. There were six units of the Ottoman army scattered throughout Anatolia, hundreds of miles apart. Some additional ten thousand men were stationed in Thrace (what was left of the Ottoman Empire in Europe), but those troops were under Allied command. The Turkish population was exhausted and their morale was extremely low.

From Samsun, Mustafa Kemal sent telegrams to Ali Fuat, the commander of the Twentieth Army Corps stationed in Ankara, and to Kâzım, who was at the head of the Sixteenth Army Corps headquartered at Erzurum. Of these two old friends and allies, Kâzım was now the key figure. A charismatic leader in his own right, he was in charge of a region of Anatolia that had been devastated by war, having been the staging area for Enver's grandiose gestures against the Russians. After the

Armenian-Turkish troubles of 1916 the population of the area is said to have dwindled to a mere 10 percent of its prewar numbers. Disease was rife, food scarce, and all matériel in short supply.

Paternal in outlook, Kâzım sought to restore some semblance of ordinary life to Erzurum and its surroundings. He adopted close to a thousand orphaned boys and saw to their care and feeding. Organizing schools for them, he had his officers give them a modicum of military training. A violinist himself, Kâzım provided these boys with training in music as well. He was very much in the old Ottoman tradition of the pasha who surrounded himself with a household that included a large number of young men being trained for his personal service, including bearing arms. Soft sensibilities aside, Kâzım remained a Turkish soldier determined to protect the Turks for whom he was responsible. When the British colonel A. Rawlinson went to Erzurum to investigate the feasibility of creating an independent Armenian state and to call for the surrender of all weapons, he found Kâzım obdurate about any such surrender. Rawlinson considered Kâzım "the most genuine example of a first-class Turkish officer that it has ever been my good fortune to meet" (Kinross 1965, p. 203).

Kâzım was obviously a force in the area and Mustafa Kemal recognized his need for assistance from him. Two days after his arrival in Samsun he telegraphed him that:

> I am hurt and sad over the gravity of our situation. I accepted the last official position in order to carry out our humane obligation owed to the nation, which we may discharge by working together. I am anxious to meet with Your Excellency as soon as possible. Since Samsun and the surrounding country may meet with disaster due to the disorder here, I must, however, remain here for a few days. Please let me know of anything that would contribute to my plans. With my warm regards, my dear brother. . . [Aydemir 1969, vol. 2, p. 21]

Another source of displeasure to Mustafa Kemal was the presence of British troops in Samsun. He decided to move his operation about sixty kilometers inland to the town of Havza on the Anatolian Plateau, which was famous for its springs. He had suffered a return of his kidney discomfort and the change, it was hoped, might be beneficial.

In a convoy of three automobiles, including an old Mercedes-Benz in which he rode, Mustafa Kemal and his retinue left Samsun for Havza on 25 May. The Mercedes was in such bad shape that it could travel no faster than 15 kilometers an hour and had to stop often for repairs. Even with a more efficient vehicle there would have been no possibility of normal travel since good roads were a rarity in Anatolia.

Those who later recalled that trip speak of how happy Mustafa Kemal seemed to be. Once, when the car broke down, he began to walk and some of the others followed him. As he walked he began to sing and urged everyone to join in. It is difficult to interpret this outwardly happy journey. He had finally arrived in Anatolia and was now embarked on a course of proving himself the savior of his country (and, unconsciously, of his grieving mother). Having reached this turning point that served to enhance his identity, he might have felt the need to celebrate and to do so by breaking out in song. On the other hand, his good cheer may have been the denial of some rather real external dangers. The song he sang was one of his favorites, and contains the lines: "The mist has fallen on top of the mountain; the silver stream, unceasing, runs; the sun is entering the world on the horizon, let us march on, my friends." Since his associations to this song are not known, one can only speculate as to why it was a favorite.

The theme of the rising of the sun (birth) appears in a recollection of how, as commander in chief of the Turkish armies, he achieved his crucial defeat of the Greeks on 30 August 1922. He speaks of the night before the battle when he and two of his most trusted generals discussed the coming showdown. "We studied the situation once more and definitely concluded that the true sun of salvation for the Turks would rise with all its splendor on the morning of 30 August" (Aydemir 1969, vol. 2, p. 21). The expression in Turkish is *kurtuluş güneşi*, "the sun of salvation," and the verb is *doğmak*, "to be born." Mustafa Kemal chose 19 May as his official birthday (Afetinan 1971, p. 3), commemorating his landing at Samsun. One can conclude that he viewed himself as the newborn sun (son) who dispelled both the mists of that early morning and the shrouding grief of his mother. The silver stream may have represented her tears. Although it was a Swedish song originally, it became the song of the Turkish revolution. Mustafa Kemal himself sang it over and over on his anxious travels across his homeland as he established himself as its savior, and even today it is sung on national holidays.

After getting settled in Havza's only hotel, Mustafa Kemal had his first opportunity to mingle with the people. He began to assume the role of a politician and he sought the assistance of the region's religious leaders. Here he made his first public declaration of distrust of the Istanbul government. Exhorting the people to participate in the resistance movement that was stirring, he protested what was happening to the empire and the Turkish nation itself. Despite the anger aroused in the populace by the Greek invasion of Izmir, Mustafa Kemal found the people apathetic and interested only in being left alone. Izmir was too far away to deflect them from their concern to get on with their farming in order to provide food. He could not strike the spark necessary to ignite intense rage and this produced feelings within him of extreme frustration. Recalling this period later, he complained of the ignorance displayed by the inhabitants and their lack of grief. He concluded that "their silence and apathy in face of this unjust conspiracy [the Greek invasion] could only be explained in a very unfavorable light for the nation. The chief thing, therefore, was to arouse them and force them to take action" (Atatürk 1927, p. 24).

While in Havza, Mustafa Kemal was visited by a delegation of Russian Bolsheviks. He spurned their attempts to convert him to their philosophy, but an important link was forged that would be invaluable later on.

Bothered by the presence of British troops in Merzifon only 20 kilometers away and by the local apathy, Mustafa Kemal abandoned Havza for Amasya. Situated 128 kilometers inland from Samsun, Amasya is a picturesque city of historical importance. One of the principal cities of the pre-Ottoman Turkish principality of Eretna (fourteenth century), it is situated in a gorge cut in the steep hills by the Yeşilırmak (Green River). The ruins of an ancient fortress and numerous tombs of Pontus kings could still be seen there. In early Ottoman times Amasya was a provincial seat to which Ottoman heirs apparent were sent, together with their tutors (*lala*s) to learn the art of government. There they built their reputations and waited for the opportunity to reign as sultan. Mustafa Kemal, the as yet unacknowledged heir apparent of Turkey's future, entered the city officially a representative of the Ottoman sultan, but spiritually the newborn son of a grieving mother/land.

Removal to Amasya had been planned with care. A committee of Amasya dignitaries was invited to meet with Mustafa Kemal in Havza prior to his departure. At the head of the committee was the mufti of Amasya, as one would expect, for the *ulema*, Muslim theologians and learned men, still played a dominant role in local affairs. Mustafa Kemal had already demonstrated his willingness to work with the *ulema* to achieve his ends. He had done so in Tripoli and he was about to do so again in Anatolia, despite the fact that he shared his father's anticlerical bias. At this stage he had no choice but to overlook their religiosity and their traditional garb. It was a time to use them and to seek their support for a common cause.

On 12 June, Mustafa Kemal and his party made the trip to Amasya. Having earlier let his identity as the hero of Gallipoli be known, Mustafa Kemal was greeted by a throng to whom he gave an impassioned speech. His mission to save the country was becoming more widely and openly acknowledged. Speaking from the balcony of the town hall, he told the people of Amasya that the sultan was a prisoner of the Allies. The nation was about to slip through the fingers of the people and he, Mustafa Kemal, had come to work with them to prevent that calamity. He then met with the leading dignitaries of the area who supported his perception of the need for an organization to serve as the focus for the resistance movement. In Amasya he was joined by Ali Fuat, Rauf, and Refet. After some discussion they banded together to issue a sort of declaration of independence which they called the Amasya Decisions. This document, composed of six articles, declared that the motherland and national independence were in peril. Only the nation's will and determination could save it. In order to coordinate the work of all who wished to save the nation, a call was issued for a congress to meet in Sivas. A preliminary congress for delegates from the eastern provinces had already been scheduled by Kâzım to convene in Erzurum.[2]

Activities such as these did not escape the attention of the Ottoman government in Istanbul. Mustafa Kemal's audacity in pushing his authority to its furthest limits caused the sultan enormous anxiety. Having placed his trust in the protection of the Allies, the sultan could not tolerate even the hint of insurrection in Anatolia. The telegraph wires were kept busy by the sultan's government and Mustafa Kemal alike as Istanbul sought to control him, and he attempted to make anybody who would listen aware of the threat to Turkish independence and national existence. On 8 June a telegram from the minister of war had ordered Mustafa Kemal to return to Istanbul. He ignored it. In a long telegraphic response to the sultan, he threatened to resign and stay among the people of Anatolia as a civilian. Escalating the confrontation with Mustafa Kemal, the government sent a secret telegram to all provincial and district governors on 23 June informing them that Mustafa Kemal had been dismissed. Since he no longer had any official status, they were told to disregard any orders he might issue.

Learning that the Istanbul government had dispatched an agent to arrest him, a retired staff colonel, Ali Galip, who was on his way to assume the office of governor of Erzincan, Mustafa Kemal and his coterie left Amasya secretly at dawn on 26 June. Upon his arrival in Tokat later that day, Mustafa Kemal took over the telegraph office to prevent the dispatch of any information about his whereabouts. After exhorting local notables to extend themselves in defense of the nation, he spent the night

[2]Mustafa Kemal later recalled how this circular was signed. He pressed Ali Fuat into signing by "assuring him that this document would be of historical value." But Refet initially declined to sign since he could not understand why and with what objective a congress would convene. Mustafa Kemal states, "It seemed incredible to me that a comrade whom I had brought with me from Constantinople (Istanbul) could take such an extraordinary view about so simple a question, especially as he understood perfectly well what we were going to do." Mustafa Kemal sent for Ali Fuat, who was in another room. Ali Fuat reproached Refet rather sharply; then, "Refet picked up the draft and put some sort of signature to it, which is rather difficult to make out" (see Atatürk 1927, p. 33).

there, making an early departure the next morning for Sivas. Before setting out, he arranged to have a telegram sent to the governor of Sivas announcing his departure from Tokat, but ordered that it be delayed for six hours (Atatürk 1927, p. 38). By that time he would have arrived in Sivas, thus thwarting any plans that might be afoot to arrest him en route. No one knew whether Mustafa Kemal would be taken into custody. An arrest would mean a court-martial, or he might be turned over to the Allies for exile on Malta or execution by hanging.

Approaching Sivas on the road from Tokat, Mustafa Kemal and his party stopped at a farm some 50 kilometers from his destination. During that halt the *vali*, "governor," of Sivas received the telegram Mustafa Kemal had arranged to be sent to him. He read the wire and handed it to Ali Galip, saying, "He is coming here now. You must do what you think proper about arresting him" (Atatürk 1927, p. 38). The retired colonel refused to accept responsibility for such a step, declining on the grounds that Sivas was not within his jurisdiction. Thereupon, the governor of Sivas suggested they ride out to greet Mustafa Kemal in conformity with the old Ottoman custom whereby arriving officials were met on the road and escorted into the city.

While at the farm Mustafa Kemal was brought up to date on the current situation by his supporters. He was informed that he had been relieved of his authority by the sultan's government, that plans had been considered for his arrest, and matters were critical. At that juncture the governor arrived at the farm by car. He implored Mustafa Kemal to rest a little longer. Seizing the initiative, Mustafa Kemal hurried his men into their cars and cleverly maneuvered the governor into sitting next to him for the trip into Sivas. The die was cast; there could be no turning back. Deprived of his authority and powerless to issue orders, Mustafa Kemal could only press on.

Hardly anyone spoke on the trip into Sivas. Mustafa Kemal was busy with his own thoughts. Who would be waiting in Sivas—soldiers to arrest him, or the people? The answer was plain as soon as they entered the city. Crowds shouted "Long live Mustafa Kemal Pasha." Nonetheless, behind the bystanders who lined the streets were posters on the walls proclaiming him a mutineer and a dangerous traitor (Atatürk 1927, p. 37).

Perceiving that he was surrounded by friends, Mustafa Kemal got out of his car and together with the governor walked through the crowds. Among those welcoming him were officers and men he had commanded at Gallipoli. They greeted him as a hero who brought with him the promise of victory. He now stood on his own among the Turks of Anatolia with no connection to the sultan's government in Istanbul. Thanks to the enthusiasm and applause of his former comrades in arms he was not arrested. Everyone was caught up in a storm of emotional excitement. The men pressed around him while the women in their traditional colorful garb watched him from a discreet distance with their faces half covered, and the children climbed the trees to get a glimpse of this famous man. Mustafa Kemal sought out Ali Galip and reprimanded him and afterward let him go. A day that had commenced with uncertainty had ended in personal triumph.

Success had so stimulated Mustafa Kemal that he spent a fitful night, unable to sleep. The next morning he set out along with his retinue for their next destination, Erzurum, almost 500 kilometers to the east. Kâzım was stationed there and awaited them. In the summer heat everything was dry and dusty. The bare hills with their yellow, orange, and gray stretches were well suited to induce a feeling of loneliness, of being diminished before the naked beauty of the terrain. On a road renowned for the bandits who terrorized it, his party met only hungry and proud villagers who had not the slightest interest in these passers-by.

Approaching the city from the west, the party could see the castle of Erzurum, built in the reign of Emperor Theodosius in the fifth century. Captured from the Byzantines by the Turks in 1071, the city was thoroughly Turkified in subsequent centuries, and under the Ottomans it was the important military center for campaigns in the east against the Iranians and Russians. Mustafa Kemal and his companions were greeted warmly on the outskirts by enthusiastic crowds. The reception was headed by Kâzım, who had ridden out a considerable distance from the city as a mark of respect. The fact that he was accompanied by his entire staff could only have been a source of comfort to Mustafa Kemal.

Enthusiastic though his reception was on that Sunday, 3 July, Mustafa Kemal was still uneasy. Along the road from Sivas to Erzurum he had received several telegraphic communications from the sultan and his officials in Istanbul, who pressured him to return to the capital or resign. Threats and bribes underlay the appeals made to him by a host of government officeholders. Despite the fact that telegrams had been sent to the provincial governors of Anatolia informing them that Mustafa Kemal had been stripped of his authority, he himself had not yet received official notification affecting his status. Consequently, he arrived in Erzurum wearing his military uniform and all his decorations. On the next day which was the anniversary of the sultan's accession, Mustafa Kemal held court and received felicitations on behalf of the sultan. The Ottoman sultans had been absolute rulers for centuries, and among the populace of Anatolia who were still bound up in the notion of folk Islam, the sultan/caliph was a supreme figure against whom rebellion was virtually unthinkable.[3] The people of Erzurum offered their allegiance to

[3]Modern western society knows a tripartite division of government—legislative, executive, and judicial. No such division exists in Islam. Traditionally the Ottoman sultan was an

him through Mustafa Kemal, who was rapidly reaching for a supremacy of his own.

For the next several days Mustafa Kemal was in a quandary about whether he should resign the commission so dear to him, or let matters run their course and wait for the sultan to dismiss him and strip him of all his honors. As a civilian, who would obey him? On whom could he rely? On the night of 8 July, he was summoned to the telegraph station in Erzurum. The sultan was personally at the other end of the wire in Yıldız Palace and wished to communicate with him. Joining the sultan was Ferid Pasha. Initiating the discussion, the sultan sent Mustafa Kemal his greetings in florid Ottoman court style, which only served to put him on guard as to the palace's real intentions. They insisted that Mustafa Kemal return to Istanbul, where great things awaited him. Mustafa Kemal refused. Then they urged him to depart from Erzurum and go on leave anywhere he wished in Anatolia.

Even from hundreds of miles away the imperial presence could be felt in Erzurum. Clearly, Mustafa Kemal was faced with a situation in which he could either resign from the miltary or be dismissed from it. Forced to act, he chose the former course despite all its political and personal risks. At 10:50 in the evening of 8 July he resigned from the army, indicating that he would continue to work as an individual in the bosom of the nation.[4] Bravado saw him across his personal Rubicon, but he was clearly shaken. He had suffered a narcissistic blow and his self-esteem was threatened by the realization that the telegram dismissing him had crossed the one in which he tendered his resignation. He had always had a uniform in which to clothe his grand self-concept. Military authority had been his leverage. Now he was without both the protective and bolstering shell provided by the military uniform that had first captured his imagination as a youngster in Salonika, and the power it had conveyed.

Rauf imparted Mustafa Kemal's recognition of the seriousness of his

---

absolute ruler whose duty it was to see that society was governed in accordance with the religious law, the Sharia. After conquering the central Islamic lands in 1517, the Ottoman sultans also assumed the title of caliph and were the protectors of the Holy Places of Mecca and Medina. In the second half of the nineteenth century, as the Ottomans began to be hard pressed by the West, the sultans began to put greater emphasis on their being the caliph of Islam which cloaked them in religious sanctity, for the caliph was the shadow of God on earth. As such, the sultan/caliph was especially revered by the common people.

[4]Mustafa Kemal later labeled the telegram exchange between himself and the authorities in Istanbul as a comedy. He recalled, "the comedy that had been going on for a month—from the 8th June to the 8th July—came abruptly to an end. . . . Henceforward I continued to do my duty according to the dictates of my conscience, free from any official rank and restriction, trusting solely to the devotion and magnanimity of the nation itself, from whom I drew strength, energy, and inspiration as from an inexhaustible spring" (Atatürk 1927, p. 43). One catches an echo of a child at the "good" mother's breast. The child, in turn, will be strong enough to save the mother so that "inexhaustible spring" can continue.

loss of authority in his memoirs (Orbay 1962–63). He reports a rueful comment by Mustafa Kemal, "If we become civilians, that is the end, Rauf—the struggle in Anatolia is going to be a military struggle. In order to give orders in such a struggle, one needs to have an official authority." Mustafa Kemal's concern and anxiety stemming from his resignation was intensified when his chief of staff stepped down the morning of 10 July, saying that in light of his commander's changed status, he could no longer serve him. Rauf, who witnessed this encounter, remarked that he had never seen Mustafa Kemal's spirits so low since the beginning of their friendship in 1909. The self-initiated departure of his chief of staff led Mustafa Kemal to remark, "Rauf, have you observed it? Have you seen the importance of government rank and position?"

Shaken by his own audacious action, Mustafa Kemal looked to those around him for signs of support and sustenance. Kâzım became the key figure upon whom everything depended. If he would support this new civilian, there was hope for Mustafa Kemal's future. If he left him in the lurch now that he had no military standing, such a defection might mark the end of any notion he had of becoming the savior of his motherland. Attended by Rauf, Mustafa Kemal paced the floor, waiting for Kâzım to make his position known. Suddenly word was received that Kâzım was arriving at the head of a cavalry unit. Mustafa Kemal and his retinue realized the crucial importance of the moment. The dramatic effect was heightened by the military trappings of the encounter. Drawing up in front of the building, the cavalry unit came to attention and saluted. Kâzım returned their salute. Then, he addressed Mustafa Kemal, "My Pasha, I am at your command. Myself, my officers, my troops, my army corps. All of us are at your command" (Aydemir 1969, vol. 2, p. 108).

Mustafa Kemal embraced Kâzım, kissing him on both cheeks. The crisis had passed, but despite the documented story of this declaration of support, there are lingering stories of suspicion existing between these two men.[5] Both appeared patriotically determined to protect the nation. Both, however, were Ottoman military men in the old tradition for whom rebellion against the sultan would have been unthinkable until this most recent turn of events.

Mustafa Kemal was now a civilian and he dressed accordingly. He had, on the day after his decision to resign, sent his new orderly, Ali, to the

[5]Kâzım handpicked an orderly, Ali, to serve Mustafa Kemal. Young Ali had worked previously for Enver, and when he first came to serve Mustafa Kemal, the latter recognized him and told him to get out; however, Kâzım intervened and thus Mustafa Kemal accepted Ali to serve him. The orderly became a devoted servant and admirer of Mustafa Kemal. However, when later he recalled the days in Erzurum, he stated that when Kâzım Pasha asked him to serve Mustafa Kemal, he also told him to inform him about Mustafa Kemal's activities. See Oranlı 1967, p. 15.

house of the provincial governor with money to arrange for some clothes. He received a black vest, jacket, trousers, and a fez, the traditional urban civilian headdress. Mustafa Kemal scorned the fez and ordered a kalpak (Oranlı 1967, p. 23), the lamb's fur hat that became his hallmark until the nation adopted the Western style hat years later. It is said that he appeared as handsome in his civilian garb as he had in his uniform, but for the first few days he was noticeably withdrawn. With Kâzım's support pledged, Mustafa Kemal began to put his depressed mood behind him and look to the future that for the moment, at least, had been assured to him.

13

Political Resistance

Reduced to the status of a private individual, Mustafa Kemal had to rely on his own inner resources and heed the direction of his narcissistic personality organization in order to accomplish his goal of saving the nation. Certainly there were others who shared his goal, and it is only fair to assume that the determinants of their ambitions and passion to play a part in the national struggle might have differed from those of Mustafa Kemal.

In fact, it would have been entirely logical for Kâzım, in Erzurum, or Ali Fuat, in Ankara, to lead the drive for independence, for both had troops at their disposal. Moreover, both had left Istanbul for Anatolia prior to Mustafa Kemal's departure. Ali Fuat had gone to Ankara in March 1919 assigned to head the Twentieth Army Corps, and he had already begun to plan the national defense of the surrounding area. Kâzım went to Erzurum in April 1919 to command the Fifteenth Army Corps, which still had about eighteen thousand men. On one pretext after another he had avoided surrendering his army's weapons to the Allies. His troops were well-armed and he enjoyed a solid reputation in the region for his exploits in World War I. In comparison, Mustafa Kemal's position was weak. He had not left Istanbul until May, and he was without a troop command. Although he had been an army inspector, he was in reality little more than a rebel.

Orders, in fact, had been sent by the sultan to Kâzım to arrest Mustafa Kemal, but he never carried them out. Mustafa Kemal simply seized the position of leadership.[1] The moment had come to realize all of the dreams he had had since his military school days and his grandiose boastings of being his country's savior—or to go down in defeat. Some consider the crisis he faced in Erzurum, from which he was rescued through Kâzım's pledge of support, to be the pivotal point in his passionate drive to be exalted above all others.

Upright and inflexible, an Ottoman soldier from head to toe who also

[1]It would be an interesting study in itself to examine why prominent people surrounding Mustafa Kemal supported his taking the leadership role. Briefly, he had proved himself on the battlefield and was truly a Turkish hero of World War I. Only Rauf (Orbay) had a similar reputation, but more than that, his personality organization played a key role. He was sure that he could save the nation and he had played the constant game of the "great organizer."

had his gentler side, Kâzım had thrown Mustafa Kemal a veritable lifeline. It is unlikely that Kâzım had any idea of the psychological forces that drove Mustafa Kemal, but it is certain that his own prestige in the eastern provinces paved the way for his friend.

Mustafa Kemal's election to the chairmanship of the executive committee of the Erzurum branch of the Defense of Rights Association provided him with immediate evidence that his resignation from the military did not necessarily force him into oblivion. More important, it was the first step in enabling him to participate in the congress of the Defense of Rights associations, which would open in Erzurum on 23 July. Two members of the Erzurum delegation resigned so that he and Rauf might attend in their places. With 54 delegates the Erzurum congress met in the classroom of a schoolhouse. Unanimously, Mustafa Kemal was chosen president of the congress.

Anticipated in part as a response to threats to the territorial integrity of the Ottoman Empire's eastern provinces, the Erzurum congress assumed political importance. Defense of Rights associations had sprung up all over Anatolia in reaction to the dangers of an alliance between minority groups within the empire and foreign powers. The Greek invasion of Izmir was the last straw that pushed local groups of Turks—and those who cherished some nationalist ideals of their own—to organize a viable structure. Meetings and congresses of those groups had been held prior to the one in Erzurum, but now, because of the military strength represented by Kâzım's army corps, the movement was becoming more cohesive. Mustafa Kemal, as president of the congress, was in a position to establish the political aspects of the resistance movement.

Despite Mustafa Kemal's open avowal of opposition to the creation of an independent Armenian state in eastern Anatolia, the local Turks viewed him with suspicion. After all, he came from Istanbul and those in the sultan's employ had not been known for their solicitous behavior toward the local inhabitants. They were farmers, small businessmen, religious functionaries, and tribal leaders representing the interests of local Turks as well as of the Kurds and Lazes. Some of the local people had been members of the Committee of Union and Progress. As a result, they still harbored a grudge against Mustafa Kemal and considered him to be an adversary. In the eyes of the people of Erzurum and its environs, the Erzurum congress was a local affair designed to accomplish such objectives as strengthening resistance to the Armenians, liberating and storing arms, and restoring law and order in the neighborhood. Rebellion against the sultan/caliph was not on their agenda.

Aware of their attitude, Mustafa Kemal was cautious not to proclaim himself in open rebellion to the sultan. Therefore, he declared publicly that, since Istanbul was under foreign occupation, he was merely trying to save the sultan from nefarious foreign influence. Furthermore, he went along with the show of religious observance. The congress was opened with prayers by a leading religious dignitary, and Mustafa Kemal concluded his speech with prayers for the well-being of the Turkish nation and the sultanate and caliphate.

Opening on the anniversary of the restitution of constitutional monarchy in 1908, the Erzurum congress was seen as part of a large-scale threat to the sultan's prerogatives. The grand vizier issued an order to the country that all such congresses should be prevented from taking place. Seeking to diminish the uproar in Istanbul, the Erzurum congress sent telegrams in its name to the sultan and the grand vizier, assuring them that no action that was inimical to the sultan's rights was being taken.

For the next two weeks the congress went about its business, though often the sessions were far from tranquil. Not only was there a lack of mutual trust among many of those involved, but there was also a group that clung to its connections with Istanbul and wanted to preserve them in order to ensure a continued livelihood. The harsh terms imposed upon the Ottomans in Paris would ultimately undermine this antinationalist group, but meanwhile, at the congress in Erzurum, they held strong to their position. Nonetheless, they were unable to block the significant work of the congress—the issuance of an important resolution that would become known as the National Pact, which called for: the preservation and inviolabilty of the Ottoman "frontiers" (i.e., those areas of the empire inhabited by Turks at the time of the Mudros Armistice); the election of a provisional government; the revocation of privileges previously extended to the minorities within the empire; and, by implication, insistence on the right of self-determination for the Turks. The congress then elected a nine-member standing committee, and Mustafa Kemal was elected committee head by his fellow committee members.

Damad Ferid Pasha's performance at the Peace Conference in Paris in June 1919 was abysmally poor. His demeanor was that of a criminal before the bar of international justice. He spoke of Ottoman Turkey's entry into the war as a crime, indicated that the Ottoman people had committed crimes in the conduct of the war, and placed the blame for these actions on the members of the Committee of Union and Progress. He pleaded that, if the Ottoman Empire were allowed to disintegrate its collapse would bring deterioration in the Middle East and put an end to any hope for tranquility there.

Clemenceau of France dealt mercilessly with Damad Ferid Pasha. He indicated that in his view the Turks had been a barbarous people, and he sent the Ottoman grand vizier home empty-handed. The news about the treatment of Damad Ferid reached Erzurum, where it heartened Mustafa Kemal's camp. It was becoming more questionable every day whether the sultan's government could protect the interests of the Turkish nation.

Resolutions made at the Erzurum conference in the form of the National Pact were properly applicable to the six eastern provinces of the Ottoman Empire. Mustafa Kemal now wanted to extend them to the entire nation, and, to advance that possibility, a national congress was held at Sivas. Acting in his capacity as president of the Erzurum congress' standing committee, Mustafa Kemal began preparations for it. On 29 August he left Erzurum for Sivas, arriving there on 2 September, much to the chagrin of the governor, who nevertheless greeted him on his approach to the city and allowed the demonstrations hailing Mustafa Kemal's arrival to take place.

The Sivas congress was not the success Mustafa Kemal had hoped for. Although two hundred delegates had been invited, only thirty-nine were on hand for the opening ceremonies on 4 September. Many were prevented from attending by the fighting going on in the region around Izmir or in areas in the possession of the British, French, and Italians. With about a third of the delegates being in Mustafa Kemal's own entourage, the Sivas congress was hardly a representative body, though it did reflect the concerns of those who were moving more and more to support Mustafa Kemal's position. The resolutions of the Erzurum congress were accepted after Mustafa Kemal was elected chairman. There were three dissenting votes to his election, but it was hardly the beginning of an opposition movement. Rauf, who was elected vice-chairman, as he had been at Erzurum, tried to get Mustafa Kemal to decline the leadership of the Sivas congress because he was concerned that Mustafa Kemal might appear too autocratic. Democratic principles would be better served, Rauf argued, if the chairmanship were to rotate from time to time. Mustafa Kemal took the occasion to insist that the participation of a number of leaders would be unfortunate, for in all great enterprises it is the presence of a single leader that brings success.

Along with Kâzım and Ali Fuat, Rauf was at this period a key figure in the life of Mustafa Kemal. He had been minister of the navy at the end of World War I, and he had represented the Ottomans during the negotiations that led to the armistice signed in November 1918 at Mudros. He firmly believed that the British would keep their word. Later, he associated himself with Mustafa Kemal in Istanbul and by agreement did not accompany him to Samsun by ship, but traveled overland. He collected firsthand information that was invaluable to Mustafa Kemal, especially about the Greeks' landing at Izmir and their penetration inland. On his arrival in Ankara he joined Ali Fuat, and together they rendezvoused with Mustafa Kemal in Amasya. Rauf remained at the side of this new dynamic leader, but a silent rivalry began to grow between them.

A cool and quiet man, Rauf was widely traveled. He had studied engineering in the shipyards of Danzig and had had the opportunity to observe democratic societies personally. Emerging from World War I as the only military commander besides Mustafa Kemal whose record was unblemished by defeat, he no doubt felt entitled to the leadership of the nationalist cause in his own right. At the same time he must have sensed that Mustafa Kemal would not and, indeed, temperamentally could not share his supremacy with anyone. For the time being, Rauf accommodated himself to the situation.

Another man close to Mustafa Kemal at this juncture was Arif, one of the military men who had made the trip with him on the *Bandırma* from Istanbul to Samsun. The relationship between the two men was unusual. With Arif, Mustafa Kemal seemed to set aside his professional persona. He treated Arif as though he were a twin brother, pouring out to him his hopes and fears with very little restraint. Each man kept a revolver on his person at all times, and one would guard the other as he slept. Arif was a combination of friend and bodyguard. More important, he was a receptacle for Mustafa Kemal's discharge of emotional response about the new precariousness of his life.

Rounding out the group close to Mustafa Kemal in those early years of the nationalist struggle was Refet, another person who had accompanied him from Istanbul to Samsun. He was a highly cultivated gentleman of deceptive mien. A bundle of energy held together by just skin and bones, Refet was wondrously wily. Some doubted whether he could grasp the subtleties of Mustafa Kemal's mind, and others thought his allegiance to the nationalist cause stemmed from ambition rather than ideology, but his unquestioned bravery and cleverness were at Mustafa Kemal's disposal.

It was clear that Mustafa Kemal would need as many brave and loyal men as he could get. Out of the Erzurum congress had come the National Pact. The Sivas congress was now faced with the issue of mandates, more specifically an American mandate over territories inhabited by the Armenians, or one that might include the Arab provinces of the Ottoman Empire, or even an American mandate over Istanbul or Anatolia. The idea of mandates was beginning to capture more popular support. İsmet referred to it as the gilded pill of the moment.

In Istanbul, Halide Edib (Adıvar) was one of the Turkish patriots who favored the notion of an American mandate. She and others viewed a physical struggle against the occupying forces as hopeless, and they looked to an American mandate as a way to avoid the disintegration of the Turkish nation. Halide Edib wrote to Mustafa Kemal in Sivas to acquaint him with her views on the mandate issue. She arranged for Louis E. Browne to attend the Sivas congress as a correspondent for the Chicago *Daily News*. In reality, he represented Charles Crane, a member of the King-Crane Commission appointed by President Woodrow Wilson to investigate the mandate question and the local receptiveness to an

American mandate over the former Arab provinces of the Ottoman Empire.

Although he was opposed to the idea of a mandate, Mustafa Kemal nevertheless agreed to meet with Browne. He impressed on Browne his willingness to accept American aid that had only economic and social, but no political implications. Turkey could not publicly admit a need for foreign assistance in unraveling its ensnarled government.

In addition to the mandate issue, Mustafa Kemal had to deal with the plots of the Istanbul government to disrupt the work of the Sivas congress. One such plot involved Ali Galip, who had been sent to arrest Mustafa Kemal upon his arrival earlier in Sivas. Now, as governor of Erzincan, Ali Galip was ordered to proceed to Sivas and take Mustafa Kemal into custody with the aid of a large force of Kurds recruited for that purpose. He had with him a British major, E. W. C. Noel, who attempted to play a sort of Lawrence of Arabia role with respect to the Kurds.

Nationalist troops loyal to Mustafa Kemal managed to send Ali Galip scurrying for the mountains around Malatya. He left behind him documents that incriminated the sultan's government in this attempt to suppress Mustafa Kemal and the nationalist movement. Major Noel was escorted to the Ottoman frontier and allowed to rejoin the British forces. He provided living proof of Allied connivance in the sultan's attempts to rid himself of the nationalist opposition.

Mustafa Kemal seized upon this event as a means to undermine the grand vizierate of Damad Ferid Pasha. Much later, Mustafa Kemal, after producing some documents, reported:

> I am sure that these documents will leave no doubt at all in your minds that Ali Galip's enterprise was arranged with the consent of the Padishah (sultan), Ferid Pasha's Cabinet and foreigners. There is no doubt, also, about our action against the orginators of this treachery without distinction of persons. But it was necessary that we should avoid as far as possible such a direct frontal attack at this phase. It was wiser to concentrate our endeavors on a single point and not scatter our forces.
>
> Therefore, we chose Ferid Pasha's Cabinet alone as our target and pretended that we knew nothing about the complicity of the Padishah. Our theory was that the Sovereign had been deceived by the Cabinet and that he himself was in total ignorance of what was really going on.
>
> We wanted to give the impression that we were convinced that he would summarily punish those who had deceived him as soon as he was made clearly aware of the facts. [Atatürk 1927, p. 119]

Engaging in politics by wire, Mustafa Kemal spent hour upon hour in the Sivas telegraph office. The telegraph key was metaphorically the key to the heart of the nation. Mustafa Kemal sent out his message concerning the Ali Galip affair. Soon Istanbul was beseiged by thousands of telegrams demanding Damad Ferid's resignation. At one point Mustafa Kemal carried on a "conversation" by wire with one of Damad Ferid's representatives who tried unsuccessfully to persuade him to meet with the grand vizier and a third party designated by the sultan. Mustafa Kemal took the position with the grand vizier that his cabinet was coming between the people and the sultan. He warned Damad Ferid that the whole country would break relations with his "illegal" cabinet. At one point Istanbul refused to accept such strident messages. Unabashed, Mustafa Kemal warned that, unless his messages were put through, all telegraph lines between Istanbul and Anatolia would be cut.

In this protracted attack upon Damad Ferid, Mustafa Kemal maintained that he was acting as the president of the congress, but in fact he was acting on his own. Kâzım complained to him at one point that the communications and circulars sent from Sivas were sometimes drawn up in the name of the committee of the Sivas congress, but at other times only in Mustafa Kemal's name. Kâzım warned his friend that the communications signed in Mustafa Kemal's name were causing loyal but frank criticism even among those who loved and respected him most. Mustafa Kemal, however, had no time for democratic niceties, having firmly seized the reins in his own hands as a leader without the need of help or advice from others save in the implementation of his designs.

Success crowned Mustafa Kemal's offensive against Damad Ferid when the grand vizier and his government were toppled on 2 October. He was succeeded by a general who was more neutral in his political views. When Dr. Volkan interviewed some of the telegraph clerks who had played a part in this politcal war by telegraph, he could sense the pride they still felt in having helped Mustafa Kemal at that early point (and later on in the war of independence as well), even though they were old men by 1974 when the interviews were conducted. Some of them described having spent long hours or even days without sleep in the telegraph offices, which they protected with their own lives. People loyal to the sultan were still abroad in the land, and the telegraph offices were always in danger of attack by forces who opposed the nationalists.

Self-sacrifice on the part of these telegraph operators and others was beginning to show results. The new government that replaced the cabinet of Damad Ferid Pasha was led by Ali Riza Pasha, who was initially conciliatory. The Sivas congress had concluded its work on 11 September, demanding that new elections be held immediately for the chamber of deputies. Ali Riza consented, but insisted that the new parliament continue to meet in Istanbul, thus opposing Mustafa Kemal's wish that it convene somewhere in Anatolia.

Many of the differences between Mustafa Kemal and Ali Riza's government (Salih Pasha, minister of the navy, represented Ali Riza) were negotiated at Amasya. Although the trip to Amasya had gotten off to a shaky start (Oranlı 1967, p. 36), the rest of Mustafa Kemal's stay there was a huge personal triumph. Upon completion of the negotiations, Mustafa Kemal called for entertainment. The people of Amasya gathered in the town square for a demonstration of wrestling, which Mustafa Kemal especially enjoyed.[2] Other entertainments that evening included horse racing and *cirit*, a pololike game played on horseback. The festivities had been announced by town criers, whose exhortations had insured a splendid crowd. Groups playing the traditional *davul* and *zurna* (drum and flute) added to the excitement. Mustafa Kemal was at the center of everything that evening.

Some British officers and troops had accompanied the Ottoman naval minister to Amasya, where they were treated to a surprise of quite another sort. Some villagers armed with hunting rifles and sticks swooped in on the British detachment and "arrested" them. With their hands tied behind their backs, the British troops were paraded before Mustafa Kemal and his guests, including the British officers. The sight of this ragamuffin group of villagers with their captives had a tragicomic aspect to it and was thoroughly lacking in dignity. Intended as a special treat for Mustafa Kemal, it must have angered him, as he proceeded to free the "arrested" soldiers. Even this absurdity could not diminish the triumph Mustafa Kemal experienced at Amasya. On the return journey, according to his orderly (Oranlı 1967, p. 40), Mustafa Kemal began to sing the song of the nationalist cause, "The mist has fallen on top of the mountain," as snow fell on his Sivas-bound party.

Despite all his hectoring, Mustafa Kemal was unsuccessful in winning one of his major points. He harbored a deep personal distrust of and distaste for Istanbul and wanted the new parliament to meet in Anatolia. The grand vizier's insistence on Istanbul paradoxically had much support among Mustafa Kemal's closest advisers. Kâzım, Rauf, and Ali Fuat believed that the Allies would probably suppress the parliament, and that would then serve as a pretext for the nationalists to convene a new parliament in Anatolia. In the end, Mustafa Kemal went along. He was elected a deputy from Erzurum, but, fearing that the government would not respect his parliamentary immunity, he refused to attend the sessions

[2]Wrestling is the Turkish national sport and, as president of the republic of Turkey, Atatürk would often ask the soldiers assigned to protect the presidential palace to wrestle and sometimes even wrestled with them.

in Istanbul. In an attempt at reconciliation, the new government restored his rank and decorations to him.

Within seven months of landing at Samsun, Mustafa Kemal was able to bring down the Damad Ferid Pasha government that had dismissed him from the army. He was instrumental in replacing it with a new government that felt compelled to give him back the rank and status as military hero that was so meaningful to him. All of this was effected right under the noses of the Allies. Although the Allied high commissioners in Istanbul knew something of what was taking place in Anatolia, they sensed no danger from the nationalist Turks. They thought that the Greeks in and around Izmir were being harassed by a group of Turkish bandits rather than by any organized Turkish army. It was felt that the Allies could ensure victory for the Greek forces any time they wished, although after the devastation wrought by World War I there was a longing among the Allied powers for peace.

The signing of the Treaty of Versailles on 28 June 1919 did not, however, mean an end to the peacemaking process. The Council of Four was replaced by the Council of Heads of Delegations. They continued to wrestle with the problems of the Middle Eastern settlement which had been intensified by the growing victory of the Bolsheviks in Russia, the onset of Woodrow Wilson's illness, and America's disenchantment with the notion of assuming any mandate over any former Ottoman domains.

Peacemaking could proceed without the United States, which had never declared war on the Ottoman Empire. Strictly speaking, therefore, the United States need not sign any peace treaty with Turkey. As matters dragged on, Lloyd George sought an accommodation with the French that would reduce the British commitment in Anatolia. In September 1919 an Anglo-French agreement was reached by which France was promised Syria and Cilicia. In return, the French gave up their interests in the area of Mosul and in Kurdistan as well. This left the French less interested in the problems of the Armenians, while the Kurds continued to concern the British. Mustafa Kemal had indirectly demonstrated his displeasure with British meddling in the affairs of the Kurds, who inhabited important areas of southeastern Anatolia, when troops loyal to him captured Major Noel and escorted him to the frontier. The French in Cilicia would soon experience his wrath over their continued presence on Turkish soil.

14

The Sun Shines over Anatolia

CONSCIOUS OF SECURITY PROBLEMS MORE THAN EVER BEFORE, MUSTAFA Kemal realized that the time had come to relocate the center of his activities. Ankara, though he had never seen it, had much to recommend it. Its people were known to be fully committed to the nationalist cause. Communications were excellent, enhanced by Ankara's location on a main rail line. In addition, Ankara was far enough inland to be reasonably protected from whatever attack might originate from either Istanbul or the Black Sea area, while at the same time it was fairly centrally located with respect to the anticipated military action.

On 22 December the three-car caravan of Mustafa Kemal and his entourage set out from Sivas in the direction of Ankara. Their departure was made possible by the timely arrangement of a bank loan on that very morning. Spirited and enthusiastic as this small band was, their financial situation was in a shambles. Economics was not one of Mustafa Kemal's strong points, but somehow he had faith that his needs and those of his followers would be met. This attitude was in accord with the basic structure of his personality.

En route to Ankara, the group was met with a tumultuous reception in Kırşehir. There was a candlelight procession, with speeches and merry-making. Swept up in the emotions of the occasion, Mustafa Kemal paraphrased a bit of poetry from Namık Kemal, "A Kemal [Namık] who came from the midst of this nation said: 'The enemy put his knife at the throat of the country, there is no one to save the ill-fated mother.' Again a Kemal [Mustafa] coming from the heart of this nation says: 'The enemy put his knife at the throat of the country, there is someone to save the ill-fated mother.' "[1] Evocation of the twin themes of savior and an ill-fated mother apparently resonated deep within Mustafa Kemal as he traveled to the city that would become the center from which he would realize both these objectives.

As Mustafa Kemal's car approached the eastern outskirts of Ankara on 27 December, he ordered his driver to stop so that he could gaze on the city for the first time. His traveling companions included Rauf, several other members of the representative committee from the Sivas congress,

[1]Kinross 1965, p. 330. See Atatürk 1952, pp. 3–4, for Kırşehir speech.

his orderly, and his military doctor, Refik Saydam, who always accompanied him because of his physical problems. The party was met at the outskirts by Ali Fuat, then headquartered in Ankara. On that day near the end of December the nearby mountains were covered with snow, but the sky was clear and the sun shone radiantly.

Both Mustafa Kemal and the people of Ankara unconsciously perceived the symbolic identification of the hero of Gallipoli with the sun. He was the warming, rising sun that would dispel the mists. It was a case of remarkable correspondence between a leader's self-image as a savior and the perception of him as such by the masses. Two days after Mustafa Kemal's arrival in Ankara, the provincial newspaper commented that:

> The dawn of this daylight-creating sun took place in Erzurum. Glistening in Sivas, it illuminated the nation. Every place opened its heart and soul to that sun of reality. The Turkish world was turned entirely into a single mass of radiance. [Aydemir 1969, vol. 2, p. 201]

Recently, Isaiah Berlin has commented on this close association between charisma and light:

> the wounds inflicted upon one society by another, since time immemorial, have not in all cases led to a national response. For that, something more is needed—namely, a new vision of light with which the wounded society, or the classes or groups which have been displaced by a political and social change, can identify themselves, around which they can gather and attempt to restore their collective life. [Berlin 1979, p. 353]

The wounded people of Anatolia recognized Mustafa Kemal as the catalyst of this new vision—the charismatic leader.

From 27 December onward, the history of Mustafa Kemal, the struggle of the Turkish nation, and the fate of Ankara were intertwined. It can be said that present-day Ankara is Mustafa Kemal's creation. All his reasons for going to Ankara cannot be known, but Sivas suffered from being too much to the east. Midway between Ankara and Erzurum, Sivas was not close enough to where Mustafa Kemal expected the action to center. He could move more to the west and leave the eastern section in the competent hands of Kâzım. Moreover, Mustafa Kemal welcomed the opportunity to put some distance between himself and Kâzım. He was uneasy about the competitiveness he sensed in Kâzım who had questioned his authority with respect to the transmission of a number of telegrams signed only by Mustafa Kemal and not by the representative committee. The desire to be away from Kâzım was unconscious, but it nevertheless influenced his decision to leave Sivas for the more westerly city of Ankara.

On the conscious level he explained later (Atatürk 1927, p. 290) that he had gone there to be as close as possible to the dangers that threatened—an invasion by the Greeks or the sultan and whatever he represented in Istanbul. Mustafa Kemal felt that those who were responsible for the organization and execution of any plan that involved danger should themselves be in the actual danger zone. Ankara, therefore, was a suitable place for him.

With the move to Ankara, Mustafa Kemal drew closer to Ali Fuat as his staunchest supporter. Although the government in Istanbul had stripped Ali Fuat of his official position as commander of the Twentieth Army Corps and had replaced him with an acting chief, he continued to exercise practical authority over all troops between Ankara and Istanbul. His support would be crucial in both the military and the political arenas.

Ankara is situated in a hollow ringed by mountains that command the Anatolian Plateau. Today the population is about two million, and the city is still growing. The texture of Turkey's major cities has been altered greatly over the past two and a half decades by the migration of rural peoples into urban areas, and Ankara is no exception. Ankara's outlying districts are now covered with settlements called *gece kondu*, which means "built overnight" and refers to the dwellings hastily put together by migrant peasants. Starting out as communities of shacks without any facilities, these neighborhoods have now been stabilized by the extension of water, electricity, and other amenities to them. In such neighborhoods one sees men dressed in dark baggy pants, and women wearing sweaters, coats, and scarves through all the seasons, summer included. But to the traveler who reaches the center of the city, now a symbol of Atatürk modernization miracle, a different prospect presents itself from these jerry-built peripheral neighborhoods. The heart of Ankara is a westernized city not very different from many European capitals, with their spacious boulevards, stately buildings, and embassy rows. On a central hillside there is an impressive mausoleum in which Atatürk's body is buried. It is a fitting resting place for Turkey's savior.

When Mustafa Kemal first saw Ankara, its most impressive feature was the citadel reconstructed several times by the Byzantines and often repaired by the Seljuk Turks, who had taken the city about 1073. The Ottomans had been in possession of Ankara since 1354. In 1919 the population of Ankara and the immediately surrounding area was about twenty thousand. In addition to the Turkish quarters of the city there was a Jewish section, and the Armenian quarter was swept by fire in 1915. As a site, Ankara had been continuously inhabited for over 4,000 years. It is said that Alexander the Great had stopped there, or nearby, on his way east.

Despite its long and proud history, Ankara shared in the decline common to Ottoman Anatolian cities. Although it boasted a few inns like those still seen in small Anatolian towns today, it had nothing that could be called a hotel or restaurant when Mustafa Kemal arrived. The *kervansarays*, "inns," were caricatures of their former glory. In the early twentieth century they were places where horses could be tied up or the occasional automobile could be parked; the typical surrounding two-story building had sleeping quarters upstairs, with a coffeehouse or place for trade below, and only rudimentary toilet facilities.

Such squalor was not for Mustafa Kemal. He was taken to a two-story building on the far side of the city that housed an agricultural school. From there he could see the flocks of famed Angora goats grazing at the city limits. Their shepherds looked like stately scarecrows in their traditional garb, and they were accompanied by powerful Turkish sheep dogs with metal spikes in their collars to protect them from the attack of wolves.

As he made his way to his lodgings through the streets of Ankara, Mustafa Kemal was mobbed by the throngs who had come to welcome him and to be warmed by this new sun. Even then he had become what psychoanalysts call a "transference figure"—someone who is invested with exaggerated magical powers and represents to his followers what they yearn to see in him, being a target of projected childhood memories of omnipotent parental figures. The charismatic personality offers followers a combination of masculine and feminine qualities (Abse and Jessner 1961), and thus reflects a parent of either sex, and responds totally to the emotional needs of the group. The fiercely manly Mustafa Kemal was no exception, having small, almost dainty hands and feet and a voice that had a suggestion of femininity. He was intensely interested in his personal appearance, taking great pains with it as his mother had done during his childhood. On the other hand, he took the lead aggressively, tacitly commanding others to follow him. Although he was of medium height (5 feet, 9 inches), he always managed to be conspicuous in any group and to seem taller than average. His blond hair, unusual in a Turk, caught the sunlight. He was the "father sun" who could burn the enemies of one's childhood, but he was also the "mother sun" who could warm and soothe the child that remains within everyone. It was said that one could no more look directly into his blue eyes than one could gaze into the sun without blinking.

During his research in Turkey, Dr. Volkan came across several people who had on occasion met Atatürk in group situations where the excitement and group regression were contagious. They reported being unable to look him directly in the eye. A physician suggested to Dr. Volkan that Atatürk probably had a slight strabismus (Göksel 1975) and that this may have been the "kernel of truth" behind the myth that trying to gaze into his eyes gave one an odd feeling. Atatürk must have been aware of some deviation, for later in his life when photographs of him were taken, he would insist on offering his "good" profile.

Even at this early period Mustafa Kemal followed the pattern typical of a charismatic leader. For example, he was both intimidating and encouraging, shy and aggressive, alternating rapidly between these opposing approaches to people. Abse and Ulman have written on this characteristic of the leader: "His charm is based on his inspiring both awe and love, and occasional glimpses of brutality only heighten it. The man of action's genius for leadership is a two-faced thing, as the close associates of any great leader can often testify" (Abse and Ulman 1977, p. 41).

As Mustafa Kemal was adjusting to his new environment on the outskirts of Ankara, the newly elected parliament was preparing to open its first session in Istanbul. The majority of its members now belonged to the nationalist movement. Rauf went to Istanbul to organize the new members of the Ottoman parliament into giving official approval to the principles accepted by the congresses of Erzurum and Sivas. From the start of January 1920 a number of deputies began making their way to Ankara to confer with Mustafa Kemal prior to the opening of parliament. Not all the deputies trusted him, but they continued to arrive, thereby putting the dusty little city in the middle of the Anatolian Plateau on the political map. Mustafa Kemal urged the nationalist members to elect him president of the parliament. He had no intention of going to Istanbul, for it would be too dangerous, but he wanted influence.

Parliament's opening on 11 January 1920 placed Mustafa Kemal in a peculiar situation. He himself had urged the new elections, but now that they had taken place and the new parliament was in session, the representative committee, elected by the Sivas congress and headed by Mustafa Kemal, no longer had any reason to exist. If he were to dissolve the representative committee, he might lose influence by staying in Ankara while the action was going on in Istanbul. He was also under some pressure from others to disband the committee. On 23 Feburary Kâzım wired him to leave everything to parliament. Although parliament publicly recognized the validity of the basic principles announced in Erzurum and Sivas, Mustafa Kemal had no intention of giving up his representative committee. He knew that the Greeks had landed more troops in Izmir during mid-Feburary, and early in March he learned from İsmet, who was still working in the war ministry in Istanbul, that the British might soon take over the Ottoman government. Clinging to his own "government" in Ankara, Mustafa Kemal predicted that things would turn sour in Istanbul. He did not have long to wait to see his prophecy realized.

Woodrow Wilson's illness delayed the talks planned among the Allies to deal with the Ottoman issue, but Lord Curzon kept urging that a draft of a Turkish peace treaty be prepared. More and more Allied vessels put in at Istanbul, but there were also signs of softening in the French view of the situation in Anatolia. Parisian papers began to take a more sympathetic view of the nationalist movement led by Mustafa Kemal. Accordingly, he decided to press the French in hopes that they might then evacuate Anatolia. A nationalist guerrilla band reinforced by some Turkish gendarmes attacked the French-occupied city of Maraş, 450 kilometers south of Sivas. Armenian forces assisted the French in their defense of Maraş, and the Turkish forces set fire to the Armenian quarter of the city. The bloodshed that ensued lasted for three weeks, ending with the French in retreat from the city. The day after withdrawing from Maraş, the French began to evacuate other Anatolian cities. By the end of May they had no choice but to seek an armistice with the nationalist Turks and sent a delegation to Ankara.

Cooperation among the Allies in Istanbul was getting more difficult. The Italians also were becoming more open in their support of Mustafa Kemal and the nationalist cause. Antagonistic to the imperial concerns of Greece, the Italians acted in concert with Turkish bands seeking to liberate arms from important caches. These developments led the British to take more drastic measures. They prepared to effect a complete occupation of Istanbul, which would include the arrest of deputies to the parliament. When news of this plan reached Ankara, Mustafa Kemal urged the members of parliament to leave Istanbul for Ankara.

On 6 March the British began to occupy Ottoman government buildings in Istanbul. They met with little resistance as they completed their occupation of the Ottoman capital. A line from the central telegraph office in Istanbul kept Mustafa Kemal informed until it was put out of commission by the British. Many deputies were arrested, including Rauf. It is difficult to know why Rauf, whose friends attempted to persuade him to escape, remained behind to be arrested. With other leading deputies he was packed off to internment on Malta while Istanbul was placed under martial law. In retaliation, Mustafa Kemal ordered the arrest of all British officers in Anatolia.

Two days after Rauf's arrest the depleted Ottoman parliament met again. There was pandemonium. Salih Pasha, the grand vizier who had replaced Ali Riza Pasha, refused to disavow Mustafa Kemal, as requested by the Allies. He resigned in protest. This allowed the sultan to bring Damad Ferid Pasha back to the grand vizierate. The first act of his new government was to dissolve what would prove to be the last Ottoman parliament. Relying upon Allied support, Damad Ferid then initiated what he hoped would be an all-out campaign against Mustafa Kemal and the nationalists. It was, instead, the initiation of a civil war in which one of the opening salvos was a declaration by prominent Ottoman religious leaders that Mustafa Kemal and his associates were infidels who should be shot on sight.

What the British occupation of Istanbul succeeded in doing was to step up the stream of Turks heading for Ankara to join Mustafa Kemal and the resistance. What had been a severe housing problem in Ankara was eased as soon as Jewish and other minority homeowners began to offer rooms to Muslim Turks arriving in the city. Before long, the newcomers outnumbered the natives. By the time of the first official census in 1927, Ankara's population had burgeoned to over seventy thousand, almost four times the number at the start of 1920.

Among those who arrived in Ankara was İsmet, who came this time to stay. Mustafa Kemal's orderly, Ali, recalled İsmet's welcome appearance in Ankara (Oranlı 1967, pp. 53–54). Informed that a man named İsmet had just arrived and was asking to see Mustafa Kemal, the orderly went outside to find a man dressed as a peasant, sitting under a tree, unshaven and with unkempt hair. When İsmet identified himself, the orderly admitted him to the building after searching him for weapons. When Mustafa Kemal clasped İsmet to his chest with great pleasure, the orderly realized that this was an important person. There was some difficulty in finding suitable clothing for İsmet, for there were no ready-made clothes available in the marketplace. The orderly saved the day by altering a pair of military trousers Mustafa Kemal had given him. He brought them out for İsmet, and someone else found him a jacket.

With the dissolution of the last Ottoman parliament in Istanbul it was time to summon a new one. Mustafa Kemal took great care to legalize his position as the country's leader. He proved to have as uncanny an ability at legal matters as he had in military affairs, and he was able to achieve legal entitlement to the position he so passionately wanted.

Among the escapees to Ankara was the last president of the chamber of deputies. He contended that the parliament had been dissolved illegally. That was enough reason for Mustafa Kemal to declare that the constitution had been violated and to call for the establishment of a new parliament. This one, naturally, would be under the control of the nationalists in Ankara.

Elections were held and a new parliament, called the Grand National Assembly, convened in Ankara on 23 April 1920. It had 190 newly elected deputies, representing nationalist resistance groups from all over the country. They were joined by some 100 former members of the old parliament who had managed to avoid the Allied dragnet and reach Ankara. Mustafa Kemal was elected president of the Grand National Assembly, and a parliamentary commission was organized to prepare a new constitution, which was enacted on 20 January 1921.

Mustafa Kemal's superiority lay in the way he could transform into reality the demand of his personality organization that he become preeminent. Time and again he was able to test the borders of the reality principle and refrain from acting impulsively to his detriment. He found it acceptable to act on intuition, but not on impulse. Whenever his intuition or the demands of his personality organization crossed the border of the reality principle, as they did on occasion when he claimed leadership, he was able to maneuver in such a manner that the limitations of the real world were expanded to meet his needs. This adaptability made him a true leader. Kâzım, Ali Fuat, or other key figures would never dare to act as Mustafa Kemal did; even had they dared, they lacked the necessary flexibility.

Only a few short months after Mustafa Kemal had arrived in Ankara, the city became, for all practical purposes, the capital of the nationalist movement. As Mustafa Kemal's stronghold, it became the focus of attention for the Turks and the Allies as well. The sun had indeed begun to shine over Anatolia, but some lingering mist still threatened to turn into black clouds.

15

Life in Ankara during the Civil Wars

Mustafa Kemal's headquarters in the agricultural school on the outskirts of the city continued to serve as the nerve center of the new Ankara. His male secretary occupied a room on the first floor next to a telegraph center installed as the point of convergence for a web of such offices throughout Turkish territory. Nationalist telegraphers maintained a round-the-clock vigil in their offices, becoming, in effect, a soldiery of paramount importance to the nationalist cause.

Mustafa Kemal's personal quarters were on the second floor. There he lived and worked in spartan surroundings with only a couch, a desk, a few armchairs, and a wood-burning stove. There was no electricity. When the sun went down, light was provided by lanterns or by the moon.

Another occupant of the building was Mustafa Kemal's personal physician who was on twenty-four-hour call to look after the pasha's physical condition. Equally in need of constant care were the chronically empty nationalist coffers. The short supply of money had its impact on life in that building. Meals were served cafeteria-style for all, and the menu usually included boiled dried beans or chick peas dressed with tomato sauce and served over a pilaf of cracked wheat (bulgur), with bits of meat when the budget permitted. Grapes boiled in sweetened water were occasionally offered for dessert. Mustafa Kemal took a fancy to this diet and adhered to it later, preferring this simple meal to more elaborate ones he would soon be able to afford. He smoked heavily and drank a great deal of Turkish coffee, so much that throughout the days of the nationalist struggle his orderly was always expected to carry a *cezve*, a small pot in which Turkish coffee is prepared. During this period Mustafa Kemal appears to have refrained from the consumption of alcohol.

Into this spare environment of hard work and no amenities, there was interjected one night an even harsher bit of reality. A retired officer who was assisting in smuggling arms from various parts of the country, but especially from the poorly guarded caches in and around Istanbul, brought news from the capital. A military court on 11 May had condemned Mustafa Kemal and five others to death. That death sentence was signed by Damad Ferid and approved by the sultan himself on 24 May. Moreover, the sentence had been upheld by a *fetva* (religious opinion) issued by the *şeyh-ül-islam*, the chief religious dignitary of the

Ottoman Empire. It thus became the religious duty of any Muslim to kill Mustafa Kemal on sight, as well as those condemned with him. That list included Ali Fuat and Halide Edib. She and her husband were among the newcomers to Ankara. On 6 June İsmet and a few others were added to the list of those whose execution would guarantee a place in heaven to their executioner.

Halide Edib had achieved overnight prominence through her emotional speeches given at meetings in Istanbul that followed news of the Greek landings at Izmir. Her memoirs (Adıvar 1928) of those crucial days have secured her a permanent place in the historiography of that period. In later life she became a novelist and one of Turkey's foremost literary figures. She and her second husband, Dr. A. Adnan (Adıvar), had made their way to Ankara from Istanbul, crossing the Bosporus disguised as an old *hoca* (Muslim priest) and his wife. They had eluded the Allies and Greek bandits as they traversed the 450 kilometers to Ankara. Adnan had at one time been a professor at the medical school in Istanbul, having had some medical training in Berlin. He had known Enver during his rise to fame as leader of the Committee of Union and Progress. During the war Adnan had served as a Red Cross officer, traveling widely in that capacity. He also had a strong interest in the history of Ottoman science.

Recollections from Dr. Adnan and Halide Edib were given by Dr. Fuat Göksel, who told them to Dr. Volkan in interviews in September 1975 (Göksel 1975). At that time, Dr. Göksel was professor of psychiatry in the medical school of the University of Ankara.[1] In 1955 he had been assigned to care for Dr. Adnan for two months, day and night, during his terminal illness. Along with Halide Edib, he had been at Dr. Adnan's side, first in a university hospital and then in the couple's home, until Dr. Adnan's death. During all that time, Rauf was a daily visitor. Ali Fuat visited on several occasions, as did Refet. Struck by Dr. Göksel's inquiring mind, Dr. Adnan talked with him at considerable length about his experiences with Mustafa Kemal. Halide Edib was also generous with her reminiscences.

Dr. Adnan made special mention of an incident connected with his first meeting with Mustafa Kemal in 1912. He had been on a mission to inform Fethi about Enver's wish to overthrow the Ottoman government. Both men were members of the Committee of Union and Progress. As they met aboard a ship, Dr. Adnan noticed a young lieutenant with blond hair and blue eyes whom Fethi introduced as Mustafa Kemal, saying, "He is one of us. You can speak freely." When Adnan reported Enver's plans, Mustafa Kemal responded nervously, saying, "All right, all right," in

[1]Later Fuat Göksel became professor of the history of medicine in the same medical school.

No time to rest. Mustafa Kemal and part of his retinue, including Halide Edib, at Gebze station.

English, and then, in Turkish, "Very appropriate." It struck Dr. Adnan disagreeably that this young man was breaking tradition in preempting the exchange. Protocol demanded that Fethi, who outranked him, should respond first. Adnan's first impression of Mustafa Kemal, accordingly, was of a brash upstart. In turn, Mustafa Kemal's first impression of Adnan was of a conspirator. This initial standoff may have had something to do with the ambivalence that characterized their later relationship.

Mustafa Kemal met Adnan and his wife at the train upon their arrival in Ankara from Istanbul. He helped Halide Edib descend from the train. Later, she recalled being surprised by this man who was so different from the others in the welcoming party.

> A vast crowd, which looked somber in the shadow of the approaching night, and a slender gray figure which merged into the dim Angora twilight met my gaze. The gray figure moved quickly toward the train, pulling his gloves off. His face, with its large-cornered kalpak, had become indistinct and colorless in the dusk. . . .
>
> The door of our compartment opened suddenly and Mustafa Kemal Pasha's hand reached up to help me down the step. In that light his hand was the only part of him I could see distinctly, and it is that part of him which is physically most characteristic of the whole man. It is a narrow and faultlessly shaped hand, with very slender fingers and a skin which nothing darkens or wrinkles. Although it is not effeminate, one would not expect it to be a man's hand. . . . It seemed to me that the merciless hunting of the human tiger in Turkey had its answer in this hand. It differed from the large broad hand of the fighting Turk in its highly strung nervous tension, its readiness to spring and grip its oppressor by the throat.
>
> "Welcome, Hanum Effendi," he said in a low voice, . . . after inquiring after our health. [Adıvar 1928, p. 127]

During the War of Independence she joined the army,[2] becoming a sergeant, and continued to record her observations of what was going on and of the leaders who were bringing about so much change.

[2]Although Halide Edib joined the army and was vital to the cause because of her ability to translate from many languages and was even regarded by Mustafa Kemal as a good luck charm whose presence he often requested at the front, she never personally used a weapon in combat. In fact, she had an abhorrence for violence and the infliction of physical pain on other human beings, even if administered as punishment or revenge. Mustafa Kemal saw this as her "supreme weakness" and often criticized her to others for it. Once a deputy reported to her, "Pasha deplores your weak heart, which cannot bear violence," to which she replied, "What Pasha calls weakness is my supreme strength. When the general trend of the world is for violence, it does not need courage to promote it—to stand against it alone is strength" (Adıvar 1928, p. 357).

Halide Edib's psychological insight is readily apparent in her writings, and her observations on Mustafa Kemal can be reinterpreted by psychoanalysts today as evidence of his use of the mechanism of splitting. Narcissistic persons use this defensive mechanism to keep separate and apart constellations of opposite character (e.g., grandiosity versus dependency).[3] By splitting, Mustafa Kemal could champion one thing for a time, if it seemed to maintain the cohesiveness of his grandiosity and to help him avoid anxiety; then, he could champion something exactly the opposite if it seemed useful to do so.

Halide Edib had observed this penchant for splitting in Mustafa Kemal's personality, but she could only describe it without giving it a name. She wrote, "his mind is two-sided, like a lighthouse lantern. Sometimes it flashes and shows you what it wants you to see with almost blinding clearness; sometimes it wanders and gets itself lost in the dark. . . . And I thought to myself: 'This man is either hopelessly confused or too complicated to be understood at once.' I wanted to believe the latter" (Adıvar 1928, pp. 128–29). She concluded that Mustafa Kemal seemed to have no firm convictions whatsoever, but was able to espouse one course and then another. He invested in whatever line he adopted the same amount of energy as long as he thought that what he currently espoused would benefit him and his cause. He treated those around him in the same manner, accepting them when they served his purpose and dropping them for others, often very different, who might be more useful to him.

During these early days in Ankara Mustafa Kemal initiated his habit of gathering people around a table during the night hours for discussions which he himself would dominate. Cynical for a moment, then amusing, and then boringly earnest, even sometimes shy, he charismatically engaged his audience while uncannily assessing the advice given him.[4] Although he believed in the superiority of his own ideas, he was capable of synthesizing what he learned from others into some reality-oriented conclusion that was both acceptable and practical. He continued to follow

[3]The mechanism of splitting is not seen, for practical purposes, in the repertoire of defenses of the neurotic person who instead simply represses from consciousness to his unconscious the unacceptable aspect of opposing elements of his dominant personality. The repressed part later may manifest itself in symptom formation.

[4]Halide Edib's description of Mustafa Kemal at his dining table is as follows: "The evening meals were more sociable and pleasant. One of the biggest rooms downstairs was turned into a dining-room, and there we all dined round an enormous horseshoe table. It was then that every one relaxed and talked of past experiences. Mustafa Kemal Pasha can be a brilliant talker at times, and he was at his best at those meals. Throughout his anecdotes and reminiscences of past life ran a dominant vein of bitter irony at the expense of many well-known personalities. He spared no name. And, as the evening passed, I began to wonder vaguely whether there was any well-known man of whom Mustafa Kemal Pasha had something good to say" (Adıvar 1928, p. 136).

this round table way of pounding out a course of action even when he became president. He often used İsmet to buffer his grandiosity. İsmet's slow, gentle, and cautious manner made him the perfect person to serve as a bridge between the leader and the others.[5]

Intuitively, Mustafa Kemal had grasped his need for İsmet, but other leading figures in the coterie felt resentment. When the Grand National Assembly convened, Mustafa Kemal's choice of İsmet as chief of staff met with resistance. He was younger than Kâzım, Ali Fuat, and Refet. All of them were already generals and had given Mustafa Kemal critical support at the inception of the nationalist undertaking in Anatolia. They failed to recognize what Mustafa Kemal knew, albeit unconsciously, that, by placing İsmet ahead of them, he acknowledged the congeniality of İsmet's personality and affirmed his doubts that any of the other three could function unthreateningly as an extension of himself.

It was Arif, however, who was most jealous of İsmet's selection. The "twin brother" had been bypassed. Hanns Froembgen gives more information on this in his biography of Mustafa Kemal:

> Mustafa slept only when Arif was there to keep guard over him. At nightfall Arif settled down to sleep for a few hours, while Mustafa rose and watched over him. When the chilly hours of dawn approached, Mustafa again retired to bed and Arif, with a loaded revolver in his hand, again stood guard. He first tasted each dish of food and each drink before passing it on to his friend. When Mustafa's fever rose (at that time he was suffering from attacks of malaria, an illness from which many in the district of Ankara suffered), he placed the tablets between his parched lips, until he was fit enough to stand up and apply himself to his work. Wherever he went he was guarded by Arif, whose suspicious eyes were everywhere. [Froembgen 1937, pp. 151–52]

Although one cannot be sure whether Froembgen, who wrote his study in the 1930s, exaggerated the intensity of the relationship between the two men, his description gives evidence of the spirit of "twinship" they

[5]Halide Edib described her first impressions of Colonel İsmet: "He had a wistful dark face with two wondering childish eyes. He had the charm of very simple and Old World Turkish manners, and a modest way of talking the most expressive and colloquial Turkish. His eyes were thoughtful and had a distant look til he began to speak; but then one had the flattering impression that he was giving one his whole attention. He was slightly deaf and bent his head forward to listen" (Adıvar 1928, pp. 131–32). At the dinner table İsmet differed from Mustafa Kemal: "In contrast to the strong satire of Mustafa Kemal Pasha, Colonel İsmet had a subtle humor which never became bitter, and the gentle innuendoes of his very able appreciations of character made his conversations a delight" (Adıvar 1928, p. 136).

shared. Halide Edib, who was a witness to these events, confirms this twinship as she observed the two men together: "He (Arif) leaned over the pasha's shoulder, his face looking like that of a twin brother" (Adıvar 1928, p. 292). Arif was far from being a sophisticate, as might be gathered from his habit of keeping a pet bear, Gray Boy, with which he wrestled. It is interesting that Mustafa Kemal was able to relate to Arif and yet keep this relationship remote from his serious association with men of worldly influence. He refrained from contaminating his professional activities with regressed behavior such as he enjoyed with Arif. It must have been small consolation for Arif to see so intimately one of Mustafa Kemal's most dominant (and hurtful) traits. He could be personally close to a man, but he was always able to split his allegiances and turn away from a former confidant when this served his interests in both the real and psychological senses. To Mustafa Kemal, Arif and his group were drinking companions in whose company he was able to feel superior. With İsmet and that group, he could put on another face and relate to them soberly as champions of a common cause. Even when he became president, he continued to surround himself with rough cronies as well as with statesmen or scholars, adapting himself to the expectations of each group, and keeping them apart.

Additional evidence of Mustafa Kemal's chameleonic nature is provided by the incident involving Fevzi Pasha's defection to the nationalist cause.[6] While Mustafa Kemal headed the nationalist movement in Anatolia, Fevzi was the minister of war in the Ottoman government. During World War I he had followed Mustafa Kemal to Gallipoli, and they knew each other on the eastern front. When Mustafa Kemal rejected the command of the Seventh Army, Fevzi Pasha assumed it. He was clearly against the nationalist movement in Anatolia at the time of the Sivas congress, and when the Grand National Assembly convened in Ankara, he still gave no indication of any change of heart. A few nights after the opening of the assembly, however, he unexpectedly appeared at Ali Fuat's headquarters between Istanbul and Ankara. Ali Fuat later recalled commenting to his distinguished caller, "A mountain doesn't come to another mountain, but a man comes to another man" (Cebesoy 1953, vol. 1, p. 368). When Fevzi Pasha's arrival at Ali Fuat's headquarters was reported to Mustafa Kemal, he sent a wire to Ali Fuat, saying harshly that he had no inclination to see Fevzi. Nonetheless, Ali Fuat tactfully arranged for Fevzi to join the group. When Fevzi arrived at Ankara on 27 April, he was met at the station by Mustafa Kemal and deputies from the assembly, accompanied by a military band.

[6]Fevzi Pasha later was known as Field Marshal Fevzi Çakmak. He was born in 1876 in Istanbul.

Fevzi was then escorted to the Grand National Assembly, where he was introduced in glowing terms by Mustafa Kemal. Having recently fiercely opposed Fevzi, Mustafa Kemal now espoused him, knowing that he could "use" this important man who had been the Ottoman minister of war only fifteen days earlier. Welcoming Fevzi gave Mustafa Kemal an opportunity to humiliate the Istanbul government through this change of allegiance. Increasing the value of the defection was the fact that Fevzi was a devout Muslim. His influence, therefore, reached not only into the military and the bureaucracy, but into the religious sector as well.

After Mustafa Kemal concluded his welcoming address, Fevzi took the podium and spoke of the confusion in Istanbul. He blamed the British for trying to turn Turk against Turk without "one English soldier even having a nosebleed." "I pray to God," he exclaimed, "that the British will fail again, as at Çanakkale [Gallipoli]" (Aydemir 1969, vol. 2, p. 261). With its graceful reference to Mustafa Kemal's triumph there, it is not surprising that his speech was ordered printed and distributed throughout Anatolia. Fevzi was then elected minister of national defense on 3 May, thus ranking second only to Mustafa Kemal. On 25 May the sultan added the name of Fevzi Pasha to the list of those condemned to death.

A strong military presence was needed, for at this time the number of uprisings in Anatolia escalated in the wake of the collapse of the last Ottoman parliament. It has been estimated that in the early 1920s there were sixty such uprisings, some having nationalist aims, some in support of the sultan, and others seeking economic gain. The government in Istanbul created an extraordinary Anatolian inspectorate and a new security army to quell this unrest, but also to put down the nationalists. With the help of the British this army was enlarged and took the name of the Caliphal Army. At first it might appear that Anatolia was caught up in a civil war, but it would be better to characterize the situation as a series of skirmishes engaged in by a number of private armies.

One of the leading "private armies" was the Green Army (*Yeşil Ordu*), originally organized early in 1920, largely by former members of the Committee of Union and Progress. Initially, they enjoyed the support of Mustafa Kemal, who felt they might be useful to the nationalist cause. The leaders of the Green Army had some notion of unifying the Islamic world and establishing therein a socialist union modeled on recent developments in Russia. The organization soon came to include people opposed to Mustafa Kemal, and by late in 1921 he saw to the dissolution of the Green Army, but some of its elements remained intact.

Migrations of Circassians from the Caucasus Mountains into Anatolia during the mid-nineteenth century provided the background for the emergence at this time of two Circassian private armies. One was led by an elderly man named Anzavur, whose base was south of the Sea of Marmara, where Circassians had settled. The other army was led by Çerkes Etem (Etem the Circassian). He received assistance from the nationalists in getting rid of Anzavur's army, which was still in existence at the time of the Sivas congress. Etem worked for nationalist goals at the outset, but later became a problem for Mustafa Kemal.

Anatolia also saw a number of communist movements. Soon after Mustafa Kemal had landed at Samsun, he was visited by a representative of Russia and later by an agent for the United States. Opposed to the communists on principle, Mustafa Kemal nevertheless realized his need for their help. Most of the arms used in the war of independence would come from Russia. In 1920 the Turkish communists joined with the old Union and Progress group to form the People's Communist party. Subsequently, another communist party was formed with Mustafa Kemal's blessings and somewhat under his control, unlike the first. It was said that the establishment of the second communist party was part of a divide-and-conquer maneuver mounted by Mustafa Kemal. When the first group's activities increased in Anatolia, Mustafa Kemal began to criticize communism openly, and he even had some of the leadership brought to trial. This angered the Russians, but did not prevent them from signing a treaty in March 1921 that assured the Turks of a steady supply of Russian arms. Thereupon, the communist leaders who had been tried received relatively light sentences.

In response to serious insurrections throughout Anatolia, the nationalists set up a series of emergency independence tribunals. Four months earlier, on 29 April, the Grand National Assembly had passed a law dealing with treason, but the uprisings continued. Many fugitives from the regular army formed bandit groups and terrorized the countryside. Such lawlessness pointed up the need for special tribunals that could dispense justice on the spot.[7]

In view of the widespread turbulence it is surprising that no serious measures were taken at first to protect the agricultural school building where Mustafa Kemal continued to be a leader without an army of his own. In fact, some ninety irregulars made up the security force. The headquarters of Ali Fuat were a good distance away, and those who worked in the school building had many anxious moments, fearing attacks by bandits or private armies. Once, they confused a herd of cattle on the horizon with imagined bandits or Ottoman loyalists come to seize them.

Minor inconveniences and mishaps increased the paranoia. Telegraph

[7]For a detailed examination of the reasons for the establishment of the independence tribunals, see Aybars 1975, pp. 54–60.

lines connecting the school building with Ankara were often cut at night, and at times watchdogs were poisoned. Mustafa Kemal became nervous and tense, a tiger in a cage. Kılıç Ali arrived with seventy mounted men to serve as a reinforcement, but did little for the general emotional atmosphere in the building, especially as Mustafa Kemal became prone to sudden "depressive" attacks. It was decided that he and his entourage should leave Ankara and go back to Sivas, but they postponed their departure because roads were dangerous. At that point Refet returned to Ankara, and his arrival once again restored everyone's spirits, but bad news continued to pour in.

Dr. Adnan and his wife left their comments on how Mustafa Kemal reacted to the tiresome messages (Göksel 1975). They described him as having panic reactions, hitting the palm of one hand with the fist of the other. Appearing nervous and despondent, he would suddenly stand up, as if discharging the panic reaction, and say, "Now let us attend to our own tasks." After he said this, a complete change would come over him, and he was able to continue with his work without any evidence of panic, suddenly appearing as someone in complete control of himself as well as of others. He had an uncanny ability to move quickly from one level of functioning to another which was more integrated. He could also keep one level uncontaminated by affect that pertained to the first and less controlled level.

Growing awareness of the physical dangers involved in staying at the agricultural school led Mustafa Kemal finally to move into the city proper, relocating in a building next to the railroad station. Although we do not know the exact date of the move, he was established there in mid-June 1921 by the time Fikriye arrived in Ankara to provide a woman's touch to his living quarters and to give him female companionship.

Mustafa Kemal called his new headquarters Direksiyon. The quarters were so spartan that a bed had to be moved in from the agricultural school for his use. It was little more than a black iron frame in which wooden boards served as spring and mattress. He was concerned about the lack of bathroom facilities. A German engineer known as Monsieur Jack designed a simple arrangement for bathing according to Mustafa Kemal's suggestions. Soon, however, a well-to-do native of Ankara saw the limitations of the place during a visit. He had a white painted bed sent in, and others soon began offering furnishings. The donor of the bed, as it happened, owned a house at Çankaya, a hilly site on what were then the outskirts of Ankara, and before long Mustafa Kemal and Fikriye moved there to what eventually became the nucleus of the presidential palace.[8]

[8]In 1932 an addition to the palace was built. It was painted pink, like the young Mustafa's house in Salonika.

The Çankaya house was luxurious after the austere surroundings of Direksiyon. Situated on a hill with shade trees and artfully arranged flower gardens, the house overlooked sloping vineyards that occupied the nearby hills of Ankara at that time. Resembling English Tudor style, the front of the house was constructed of mortar with parallel wooden beams, adorned with leaflike designs of wood within the stucco panels. The lower level, sides, and rear of the house were more simply constructed in stone and mortar. Topping off the sprawling structure was a red tiled roof.

Fikriye, who was related to Mustafa Kemal through his stepfather, was about eighteen years his junior. After the death of her sister Julide left her with no real family, she had written to Mustafa Kemal that she would be happy to act as his housekeeper. She came to Ankara on that pretext. It is impossible to ascertain what Zübeyde thought of that move. Although she liked Fikriye, she could not have considered her a proper match for her pasha son, since, having once been married, Fikriye was no longer a virgin. Zübeyde's religious and cultural attitudes would have led her to insist on a virgin bride for her son. In any case, the girl who had offered herself as a housekeeper and who had in a way been adopted by Zübeyde was viewed by Mustafa Kemal as a "guest" he would be glad to welcome. On the day she arrived he was busy at the Grand National Assembly, but sent his orderly to help her from her carriage and install her in a room—formerly his own—at Direksiyon (Oranlı 1967, p. 89). The room was furnished with just a shabby bed, but it served the "guest" until the group's removal to Çankaya.

At that time Fikriye was twenty-two, a rather tall and beautiful young woman resembling Greta Garbo with her wistful, sad eyes and delicate oval tawny face framed by dark brown waves of hair. She had a small nose, a dainty chin, and an exquisite mouth that smiled often. Halide Edib speaks of the gravity of her contralto voice and her dark eyes with their long, curly lashes, portraying a sadness far beyond her age. Dr. Adnan speculated as to whether the sadness in her eyes might not indicate a tendency toward tuberculosis, which had claimed her sister.[9]

[9]Halide Edib first saw Fikriye in a carriage with fine horses. The carriage belonged to Mustafa Kemal, but he rarely used it since he preferred to ride in his car. Halide was riding her horse when the carriage approached and nearly touched her horse. She wrote: "I saw in it not Mustafa Kemal Pasha but some one with a very pretty face, though she looked very tired and very cold—the tip of her nose was almost blue and the lips had no color. Framed in black, the delicate lines of the oval face were at their most effective. The eyes, dark brown, and with very long and curling lashes, stirred in me some dim memory of the distant past. I thought that she must be the cousin, Fikrié Hanum, the proper sort of sensibly brought up and sensible girl. She certainly looked it, so tastefully and simply attired, and so different from the very colorful female friends of Mustafa Kemal Pasha. But whom did she resemble? Why did her face trouble me so? She looked at me with something of a smile on her wan face, and when she had passed I was haunted by the ineffable sadness of her look. Her eyes

Fikriye made Mustafa Kemal the object of her hero worship. Her chief aim in life was to please him. When she took over the work of keeping the little station building clean and its occupants fed and cleanly dressed, he was pleased to find someone who adored him uncritically. She was, of course, no Corinne, but she had had some education and was even able to play the piano after a fashion. When they moved to Çankaya, he had a piano brought to the house for her. No doubt, whether consciously, or not, he was encouraging her westernization just as he would do later with his own adopted daughters. After the move to Çankaya, Fikriye shed the traditional *çarşaf*, "head covering," altogether. At Direksiyon she had not worn it at the dinner table.

She soon began to dress in a skirt, with a short jacket over her blouse. It was a style flattering to her slender body. Like Mustafa Kemal, she enjoyed riding horseback, and she could use a revolver competently. This small figure riding around Ankara caused considerable comment. She dealt with Mustafa Kemal's narcissism by feeling enhanced in her own self-esteem through association. It is always risky, however, to love someone with a narcissistic personality organization, since their investment in others is transient, and the association is apt to be short-lived. The narcissistic male in psychoanalysis often tells of being fascinated by "the most beautiful woman I ever saw in my life," only to report shortly that some trivial flaw has made her unacceptable and has led to her total rejection (Volkan 1976, pp. 239–71; 1981). Mustafa Kemal "loved" steadfastly only one woman—the Turkish nation that represented the idealized mother of his childhood, to the reparation of whom he devoted his life. Other women would come and go. Fikriye's downfall was predictable.

During the summer of 1920 there was, in addition to the many uprisings, an evident expansion of Greek forces. It is clear that in those days Mustafa Kemal had no desire to initiate military action. The organized Turkish army was unequal to the conduct of a major war, and he had no interest in being another of the many "leaders" involved in uprisings. Instead, Mustafa Kemal was bent on the organization of a new government. He did not lack critics since the confusing and dangerous situation in Anatolia had disillusioned some of his followers. The "savior" they had seen in him had done nothing for them thus far, and he seemed more involved in politics than in bringing peace to the land by military action.

---

particularly I could not get away from; then at last I knew. They were like the eyes of my mother, who had never been anything more than a shadowy vision in my life. When I told Dr. Adnan about it he smiled. 'Well,' he said, 'I don't wonder at it. You tell me your mother was consumptive, and Fikrié Hanum is nearly that.' But she could be nothing other than the nicest of girls. She had her eyes" (Adıvar 1928, pp. 223–24).

Some even regarded him as helpless. The first group of Grand National Assembly deputies were a heterogeneous group; there were communist sympathizers, others who still believed earnestly in the sultan, and some who were merely personally ambitious. Eighteen percent were religious leaders and about the same proportion were former soldiers. Most were bureaucrats. Kalpaks, turbans, and fezes adorned their heads. Group pictures of the assembly reflect the great diversity of characters and cultural backgrounds represented.

Individual psychology and group psychology have their similarities, but many important differences are all too often overlooked. Rochlin (1973, p. 260) notes that a group is far readier to invest its interests in a leader, a cause, or a purpose, than an individual is ready to fall in love or to give devotion to a work objective. What is germane here is the readiness with which group narcissism can withdraw from a choice. To some extent this was going on in relation to Mustafa Kemal. The Allies' offer to the Ottoman government of a peace treaty that would bring a bleak future to the Turks, however, enabled him to continue to hold the attention of the masses. When the Ottoman government accepted the Treaty of Sevres on 10 August 1920, a new wave of humiliation spread over Anatolia, inducing rage and indignation. Mustafa Kemal was ever ready to grasp such opportunities and to continue as the only man able to erase this humiliation.

16
From Mustafa Kemal to Ghazi M. Kemal

MISCONCEPTIONS ABOUT WHAT THE TURKISH RESPONSE TO INVASION BY THE Greeks would be, the depth of Turkish feelings about such aggression by their former subjects, and Turkish resilience in the face of what they perceived to be a life or death situation set the Allies on a road from which there was no turning back. Politics had become embroiled in ethnic conflicts as little understood today as they were at the end of World War I.[1]

With their vision blurred by their own intense desire for peace, having lost the taste for war and even the will to rule, and taken in by Greek assurances that they could subdue the Turks quickly and efficiently, the British first backed the initial Greek landings at Izmir and then blundered on with their own occupation of Istanbul. Lord Curzon mounted an intense campaign to work out a treaty for the Ottoman Empire that would be the ultimate answer to the Eastern Question—what to do with the Ottoman territories once "the sick man of Europe" expired.[2]

Another Allied misconception was their notion that Mustafa Kemal's nationalist movement had been fostered by the Istanbul government in order to lessen the harshness of the treaty terms. With Istanbul occupied and the Ottoman government in a shambles, the Allies sought to produce and impose a peace treaty before the Turks could mount any significant resistance. There was a forlorn hope that even if Mustafa Kemal could not be controlled, swift signing of a treaty would convert chaos into stability. Belief in magic is not restricted to primitive societies.

It would not have required the haruspical examination of animal entrails to foretell the failure of the treaty finally arrived at as the result of a number of Allied conferences, the last of which was held at San Remo, Italy, in April 1920. There was distrust among the Allies, and a variety of opinions within the ruling circles of the main Allied powers. The British were especially divided. Lloyd George was totally committed to the

[1]For another eruption of Turkish-Greek conflict see Volkan 1979.

[2]The term "sick man of Europe" stemmed from a remark made by Tsar Nicholas I to the British ambassador Sir George Hamilton Seymour in conversations they had early in January 1853 about the future of the Ottoman Empire. See Henderson 1947, pp. 1–14. The Russians considered the empire on the verge of death, and they thought it would be best to arrange for the distribution of Ottoman territory in order to avoid war after the fact.

Greeks, whereas Curzon was most apprehensive about any extension of Greek rule into Asia Minor. The British army and navy were at odds over who should control their part of the operation. Politicians representing British interests in India were concerned about the effects a harsh settlement would have on the Muslims of the subcontinent and sought to preserve a larger Turkish presence in Istanbul.[3]

Relations among the Allied powers were not better. Italy deeply resented the extension of Greek influence in the Aegean and the Mediterranean. The French, with Syria their major concern, were suspicious of the British. Unwilling to commit more of their resources to Asia Minor than was necessary, the French supported the cause of the Armenians in Cilicia, hoping that they would supply the necessary manpower. The British were rapidly growing weary of the mess. Their military presence in Asia Minor consisted predominantly of Indian troops.

Against this background a treaty was hammered out and presented to the government in Istanbul for its signature. Few defeated nations have ever been presented with so Carthaginian a treaty. The 150-page draft document divided the Ottoman Empire into pieces as though it were a pie. Only a thin slice, a veritable crumb, was left to the Turks. What was not given away outright was left under foreign control or influence. It was the same sort of imperialism that had contributed so greatly to the origins of World War I.

Eastern Thrace, except for a small toehold in Europe radiating out from Istanbul, was assigned to Greece. This included the symbolically important city of Edirne, which had served the Ottoman Empire as its capital prior to and even after the conquest of Constantinople. For centuries Edirne had been the Ottoman staging area for the massive imperial campaigns that had brought the Balkans under Turkish sway. Greek ambitions were also satisfied in the area of Izmir. True, for the first five years there would only be Greek adminstration, but then a plebiscite would be held for union with Greece. Eight Turkish islands in the Aegean would also be assigned to Greece.

Other territorial arrangements brought Italy the Dodecanese Islands, as well as the Aegean coastal area south of Izmir, and the Mediterranean coastal region of Anatolia all the way to Adana. These areas in Anatolia would be theirs as zones of influence.[4] The French zone of influence would begin at Adana and extend to Sivas. An independent Armenia would be established with borders to be set later by the United States.

[3]The Muslims of India supported the Kemalist movement. See the relevant chapters in Busch 1976.

[4]A "zone of influence" was an area in which the dominant foreign power's economic, diplomatic, and political interests would take precedence over those of other nations.

Kurdish autonomy was recognized, Kurdish borders to be delimited later. In addition, the Ottoman Empire was stripped of all its Arab lands.

Further provisions called for the straits to be placed under international control. Turkey's finances would also be under Allied control. The Turkish army would be greatly reduced and the gendarmerie would be staffed by foreign officers. It was a totally humiliating document that was handed to the sultan's government on 10 June. They were given one month in which to sign it.

Objections to the treaty were raised by the sultan's government, as was expected. Signature of such a disastrous treaty without any revisions would signal the end of the Ottoman Empire and acceptance by the sultan of the end of the House of Osman. The attitude of the Grand National Assembly had already been made clear. Soon after its opening, the assembly had announced that any treaty or other obligation signed by the government in Istanbul after 16 March 1920 would be null and void.

Determined not to allow Mustafa Kemal time to organize resistance to the treaty, the Allies decided to mount massive pressure on the sultan's government for a quick signing. The pressure would come in the form of an offensive by the Greeks northward from Izmir, directed against the nationalist forces that had managed to threaten the British forces at Izmit, the port city that held the key to the Gulf of Izmit and Istanbul beyond it. Venizelos, the Greek premier, had convinced the Allies that his divisions could accomplish the task. In the face of Allied unwillingness to commit their own forces, Venizelos's optimism was readily embraced. On 22 June the Greeks crossed the Milne Line, a boundary previously established by the Allies between the Turks and the Greeks in the Izmir region.

Greek forces met with only slight resistance as they rolled over Ali Fuat's meager and poorly supplied army. Venizelos indeed appeared to be the confederate he had claimed to be. The Turks fell back to Bursa. Snuggled against the slopes of Mount Olympus, Bursa is a place of considerable emotional importance to the Turks. Seized by the Ottoman Turks from the Byzantines in 1327, it became the first substantial Ottoman capital. As such it was embellished by handsome inns, spas, baths, bridges, and buildings devoted to a variety of religious functions, including the famous Green Mosque.

Its ancient glories could not defend Bursa. On 8 July the city fell to the advancing Greeks. Panic gripped Ankara. How could Bursa have fallen so quickly? There was an outcry against Mustafa Kemal's leadership. The rostrum in the Grand National Assembly was draped in black as a sign of mourning, and one speaker after another declared that the pall should cover the rostrum until Bursa was freed. There was much talk about guerrilla warfare as a means of halting the Greeks, since Ali Fuat's forces had failed to block their advance.

Mustafa Kemal had little patience with anyone who failed. Failures were not acceptable extensions of his grandiose self. The status of Ali Fuat was condensed with Mustafa Kemal's realistic assumption that his old friend might be able to set himself up as a warlord if he could effect a working combination of irregulars and guerrillas. Such an action by Ali Fuat would obstruct the plan for a more cohesive nationalist resistance. The time had come to drop him. Mustafa Kemal's personality makeup made it easy for him to rid himself of former associates without significant emotional travail or feelings of guilt.

In November 1920, therefore, Mustafa Kemal had Ali Fuat summoned to Ankara. He met him at the railroad station, and they sat in a train compartment for a private talk in which he tactfully told him that he was to become ambassador to Moscow.[5] Ali Fuat had little choice in the matter. He was obliged to leave his military post and become a civilian. Having rid himself of the first of his four friends from the early days of his arrival in Samsun, Mustafa Kemal stood alone in Ankara flanked by two more recent friends, İsmet and Fevzi, both of whom approved of his plans. Rauf was in British hands on Malta, Kâzım was on the eastern front facing the Armenians, and Refet was in the field.

Sensing that it was important to permit the deputies to discharge their feelings, Mustafa Kemal "allowed" them to speak at the black-draped rostrum of the Grand National Assembly. Afterwards, he would take the rostrum and counter any dissent they had offered, with an adroit alternation of threats and charm, logic and charisma. He would tell the assembly the realities of the situation and ask it to think logically about the matter. He explained that the Greeks and the Allies could land more troops in Anatolia at will, since they had control of the seas. Claiming that no front in history was impregnable and noting the hole in the Greek front around Bursa, he said that the Turks could be expected to strike at this hole. He suggested that, given the unpreparedness and weakness of the Turkish forces, an offensive at Bursa would be inadvisable. Thus, the deputies should not see the quick recapture of Bursa as a goal, but should focus on the defense of Anatolia. An attack upon the enemy should occur only at an appropriate time in an appropriate place, and only after emotions had cooled off. His words calmed the assembly.

[5]Mustafa Kemal's "official" recollection of this event is as follows: "I was convinced that Ali Fuat Pasha could no longer hold the command of the troops on the Western front. At this time it was thought necessary to send a diplomatic mission to Moscow, and here was an opportunity of sending him there as our Ambassador" (Atatürk 1927, p. 429).

As bad as things were for Mustafa Kemal and the nationalists, they were worse for the sultan and his government. The Greek offensive in Anatolia was designed to pressure the sultan into signing the peace treaty. That offensive was only one part of Venizelos's plan. The other was a quick offensive in Thrace that forced the surrender of Edirne on 26 July. Only the Russians in 1876 and the Bulgarians in the Balkan Wars had come closer to Istanbul. On 10 August the sultan's government accepted the inevitable and signed the treaty at Sevres.

Signature of the Sevres treaty had to be followed by its ratification in Istanbul and its acceptance in Ankara by Mustafa Kemal. Maneuverings in Istanbul to build a majority willing to ratify the treaty brought about the resignation of Damad Ferid Pasha, while in Ankara Mustafa Kemal made it plain that he did not recognize the treaty. Such a stalemate created tensions within the Allied camp. France and Italy, already dismayed at the Greek advance in Anatolia, were searching for ways to settle their differences with Mustafa Kemal's government and to emerge from the conflict with both their honor and economic positions intact. Lloyd George still gave the Greeks full diplomatic support, but he could not provide them with what they needed most—men and matériel.

Enthusiasm emanated only from the Greeks, who were prepared to press on with the attack in Anatolia. While the Allies pondered concessions in interminable conferences that included one in London attended by representatives of both the sultan's government and Mustafa Kemal's, the Greeks looked to military victory in the field to bring them even more than was allotted to them by Sevres.

Hard pressed by the Greeks in the east and by the establishment of an Armenian state in the west, Mustafa Kemal had been casting about for possible sources of supplies. Near enough to deliver and disposed to help on ideological and practical grounds, the Soviets presented themselves to Mustafa Kemal as his best hope. In May 1920, he had dispatched a mission to Moscow under Bekir Sami, the son of a former tsarist officer who had taken refuge in the Ottoman Empire after falling out with his superiors. Bekir Sami, who would later represent the Ankara government at the conference in London in February 1921, reached Moscow in July 1920 after a long and arduous trip through parts of Russia ravaged by the struggle with the White Armies of Denikin and Wrangel. After some delay Chicherin received the Turkish mission. He had no illusions about Mustafa Kemal's being a socialist or a communist, but it suited a number of his policies to aid the Ankara government at this juncture. Aligned in a symbolic relationship, Mustafa Kemal was prepared to make the best of it while he sought Soviet arms and gold.

Mustafa Kemal and the Soviets were united also by their opposition to the establishment of an independent Armenian state. Realizing that the

Soviets had designs on as much Armenian territory as they could get, Mustafa Kemal decided to march on his eastern flank to expand and maintain his own borders in the face of possible Soviet expansion. The Russians had already indicated an interest in the regions of Van and Bitlis. To forestall them, Mustafa Kemal finally sent Kâzım's army into action in an attempt to recover Kars, Ardahan, and Batum, areas lost at the conclusion of World War I. Kâzım's forces initiated their advance late in September and quickly took Kars. Abandoned to their fate by the Allies and with America unable to assume its proposed mandate, the Armenians watched their dreams of an independent state slip away. On 3 December, the fledging Armenian state and the Ankara government signed the Treaty of Alexandropol. Turkey's eastern frontier was fixed at the traditional border of the Arpa Çay and Aras rivers. Subsequent fighting brought Ardahan and Artvin to the Turks, but the Russians put on a sustained drive and took Batum. On 16 March 1921 the territorial arrangements were delineated in the Treaty of Moscow signed between the Soviet Union and the nationalist government.

The Allies had hoped that problems in the east would preoccupy Mustafa Kemal and prevent him from dealing effectively with the Greeks, but again they had misjudged the situation. Mustafa Kemal was able to devote attention to conditions in the west as well. Militarily the Turkish position had worsened, but the Greek political situation had degenerated drastically. Venizelos had been driven from power in an election that showed the degree to which the Greeks were wearying of massive mobilizations that had produced no permanent territorial acquisitions. King Alexander died suddenly in October 1920 of complications from a bite inflicted by a pet monkey. This opened the way for a plebiscite that restored Constantine, who had few friends among the Allies, to the throne.[6] Taking advantage of the restoration of this man who had sided with Germany, the French and the Italians refused to support the Greeks any longer in their Anatolian adventures. Lloyd George was left as the only, but increasingly reluctant, pro-Greek advocate among the Allies. King Constantine purged the officers' corps of its pro-Venizelos elements and prepared to renew the offensive in Anatolia, unfettered by Allied restrictions.

As the Greeks prepared their offensive, Mustafa Kemal had to deal again with the threat posed by Etem, the Circassian leader. An implacable enemy of İsmet's, the Circassian had refused to place his irregulars under İsmet's command when he took over Ali Fuat's forces. Etem sent Mustafa Kemal a telegram informing him that Ali Fuat's removal and his

[6]The Royalists defeated the Liberals in an election held one month after the death of King Alexander, and they formed a Royalist government. In December 1920 they brought Constantine back to the throne.

designation as ambassador to Moscow was being interpreted as evidence that Mustafa Kemal sought to become a dictator (Atatürk 1927, p. 463). Seeking a confrontation with Mustafa Kemal, Etem called upon him with a contingent of his followers. Mustafa Kemal was sick in bed at the time. Threateningly, he reached for a revolver that was under his pillow, and Etem, realizing that help had been summoned, backed off when he heard the sound of rifles being loaded. Feigning concern for Mustafa Kemal's health, he withdrew. Following this incident, a bodyguard was established for Mustafa Kemal composed of fearless Lazes from the mountains of the Black Sea coast near the Russian border. These tall, handsome, dark-skinned men made a striking appearance in their black uniforms and black turbans.

No sooner had Mustafa Kemal checked the pretensions of Etem and his Circassians than he had to turn his attention to a renewed Greek attack launched early in January 1921. Seeking to consolidate their front lines and gain control of important railheads, the Greeks pushed out from Bursa, aiming at Eskişehir. Outnumbered three to one and behind in firepower, the Turks met the Greeks at the small town of İnönü. Under the command of İsmet, they held firm despite shortages in ammunition and other supplies and won a crucial victory, the First Battle of İnönü.

Incredulity characterized Lloyd George's reaction to the Greek defeat, while the response of the other Allies was shock. They decided to invite the Greeks and the Turks to London to discuss the Treaty of Sevres and any modifications that recent events—meaning the success of the nationalist cause—might require. Commencing in February 1921, the conference almost foundered when Mustafa Kemal insisted that his government alone represented Turkey. A compromise was reached with both the sultan's government and the Grand National Assembly represented. They occupied different floors of the Savoy Hotel.

Incapable of understanding the new conditions in Anatolia, the Allies met the demands of the Ankara delegation—Greek withdrawal from Izmir, restoration of full Turkish sovereignty over the straits, and the evacuation of all foreign troops from Istanbul—with derision. Lloyd George, still the philhellene, continued to believe that the Greeks could march into Ankara with ease and tame the rebellious Turks. No agreement was reached on the modifications to the Treaty of Sevres demanded by the nationalists, and the London conference broke up on 12 March 1921.

Self-delusion continued to dominate the Greek perception of the situation in Anatolia after the London conference had left the Greeks with only British support. On 23 March the Greeks initiated an offensive that King Constantine hoped would bring the "great idea" to fruition. On 27 March Greeks and Turks clashed again at İnönü in the Second Battle of

İnönü. An important political event had intervened between the two battles. The Grand National Assembly had adopted a constitution stating that Turkey was to have a people's government to be known as the Turkish Grand National Assembly government. The seeds of the future republic of Turkey had been planted.

Fighting now for a more clearly defined future, the Turks put up an inspired resistance that lasted three days. On 1 April, İsmet sent Fevzi a telegram reporting that "The enemy has left the field to our troops; it is covered with the bodies of thousands of Greeks who have been killed" (Atatürk 1927, p. 492).[7] In 1934, when a law was passed requiring all Turks to take last names, İsmet, at Atatürk's urging, chose as his surname İnönü, commemorating his feats of military leadership at the first and second battles of İnönü.[8]

On receipt of the news of the Turkish victory, Mustafa Kemal wired İsmet that his conduct of the battle had been the work of a genius and that rarely in the history of mankind had a commander assumed so heavy a responsibility. He stated: "You have not only defeated the enemy, but at the same time have reversed the unhappy fate of the nation" (Atatürk 1927, p. 492). Then he concluded his message: "I want to tell you here that the high pinnacle on which you stand is not only overlooking a glorious battlefield strewn with the bodies of thousands of the enemy, but from its summit the eye can also discern the horizon of a future for our people and yourself that is resplendent with glory" (p. 493). The excitement in Ankara was great and the morale high. A new and glorious Turkish army had been able to reactivate the traditional fighting spirit of the Turks.

Exultation had seized Mustafa Kemal, but the nation's "bad luck" still plagued it. While İsmet had been successful in the northern sector of the western front, Refet had had no such good fortune in the southern sector. Unable to tolerate failure, Mustafa Kemal maneuvered to remove Refet from battle, making him minister of defense in Ankara, where he would be under the leader's thumb. İsmet was then given command of the entire western front, having replaced Refet as well as Ali Fuat.

Undaunted by their defeat and Allied neutrality in this latest con-

[7]After Ali Fuat was sent to Moscow, the entire front facing the Greeks "was divided into two parts, of which İsmet Pasha was given the command of the most important one, called the Western front, while the Southern portion of it could be given to Refet Bey . . . and both fronts were directly under the General Staff. Fewsi [Fevzi] Pasha, Minister of National Defence, could undertake the adminstration of the General Staff" (Atatürk 1927, p. 430). This is why İsmet sent Fevzi the telegram mentioned here.

[8]Many military men followed İsmet's lead and chose (or were given by Atatürk) as a surname the name of a place where there had been a military engagement in which they had achieved glory.

frontation with the Turks, the Greeks were in no mood to withdraw from Anatolia. King Constantine left Athens for the front and became the first Christian ruler to set foot in Asia Minor since the Crusades. Encamped where Richard the Lionhearted is supposed to have landed, King Constantine and his staff devised a new offensive that would strike to the south against Afyon and Kütahya and take Eskişehir from the south rather than from the west. On 10 June the Greeks struck, this time with greater success. On 27 July Constantine was able to meet with his conquering commanders in Kütahya. They decided to press the attack, with Ankara as their objective.

Confident that the Turks were finished, the Greeks watched floods of refugees head inland. Centuries-old Greek rage against the Turks was unleashed, and local Greeks living on land newly liberated by Greeks from the mainland vented their hatred in atrocities against the Turkish inhabitants. Panic swept Ankara, and İsmet was in a mood of deep depression. It was while visiting him at the front that Mustafa Kemal unhesitatingly ordered the Turkish army to retreat across the Sakarya River, the last natural obstacle between the enemy and Ankara. Later, in his famous marathon speech, he explained that this order for a general retreat, which had been highly unpopular at the time, had been necessary to put a great distance between the Turks and their enemy in order to maximize the Greeks' disadvantage of being far from their main base and without adequate arrangements for transport. Moreover, *systematic* retreat kept the Turkish army together. He pointed out: "The disadvantage of such tactics would be the moral shock which might be produced in public opinion by the fact that a wide territory and places so important as Eski-Shehr [Eskişehir] would be abandoned to the enemy." He then added, "But these disadvantages will automatically disappear in a short time as the result of the successes which we shall achieve" (Atatürk 1927, p. 515).

No one else could have ordered such a retreat, but once Mustafa Kemal had decided it was the best move, he gave the order without hesitation. Audacious and extremely risky, his order threw the Grand National Assembly into disarray. Mustafa Kemal recalled later:

> The first excitement became apparent in the Assembly. Above all, the representatives of the opposition immediately began to make pessimistic speeches and express themselves in all possible tones: Where is this army going to? Where are the people being led? There must surely be somebody who is responsible for what is being done! Where is the person? He is invisible. We would like to see at the head of the army the actual originator of the sad and deplorable position in which we are today. [Atatürk 1927, p. 515]

Kâzım, just returned to Ankara after his success on the eastern front, became the voice of the opposition to Mustafa Kemal, whose powers he wanted reduced. Many felt that Mustafa Kemal should be leading the army himself. He realized this and said later:

> Imbued with this conviction, they wanted to relieve themselves by pouring all their wrath upon me; they wanted me to perish at the head of the army which, as they thought, was in danger of dissolution and could not be saved. On the other hand, there were others—I might well say the majority—guided by their feelings of confidence and gratitude, who wanted to see me at the head of the army. [Atatürk 1927, p. 515]

As usual, Mustafa Kemal waited for everyone to speak and then gave his famous memorandum to the Grand National Assembly. Undaunted by the prospect of failure, he announced that he would become commander in chief on the condition that the assembly grant him total authority. In simple language, he wanted authorization to become a dictator, but, by utilizing one of his great strengths, he was able to place limitations on his grandiose demands. He requested that the authority he sought be granted to him for *only three months*. Opposition to his demand for total authority for that limited period met his unyielding resistance. On 5 August 1921 the Grand National Assembly voted him such authority. He was forty years old when he legally became dictator for three months. No other Turk could take action against the impossible odds that prevailed, defeat the enemy, and save the nation. Taking the rostrum, he made a speech in which he promised to succeed and show everyone that he merited the trust of the assembly.

> My confident belief that we shall be able completely to defeat the enemies who want to subjugate our unhappy nation has not been shaken for a single moment. I declare this unshakable faith of mine on this occasion in the presence of this High Assembly, before the entire nation and before the whole world. [Atatürk 1927, p. 519]

Communicating his confidence to the Turks, Mustafa Kemal was able to galvanize them into action. Everyone gladly sacrificed, and contemporary newsreels show the Turks working like ants in preparation for the defense. Supplies from Russia were insufficient to meet the enormous needs, and so primitive Turkish factories worked overtime and the people made up with muscle and sweat what they lacked in matériel. People of all ages were caught up in the effort; ox carts, camels, farm trucks, and donkeys were pressed into service to augment the trains in getting ammunition, troops, and supplies to the front.

That front was about 100 kilometers wide and 20 deep. Mustafa Kemal and Fevzi made their headquarters at Polatlı, near the place where Alexander had cut the Gordian knot. They arrived there on 12 August. İsmet was assigned to direct the troops at the line of battle. The distance between Ankara and Eskişehir is about 200 kilometers, and Polatlı is roughly in the middle.

On the day Mustafa Kemal reached Polatlı, he rode on horseback to a hilltop to inspect the enemy's lines ranged on the opposite side of the Sakarya River. His mount became frightened when he lit a cigarette and threw him to the ground. In the fall Mustafa Kemal broke one of his ribs. The broken rib pressed on his lung, giving him great pain and affecting his breathing. His doctor told him that he would die if he failed to take care of himself, but Mustafa Kemal had no time to exercise care. He persevered, as he had done at Gallipoli after being hit by shrapnel. Although he was rushed to Ankara for treatment, he was back at the front, bandaged, within twenty-four hours, obliged to keep up the cohesiveness of his personality under stress. There is evidence that at this time his trust in certain personal superstitions was marked. He fancied, for example, that at the spot where he had broken his rib the resistance of the enemy would also be broken. Events bore out this belief. He also clung to a green flag given to him years earlier by some unidentified Muslims, possibly in Libya, and adopted as a talisman of his success. He seemed to need his eccentric beliefs in magic as patches for the weakening borders of his personality organization strained under the (internalized) influence of external stress.

On 23 August the Greeks initiated a battle that raged until 13 September. The din from the battle of the Sakarya could be heard as far away as Ankara, where panic gripped the city. The inhabitants began to flee by whatever means were available. Questions were raised whether the Grand National Assembly should relocate, but the deputies decided to remain in Ankara.

Mustafa Kemal chose to fight the battle according to a principle he enunciated: "there was no line of defense but a plain of defense, and this plain was the whole of the country. Not an inch of the country should be abandoned until it was drenched with the blood of the citizens" (Atatürk 1927, p. 521). His message, that the soldiers should not dig in but should try to protect the entire defense surface, was a novel idea. Arif was at his side during the battle, as was Halide Edib, who held the rank of sergeant. Arif had become familiar with the contours of every hill and valley over which they fought, and the location of each waterhole. This made him invaluable to Mustafa Kemal, but his prime service to the commander in chief was again being his "twin brother," another "green flag" giving Mustafa Kemal the psychological reassurance he always needed. He used

Arif to retain his grandiose cohesiveness by seeing his reflection in his "twin" and by projecting onto him his unwanted impulses.

Just as he had at Gallipoli, Mustafa Kemal ordered his men to defend every inch of ground. The lives of individuals were expendable in defense of the nation's security. Thousands died, but the Turks won, and the Greeks retreated to the west bank of the Sakarya. Triumphant, Mustafa Kemal returned to Ankara, where he was received by the Grand National Assembly and given the title of Ghazi. That term, meaning one who engages in combat against the infidel, was coveted by the earliest Ottoman sultans whose driving impulse had been waging war against non-Muslims. Mustafa Kemal was also made marshal of the army. As an Ottoman officer he had worn elaborate uniforms, but during the nationalist struggle he dressed in khaki like a private.

Among all his titles and ranks, that of Ghazi had special appeal for Mustafa Kemal. He used it as part of his signature for some time. Children often called him Ghazi Baba (Ghazi Father), and mothers warned their children that he would think poorly of them if they behaved badly or be proud of them if they were good. "Little Mustafa" had become Mustafa Kemal, the perfect man. His name kept undergoing alteration in accordance with his enhanced self-perception, and he could at last feel that he had saved his grieving mother and become the savior he had wanted to be—a true Ghazi. Such perfection reflected his defensive use of grandiosity to deal with deficiencies he had experienced in his mothering, and perfection had finally become his character. It can even be said that after the victory at Sakarya, when he began signing his name as Ghazi M. Kemal, the deprived "Little Mustafa" had virtually disappeared.

Observing Mustafa Kemal's triumphant return to Ankara after the battle of the Sakarya, Dr. Adnan noted the excitement of the welcoming crowd and remarked to a friend, who recalled the comment later, "We will never be able to stop him from now on" (Göksel 1975). Although he came to hate Mustafa Kemal, Dr. Adnan remained stubbornly honest enough the rest of his life to insist that Mustafa Kemal was unique, a nonpareil.

Unexcelled, Mustafa Kemal had kept his promise to defeat the enemy, but it would take another year for him to achieve final victory. The success of the Turks at the Sakarya heightened the opposition of the French to the Greeks and strengthened their inclination to recognize the nationalists. There was clearly a new reality in Anatolia, and the French had to take this into account. A French diplomat, Franklin-Bouillon, who had served as minister of propaganda in 1917, arrived in Ankara and signed a treaty with the nationalist government on 20 October. This agreement called for the French to withdraw from Cilicia and fixed the northern border of Syria, giving the Turks more than had been granted by the Treaty of Sevres.

The British foreign secretary, Lord Curzon, was dismayed at the French arrangement with the Turks and protested to the French ambassador about it, but to no avail. Winston Churchill recommended that some accommodation be reached with Mustafa Kemal, but the British were reluctant to cut their ties to the Greeks. Unable to detail more troops for service in Anatolia, and unwilling to withdraw, the British offered the Greeks their sympathy, but not much else. The realization that Sevres would have to be modified significantly was clear, but the British feared that any sign of weakness would be taken by Mustafa Kemal as an invitation to raise his demands in any conference that might be arranged. Ṛefet did meet with some British representatives at the Black Sea port of İnebolu, but only an agreement to exchange some prisoners was reached.

Interned on Malta for the past eighteen months, both Rauf and Fethi, the ambassador to Sofia during Mustafa Kemal's service there, returned to Ankara. All the main actors in the nationalist struggle, except for Ali Fuat, who was ambassador to Moscow, were in Ankara. Others joined them. Abdürrahim Tuncak was among them. In his interview with Dr. Volkan he was unable to recall the exact date of his departure from Istanbul, but he did remember leaving with the son of Mustafa Kemal's first aide-de-camp, some women, and a railroad inspector. Having left Zübeyde behind in Istanbul, the young boy and his companions boarded an Italian ship. They were supposed to land at İnebolu, but put in at Samsun because of a storm. Since they could not make it overland to Ankara because of bandits, they were taken by the ship to İnebolu, where some Lazes sent by Mustafa Kemal accompanied them to Ankara. Abdürrahim's arrival there came a few months after Fikriye's.

Abdürrahim found Fikriye established as the "lady of the house" (Tuncak 1974) at Çankaya. She carried out her housekeeping duties with dignity and grace. Her attachment to Mustafa Kemal was obvious, and she commanded the respect of the people of Ankara. She was popular, but her health was poor. She had grown pale and much thinner, and the consumptive look Dr. Adnan had noticed in her eyes now had become obvious. Abdürrahim remembered her drinking a glass of warm milk each night before retiring. Shortly after the victory at the Sakarya, Mustafa Kemal's enhanced stature made it possible for him to send to Istanbul for his mother. She joined the group in Ankara about six months after Fikriye's arrival. Zübeyde's belief at one point that her son was dead had led her in her grief to become reabsorbed in religious devotions.[9] This must have awakened in her son the old wounds of seeing her grieve for

[9]This was due to the sultan's propaganda designed to suppress nationalist sentiment.

her other lost children, and the situation must have been painful for Fikriye, too. She tried to please Zübeyde, but suffered under the disadvantage of being ineligible as a marriage partner for Mustafa Kemal. Zübeyde, who dressed only in white,[10] tried to gain control of the household with the help of her long-time maid and companion who accompanied her to Ankara.

It is reasonable to assume that Zübeyde understood little or nothing of what her son was trying to accomplish. She would flinch when any disrespect to the sultan was voiced, although she came to speak favorably of the nationalist movement simply because it was expected of her. Hanns Froembgen wrote of her (1937, p. 185), "Frequently she found fault, and not infrequently it was the Ghazi himself who was made to feel the weight of her displeasure. Today she still expected obedience from him, and his exalted rank still did not alter the fact that he was her son." He also noted that, "Mother and son lived side by side like two friendly Great Powers. Each respected his own frontiers, but immediately showed his teeth if the other attempted to violate those frontiers."

That is a good assessment of the psychological state that existed between mother and son. Each *had* to distance the other.[11] Although he tried to keep her away, he was unable to remain completely outside her orbit. Before long he fell into a morning ritual, on rising he would shave, dress with meticulous care, and visit his mother, who lived in an adjoining house rather than under the same roof. He would kiss her hands in the traditional manner, paying homage to the religious mother, before departing to care for the nation's business. This ritual was a repetition of the first memory of his life. Paying homage to his mother was a representation of bowing to her will when he attended the religious school before following his own inclinations with his father's help. In this instance he was paying homage to the "bad mother" prior to going about his affairs which were identified with fatherly functions. This particular ritual came to an end, however, when one day Zübeyde tried to kiss his hand, saying that it was only proper for her to do so, for he was the savior of the country and its leading personality. By this action she spoiled his repetition of his earliest memory.

Zübeyde's demonstration of respect for him would alternate with her treating him like a child, calling him "my Mustafa" and scolding him as though he were a naughty boy living under her care and protection. Meanwhile, he was attempting to move away from the Mustafa identity

[10]Halide Edib tells us in her memoirs that Zübeyde refused to have a new dress made until her son Mustafa delivered her beloved city Salonika, for which she mourned, from captivity; Adıvar 1928, p. 343.

[11]This was, we believe, a defensive-adaptive response against the anxiety of a symbiotic pull toward each other.

to the Ghazi identity. What he did not consciously recognize was that although this hand-kissing ritual distanced him from the "bad mother," he was investing the rest of his time in repairing the idealized mother—the Turkish nation. He could be loyal only to the idealized image of his mother. When Fikriye hinted at marriage he declared that he was already married, and the Turkish nation was his bride.

17

"Armies, Your Primary Objective Is the Mediterranean"

FOLLOWING THEIR SUCCESS AT THE SAKARYA, THE TURKS PLUNGED INTO preparations that lasted a year for a great offensive designed to drive the Greeks out of Anatolia. Ghazi Mustafa Kemal recognized the need for time to prepare his army for so daring an undertaking, but there were many who did not. At the battle of the Sakarya the Turks had lost most of their officers who had been in the front lines. They would have to be replaced, and new supplies and weaponry had to be obtained.

Mustafa Kemal also recognized the need to prepare the nation psychologically for the offensive. Although some wanted to pursue the retreating Greeks across the Sakarya River immediately, others favored acceptance of the peace proposals offered by the Allies. By far the strongest opposition to the offensive came from those who found Mustafa Kemal's personal power abhorrent. Kâzım and Refet, who had won election as deputies to the Grand National Assembly, joined Rauf in leading the criticism against the Ghazi. Rauf was the key person in organizing the opposition in the assembly. Mustafa Kemal made a habit of visiting the assembly daily, warily assessing the opposition, which he appeared to tolerate. He called upon his oratorical powers, using long and elaborate sentences to preach, to explain, to threaten, and sometimes to disparage. He could be short with those who came to the assembly to shout and banter with the speakers. Once, in defense of his own plans, he haughtily pointed out to the leader of the opposition that discussions were not to be conducted in the parliament as though it were a coffeehouse.

Ghazi Mustafa Kemal's powers as commander in chief had twice been renewed by the assembly for three-month periods, but when the time arrived for a third renewal, serious opposition arose. Men from both camps came to the assembly with revolvers tucked in their waistbands. It was not impossible that in the passionate heat of discussion someone might try to shoot Mustafa Kemal. His oratorical magic and his shrewd proposal that Rauf become the chairman of the ministry council, in effect, prime minister, carried the day. The Ghazi had held that position as well as the presidency of the assembly. He now proposed to surrender some of his power to Rauf, with whom he was still, at least on the surface, friendly. Rauf initially refused, fearful that the Ghazi would interfere with his conduct of the office, but he accepted after Mustafa Kemal promised to refrain from doing so, and in fact Mustafa Kemal kept his promise. The Ghazi was seeking a common front in the assembly for national goals in the face of the continuing Greek threat. During the year he brought Ali Fuat back from Moscow to head the deputies loyal to him and to deal with the opposition in the assembly.

Shedding his concern with parliamentary infighting, Mustafa Kemal wanted to be free to concentrate on military preparations for the great offensive. Although he continued to confide in İsmet and Fevzi on military matters and went through the motions of consulting other military leaders, the plans were entirely his own and the coming battle would be one he would devise.

Despite his absorption in military matters and politics, the Ghazi managed to conduct a life full of personal satisfactions. The backward and neglected Anatolian town of Ankara was changing rapidly. In his house in Çankaya Mustafa Kemal surrounded himself with beautiful things, Turkish carpets, marble tables of ornate design, tiles from Kütahya, and other embellishments. Fikriye, who adored him and who was uncomplaining about absenting herself when he and his guests talked business and drank rakı until late at night, cared for his needs.

At this point, Mustafa Kemal began drinking regularly every night. It relaxed him and facilitated his social interaction. He would have a bowl full of salty roasted chick-peas brought to him to accompany his slow sips of rakı, drunk in the traditional Turkish ritual that makes convivial gatherings last for hours. When drinking with his friends, he would scoop up the chick-peas with two fingers and the thumb of his right hand, or occasionally toss one in the air and catch it in his open mouth. His favorite toast was "Chin, chin," which he adopted from the British and which sounded gratifyingly Western to his ears. Although he certainly relaxed, and even regressed, in the sociability of such drinking before meals, often becoming nostalgic about his youthful days in Macedonia, he knew when he had had enough, and there are no stories of his making a drunken fool of himself. He began to use these gatherings as an opportunity for serious talk as well as for socializing, and later they became known as "The President's Table" (see chap. 27). In the background hovered Fikriye, her dark eyes full of adoration for him, patiently waiting for her lover to come to her whenever he needed her. Her abandonment of the traditional veil was copied by the nationalists' wives and became fashionable. Ankara was changing in other ways, too. New housing sprang up between the Anakara fortress, which was the center of the old town, and the slopes of Çankaya hill. The road bustled with people on horseback or in carriages making a sort of pilgrimage to the new Mecca coming into being around Mustafa Kemal.

Mustafa Kemal was careful to keep his contacts with Western women separate from his contacts with Eastern women, including his mother, as he had done previously in Istanbul. Zübeyde was isolated in the house adjoining her son's, and he continued to relate to her in a ritualistic manner, while he entertained Western women in his guesthouse in Çankaya. One of his guests was a French journalist, Madame Berthe Georges-Gaulis, who wrote three books on her observations of Turkey in those days (1921, 1922, 1924). His conversations with her no doubt recalled memories of Corinne. An Englishwoman, Grace Mary Ellison, also visited him and later, like Berthe Georges-Gaulis, wrote on life in Ankara (1923). Sooner or later he would speak to these foreign women about his childhood, talking of his mother's intense love for him and of his troubles as a youth.[1]

Social life in Ankara, especially that revolving around the growing diplomatic community, was on the upswing. Orthodox Muslims and those who were politically opposed to the Ghazi criticized his frequent attendance at the embassy parties of the Soviet Union and its satellite republics. These parties featured vodka, wine, and women, and Mustafa Kemal's obvious enjoyment of these pleasures outraged some significant segments of public opinion.

Dependence on Soviet aid entailed Mustafa Kemal's presence at those social functions given by the Russians. He became rather close to Aralov, the Soviet ambassador. The Ghazi took delight in teasing him and displaying cynicism about communist dogma. At one party held at the Soviet embassy, he challenged Aralov: if the Soviet revolution meant true egalitarianism, he should include the embassy cooks and other servants in the festivities. Aralov humored the Ghazi and invited them all to join the party (Kinross 1965, p. 338). Possibly in an effort to get even, Aralov, who had been pressing a reluctant Mustafa Kemal to politicize the army, harangued the Turkish army on the glories of the Bolshevik revolution while on a visit to the front.

Another important delegation that arrived in Ankara was one from the Ukraine under the leadership of General Frunze. The Allies interpreted his mission as part of a Soviet plot to return Enver Pasha, who had made his way to Russia, to Ankara and to install him in the Ghazi's place. General Frunze arrived on 13 December 1921. Some eight months later, Enver, who had quixotically organized a pan-Turanian emirate in

[1]One might almost believe that in his own indirect way Mustafa Kemal discussed his fear of being engulfed by his mother and that he conjured up in these foreign women an idealized mother image distinct from that of the engulfing mother. One should not, however, overlook the importance of such foreign writers in promoting his cause and the "new" Turkey since their books served as positive public relations statements.

Bukhara, would be killed in combat against Russian forces in the summer of 1922.[2]

General Frunze's visit put Mustafa Kemal and the dusty town of Ankara gratifyingly in the limelight. On 4 January 1922, shortly after Frunze's return to the Ukraine, the Ghazi wrote to Lenin lauding General Frunze for his sympathy with the Turkish cause. He went on to compare the Turks and the Russians, and the two revolutions they had brought about, indicating that the true meaning of both revolutions would elude the West since they had been initiated in response to an imperalist attack by a foreign power. The letter went on to talk of the congresses of Erzurum and Sivas at which the people had decided their own fate, just as Lenin had led his people to do in the aftermath of World War I. Acknowledging past antagonisms between the Turks and the Russians, Mustafa Kemal spoke of a new friendliness between the two nations that would greatly surprise the expansionist West, which was directing both overt and covert attacks against Turkey for revealing to all oppressed peoples by its own exemplary actions that the road to freedom lay ahead. On this account, as long as the West saw the Turks as enemies, the Soviet Russians were the only people the Turks could trust.

Oppressed people of the east were indeed looking to the example of Turkey.[3] Afghanistan had already sent an ambassador to Ankara, and the Muslims of India were represented there as well. Mustafa Kemal's name was beginning to inspire awe throughout the Muslim world. The man

[2]Enver had escaped from Istanbul on 2 November 1918 in a German torpedo boat. He went first to Odessa and then reached Berlin in December. He went to Moscow early in 1920, and there he had conversations with Mustafa Kemal's representative Bekir Sami and with Lenin. In time, he worked within the Soviet framework, organizing the Union of Islamic Revolutionary societies, and was in Batum, where he attended the Congress of the People of the East, a gathering spurned by Soviets. Enver returned to Berlin, where he tried to organize a military campaign for the Caucasus. He also toyed with the idea of trying to take over the resistance movement in Anatolia, but his support in Trabzon evaporated. There were some former Unionist officers in Ankara who would have welcomed Enver, but once Mustafa Kemal's force had defeated the invading Greeks, Enver's cause was hopeless. In October 1921 Enver arrived in Bukhara, where he quickly rallied some anti-Soviet forces. He put himself forward as the deputy of the exiled emir of Bukhara and commander in chief of his army. Demanding Russian evacuation of Bukhara, he went into battle against them. He was killed in a calvary charge on 4 August 1922.

Frunze's arrival in Ankara could be viewed as an attempt to test the waters for Enver, but Mustafa Kemal's faction was too secure. Mustafa Kemal relied greatly upon the Soviets for military assistance, but he was not their puppet. If Enver had succeeded in replacing Mustafa Kemal, the whole issue of the straits would have been injected into international politics again. See Rustow 1965.

[3]Anwar el-Sadat (1979, p. 12) noted in his autobiography that Mustafa Kemal's portrait hung in his parents' home in Egypt and that he grew up idealizing the Turkish leader, having heard from his father that Mustafa Kemal was a great leader.

whose eyes often turned toward the West for inspiration even as he fought Western armed forces was paradoxically becoming the hero of the East.

Diplomacy, partying, and revelry occupied only the surface of Mustafa Kemal's attention. Beneath that frivolous exterior he was busy preparing his army for the final push against the Greeks. As the year he had estimated it would take to prepare for battle drew to a close, his attention was drawn to the city of Afyon, about 250 kilometers west of Ankara. Afyon, which means "poppy," is located in the midst of the Turkish poppy fields. In the summer of 1922 it was held by the Greeks and commanded a direct rail line for supplies to Izmir. The Greeks had prepared a strong defense there which British engineers had declared impregnable. If the Turks were reckless enough to attack Afyon, their doom would be sealed.

South of Afyon lies Turkey's lake district. One of the lakes, Akşehir Gölü (White-City Lake), is some 100 kilometers to the southeast. Troops commanded by İsmet had made their headquarters in Akşehir, the city from which the lake took its name. During the last week of July 1922, the Turkish military leadership secretly gathered there, using attendance at a widely publicized soccer match as cover (Atatürk 1927, p. 564). Among the spectators was Ghazi Mustafa Kemal, who had come to join İsmet. Fevzi arrived by another route, and other commanders drifted in to be with the top military trio which had achieved its most recent fame with the victory at the Sakarya.

When the soccer match was over and night had fallen, they all joined Mustafa Kemal in a hut. They gathered around a map to see the plans for the great offensive, which called for a surprise attack by almost the entire Turkish army. Some opposed the plan because it placed the entire army in jeopardy. İsmet, ever cautious, was not sure that a decisive Turkish military victory was possible at the time and preferred to wear the Greeks down gradually. Standing firm, the Ghazi had his plan approved. He then returned to Ankara and acquainted the cabinet with his plan to attack the Greeks. At this time he did little to suppress or counter those who opposed him in the Grand National Assembly or who believed the Turkish army was not ready for such a move. In fact, he wanted to have such doubts expressed publicly in Ankara (Atatürk 1927, p. 565). He knew that Greek spies were present in the city, and, as long as political problems persisted in the Grand National Assembly, the Greeks would, no doubt, discount the possibility of a Turkish attack, thus increasing the chances for surprise.

Part of the plan was an elaborate hoax designed to misdirect Greek attention (Atatürk 1927, p. 566). The main Greek strength was located between Eskişehir and Akşehir, cities approximately 170 kilometers apart. Considering Afyon impregnable, the Greeks expected that Eskişehir would be the most likely target of any Turkish attack. Undaunted, Mustafa Kemal planned to hit the Greeks at their strongest point, Afyon. Success there would convey great military advantage, for it would ensure control of the supply lines for the follow-up drive aimed at Izmir. In order to have the Greeks anticipate a Turkish attack against Eskişehir in the north, he devised a maneuver that was carried on for a month following the soccer match. During the daylight hours, the Turks moved troops from around Afyon toward Eskişehir openly so that they would be easily spotted by the Greeks. When night fell, however, the troops secretly returned to their previous positions as stealthily as possible. Based on what they could see of the Turkish movements, the Greeks would surely conclude that the enemy was readying all its forces against Eskişehir. It was hoped that the Greeks would then move their own forces to that sector, unaware that the Turks were really poised for an attack on Afyon. This plan may have been inspired by General Allenby's attack upon the Turks in Syria, similarly disguised and thoroughly devastating. Besides the identification with the aggressor seen in this plan,[4] the ethos of Mustafa Kemal's notion to attack the strongest enemy position was in accord with his personality organization: he was going to achieve something of dazzling brilliance.

Fevzi returned to Akşehir on 13 August and was joined there by the Ghazi a week later. Mustafa Kemal had left Ankara in secret. Mr. Tuncak still remembers being told one morning that he was to tell no one that the Ghazi had left Çankaya (Tuncak 1974). Ali Fuat, who remained behind, pretended that he had dined with Mustafa Kemal at a time when he was already en route to Akşehir. Once İsmet, Fevzi, and the Ghazi were together, it was decided to launch the attack early in the morning on 26 August. When some objections to that date were raised, the Ghazi flared up, declaring that "Those who don't have trust should resign. I take all responsibility on myself."[5] That was on the evening of 21 August, after he had been reading on and off for several days a popular Turkish novel entitled *Çalıkuşu*, published in 1922 (Güntekin). In an effort to retrace some of the associations Mustafa Kemal may have had at this time, it is interesting to note that this is the story of an orphaned daughter of a calvary officer who breaks off her engagement to a young man and

[4]The concept of identification with the aggressor was first described by Anna Freud (1936). Identification is an unconscious mental process whereby an individual becomes like another person in one or several aspects. Identification with a person who was previously an aggressor toward the invidual enables him to be like the aggressor and enriches his capacity to deal with the world.

[5]Mahmud Saydam, then a major, kept personal notes on the Ghazi's activities just before the great offensive. These notes appear in Aydemir 1971, vol. 2, pp. 528–29.

seeks a teaching post in Anatolia. The director of education is thoroughly surprised to find a young woman interested in going to Anatolia of her own free will. In a later scene a foreign journalist meets her in Anatolia. He remarks, "The conclusion I draw from this is that there is in Istanbul a set of modern young girls who have had a good European education: they belong to an entirely different generation from the generation which destroyed itself with useless melancholy. . . . They prefer action to empty dreams, and they'll give up their prosperity and happiness in Istanbul, to come and arouse Anatolia, of their own intiative. What a beautiful and lofty example of renunciation!" (Güntekin 1949, pp. 205–6). A Turkish officer falls in love with her, but she refuses his offer of marriage. Subsequently, he is wounded and disfigured. The heroine nurses him back to health and suggests that they get married. He views this as an act of pity and rejects the suggestion.

There is much in this masterpiece of late Ottoman literature with which the Ghazi could identify. Like the heroine, he had come from Istanbul to Anatolia to arouse the country. She reflects the Ghazi's perception of himself. Like her, he had renounced the melancholy of his mother's religion to seek a modern, westernized education. Mustafa Kemal could also see himself in the officer who loves but is not loved in return (by his fellow officers who opposed him and, on another level, by a grieving mother who unconsciously felt that she could also lose him and hence should not love him too much), and then turns his back on the possibility of happiness.

As Mustafa Kemal made ready for the day of the offensive he drank large amounts of coffee, smoked a great deal, and read his novel. It is interesting to note that he put aside his rakı. It would be inaccurate to say that at this time of his life Mustafa Kemal was addicted to alcohol, for he was able to stop drinking, especially at the battlefront. He could postpone the gratification that alcohol offered him in order to carry out this task in the real world which promised, if accomplished successfully, to raise him once again to radiant glory as the "savior sun."

On the morning of 25 August the Ghazi again inspected the front with Fevzi. The plan was to strike against Afyon's southern flank, the most heavily defended sector of the city's perimeter. If it succeeded, Afyon would be cut off from the rest of the Greek army, and a deep wound, both military and psychological, would be inflicted on the Greeks.

Mustafa Kemal's orderly awakened him and his staff at 2 A.M. on the decisive day. At 3 A.M. Fevzi went to the Ghazi's tent to learn whether the cavalry was in position. When word came that all was ready, the two leaders and their staff mounted and rode to a hill some six or seven kilometers distant, one appropriately named Kocatepe (Lofty Hill). From there the troops could be seen, waiting tensely in the distance, their

With the outcome still in doubt, Mustafa Kemal Pasha ponders the terrain at Kocatepe. The offensive against the Greeks rages on.

horses whinnying with excitement. The Ghazi and Fevzi dismounted and walked to a nearby outlook where Mustafa Kemal once again gazed at his maps in the light of a lantern. Fevzi, a devout Muslim, drew a Koran from beneath his shirt and began to read it. When dawn broke, the Ghazi interrupted his reading, saying, "The time has come, hocam," addressing Fevzi by his pet name of "my (religious) teacher" (Oranlı 1967, p. 115).

Surprise was total. The Greeks had no idea that the Turks had gathered their main forces south of Afyon. Urged on by the presence of Mustafa Kemal, the Turks captured most of the important commanding heights by mid-morning. Covering as much as fifty kilometers in a day, they drove the Greeks before them. Afyon fell easily, and on 29 August the Ghazi met there with İsmet and Fevzi to make further plans. The Turkish population was in a state of great exuberance, pouring out their affection on the conquering troops. Mustafa Kemal predicted, as he plotted the advance of the Turkish troops to close the ring on the retreating Greeks, that the "real *savior sun* of the Turks would dawn on the morning of 30 August with all its splendor" (Atatürk 1952, 2:174; italics added). The battle that was initiated that day with Mustafa Kemal himself leading the charge is known in Turkish history as the Battle of the Commanders in Chief.

As at Gallipoli, Mustafa Kemal's narcissistic personality organization was an immense asset to him as he personally led the great offensive. His grandiosity allowed him to disregard discouraging "realities" and to envision successes others could not conceive of. It also permitted him to see himself as embodying the honor of all Turks, wrapped in a protective mantle bestowed upon him by the motherland. Projecting this air of invincibilty, Mustafa Kemal was capable of imbuing himself and his troops with an inordinate sense of hope and purpose.

This complex process at work has been captured in a reminiscence of his orderly Ali (Oranlı 1967, pp. 121–22). During the night of 28 August the Ghazi and another general, Fahrettin Pasha, along with some staff members, came upon a modest village home in the darkness. Made of mud and hay, it had just one bedroom. Its occupants, an old couple, were anxious when a knock came on their door. The military men were weary and in need of rest. In spite of their anxiety, the old couple hospitably offered their meager resources to the generals whom they did not recognize. The visitors slept that night on quilts spread on the dirt floor. The Ghazi is reported to have said to the man and woman, "I have no father and mother [despite the fact that his mother was still alive]. Would you be my parents?" The pair agreed that the Ghazi could be their "son." This encounter suggests that he created in the old couple a "good" Turkish mother and father who symbolically represented the Turkish nation and that his assumption of the role as their son pointed to him as the savior son, and promoted his vision of himself saving the grieving mother.

By 31 August everything appeared to be over for the Greeks. Swift and ferocious, the battle left its mark on the immediate area. Mustafa Kemal recalled his feelings when he observed the scene after the victory:

> When I walked on the battleground, I was deeply affected by the greatness of the victory our army had gained, and in comparison to this, by the horror of the tragedy the enemy army had experienced. All the valleys, streams, and the protected places behind the ridges, strewn with all the abandoned cannons, vehicles, and endless equipment and supplies, and amidst all this debris left by the dead, the heaps of corpses and the groups of prisoners being sent in droves to our headquarters, made the scene resemble the gathering on the Day of Judgement. [Aydemir 1969, vol. 2, p. 541]

Those who recalled seeing Mustafa Kemal on that day have described his genuine shock. It is reported that he confessed hatred of war to his aide-de-camp after observing the desolation and that he philosophized on the frailties of mankind, especially those of the Greeks. Shaken as he may have been by the ferocity of the battle, he remained resolute and reminded his troops of their goal in his order of the day, "Armies, your primary objective is the Mediterranean. Forward" (Atatürk 1964, vol. 4, p. 450).

While Mustafa Kemal had been at the front in the uniform of a simple soldier, urging his men to die for their country if need be, the Greek commander in chief, General Hajianestis, directed his side of the battle from a yacht in the harbor of Izmir. He was a political appointee who was subject to delusions, one of which was that his body was made of glass. It is said that he sometimes refused to rise from bed in the morning for fear of being crushed. It is known that the orders he issued were confused and confusing. The operational Greek command at the front was under General Tricoupis. He and another Greek general, Dionis, were both captured during the initial days of the battle and were the highest ranking captives. Many eyewitnesses have left accounts of their being brought before the Ghazi on 2 September, along with some 50 other Greek officers and 150 troops.[6] They anxiously awaited an audience with Mustafa Kemal outside his tent, dressed so smartly that one Turk remarked that they were ready to go anywhere, "Even to a ball" (Oranlı 1967, p. 128). The Turkish soldiers who guarded them were dressed rather shabbi-

[6]See Adıvar 1928, p. 346, and Ünaydın 1957, pp. 102–4. Mustafa Kemal himself refers to this event in his speech with only one sentence, "Among the prisoners of war was General Trikupis, commander in chief of the enemy's army" (Atatürk 1927, p. 566).

ly, using bits of rope for belts and lacking buttons for their shirts. The contrast between the conquered and the conquerers was staggering.

Meagerly furnished, the Ghazi's tent contained only a desk and a few folding chairs. Some Turkish officers were obliged to sit on the ground. An officer who knew Greek was summoned and asked to introduce the Turkish commanders to the captive Greek generals. All accounts of the meeting indicate that Fevzi and İsmet stood on either side of the Ghazi. Only Mustafa Kemal deigned to shake hands with the Greeks. He also restrained Tricoupis from trying to bow before him. A trunk was sent to serve as a seat for Tricoupis, and Mustafa Kemal offered him cigarettes and coffee. Tricoupis is said to have remarked that he had not realized how young Mustafa Kemal was. Mustafa Kemal was able to inform Tricoupis that Hajianestis had been dismissed and that Tricoupis was commander in chief in his place. Their conversation lasted for some time and included talk about the tactics of the battle. The Greeks were impressed that he had conducted the battle from the front lines himself. They reported that they had been unable to communicate with Izmir because the Turkish cavalry had cut the telephone lines. Graciously, Mustafa Kemal asked Tricoupis if there was anything he could do for him. The Greek general asked that his wife be informed that he had been taken prisoner, and Mustafa Kemal promised to do that.

Leaderless and in disarray, the Greek army retreated toward Izmir with the Turks in hot pursuit, but even the Grand National Assembly in Ankara did not learn until the beginning of September that the battle was virtually won. Always cautious about security, Mustafa Kemal kept the great offensive out of the news, and even his own people remained in ignorance of what was going on until success was assured. The Allies once again found it difficult to believe in the Turkish victory. The British foreign secretary, Lord Curzon, was told by Sir Horace Rumbold, the high commissioner in Istanbul, on the basis of news from the British consul in Izmir, that the Greeks "went to pieces altogether," and left "a sickening record of bestiality and barbarity" (Kinross 1965, p. 362) in their wake.

No doubt there were psychological reasons for their extreme inhumanity. After living for centuries under Ottoman domination, they had at last recaptured part of Anatolia, revitalizing their hope of reestablishing the Byzantine Empire. Boundary lines between reality and this passionate wish became blurred, creating a shared psychological world that could sustain Greek self-esteem. The collapse of the Ottoman Empire seemed to provide the West, and especially the British, with an opportunity to be of assistance to the Greeks. In the end it had taken but a few days to put an end to the gloriously anticipated return of Hellenism, to crush all hope, and thus to induce a shared narcissistic rage among the disappointed Greeks. They left a chilling devastation behind them. Uşak and Manissa are two large cities on the road to Izmir from Afyon. One-third of Uşak was razed and all but 500 of 18,000 buildings in Manissa were destroyed by the retreating Greeks. Halide Edib described Alaşehir, a small city not far from Izmir:

> The city is a pile of ashes. . . . Neither Greeks nor our people had found time to bury the dead, the Turkish army running at top speed to save Turkish cities from being burned. The Greek army is escaping from the fires it started, and from atrocities. But each side shows no mercy to the other. . . . The people are confused. Women mindlessly try to dig the ground with their fingers. It is as though hell had come to earth. . . . I remember Alaşehir as an oven stinking with burned human flesh. [Adıvar 1928, p. 367]

Before the great offensive began, Mustafa Kemal predicted that he would rid Anatolia of the Greeks in fourteen days. He fell short by only one day. Turkish soldiers reached Izmir on 9 September. The Ghazi, Fevzi, and İsmet surveyed Izmir from a distance through their field glasses. Seeing no sign of fire, they felt immense relief. Mustafa Kemal had indicated that he would be saddened if anything happened to Izmir. That city's tragedy was yet to come.

Spending the night at Nif, which was renamed Kemal Pasha, the Ghazi wanted that evening to be marked as unlike any other. He encouraged his staff to sing. On the following day, 10 September, he entered Izmir. On the same day, Bursa was liberated by Turkish forces. When that news reached Ankara, the black cloth was removed from the assembly's rostrum. The new Turkey's first experience with mourning was over, at least symbolically.

18

Love's Flame among the Flames That Burned Izmir

When Mustafa Kemal entered Izmir on 10 September 1922 in an automobile decorated with olive branches, the city was not yet securely in Turkish hands. With his staff, he went directly to the government building, surprising the Turks there, as well as the foreign consul and other dignitaries, by his prompt arrival. The nearby square was filled with Turks, young and old, all cheering in a virtual frenzy. They kissed the soldiers, pressed flowers upon them, and hugged them. The convertible given to the Ghazi by the Turks of Izmir overflowed with roses and carnations in the Turkish colors, red and white. With tears of joy streaming down their cheeks, people crowded forward to touch and even kiss the car as though it were the person of the hero himself. They even embraced the cavalry guard and their horses.

Contrasted with this scene of boundless joy was the less fortunate predicament of the crowds of Greek refugees who had arrived from the interior in the wake of the retreating Greek army. Although a large contingent of the Greek army had been evacuated by ship on the preceding day, some troops had been left behind, along with thousands of refugees. Allied warships still lay in the harbor. People frantic to leave Izmir jumped into the water in an attempt to reach the overladen boats making runs to those vessels. Even when those boats managed to pull alongside the warships, the refugees were not permitted on board. The day was one of overwhelming confusion, joy, excitement, and tragedy.

While Mustafa Kemal and his staff were in the government building, there was a flare-up of gunfire and an increase in the clamor of fighting. Everyone grew tense and wary. It was learned later that about three thousand Greek soldiers, pursued by a Turkish guerrilla band, had just arrived in Izmir unaware that the Turks had entered the city. A battle broke out, but was quickly ended. Had the Greeks known that Mustafa Kemal was in the government building, his situation might have been difficult in the extreme.

Feelings ran high among the Turks, Greeks, and Armenians in the liberated city. Mustafa Kemal tried to prevent gratuitous insults to the Greeks and their flags, and he issued an order to the effect that any Turkish soldier who molested a noncombatant would be dealt with severely, but the situation was not so easily controlled. The fear of massacre was on all minds. Representatives of the French government arranged to talk with Mustafa Kemal, who gave assurances that he would protect the Christian population. The British representative was ordered by his government not to pay an official visit to Mustafa Kemal, but managed to have an unofficial encounter. The Ghazi berated the British consul, telling him that without the British the Greeks would not have been able to land in Anatolia. He added that the Turks were still technically at war with the British. When Turkish soldiers prevented the British admiral Osmond de Beauvoir Brock, whose ship was in the harbor, from landing, the British flagship trained its guns on the city. Admiral Brock demanded written clarification from Mustafa Kemal as to whether the terms of the Mudros Armistice were to be observed, or whether Turkey and Britain continued to be at war.

Amidst all this confusion, on the afternoon of 10 September, a young woman entered the room of his aide-de-camp next to the one where the Ghazi was engaged in discussion with representatives of the foreign powers and his own staff and demanded to see him. A small woman of about twenty-three or twenty-four, with brown eyes and a slightly plump figure, she wore a stylish purple *çarşaf*, a head covering, but no veil. Her obvious determination struck the aide-de-camp, Salih, as outrageous. He explained that what she asked for was out of the question. The Ghazi was still engaged in a war and had no time for her. He offered her a compromise, saying that if she could wait for a day or two he would see what could be done about her request. She stood firm and so harangued the aide that he finally announced her to the commander in chief. Mustafa Kemal asked his aide what she wanted to see him about, and when he replied that he had no idea, the Ghazi told him to get rid of her.

His order came too late, however, for the young woman was already in the room, identifying herself as Lâtife, the daughter of Uşakizade Muammer Bey, a well-known Izmir businessman. She declared that she had made a pact with herself not to leave without kissing the Ghazi's hand, even if she were to be killed for her boldness. Mustafa Kemal asked her to be seated. Such a concession on the part of a thoroughly preoccupied general at a time of crisis can only be a matter for speculation. Perhaps he was flattered, and perhaps this well-dressed Turkish woman without a veil gave him some comfort after the brutal battle he had been engaged in for fifteen days. He was certainly impressed with her family connections, being familiar with the name of Uşakizade Muammer Bey. We suggest, however, that she reminded him of himself as he had been as a young man in Istanbul—brash, abrupt, and heedless of protocol, making pacts with himself to save the country and barging into bureaucratic offices to announce his dream. He was drawn to this young woman who had pushed her way through frenzied crowds and had overcome his protective aide-de-camp to burst into his private world.

Lâtife told him she was the oldest daughter of Muammer Bey and that she was studying law in France. She spoke French like a native and was proficient in English as well. While in France, she revealed, she kept dreaming about Mustafa Kemal who told her not to worry, that he would save the country. Those words added to the rapport based on her resemblance to a younger Mustafa Kemal. In effect, she had voiced a frank expression of her belief in his superiority. She could very well have been an extension of himself!

His success at the Sakarya had elated her. When the great offensive seemed imminent, she insisted to her parents that she return to their country and witness the Ghazi's rescue of it with her own eyes. Summering in Biarritz, they were unable to prevent her from returning to Turkey to work for Mustafa Kemal. The family maintained a home in the Göztepe district of Izmir, and she invited him to move there. Moreover, she told him that the Greeks had treated her rudely on her return to Izmir, searching not only her baggage, but her person as well. They had found Mustafa Kemal's picture, clipped from a French newspaper, in a locket she was wearing, which displeased them greatly. She showed the picture to him. The Ghazi found the gesture charming and went so far as to agree to give serious thought to becoming a guest in her family's home.

Pleased with this encounter, Mustafa Kemal told Halide Edib about it. She later wrote that at this moment of his glory Mustafa Kemal should have known that thousands of young Turkish girls carried his picture and his image in their hearts (Adıvar 1928, p. 384).

In the meantime, the Turks of Izmir had found another site for Mustafa Kemal's headquarters in Karşıyaka on the other side of Izmir's harbor. It was a house across the bay from Göztepe, in a section populated by many foreigners. It had been lovingly prepared for his occupancy. The Turks in Izmir wanted him to make a ceremonial parade to his residence in the new convertible. The route passed through old Izmir, making a loop from the government building to Karşıyaka along the shoreline. Since the British had a garrison in old Izmir at the tip of a thumblike incursion of the bay, he would have to pass by the British.

Mustafa Kemal had always wanted to save his country and be the undisputed leader of his people. The time had now come. Arriving at the pinnacle of his long anticipated success, he seemed to become an innocent child free of cynicism. Psychologically it was as if having saved the grieving mother from her grief, he could relax and in turn be saved by the mother he had rescued. External events do not necessarily alter the internal structure of an individual, but they may correspond with his inner wishes, at least temporarily, enabling him to rejoice in being alive and to feel gratified inwardly. Thus, Mustafa Kemal agreed to drive the loop to Karşıyaka in his new car. The cavalry accompanied him, lances in hand, making a dazzling spectacle. He sat in his car in godlike splendor, clad in a light grey overcoat that associated him with the grey wolf of Turkish myth. That story revolves around a Turkish tribe that had been lost in a valley from which there was apparently no way out. The people multiplied there, but were unable to leave the valley until a grey wolf's appearance pointed to the existence of a passage to the world outside. Following the wolf, they made their escape. The grey wolf became a Turkish national symbol and provided Mustafa Kemal with another sobriquet. Despite the grey wolf (phallus) image with its connotation of the fierce and the swift, he managed in his car full of flowers to suggest the radiance of an innocent bride on her way to a wedding festival. The Ghazi combined male and female elements and thus offered his Turkish followers a wholly satisfying parental image.

On his arrival at the house in Karşıyaka, Mustafa Kemal was asked to mount the marble steps between the ranks of people waiting to catch a glimpse of him. He noticed that a Greek flag had been spread out for him to walk on. This angered him, for he was far too scrupulous to step on the flag of his enemy. He was told that this house had been chosen for him because King Constantine of Greece had stayed there and had trampled on the Turkish flag upon entering it. Composing himself, the Ghazi declared that King Constantine's mistake was one he did not propose to repeat. A flag, he said, represents a country's honor and should not be trodden upon. The Greek flag was removed by his orders (Kinross 1965, p. 367).

On the following day he was in a happy mood, feeling again like a joyous young man, full of mischief. Prior to the commencement of the great offensive, he had promised friends that he would eat and drink in Izmir's well-known Kramer Hotel. When he went there, dressed simply and attracting no attention, he found the hotel was full of foreigners, among them many Greeks. A waiter who did not recognize him told him there were no vacant tables, but then everyone recognized him, much to his delight, and tables were found for his party. He asked for a glass of rakı and, standing up, held his glass aloft and asked the people in the room, "Did King Constantine ever come here to drink a glass of rakı?" When they said no, he laughed, "Why then did he bother to take Smyrna [Izmir]" (Kinross 1965, p. 367).

A tragic event took the joy out of the Turkish victory. A terrible fire broke out and spread through Izmir. The Kramer Hotel was among the buildings burned to the ground, and the fire threatened the Ghazi's headquarters. Responsibility for the fire has been disputed; the Turks blame the Greeks and the Armenians, the Greeks and the Armenians accuse the Turks. Eyewitnesses report both sides committed brutalities. As usual with ethnic conflicts, the truth is obscured by special pleading on both sides.

Strong winds fanned the flames that reduced thousands of homes to ashes. When the fire came dangerously close to Mustafa Kemal's headquarters, his staff prevailed on him to relocate. Falih Rıfkı (Atay), a journalist who had just arrived in Izmir from Istanbul, detailed the Ghazi's flight to Lâtife's house in Göztepe (Atay 1980, p. 323). A large truck and a few cars were dispatched to the Ghazi's establishment in Karşıyaka. With Mustafa Kemal in one car, the party followed the truck which opened a way through the crowds. The caravan had to negotiate the entire loop along the shoreline to Göztepe. The journey was not easy. Falih Rıfkı feared that the waves of panic-stricken people would overwhelm the Ghazi and smother him, but the party managed to reach Lâtife's house safely.

The white house, as it was called, was indeed a stately mansion. Built in the European Mediterranean style, this three-story structure must have impressed Mustafa Kemal. The doorway on the street level was elaborately decorated with wrought iron panels. Rising on the sides of this entrance were two semicircular, grand stairways with white wrought iron railings leading to the first level portico and main entrance of the house. A railed portico shaded by an arbor ran the length of the house.

İsmet and Fevzi soon joined the Ghazi at Lâtife's. She met them at the stairway with adoring eyes. Falih Rıfkı recounts that Mustafa Kemal was taken to his room and later came down in a beautiful Russian silk shirt to meet the people crowding into the house. His eyes had a faraway look for a few minutes and then he became intent. Falih Rıfkı thought of him as a god. When nighttime came, Lâtife acted as a proper hostess in the dining room, sitting at the right hand of her hero, between the Ghazi and Fevzi, while İsmet sat on Mustafa Kemal's left.

Falih Rıfkı and another journalist, Yakup Kadri (Karaosmanoğlu), were asked to stay that first night. Although it was the first time either sat with Mustafa Kemal at a dinner table, they often appeared later at the presidential table. Mustafa Kemal's capacity for recall astonished Falih Rıfkı when he recollected in detail a chance meeting between them years earlier. The journalists' first impression of the hero was that he was a happy man who successfully sought to make everyone feel at ease, but they noticed something else, as Halide Edib had done when she first met Mustafa Kemal. Falih Rıfkı gives further evidence that Mustafa Kemal used the splitting mechanism and behaved as if he were two people. Falih Rıfkı wrote:

> Even on our first night together, we felt close to him [Mustafa Kemal] as if he were an old friend. But with one gaze, with one word, we sensed how he could distance himself as much as he wished. These *two men* always stayed intertwined. . . . His real personality (the one who possessed great responsibilities) would not leave him alone even during the nights of entertainment. His mind always seemed to be hooked on some thought. These *two men*, one of whom would be nicknamed "debauchee" by some souls, have shortened each other's lives. [Atay 1980, pp. 326–27; italics added]

Falih Rıfkı felt that the two men in Mustafa Kemal's character had found a balance. That night the leader chose to discuss the comparison between love and pity. The journalists, who had thought of him previously as a mighty warrior, were now seeing his human side. As the night wore on, Mustafa Kemal began to sing and he seemed lost in memories of his own. Then he got up and danced a *zeybek*, a folk dance of Aegean Anatolia, not making certain of the traditional movements as though westernizing the dance. No one went to bed before dawn.

Mustafa Kemal's relationship with Lâtife has been depicted by İsmet Bozdağ (1975*a*). He describes a scene between Mustafa Kemal and his hostess. When Izmir burned, some of the buildings consumed by the fire belonged to Lâtife's family. Seeing her crying, the Ghazi sought to console her. She supposedly responded by saying that she wept not for the material loss, but because her country had been saved. She had dreamed about the Turkish flag again waving over the city, and her tears were tears of joy. She then suddenly embraced her hero, resting her head on his shoulder. Since his personality organization would not allow him to acknowledge affection openly (except toward children and animals), Lâtife's gesture must have taken him aback. Bozdağ suggests that she may have reminded him at this point of Miti, whom he had known in Sofia. In the days before Gallipoli, before he was hit by shrapnel, and before his grandiosity and convictions of immortality had crystallized, he had wanted Miti, a Westerner, to be his wife so that he could turn his back on a grieving, oppressive mother. Bozdağ tells a story of a walk Mustafa Kemal took with Miti in the King's Park in Sofia. When they came upon a child playing with a bird tied by a string attached to its leg, Mustafa Kemal bought the bird from the child and set it free, whereupon Miti began to cry and hugged him. Now Lâtife was hugging him, and perhaps for a moment she took him back to a gentler time of his life. Bozdağ reports that Mustafa Kemal softly disentangled himself from Lâtife's embrace to join his comrades in conversation and drink. From that day on, he called her *Lâtif*, dropping the feminine ending of the Arabic word meaning

Two couples, four lives. Mustafa Kemal and Lâtife Hanım pose with Fethi Okyar and his wife.

"pleasantry" and giving her a name that meant "beautiful" and even "ethereal."[1]

Soon people began to notice the developing relationship between Lâtife and Mustafa Kemal. Most seemed to approve. Fevzi and İsmet were there at the time, Halide Edib dropped by often, and later, Rauf and Ali Fuat were visitors. Mustafa Kemal told Rauf that the war was over and that as soon as peace really came, he would probably buy a small farm on the Aegean coast and raise fruit there. He gave the impression of trying to be a family man. One day, while in a jovial mood, he ordered Halide Edib's promotion, and Lâtife sewed the badges of her new rank onto Halide's uniform.

Each morning Lâtife would pore over the newspapers, especially those from Europe, and would give Mustafa Kemal a summary of world events

[1]Also by dropping the *e*, which is the feminine ending in Arabic (preserved in Ottoman Turkish), Mustafa Kemal seems to be attacking Lâtife's femininity—for every woman had the possibility of turning into his grieving/bad mother. He could not get too close to any woman. Another explanation for his dropping the *e* might be due to his attempt to identify her as a representation of himself as a young man, and in some of the existing pictures of her, Lâtife indeed appears rather masculine.

as she brought him his breakfast. He called her his "talking newspaper." She was like a Western woman, and as he had been in the habit of doing with Western women, he spoke to her about his childhood, his mother, and their relationship. Those conversations took place when the two dined alone. Their relationship was becoming sexualized. Students of this period of Mustafa Kemal's life generally discuss his desire to go to bed with Lâtife, and her refusal to do so before being married to him. This refusal cannot be documented, but it is likely, given Lâtife's background.[2]

The electricity in Mustafa Kemal's personal relationships was matched with increasing tension in the diplomatic realm. Advancing Turkish cavalry and infantry units had made contact with the British forces dug in around the town of Çanak, an important base for control of the straits. The issue was clear: would the Ghazi halt the Turkish advance, or would the British fire upon the Turks, thus risking the resumption of all-out warfare.

On 18 September, General Pelle, the French high commissioner in Istanbul, went to Lâtife's house in Izmir to call on the Turkish commander in chief, a gesture that emphasized French recognition of the Ghazi as the head of his country. General Pelle, a proud man more comfortable with the formalities of the sultanate in Istanbul, found this task repugnant. He was concerned about how he would be received. Falih Rıfkı's account of the meeting (Atay 1980, p. 329) tells us that Mustafa Kemal descended the stairs to help Pelle the Frenchman, who found himself pale and dizzy at the confrontation. Pelle asked Mustafa Kemal to keep the Turkish troops from pressing on toward the Sea of Marmara and Istanbul. Mustafa Kemal replied that in fourteen days his armies had advanced 550 kilometers against an enemy force of 140,000 to 150,000 men. The foot soldiers had kept pace with the cavalry and even if he wanted to stop them, it was beyond his power to do so.

Perhaps most at issue was Thrace.[3] General Pelle asked Mustafa Kemal how much territory he was prepared to assign to the Greeks in what had

[2]At the same time, and even now, the virginity of an unmarried woman is a most important issue among the Turks. Lâtife came from a well-bred family and the tradition and cultural norms would not allow her to lose her virginity prior to marriage. Even though she adored Mustafa Kemal, she would have been giving up her self-esteem, and thus would not be worthy of her lover if she had sexual intercourse with him out of wedlock.

[3]On 5 September 1922 Mustafa Kemal sent a telegram to Rauf, then president of the Council of Ministers, and stated, "The Greek army has been decisively defeated in Anatolia. . . . There is no reason to enter into any negotiations with regard to the question of Anatolia. The armistice can only be discussed with reference to Thrace" (Atatürk 1927, p. 567).

[4]Pelle did not have the backing of the French foreign office, which did not want to promote Mustafa Kemal; Busch 1976, p. 350. See also the still informative article by Davison 1953, pp. 172–209.

been the Ottoman presence in Europe.[4] This led Mustafa Kemal to the harsh declaration that although the French, along with the British, were responsible for Turkey's tragedy because they had abetted the Greek landings in Anatolia, Pelle now seemed to place the host and the thief who had robbed him on an equal footing. Mustafa Kemal's interpreter tried to soften the Ghazi's words in translation, but the Ghazi caught him up, saying, "You are giving a false interpretation. Just tell him exactly what I say" (Aydemir 1969, 3:23). In their discussion Mustafa Kemal made it rather clear what he would accept from the Allies—the Greeks in Thrace would have to withdraw west of the Maritsa River.

Mustafa Kemal enjoyed playing his role of the superior. Although the British remained in Gallipoli, the French removed their troops on 19 September. The principal remaining problem was the presence of sixty-four enemy ships in the harbor of Izmir. Lâtife was instructed by the Ghazi to write an ultimatum to the Allies in English demanding their departure within twenty-four hours. His followers were anxious should the British refuse and initiate a new war, but the Ghazi's narcissistic personality organization once again saved the day by enabling him to discount any uncongenial realities that might threaten the execution of his will. During the ensuing twenty-four hours of generalized anxiety, he busied himself with other matters, and at last word came that the ships were departing the harbor after saluting the city. Continuing his work without interruption, Mustafa Kemal showed little interest in their departure. His personality was such that he had had no doubt that the enemy would comply with his ultimatum.

Turkish negotiations with the French were expedited when Franklin-Bouillon arrived in Izmir on 28 September. He was already known to the Ghazi, who met him at the dock with Rauf and İsmet. The Ghazi agreed to a conference to be held at Mudanya at which the Turks and the Allies would lay the groundwork for peace. On 29 September the Ghazi left for Ankara, arriving there on 2 October.

During most of his twenty days in Izmir, Mustafa Kemal had been Lâtife's guest, but despite her hospitality, he refused to let her accompany him to Ankara. Fikriye awaited him there. Had he allowed Lâtife to return with him, all sorts of complications would have arisen. He had to deal with Fikriye before his relationship with Lâtife could develop further.

Ankara turned out to give Mustafa Kemal a hero's welcome. On 4 October he gave a speech before the Grand National Assembly. Like a good teacher, he shared his thoughts and plans with the deputies. On the same day peace talks opened at Mudanya, a sleepy town north of Bursa on the Sea of Marmara. To the surprise of all, Mustafa Kemal chose İsmet, who had no previous experience in diplomacy, to represent the new Turkey. İsmet joined the delegates of the Allies in the house of a man named Alexander Ganyanof, a Russian merchant who lived in Mudanya.

In Ankara, meanwhile, Fikriye was pondering Mustafa Kemal's changed attitude toward her. She now knew that she had tuberculosis and may have attributed his coolness toward her to some anxiety about infection. She had, however, heard about Lâtife, with whose family connections she could not compete. Having obtained a picture of her rival (Bozdağ 1975*a*, pp. 49, 184–85), Fikriye must have realized that she faced not only a struggle against her own illness, but also a formidable challenge for the affections of her lover.

19

The Sultan, the Mother, and the Oedipal Son

MUSTAFA KEMAL'S RETURN TO ANKARA AS A HERO CONTRASTED WITH A COUP d'etat in Athens led by Venizelist officers. King Constantine was toppled and replaced by George II as the Venizelists promised to punish those responsible for the debacle in Anatolia. The Ghazi had not only altered the history of his own country but also brought a new regime to power in Athens.

Defeat of the Greeks by the Turks introduced new tension into the relationships among the Allies. The French supported Mustafa Kemal even more openly than before. Italy had already given the Ghazi a pledge of neutrality. Both the French and the Italians had pulled their forces out of Çanak, leaving the British flag flying alone. Lloyd George refused to believe in the total defeat of the Greeks. Churchill, who had supported the Turks in opposition to Lloyd George, was galled by the humiliation of defeat and joined those in the British cabinet seeking to stop Mustafa Kemal. Britain's plans to raise troops from the Balkan states and the dominions came to nothing. General Harrington, who was negotiating for the British on the scene, remained calm and refused to deliver to the Turks any ultimatum for their withdrawal. In the end, there seemed no recourse but to agree to a conference at Mudanya.

Almost continuous negotiations led to an agreement on 11 October. İsmet cabled the news to Ankara that the war had been brought to an official conclusion. In the Grand National Assembly the deputies rejoiced, hugging and kissing each other in their delight at having reached a victory they regarded as richly deserved. The Mudanya agreement brought a halt to the fighting between the Turks and the Greeks and allowed Turkish forces to occupy Thrace up to the Maritsa River, giving the Greeks fifteen days to withdraw. Allied forces would remain for a month to ensure a calm transfer of power. An Allied presence would still remain in Istanbul and Gallipoli until peace between the Allies and the new Turkey was concluded.

As the Turks prepared to occupy Thrace, the Lloyd George government collapsed. Gone were his hopes for the resurrection of a Greek empire, and gone, too, was his support in the cabinet, Parliament, and the country. Lloyd George was brought low by Mustafa Kemal and the host of problems, both internal and external, that plagued postwar Britain. On 23 October, four days after Lloyd George's fall, Andrew Bonar Law assumed responsibility for the government and the new elections that would take place in mid-November.

While this political infighting was taking place in Mudanya and London, Mustafa Kemal faced some delicate negotiations of his own in Ankara concerning Fikriye and Lâtife. During his stay in Izmir he had been greatly impressed with Lâtife, but if he were to make her his consort, he would have to banish Fikriye, whose tubercular condition was no longer a secret. Mustafa Kemal abhorred illness in anyone, but that repugnance was intensified with respect to a sickly woman, for it no doubt reminded him of the grieving mother of his early childhood. He had learned to distance himself from such women even as he worked to save their mental representation, displaced to the nation itself. Upon his return to Ankara, he urged Fikriye to go to Switzerland for a cure. He got her physicians to agree that treatment in a modern tuberculosis sanatorium would be beneficial. In the end, she decided to become a patient in a private Swiss clinic but refused to enter a sanatorium. The Ghazi instructed Salih, his chief aide-de-camp, to make arrangements for her in Switzerland. At the same time he had him send a telegram to Lâtife in Izmir telling her to meet him in Bursa on 12 October to take part in the anticipated celebration for the agreement that would be reached in nearby Mudanya. Fikriye reluctantly accepted his plan to seek treatment in Switzerland, but as the situation developed, it made further demands on his "diplomatic skills." At the last minute Fikriye changed her mind. She insisted that they have one last trip together, to Bursa, before she departed for Switzerland. Then, after leaving Bursa, she planned to visit relatives in Istanbul to say farewell.

Obliged to agree to this, the Ghazi had another telegram sent to Lâtife, telling her not to join him in Bursa after all. The telegram arrived while Lâtife was in a state of elation over the prospect of joining her pasha. Her suitcases were packed for the journey, and the car in which she was to travel was ready. That message chilled her and threw her into despair, suggesting to her that the cancellation of the Bursa trip meant that the Ghazi was ill. Although she sent a telegram to the aide-de-camp expressing her wish for Mustafa Kemal's quick recovery from the supposed illness, Lâtife was curious enough to call the news agency in Izmir and learned that Mustafa Kemal was in Bursa. Her despair deepened at this information, for by now she had heard much about Fikriye. Handling the situation with her own diplomatic skills, she wrote to Mustafa Kemal, telling him that she had heard of his arrival in Bursa—news that had allayed her fears about his health. His original invitation to join him in Bursa had given her two very happy nights before it was cancelled, and in any case, she would be loyal to him forever.

Even as Mustafa Kemal wrestled with the problem of keeping his two women apart, he was able to remain highly effective in testing the realities of the national situation. He appointed İsmet, who had been successful at Mudanya, to represent the new Turkey at the peace conference that was to convene in Lausanne. Rauf, the prime minister, had expected to attend the conference himself accompanied by his own minister of foreign affairs. Short-circuiting Rauf, the Ghazi had met with the foreign minister, who agreed to step aside and be replaced by İsmet. Mustafa Kemal was more comfortable with İsmet and felt he could control him more effectively.

Accompanied to Bursa by Kâzım and Refet as well as Fikriye, the Ghazi was met there by Fevzi and İsmet. They all made an appearance before the ten thousand or more Turks crowded together for a victory celebration that lasted all night and included a tumultuous demonstration.

Mustafa Kemal was the houseguest of Bursa's mayor. Fikriye was given a bedroom next to his. After everyone had retired for the night, she went to his bedroom and had what was apparently an attack of "hysteria." Unable to speak coherently, she kept muttering, "My Pasha, my Pasha," until a physician sedated her. Supposedly, before breaking down, she told the Ghazi that she knew she was about to die and wanted to spend the remainder of her days with the man who was beloved by everyone, so that she could die in happiness (Bozdağ 1975*a*, p. 77).

Mixed feelings must have been aroused in Mustafa Kemal by this confrontation. The plight of Fikriye, who had loved him slavishly, no doubt appealed to his savior fantasy and possibly evoked his carefully concealed capacity for tenderness, but he had transferred his savior fantasies to the saving of the nation. Moreover, since childhood he had distanced himself from grieving (ill) women. He refused to change his mind and insisted that Fikriye go to Switzerland as planned. She complied.

Some semblance of order having been restored to his personal life, the Ghazi turned again to politics, but politics tinged with his own concerns. He appointed Refet, who had not participated militarily in the great offensive, as special representative to the Grand National Assembly. Refet was also ordered to Istanbul and then Thrace as special commissioner for the Nationalists, making him the first Nationalist figure of prominence to enter the former Ottoman capital in Europe. Refet's departure for Istanbul served a dual purpose. The incipient opposition to the Ghazi was appeased by Refet's appointment to a place of honor, and he would be able to escort Fikriye on the first part of her journey to Switzerland. Accompanied by a hundred Nationalist gendarmes, Refet arrived in Istanbul on 19 October, but he and his entourage were prevented by the British from disembarking until the following day. At that time they were given a stunning reception by the populace. Countless Turkish flags and the green banners of Islam were unfurled, and people hung from balconies, clung to rooftops, and filled the streets in an emotional frenzy.

Fikriye landed in Istanbul with Refet and his gendarmes, and she saw the tumultuous welcome. She could not fail to become increasingly aware of the idolatry given her pasha whose portrait was displayed everywhere. Halide Edib, who was in Bursa when Fikriye left with Refet, later recalled her own goodbye to the ailing woman. In grasping Fikriye's hand, she was reminded of the boyish hand of Lâtife, which it seemed to her to resemble despite Lâtife's superior health and vigor. She said of Fikriye, her "pretty little chin was a sharp blade edge, the small nose almost transparent in its thinness and squeezed, tortured air" (Adıvar 1928, p. 398). There was hurt in Fikriye's eyes: "Out of this devastated mask of pain they loomed; the lower and the upper lashes curled and intermingled more than ever; tears falling through their webby edges on the sunken and drawn cheeks" (Adıvar 1928, p. 398). The vision of that young woman who had galloped through the streets of Ankara, the object of all eyes, beloved in the Ghazi's household, in spite of Zübeyde's presence, was transformed into the image of a desperately ill woman.

With Fikriye out of the way, Mustafa Kemal began to plan his life with Lâtife. He approached his mother on the subject and asked her to go to Izmir, where she would be a guest in Lâtife's home. His rationalization was the benefit his now arthritic mother would gain from being near the sea, but in actuality he felt the traditional need to have his mother bless his intended marriage.

Ensuring Fikriye's removal from Ankara was only part of Refet's assignment. He did not neglect the political aspects of his position. Once in Istanbul, Refet refused to acknowledge the Ottoman government and made no mention of the sultan. He made reference only to the high office of the caliph when he was welcomed by a group that included the sultan's aide-de-camp, implying a recognition of the religious high office while denying the governmental power of the sultan. When visiting the tomb of Sultan Mehmed the Conqueror, who had seized Constantinople from the Byzantines in 1453, he made a speech assuring the Conqueror's spirit that no Turk would ever permit the city to fall into infidel hands.

Confident in the extreme, Refet had an audience with Sultan Mehmed VI in which he advised the discredited ruler to dissolve the government in Istanbul inasmuch as Turkey could no longer afford two government systems. The sultan continued to cling to the hope that somehow he would be saved and allowed to remain on the throne, but his hopes were dampened when the Allies asked both the Istanbul and Grand National

Assembly governments to send delegates to the peace conference in Lausanne. That invitation served to highlight the anomaly of two governments existing in the remnant of the Ottoman Empire. Aware of the hackles that such an untoward invitation would raise in Ankara, Tevfik Pasha, the grand vizier, had sought to fend off the worst by proposing to Mustafa Kemal on 17 October, before the invitations were actually received, that a common position be worked out in anticipation of the conference. Mustafa Kemal replied by cable on the following day that through the adoption of the constitution by the Grand National Assembly, the only recognized representative of the Turkish nation was, by law, the government of the Grand National Assembly.

On 27 October the Ankara government received its official invitation, as did the sultan's. Tevfik Pasha sent the Grand National Assembly a cable suggesting a joint delegation, which threw the deputies into an uproar. One after another, they denounced the Istanbul government and this flagrant attempt to divide the nation. Impassioned discussions on 30 October led to the submission of a resolution signed by eighty deputies and Mustafa Kemal, which declared that the Ottoman Empire was dead, a new Turkish nation had taken its place, and constitutionally sovereignty belonged to the nation. While Mustafa Kemal had already foreseen the demise of the Ottoman Empire, the proposal for a joint delegation to Lausanne sealed its fate by signaling recognition of the Anatolian Nationalist government in Istanbul.

Opposition to this resolution arose within the assembly, especially among two groups, the religious element and those who feared that the resolution would strengthen Mustafa Kemal's position and lead to a dictatorship. A long and acrimonious debate broke out on the feasibility of separating the caliphate from the sultanate. If the sultanate were abolished, what would become of the caliphate? Mustafa Kemal discoursed at great length on the history of Islam, the life of Muhammad, and the history of the Ottomans. He argued that the two institutions had been separate in the early history of Islam and could be separate again. Separate, of course, implied the demise of the sultanate, with sovereignty reverting to the Turkish nation, and the continuation of the caliphate without any political authority.[1]

[1]In his "Great Speech," Mustafa Kemal reproaches Rauf and Refet regarding their views on the sultanate and the caliphate. When he asked Rauf about his convictions, the latter, according to Mustafa Kemal, told him the following, "I am devoted heart and soul to the throne and caliphate, because my father has received benefits from the Padishah [sultan]. . . . It is my duty to remain loyal to the Padishah. Regarding my attachment to the caliphate, it is imposed upon me by my education." Refet supposedly entirely shared Rauf's opinion (Atatürk 1927, p. 573). It is clear that Mustafa Kemal and some of his close associates were pulling apart at this time.

On 1 November, Mustafa Kemal opened the assembly debate on the resolution that had been submitted by eighty-one deputies, including himself. Several other resolutions on the matter had been submitted as well, leading to the selection of a joint committee composed of members from the Constitutional Committee, the Judicial Committee, and the Religious Law Committee. That joint committee immediately began deliberations in a crowded chamber. The discussion was followed by Mustafa Kemal from a corner of the room. A group of *ulema* tried to sustain by scholarly discourse the proposition that the caliphate and the sultanate were inseparable. Mustafa Kemal had no patience with such arguments, which could only prolong the discussion. Recognized by the chair, he stood on a bench before the deputies and declared that power could not be granted to anyone by means of such discussion. What counted was the evident fact that by their rebellion the Turkish people had seized power in a manner that was no longer subject to debate. Loudly he proclaimed:

> Gentlemen, neither the sovereignty nor the right to govern can be transferred by one person to anybody else by an academic debate. Sovereignty is acquired by force, by power, and by violence. It was by violence that the sons of Osman acquired the power to rule over the Turkish nation and to maintain their rule for more than six centuries. It is now the nation that revolts against these usurpers, puts them in their place and actually carries on their sovereignty. This is an actual fact. [Atatürk 1927, p. 578]

He went on to suggest that if his view of things was not accepted, possibly "some heads will be cut off." That challenge became one of his most celebrated public statements. In it he spoke unabashedly as a dictator, and he could well afford to do so at the time. It was also the clearest declaration yet of the way he felt about those who exploited religion. The immediate issue was a political one, but it should not be forgotten that his lifelong antagonism to religion arose in his early years, being connected with his "Molla" mother and the religious teacher who had beaten him so cruelly.

Brought to their senses by the Ghazi's chastisement, the committee supported a resolution to abolish the sultanate, which was quickly formalized as a law and adopted by the assembly on 1 November. News of this was transmitted to the Allies in Istanbul, where the sultan's government met for the last time on 4 November. On that day the directors of many official divisions of the Ottoman government visited Refet to declare that they were transferring their loyalty to the government of the Grand National Assembly. Refet ordered the termination of the Ottoman ministries on the following day, and the Ottoman government simply collapsed. Meanwhile, Mehmed VI remained in the palace. Mustafa Kemal was reluctant to banish him summarily, considering that for centuries the Ottomans had held the sultan to be God's shadow on earth. An image that had been regarded so reverently could not be made to disappear overnight. He knew full well that, among his own supporters and friends, many had a special place in their hearts and minds for the sultan. It was the potentate himself who finally solved the vexatious problem. On 16 November, Mehmed VI wrote to General Harrington that he felt his life to be in danger and requested assistance in making his departure from Istanbul. Arrangements were made for the sultan, his son, doctor, two confidential secretaries, bandmaster, valet, barber, and two eunuchs, to leave the palace in two British Red Cross ambulances early the next morning. The party was taken to dockside and then transferred by naval launch to the HMS *Malaya*. Once the sultan and his party were aboard, the warship steamed out of the harbor bound for Malta. The last Ottoman sultan, member of a dynasty that had ruled in an unbroken chain for over six centuries, was heading into ignoble exile.

So secretly had the sultan been moved that the Nationalists knew nothing of his departure until it had been completed. The day after Mehmed VI's successful escape into exile, the Grand National Assembly deprived him of the caliphate. His cousin and heir apparent, Abdülmecid, who had remained in Istanbul, was selected as caliph with the understanding that he would serve on conditions to be spelled out by the Grand National Assembly.

Turkish traditions that had prevailed over centuries had been shaken, not without resentment among some who directed their criticism toward Mustafa Kemal. While he was not directly called to account for his action in this regard, murmurs about his role in doing away with the sultanate reached his ears. Resentment against him became even more evident in a bill introduced in the Grand National Assembly in December 1922 which stated that only persons born within the Turkish borders of that day could be elected to the assembly and that anyone, whether Turk or Kurd, who had migrated to Turkey from outside those borders would have to have five years of residence before being eligible for election. This proposed electoral law was plainly directed against Mustafa Kemal, for his birthplace, Salonika, lay outside the borders of the new Turkish nation. Mustafa Kemal flew into a rage at this action and made an impassioned speech before the assembly, saying:

> The place of my birth is lying unfortunately outside our present frontiers; besides I also have not since lived five years continuously in the same electoral district. My birthplace is

> outside our present national frontiers, but that is neither an intention nor a fault on my part.
>
> The reason for it is that we have only partly succeeded to arrest the efforts of our enemies who are aiming at the destruction and disintegration of our country and our nation.
>
> If our enemies had succeeded in realising their designs completely the country of these gentlemen who have given their signatures here would likewise be outside the frontiers, which may God prevent.
>
> In addition, if I do not fulfill the conditions demanded in this Article, that is to say, if I have not been able to live for five years continuously in the same electoral district, the reason for this is to be found in the services which I have rendered to our country. If I had made it my business to satisfy the conditions of this law, I could not have defended Ari-Burnu or Anafarta [on the Gallipoli Peninsula], which has made it possible for us to keep Constantinople.
>
> If I had been condemned to live for five years in the same place, I should not have been able to oppose the enemy who was advancing on Diarbekr after having taken Bitlis and Musch; I could not have fulfilled my patriotic duty, the result of which was that Musch and Bitlis were saved.
>
> If I should have been desirous of fulfilling the conditions demanded by these gentlemen, I should not have been allowed to form an army at Aleppo out of the ruins of the armies that evacuated Syria, which I defended against the enemy, nor could I have effectively upheld the border which we call today our national frontier.
>
> I believe that the work to which I have dedicated myself henceforth is known to all of you. I have worked so much that I could not have lived for five years continuously in the same place. I believe that I have gained through these services the sympathy and love of my people and, perhaps, of the whole Mohammedan world. [Atatürk 1927, pp. 603–4]

His wounded, narcissistic outburst turned the tide. The bill was defeated.

Critical political moves by the Ghazi in the public arena were matched simultaneously by him with maneuvers in his private life. His mother was sent to Izmir to stay with Lâtife and her family. Lâtife made elaborate preparations for Zübeyde's arrival: the walls of the house were washed, the Turkish carpets dusted, the crystal chandeliers cleaned, and the garden trimmed. The eyes of all Izmir were on the white mansion. Offers of help came from every side, and the provincial governor visited and shared a cup of coffee with the hosts. Mustafa Kemal asked Salih and his wife to accompany Zübeyde to Izmir. Mustafa Kemal also called upon a political friend who had his residence in Izmir and was a distant relative of

Lâtife's. This man was to play the traditional role of matchmaker to bring the two families together with a possible marriage between Mustafa Kemal and Lâtife in mind.[2] The party going to Izmir also included the Ghazi's orderly, Ali, and the boy Abdürrahim, as well as several female helpers and companions for Zübeyde. Years later, Mr. Tuncak (1974) recalled that, at the time they went to Izmir, Zübeyde still used him as a "walking stick." With the war just over, the train carrying the party to Izmir passed through burned villages and towns, and Mr. Tuncak never forgot the indelibly sad impression the scenes made on him.

Lâtife met the train when it chugged into the Izmir station, but she was only one of thousands who had gathered to see the national savior's mother. It was a sign of the dramatic changes occurring in the new Turkey that the dignitaries crowding the station were accompanied by their wives. Unveiled and dressed in a white *çarşaf*, Zübeyde nodded and smiled at the crowd from her train window. Although in her seventies, her big round face retained its smooth, milk-white and pink coloring with hardly a wrinkle. She resembled her son, but her eyes, behind silver-rimmed eyeglasses, were a darker blue, warmer, and more affectionate, and her mouth was kind. Nonetheless, she had a fiery temper and was not one to be reckoned with lightly, especially in matters concerning her Mustafa. On the train, she remained seated in a bamboo armchair on the advice of her doctor, who was concerned about her frail condition. She and Lâtife met for the first time in Zübeyde's train compartment. Taking an instant dislike to Lâtife, she nevertheless masked her feelings behind a facade of numerous compliments. In this atmosphere of dissimulation the party arrived at the white mansion in Göztepe that had been her son's temporary home during his stay in Izmir.

Tradition called for the presentation of a gift upon such an occasion. The Ghazi had sent a beautiful horse named Sakarya as a present for Lâtife. Custom demanded that Zübeyde give the horse to the younger woman, either as an engagement present from the Ghazi or simply as a gift to her hostess. Zübeyde saw to it that some ambiguity surrounded the presentation. Lâtife was charmed by the horse and responded with an appropriate expression of appreciation. The shrewd Zübeyde must have sensed that Lâtife was infatuated with the savior of her country rather than being genuinely in love with him. Moreover, her own long, torturous relationship with her son did not incline her to share him with another

[2]Mustafa Kemal's consideration of marriage at this point in his life may have had something to do with his saving the grieving nation-mother and now being free to individuate from her to find another woman—a wife. But we also suspect that the act of marriage to Lâtife would mean for him a binding together of himself with the feminine version of himself which he saw in Lâtife.

woman. Mr. Tuncak (1974) remembered hearing Zübeyde speak of her dissatisfaction with Lâtife to her maid companions and others. She saw no beauty in her and thought her too short to have any presence.

Their days together in the white mansion must have been stressful for both women. Lâtife was well educated, had visited Europe, was of another generation, and was accustomed to a different way of life. Zübeyde, on the other hand, was uneducated, and her Turkish was strongly accented in a manner that betrayed her Macedonian origin. She was witty in an earthy way, and her wit was often expressed through proverbs. Because she was often in pain, Zübeyde must have been rather irritable, but the real bone of contention was the unacknowledged competition between the two women. As she grew older, Zübeyde became more and more homesick for Salonika and found the luxury of the Izmir surroundings oppressive. During the first days of her visit, Lâtife's family was still abroad. When they returned from France, Zübeyde was quick to find the younger sister prettier than Lâtife, whose marriage to her son, she told Salih in a conversation never reported to Mustafa Kemal, she opposed (Bozdağ 1975*a*, p. 102).

Within ten days of her arrival in Izmir, Zübeyde asked to be returned to Ankara, but her doctor refused. Later, her health worsened. Ali was on the point of leaving for Ankara to assist the Ghazi with preparations for his own trip to Izmir. Zübeyde had already confided her doubts about Lâtife to Ali when she asked him, "Do you think this lady can make my Mustafa happy?" (Oranlı 1967, p. 141). Putting her affairs in order, she called for the chief religious figure of Izmir to be brought to her side. Supposedly, she also had a will drawn up in which she left her son a diamond ring.

Ali returned to Ankara, where word was received that Zübeyde's condition was worsening rapidly. Mustafa Kemal, accompanied by Ali and the rest of his retinue, set out for Izmir by train at 11 P.M. During the night Ali received a telegram in cipher informing him that Zübeyde had died on 14 January. He did not show it to Mustafa Kemal right away, not wishing to disturb the Ghazi with such bad news. Shortly before dawn Mustafa Kemal called for Ali and asked him if there had been any news. He replied that there had been a cipher, but it was in the process of being decoded. Mustafa Kemal said, "I know my mother has died," and he related a telepathic dream he had had during the night. He and his mother were walking in green fields, when a sudden torrent swept his mother away (Oranlı 1967, p. 142).

After the deciphered telegram was brought to him, Mustafa Kemal decided against going on to Izmir. He sent word ahead to have his mother properly buried and ordered his train to branch off to Izmit. He spent the better part of two weeks in the Izmit area, making speeches and attending to business before returning to Izmir on 27 January. Perhaps the delay was his way of denying his mother's death or dealing with his loss. His first act on arriving in Izmir was to visit his mother's grave in the garden of a mosque. He was accompanied by Kâzım and Fevzi. There he delivered an important oration, attesting consciously and unconsciously to the deep attachment that had existed between Zübeyde and her son, who now basked in glory as the savior of his motherland.

He told those at his mother's graveside that she had been a victim of oppression. He blamed the Abdülhamid administration for her suffering. He described how "the secret agents, the spies, the hangmen of tyranny" sent him away to Syria and how his mother, not being able to see her son, was left alone in her grief. He spoke of how his own and his mother's personal histories were intertwined with history on a grand scale. He mentioned that his mother had been grieved by the belief that the death sentence pronounced on him by the government of Mehmed VI had been carried out.

The Ghazi's emphasis in his speech at the graveyard was how grief-stricken his mother had been. He blamed all of this on the bad father figures, the sultans. Referring to the period following his leaving Istanbul for Samsun to initiate the Turkish struggle of independence, he said: "For three and a half years my mother cried day and night. Her tears made her lose her eyesight. Only recently I had saved her from Istanbul. Then I could rejoin her. However, she had already died in body and was only living on in spirit" (Atatürk 1952, vol. 2, p. 74). The echo of his displacement of feelings from his mother (perceived dead in life) to the nation (mother living in spirit) is clear, as is his lifelong burden of having a grieving mother.

> I am, naturally, sorry that I lost my mother. But there is something that negates my sorrow and consoles me. This something is to know that the administration which brought our *mother the country* to destruction and ruin has gone to the grave of oblivion, never again to return.
>
> My mother is under this soil, but let national sovereignty last forever. [Atatürk 1952, vol. 2, pp. 74–75; emphasis added]

Here, he blamed the oedipal father (sultan) for his mother's suffering. What survives, after the sultan has been sent to a "grave of oblivion," is the displaced mother-nation and triumphant son who saved her.

Once more, then, as is especially apparent in the last sentence, the image of the mother who dies continues in the image of the nation which survives. To heal that nation was to heal his mother, all in the service of restoring his grieving, ill mother to health so that she would be able to nurture him. It is ironic that in the process he became the nurturer of both his mother and the Turkish nation (Rustow, 1970). Mustafa Kemal finished his speech by taking an oath that it would be his duty to sacrifice his life in the service of national sovereignty.

Rustow has been interested in how Mustafa Kemal's speech at the graveside so quickly turns to a political theme. He says that in the speech:

> The authority figure is the sultan, first Abdülhamit and then Vahidettin, in the deposition of both of whom Kemal was instrumental. The relationship between these three *dramatis personae*—mother, son, sultan—thus is intimate. The sultan, one readily infers, represents the evil father figure: his emissaries are hangmen, and he is guilty of the bodily destruction of mother Zübeyde and mother country. Kemal himself appears as the loyal son, who avenges mother and country by exposing the hollowness of the sultan's—any sultan's—authority, by consigning him to "the grave of oblivion," and by replacing the sultanate with a more legitimate regime of his own creation and with himself in command. [Rustow 1970, p. 237]

We agree that here the oedipal theme is clear. What underlies this theme, however, was the substance of his personality organization that compelled him to attempt to reach an oedipal triumph on a grand historical stage.

20

Toward the Republic of Turkey

DEMONSTRATING AGAIN HIS ENORMOUS CAPACITY TO DEAL WITH DEVASTATING emotional shocks, Mustafa Kemal quickly collected himself at the conclusion of the speech at his mother's graveside. Leaving the grounds of the Osman Pasha mosque, he asked the governor of Izmir what the program was for the remainder of the day. Learning that out of respect for his mourning no official business had been scheduled, he decided to go to Lâtife's house. At that point a well-dressed man who had remained on the fringe of the group was brought forward and introduced to Mustafa Kemal as Uşakizade Muammer Bey, Lâtife's father. He paid his respects to the Ghazi and kissed his hand in the traditional fashion, and the two set off for the house that Mustafa Kemal had come to know so well.

Upon his arrival Mustafa Kemal thanked his hosts for the care and attention they had lavished on his mother during her last days. This was Mustafa Kemal's first meeting with Lâtife's family, for they had returned from France only after his departure from Izmir for Bursa. After the exchange of some formal small talk, Mustafa Kemal took Lâtife aside and announced to her that they would be married, possibly even at once. Lâtife was overcome with joy but protested that she needed some time to make adequate preparations. Remonstrating with her, Mustafa Kemal turned to Lâtife's mother and complained that she had a rather rebellious daughter who was disobeying his orders. Not knowing what had been said between them, the mother suggested that there might be some mistake. The Ghazi was enjoying himself and said, "No, there is no mistake. Let her tell you herself" (Bozdağ 1975*a*, p. 112). Lâtife blurted out that the Ghazi wanted to get married right away and that she had begged for some time, even a few hours. Everyone broke into relieved laughter as Mustafa Kemal gave in and put the marriage off for two days, until 29 January.

Probably most relieved of all was Mustafa Kemal's chief aide, Salih. He had accompanied Zübeyde to Izmir and had remained there with her. Many times she had used him as a sounding board and confidant for her feelings about Lâtife. It would have taken an extraordinary woman to be accepted by Zübeyde as a wife for her Mustafa Kemal. She had told Salih of her misgivings about Lâtife. Salih did not share them and had been in a quandary about whether he should pass her views on to the Ghazi or hope that she might change her mind. Death had overtaken her before the issue had to be resolved, and now the Ghazi had made his decision.

Preparations for the wedding started immediately. Mustafa Kemal requested that the ceremony be attended by only a few close friends and relatives. The ceremony itself would represent a departure from Turkish Muslim tradition. In the past the bride and groom did not appear together in the same room during the religious ceremony that bound them in marriage, but he and Lâtife did participate in the ceremony in the same room. Lâtife, carrying a single white rose in her hand, wore little makeup out of deference to Mustafa Kemal's wishes. Her hair was covered with a violet scarf and she had matching gloves. The Ghazi's attendants, Fevzi and Kâzım, wore their military dress uniforms, but Mustafa Kemal himself wore a dark blue, three-piece business suit with matching tie sparked by a red design. His blondish hair was partially concealed by a kalpak of grey astrakhan. In his breast pocket he wore a white handkerchief. He made an exceedingly handsome bridegroom.

At half-past three in the afternoon the *kadı* (judge) who was to perform the ceremony arrived. He met privately with Mustafa Kemal, and then together with Fevzi and Kâzım, who acted as witnesses. According to custom, Mustafa Kemal was asked by the *kadı* to state the amount of dowry he offered for Lâtife. He replied, "Ten dirhems of silver" (Bozdağ 1975*a*, p. 117), the smallest amount allowable according to some Islamic law books. He and his two friends broke into smiles. The meanness of the sum suggested that Mustafa Kemal, while ostensibly complying with the requirements of custom, was actually mocking the entire traditional Muslim process.[1] When asked what he would give Lâtife as a settlement in case of divorce, he again replied, "Ten dirhems of silver" (Bozdağ 1975*a*, pp. 117–18, 120). Kâzım joked that his friend had gotten off cheap, and Fevzi expressed his wish that the marriage be marked by serenity and happiness and in that case the divorce settlement should be fidelity and good fortune.

With these preliminaries out of the way, the actual ceremony began. A table had been arranged in one room. Mustafa Kemal led Lâtife to the seat on his right at the table. The governor of Izmir was seated at her right. Fevzi and Kâzım sat on the Ghazi's left. When all were in place, Mustafa Kemal told the *kadı* that he and Lâtife had decided to marry, and he asked him to begin the ceremony. The *kadı* then asked Lâtife if ten dirhems of silver constituted an acceptable dowry and whether she wanted to marry Mustafa Kemal, who had proposed a ten-dirhem divorce settlement. She accepted. Mustafa Kemal acknowledged the sums that

[1]It is also possible that this unconsciously reflected his negative esteem for Lâtife or women in general.

had been agreed upon and indicated his willingness to marry Lâtife. The *kadı* then declared them man and wife before God. He prayed that the marriage be blessed for the two families and for the whole nation. The formula followed in this ceremony became the model for such rites in the Turkish republic for some time, although later on there would be no mention of dowries and divorce settlements, and there would be no concession to religion.

Abdürrahim Tuncak later recalled the simplicity of the event. He had been impressed when the governor told Lâtife after the ceremony with considerable emotion, "You have conquered the conqueror of Izmir."[2]

Slowly the guests departed. Mustafa Kemal asked Fevzi and Kâzım to remain behind and dine with him and his new family. He said they would now see a demonstration of his bride's culinary skills, for "A soldier's wife spends her wedding night in the kitchen" (Bozdağ 1975*a*, p. 122). The table was decorated with flowers and a crystal centerpiece heaped with caviar. Plates of hors d'oeuvres abounded. Mustafa Kemal appeared happy and animated enough, but one of the stories he told his audience that night (Bozdağ 1975*a*, p. 122) suggests a less genial mood operating within him. He recalled that when he, Fevzi, and İsmet had approached the town of Turgutlu, near Izmir, during the grand offensive, they had noticed a Turkish flag waving from the steeple of a church. While they puzzled over why the Turkish flag still waved after the retreating Greeks had burned everything else, a bomb exploded in the church and the roof caved in. It became clear then that by flying a Turkish flag the Greeks had hoped to lure Turks into the church to be blown up by the bomb set to go off at a designated time. In recounting this story Mustafa Kemal pointed to how zealous the Turks had been when they tried heroically to save their flag from the flames. With relish he explained that the ropes holding the flag were burned and the flag flew free, landing in the branches of a tree.

Moot as the psychological implications of this story are, it is intriguing that it came on his wedding night only a few days after his visit to his mother's grave. Her death can be seen symbolically as freeing him from his psychic image of her, but almost at once he tied himself to another woman, perhaps to have again an unconscious longing for his freedom. He seemed happy enough, but it is possible that he nursed an inner rebellion against marriage, equating it with being in bondage to a woman. The story might also involve an unconscious wish to be freed from the pull

[2]Tuncak 1974. The reminiscences of Mr. Tuncak ended here in Dr. Volkan's interview on 5 December. Consequently, we have no information about Abdürrahim's relationship with Mustafa Kemal as he grew to manhood. We do know that Abdürrahim was sent to a technical school in Turkey and then to Germany for part of his education and that he became an engineer.

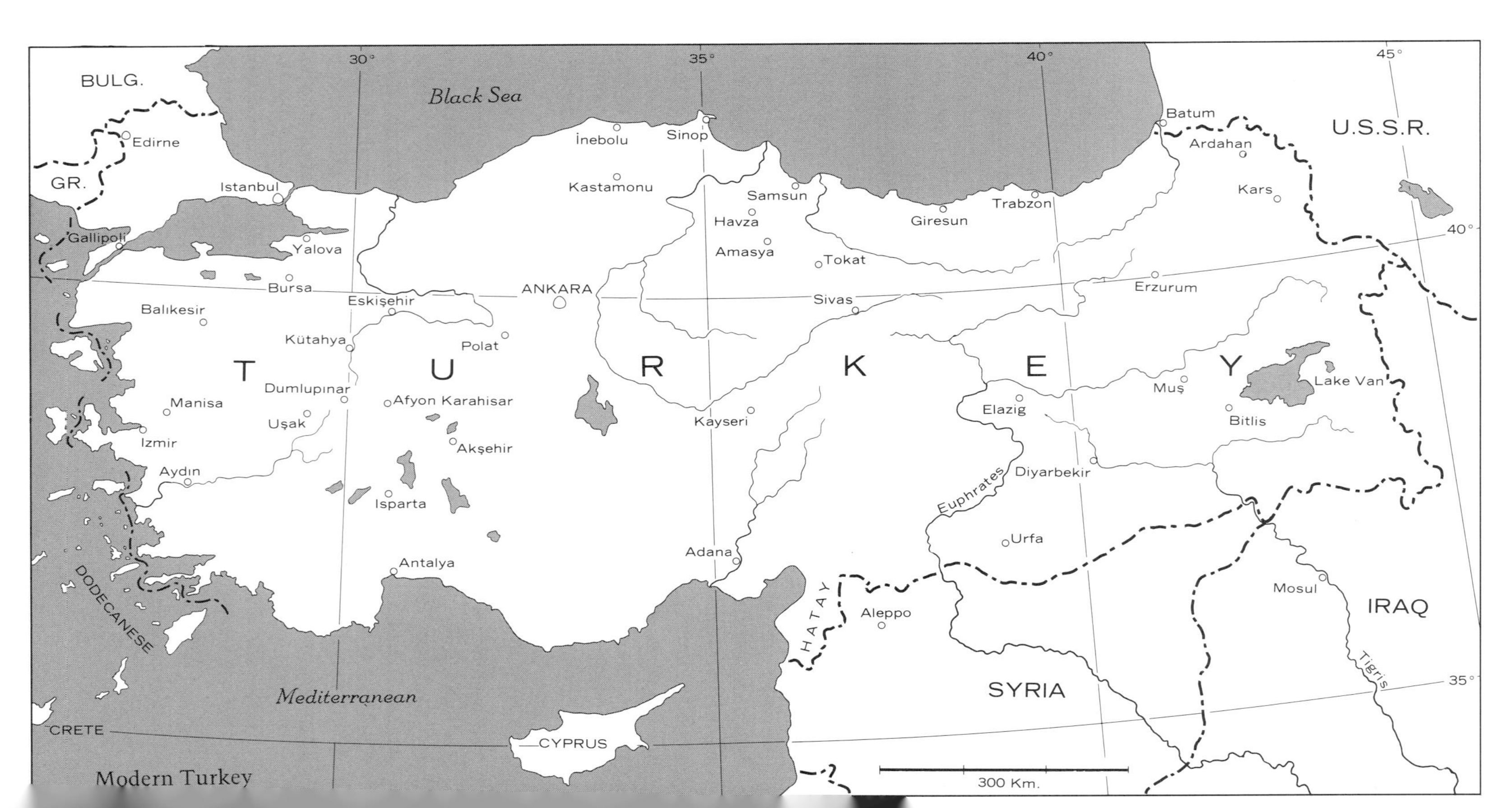

Modern Turkey

of the engulfing flames of a mother representative. Paradoxically, he married Lâtife because, on the surface, she appeared very different from his mother; her brashness even reminded him of himself, always thrusting forward and testing boundaries. Soon, however, he would experience Lâtife's engulfing qualities.

Married life had gotten off to a good start, but soon it meant changes in Mustafa Kemal's daily routine. He had been accustomed to the life of a soldier since the day he left his newly married mother in a narcissistic rage. The comings and goings of orderlies and aides had surrounded him for some time in the male society that was the military. That existence was now challenged by the presence of a wife. For example, Salih had to use a new formality in approaching his chief's bedroom, asking Lâtife for permission to enter. Meanwhile, Lâtife began to flout such traditional formalities as calling her husband "my Pasha," addressing him instead as Kemal. Having been educated in Europe, she used such familiarity easily, but it fell strangely on the ears of those around the great man. It is impossible to know how many in Mustafa Kemal's circle resented his marriage out of loyalty to the spurned Fikriye. The ceremony, however, had taken place in Izmir, where few (except for the close inner circle) knew Fikriye, and in the culture of the time there could be little disapproval since Mustafa Kemal was a pasha, and the girl he had abandoned had had no standing at all.

His marriage into a prominent family was not likely to be regretted deeply by anyone but Fikriye. Lâtife, a westernized Turkish girl, was an appropriate choice as the representative of the new Turkey. His mother's death coincided with the Ghazi's success in saving his country. He could now turn his back on both the grieving nation of old and the early grieving mother who had been such a persistent burden to him. His marriage at forty-two to a young woman of twenty-four reflected the marriage of his parents between whom there had been a similar age disparity. The marriage had been made for reasons beyond Lâtife's sexual appeal and his enjoyment of her adoration. Mustafa Kemal seems at no point to have seen Lâtife as an individual but to have viewed her as a token of his success. She surely took great pleasure in marriage to her idealized hero but had little or no desire to know him as a human being.

Mustafa Kemal had become the son-in-law in a family whose members, except for his bride, he had known for only a few days. Yet, he expected them all to conform at once to his expectations and to become extensions of himself. He began to dominate the household, even ordering rakı to be served at dinner instead of the customary wine. When Lâtife's father demurred at being denied his role as host, Mustafa Kemal firmly told him to sit down and assured him that he would take care of everything himself.

Supremely confident that he could manage his domestic affairs, Mustafa Kemal was equally sure that he would be able to steer Turkey through the final phase of peacemaking embarked upon at the Lausanne conference convened at the invitation of England, France, and Italy on 22 November 1922. The conference was still in session when he married Lâtife. The Ghazi hoped to undo the damage done to Turkish pride at Versailles, where the defeated Ottoman Empire had been dealt with harshly. Four years had brought far-reaching changes—Lloyd George had fallen from power, the sultan had fled Istanbul, military failure had brought revolution to Greece, and the Soviets were in control of Russia. Turkey, galvanized by Mustafa Kemal, had won on the battlefield a dignified place at the peace table.

Delegations were sent to Lausanne by Greece, Yugoslavia, Rumania, and Japan, in addition to Turkey. The United States was represented only by an observer. Russia's delegation arrived after the conference had begun. Lausanne's streets were thronged as people sought glimpses of renowned world leaders. Curzon was there for England, Poincaré for France, and Mussolini for Italy. To negotiate with these veterans of political infighting and diplomatic bargaining, Mustafa Kemal had named his trusted general, İsmet Pasha. A major architect of the military victory over the Greeks at the Sakarya, İsmet was surprised and dismayed at his appointment. Only thirty-four years old, he insisted that he was a soldier and not a diplomat, but Mustafa Kemal pointed to İsmet's success at Mudanya and refused to replace him. More outraged than surprised at this appointment was Rauf, who served as Mustafa Kemal's prime minister and who was interested in the assignment for himself. Mustafa Kemal silenced all opposition, and İsmet made his way to the Swiss lake resort.

As the conference unfolded, the British press showed extreme hostility toward Turkey in contrast to the French press, which demonstrated some sympathy for the Turkish case. Both the French and Turkish delegations were housed in the Lausanne Palace Hotel, which led to some speculation that the two governments were directing their policy in tandem. İsmet thought he sensed hostility among the delegates when the Turks entered the conference room only to find, in confirmation of his suspicions, that the armchairs provided for all the other delegates were denied the Turks, who were expected to sit in ordinary chairs. It appeared that the Turks were being treated as second-class delegates. If they accepted that situation, they would be laboring under a psychological disadvantage that would be extremely difficult to shed. Accordingly, İsmet inquired about the meaning of such discrimination and demanded that armchairs be provided instantly for his party or they would leave. His demand made it clear that the Turks expected equality and that times had changed since the Treaty of Sevres, when the Allies had merely dictated their wishes for the agreement of the Ottoman delegates. The new Turkey, victorious, was appearing at this conference as an equal to the other delegations. The Turks would have nothing to do with the outdated Treaty of Sevres and its mentality. They refused to regard the Lausanne Conference as one designed simply to offer modifications to stipulations arrived at earlier.

Objective reality embodied in the Kemalist political revolution failed to make any impression on Allied psychology. With the British in the forefront, the Allies continued their atavistic attempt to have Turkey accept war guilt and humiliation, while simultaneously dictating conditions for peace. They were surprised when İsmet counterattacked by refusing to enter into any discussion about war guilt. He declared that any definitive conclusion on the subject of who bore responsibility for the war would require a detailed examination of the past thirty years, an exercise in which the Turks had no intention of engaging at this point. His government insisted on Turkey's complete independence in political, economic, and military matters.

Despite his own modesty, İsmet proved to be a most capable diplomat. Crafty and blunt, he kept his more seasoned diplomatic adversaries off balance and unable to parry his own verbal ripostes to their barbed comments. Slightly deaf, İsmet displayed greater political shrewdness than physical necessity when he asked that the utterances of Allied delegates be repeated for his benefit. This gave him time to frame his responses. He infuriated those present by his obdurateness, which served to give him an advantage. His lack of diplomatic experience was more than compensated for by his determination and his moral conviction that Turkey was for the Turks. The Kemalists were willing, however, to give up all the non-Turkish provinces of the Ottoman Empire, thereby accepting, after a fashion, the defeat inflicted during World War I.[3]

Two protagonists emerged in the course of the conference; one was İsmet, the other was Lord Curzon. The other delegates seemed mere go-betweens in their confrontation. Lord Curzon did not trust the Kemalist Nationalists. He feared that they might join with the Russians to frustrate British objectives in the east. Control of the straits was the prime issue between Curzon and İsmet. The Russians, represented by Chicherin, commissar for foreign affairs, quickly allied themselves with the Turks in hopes of obtaining control of the straits through a united front. Curzon was determined to divide them, while İsmet had the unenviable task of trying to use the Russians without becoming dependent on them. He saw Chicherin almost every day, but Turkey could look for alliance to the east and the north as well as the west, according to İsmet, and that kept everyone guessing. In the end, İsmet agreed with the British on the status of the straits, refusing to succumb to Russia's blandishments. The straits would be open to all, and the Black Sea would

[3]Those provinces which were not predominantly inhabited by a Turkish population but were populated, for example, by Arabs were considered non-Turkish.

not become a Russian lake. Mustafa Kemal's Turkey demonstrated its complete independence and its entitlement to a place of international importance.

Agreement on the straits left three other major issues separating Turkey from the Allies. One of those was possession of the district of Mosul with its rich deposits of oil. Both the British and the Turks were aware of Mosul's subterranean wealth. Further exacerbating the Mosul question was the large Kurdish-Turkish population that formed a majority of the region's inhabitants. They had been included within the National Pact, the document upon which Mustafa Kemal had built his movement. İsmet was adamant in his demand for the inclusion of Mosul within the Turkish national boundaries, while the British were equally insistent upon the area's becoming part of Iraq, over which they would exercise a mandate.

Population exchange with Greece was another of the major issues defying solution. Although less intractable than the question of Mosul, the exchange of populations presented enormous difficulties. Greek officials within the Ottoman Empire had consistently overestimated the number of Greeks living in Anatolia and underestimated the number of Muslims in heavily Greek areas (McCarthy 1980). The population question was intimately associated with the issue of reparations, and racial overtones complicated the question. The Turkish efforts to effect an exchange of populations made it seem that Mustafa Kemal sought to "purify" the new Turkey for the Turks.

Emotionally, the issue of capitulations, which the Turks viewed as the most serious infringement of their sovereignty, was perhaps the most difficult. Capitulations had originated in pre-Ottoman times as a concession on the part of Islamic rulers to Western merchants as a means of fostering trade, and early Ottoman sultans continued the practice of extending certain privileges, which were then embodied as law in state documents. The most famous of these capitulations were the privileges extended by Sultan Suleiman the Magnificent (1520–66) to the French. As Ottoman power weakened and other nations sought and were granted capitulations, those privileges were woven into a pattern of life that became known as the capitulatory regime. By the nineteenth century capitulations covered almost every aspect of life engaged in by foreigners residing in the Ottoman Empire. In legal cases foreigners had the right to be tried in the counsular courts of their own nations. Foreigners paid no personal taxes to the Ottoman state, and export tariffs were established and maintained by capitulations treaties, generally at a level favorable to the foreigners.

In addition to favorable treatment in the areas of law, taxation, and tariffs, foreigners enjoyed postal privileges through the postal systems organized by their own nations, and in the nineteenth century they established educational, religious, and health facilities that also benefited from the capitulatory regime. Moreover, non-Muslim subjects of the Ottoman state sought to take advantage of this system by purchasing status as protected persons from consular agents. They would buy a *berat*, or certificate, attesting to the status, which had originally been intended to protect interpreters and consular agents recruited from the local, non-Muslim population. In time, what had been granted as a trade inducement by the sultans grew into a system of foreign exploitation characterized by extraterritorial privileges and immunities.

National sovereignty was more than a catchword with Mustafa Kemal and his colleagues. They viewed the capitulatory regime as the most disgraceful legacy from the past, which they were pledged to eradicate. Curzon little understood the depths of their feeling and had no empathy for their position. İsmet was obdurate on the issue of capitulations. The European mentality that had created and exploited the capitulations of the nineteenth century was out of touch with the twentieth-century forces that demanded their termination. Mustafa Kemal, who had already demonstrated on numerous occasions his keen sense of boundaries and limits, had placed the capitulations beyond his personal pale.

There was bound to be an irreconcilable confrontation. The Allies insisted that Turkey did not have a proper legal code that offered their nationals adequate protection as they went about their business and that Turkey was unable to manage her economic affairs. Curzon decided there was only one way out of the impasse. Having grown weary of İsmet's "deafness," delaying tactics, and other maneuverings, Curzon presented him with a complete draft of a treaty to take or leave. The draft was presented to the Turks on 31 January 1923, and Curzon scheduled his departure from Lausanne for 4 February. There followed four days of intense negotiations. In the early afternoon of 4 February, İsmet made his formal reply, accepting much that was in the draft but holding out for full recognition of Turkish sovereignty with respect to the capitulations and finances. He suggested that a treaty embodying all points agreed upon be signed, leaving the other matters to be discussed later. Curzon realized that this would be a significant diplomatic victory for the Turks and refused. There followed a series of frantic meetings. İsmet delivered his response to the Allies' "final" concessions at 1:45 P.M. At a meeting in Curzon's hotel room a few more concessions were agreed upon, and İsmet was summoned there at 5:40 P.M. Curzon tried alternately to bully and cajole İsmet into accepting the treaty, but the implacable Turk stood his ground and refused to allow any of the judicial and economic clauses, which he viewed as imposing servitude on Turkey. Curzon repaired to his train, hoping that İsmet would have a change of heart. After having delayed the train's departure for some time, Curzon gave up, and his train pulled out of the Lausanne station shortly after 9 P.M. on 4 February. The first phase of the Lausanne Conference had come to an inconclusive end.

Just before the conference broke off, Mustafa Kemal and Lâtife left Izmir on a honeymoon tour of the country. Their journey gave Lâtife her first view of the real Anatolia. She had witnessed the Turks' humiliation in Izmir at the hands of the Greeks and then their subsequent victory and the burning of the city. Whatever romantic notions she might have had about Anatolia were quickly dispelled by the harsh reality. The countryside was a wasteland. The excitement of the crowds cheering her hero was one thing, but the pervasiveness of need and poverty was another.

When the couple visited Balıkesir, north of Izmir, Mustafa Kemal delivered a speech in a mosque,[4] which was psychologically significant because it revealed his plans to separate religion from state affairs and to bring new meaning to the religion of Islam by turning away from the ways it had traditionally been understood and practiced in Turkey. On a deeper level, the speech reflects his own internal splitting. He said, "Friends! The great Prophet [Muhammad] possessed two dwellings, two abodes for his endeavors. One was his own house, the other was the abode of God" (Aydemir 1969, vol. 3 p. 77). He then went on to describe how the Prophet had separated the conduct of the state's affairs in the abode of God from the activities within his own residence. Perhaps identifying with this ability of Muhammad's to dichotomize, Mustafa Kemal seemed to have—or aspired to have—the ability to split apart the several areas of his own responsibility. He was one man when dealing with the affairs of the nation, and quite another when dealing with personal issues such as maintaining his relationships with women in "another house." It was this ability of Mustafa Kemal's to split effectively that enabled him to be a great leader, for in the middle of devastating personal problems he could continue to cope with the nation's business.

Moving on in the same speech to deal more directly with religion, Mustafa Kemal said:

> Gentlemen! mosques were not built in order for us to prostrate ourselves and then stand up again without looking at each other. Mosques were built for discussion, that is, for consultation, of what had to be done in religious and worldly affairs, as well as for obedience to God and prayer. It is indispensable for everyone's mind to be occupied with the affairs of the nation. Therefore, let us here divulge what we

[4]During this tour Mustafa Kemal gathered the people in suitable buildings and had long conversations with those present. He stated, "I requested that the population should freely ask questions on subjects that were near to their hearts. In order to answer them I delivered long speeches which often lasted for six or seven hours" (Atatürk 1927, p. 587).

> have thought about with respect to the sacred and the profane, about the future and our independence, and especially about our sovereignty. I don't want to talk about just my own thoughts. I want to know what all of you have been thinking. National aims and the national will do not stem from the thinking of any one individual. They are composed of the wishes of all the nation's inhabitants, and all their desires. Consequently, I exhort you to inquire of me freely about anything you wish to know or to ask. [Aydemir 1969, vol. 3, p. 77]

Mustafa Kemal had a talent for portraying to the people an image of himself as someone sincerely interested in hearing what they had to say. He presented himself to them in their midst, on their ground. In addition, he also appeared to them as a tolerant father who wanted his children to know his mind. Here in Balıkesir he sounded a new note on the subject of religion and its connection to the affairs of this world. He wanted to bring a new light to the house of God, to make religious people think, to change the influence religion had on daily life, and to make the house of God into a place in which temporal affairs would be discussed according to his own vision of what Muhammad had intended.

One of the unintended consequences of the breakdown of the Lausanne Conference was to cut short Mustafa Kemal's and Lâtife's honeymoon trip. İsmet, whose handling of the Lausanne Conference made him the object of the displaced wrath of many who were angry at Mustafa Kemal but unable to express their hostility toward him directly, met the couple at Eskişehir. The threesome arrived in Ankara on 20 February. After the shock of her visit to Anatolia, Ankara may not have taken Lâtife so much by surprise. Mustafa Kemal had been busily changing the face of Ankara since his establishment there, but it still reflected a long history of Ottoman indifference.

Prime Minister Rauf met the party at the railroad station and presented Lâtife with a bouquet of flowers. She was then escorted to Mustafa Kemal's house in Çankaya, referred to as his "mansion." The new bride found it no mansion, compared with the sumptuous home she had left behind in Izmir. Not only did she have to swallow this disappointment, but she had to deal with the memories of Fikriye's recent occupancy of the premises. Lâtife soon began to erase reminders of her predecessor, changing the arrangement of the furniture and getting rid of some of the appointments. She was dissatisfied with the dress of the servants and insisted that the men on the staff, most of whom were soldiers, wear white gloves while serving the table.

The debate about the Lausanne Conference reached an explosive point in the Grand National Assembly. A deputy from Trabzon named Ali Şükrü charged that the victory won by the bayonets of Turkish soldiers had been thrown away at Lausanne. He railed against Mustafa Kemal and İsmet in the assembly and in the coffeehouses of Ankara. Following a sharp exchange with Mustafa Kemal in the assembly during which the Ghazi asked Ali Şükrü what his purpose was in stirring up the country, Ali Şükrü mysteriously disappeared. Rumors reverberated throughout Ankara that he had been murdered. Those who opposed Mustafa Kemal and who suspected his hand in the transgression took the opportunity to vent their spleen at the podium of the assembly, declaring that whoever might have attacked Ali Şükrü had stained the nation's honor and deserved to die.

Such strong words called for an investigation. Rauf was able to report after a couple of days that the chief of Mustafa Kemal's personal bodyguard was the culprit. He had had Ali Şükrü strangled when he became convinced that the fiery troublemaker was planning to kill the Ghazi. In the old days of Ottoman palace intrigue such behavior might not have excited such comment, but in the new atmosphere of Ankara it proved a considerable embarrassment to Mustafa Kemal. The situation became dangerous when the Ghazi's bodyguards refused to surrender. Mustafa Kemal and Lâtife were removed to temporary quarters in the station house where he had stayed after his first arrival in Ankara. Government troops were sent against the men in the mansion at Çankaya, and the engagement ended with the fatal wounding of the chief bodyguard.

These terrible events convinced Mustafa Kemal that the Grand National Assembly had outlived its usefulness and that some deputies had overstepped their bounds. The time had come to dissolve the first Grand National Assembly and elect new deputies. Later, Mustafa Kemal recalled why he had decided on the need for a new assembly (Atatürk 1927, p. 605). On the basis of the recent chaos and the dissent over the Lausanne agreements, he had become convinced that unless the assembly was composed of newly elected delegates, it would not be able to carry out the heavy responsibility of putting the nation's affairs on a sound footing. He held a meeting with all the ministers, and on 1 April 1923, the president of the National Assembly received a bill signed by 121 deputies calling for its dissolution and the election of a new one. According to law, elections would have to take place within two months. Upon approval of the bill, the first Grand National Assembly, one in which the deputies wore kalpaks, turbans, and fezzes in a mixture of past and present, terminated. Mustafa Kemal was then ready to form a bona fide political party that would represent the new Turkey.

While dealing with the political issue of the makeup of the assembly, Mustafa Kemal also had to resolve the impasse over the peace treaty. İsmet had been criticized for the concessions he had made to the Allies as well as for the fact that he had failed to conclude peace. After consultations with the Ghazi, İsmet submitted a note to the Allies that restated the Turkish stand on sovereignty and called for resumption of the conference at Istanbul. Equally interested in finding a way out of the impasse, the Allies agreed to resume negotiations, but at Lausanne. The Turks agreed to meet there on 23 April.

With İsmet off for the resumption of the Lausanne Conference, Mustafa Kemal embarked on a tour of the countryside accompanied by Lâtife. As he went among his people, he acted as a teacher and a preacher. He might have had his difficulties with the Grand National Assembly, but out in the provinces he was in his element. He struck awe in the hearts of the people, most of whom had never seen a pasha before. They were deeply impressed with seeing the savior of their country and having him actually talk to them! All the adoration showered on Mustafa Kemal irked Lâtife. On the part of their trip that took them to Adana in southern Turkey, she gave way to her rage when she was obliged to enter their automobile *after* her husband and sit on his left (Bozdağ 1975*a*, pp. 172–73). Mustafa Kemal pointed to the protocol required in any official public appearance, but she was deeply humiliated and disappointed by his failure to treat her with appropriate consideration. She was no Fikriye, not a girl who adored the leader and was happy to be his slave. She did adore him, but she required support for her own demands, was infuriated by any neglect, and eaten by envy when his admiring public, especially the women, stood before him in awe. Clashes were inevitable when these two rather similar personalities joined together. Mustafa Kemal's narcissistic personality expected support for his grandiose self from Lâtife, while she looked to the Ghazi for validation of her own self-esteem.

Friction at home was matched for Mustafa Kemal by friction in the political arena. He now busied himself with the organization of a political party, the People's party, which would become, he hoped, a school for the nation's political training. It would also serve as a vehicle for dealing with the opposition. Politics was his major interest in Ankara, but diplomacy vied for equal attention. Ankara's government leaders watched the reports from Lausanne and grumbled about İsmet's handling of the Allied statesmen. They feared he was conceding too much, and İsmet complained that they did not give him enough latitude. In many ways the bloom was off the conference, for Lord Curzon had remained behind in London, replaced by Sir Horace Rumbold as the British representative. There was much posturing, but in reality the Allies were not prepared to go to war over any of the issues being discussed at Lausanne. As British intelligence revealed more and more that delay in concluding peace was eroding İsmet's position in Ankara, Rumbold, not seeking to undermine the new Turkish government, became more conciliatory. İsmet held his ground on the matter of complete sovereignty. He had expected to negotiate the treaty arrangements in two weeks, but the wrangling on innumerable issues of minor importance dragged the process out for three months. Much of İsmet's ability to survive the backbiting that went on in Ankara during that period was due to the personal support he received from Mustafa Kemal, which roused the ire of Prime Minister Rauf.

Skillful in an arena for which he professed to have no liking, İsmet succeeded in effecting what many consider "the greatest diplomatic victory in history." Compromising on the question of Greek reparations in order to gain for the Turks the important town of Dedeağac, near Edirne, İsmet opened the way to the final phase of the conference. After months of frustrating delay, the Treaty of Lausanne was signed on 24 July.

Signature of the treaty brought peace after nine terrible years of war and devastation. The humiliating Treaty of Sevres was wiped off the books, and Turkish sovereignty was unequivocally established over Anatolia, the straits, and much of Thrace. The capitulatory regime was ended, and, with the exception of a few foreign legal advisers who would remain for a limited time, the Turks were masters of their own judicial system. İsmet richly deserved the plaudits Mustafa Kemal would heap on him.

News of the signing of the treaty was brought to Mustafa Kemal in his home at Çankaya by Rauf and Ali Fuat on the morning of 25 July. When he heard that the two men had come to see him, he hurried to meet them without even dressing for the occasion. Everyone was stirred by the news. After drinking a cup of coffee, Rauf tried to give credit for the great accomplishment to Mustafa Kemal, Kâzım, and Refet, pointedly refraining from any mention of İsmet. In due course he indicated that he was so angry at İsmet that he would resign as prime minister and let İsmet run the country according to the new treaty. İsmet served only as a screen behind which he vented his anger with and jealousy of Mustafa Kemal. He did not want the Ghazi to become the leader of the People's party and to remain politically active. Rauf ventured to remind his chief that he had once promised to drop out of active politics as soon as peace had been attained.

What had once been promised long ago was not to be considered seriously at this point. Mustafa Kemal had no intention of renouncing politics, for his real work was only just beginning, and he still had to turn the grieving nation into a nation of joy. He had not yet satisfied his unconscious need to save the grieving mother, of whom in one sense he wanted to wipe out any lingering trace.

Infuriated by this state of affairs, Rauf resigned his post. He even refused to meet İsmet's train upon his triumphant return to Ankara, leaving the capital for Sivas with only the farewells of his fellow ministers and intimates resounding in his ears.[5] Fethi was appointed prime minister in his place, and Ali Fuat agreed to stay on as vice-president of the assembly. Within three months, however, Ali Fuat resigned, purportedly to resume his military career, but in reality it was his way of demonstrating his displeasure with Mustafa Kemal's one-man rule. Only a few of his oldest comrades remained at the Ghazi's side as he and the nation stood on the threshold of peace.

Distrust of Mustafa Kemal's intentions at home was echoed abroad. Was he going to institute his own dynasty to replace that of the house of Osman? Many in the Islamic world wanted him to declare himself sultan and caliph, and they made several pilgrimages to Ankara to encourage him to do so. Cajole him as they might, Mustafa Kemal knew where to draw the line with regard to his own ambitions. Moreover, his desire to save a grieving nation and make a house of death into a house of life did not require him to take part in limitless adventures. He realized that he was the leader of a backward nation of illiterates, a nation that had known neglect and faced devastation. Yet, it was also a nation of hope and excitement, ready to follow him to accomplish impossible tasks, a nation reborn, just as he had been reborn at Samsun as the savior sun.

In August the second Grand National Assembly opened with its new membership. Lâtife had been greatly excited by the election in which only those who were in Mustafa Kemal's newly formed political party were elected. The members again elected him president of the assembly. Mustafa Kemal joked with Lâtife lightheartedly as the election results came in from the city of Konya. He told her that 39 votes had been cast for her there. She enjoyed such recognition, and the couple could engage in happy banter as long as each maintained high self-regard and as long as Lâtife could feel herself allied with his successful activities without envy. Hearing of her Konya votes, she laughingly asked for a pen and paper and composed a telegram of acknowledgment and appreciation to be sent to the city's mayor. She wrote:

> I thank the people of Konya who gave me 39 votes in the election, and I understand this to be more of a sign of respect for and sympathy with Turkish women than a sign of favor toward me. The Turkish woman will gain new strength for the performance of her national duty due to this encouraging sign from our dear nation. [Bozdağ 1975*a*, p. 179]

[5]Mustafa Kemal referred in his "Great Speech" to the conflict between İsmet and Rauf. He stated, "Examining the documents relating to it, it appears to be difficult to explain this conflict by essential and serious reasons, and I am rather of the opinion that it must be regarded as an effect of motives of a psychological character" (Atatürk 1927, p. 620).

As it turned out, Konya was not the only district to cast votes for Lâtife. A few other prominent women received votes as well—İsmet's wife and Halide among them. This would have been unthinkable in the old Turkey. The same was true of a visit Lâtife made to the Grand National Assembly. The Nationalists saw to it that that historic event—a Turkish woman for the first time visiting government at work—was well publicized locally and internationally as well.

While Lâtife had been the first Turkish woman to visit the assembly, she had been preceded by another woman, a Westerner, the French journalist Berthe Georges-Gaulis. After Lâtife's marriage to Mustafa Kemal, the Frenchwoman returned to Ankara to interview the bride. It is said that Lâtife was terribly jealous of the journalist for having earlier been Mustafa Kemal's guest at Çankaya.

Jealousy over the journalist was nothing compared with what Lâtife experienced with respect to Fikriye. The tragic events involving Fikriye that were to occur opened a breach between Lâtife and her husband that could not be healed. Fikriye was in a sanatorium in Munich when she learned of Mustafa Kemal's marriage to Lâtife. She had heard very little from him after her departure from Istanbul. At first officials from the Turkish consulate in Munich had called upon her at the sanatorium, but their visits gradually ceased. News of the wedding reached her accidentally. She was sunning herself beside an old German woman who was reading a German-language newspaper when she spotted a picture of the Ghazi and Kâzım, with a rather short woman standing in the background. Fikriye suspected this might be Lâtife and had the German woman read her the accompanying story in the paper. She fainted at learning of the marriage, and after recovering consciousness she wept for hours.

Galvanized into action, she demanded that she be discharged from the sanatorium. She secured her release despite the protests of her physician and officials at the Turkish consulate. She then took the train for Turkey, carrying with her a number of gifts she had bought to give Mustafa Kemal when she should return to Turkey a cured woman. One was a handgun with which she would soon take her own life.

Arriving in Ankara in the early evening, she went to Çankaya, where she found Mustafa Kemal and Lâtife at home. Lâtife was astonished to have Ali announce this visitor, but she rose to the occasion, urging Mustafa Kemal to meet and welcome her. "Let's not have this lady who served you so well in the past wait for us now" (Oranlı 1967, p. 144), she said. Entering, Fikriye was numb and seemed unable to believe what she was seeing. They managed to sit at the table together for dinner while Mustafa Kemal told Fikriye that she need have no worry about finances, that a house would be readied for her use in Istanbul, and that she should have no concerns. Staying the night in that house in Çankaya where not so long before she had been mistress, she must have felt deeply humiliated. Unable to surrender her hero, she could not bring herself to leave for three days. Lâtife was so upset by this, that she voiced her rage in the hearing of the orderly and others. Fikriye's departure on the fourth day after her arrival temporarily lifted the heavy atmosphere. Fikriye made her exit without being given further opportunity to see the man she called *her* pasha and whom she could never bring herself to call Kemal with the informality of Lâtife.

Mustafa Kemal's orderly recalled a scene at the house after Fikriye had left. The Ghazi was playing with some puppies, apparently relaxed and content. In calling Lâtife's attention to the playfulness of the pups, he made a slip of the tongue, saying, "Look, Fikriye, how nicely they are playing."[6] Lâtife almost fainted when she heard him, and two days later her parents came to visit, obviously sent for by their daughter in her distress. Having soothed Lâtife, they tactfully removed themselves from this scene of marital discord.

Upon leaving the mansion in Çankaya Fikriye stayed in a hotel and made an effort to see friends in Ankara. It appeared that she was about to return to Istanbul when she decided she must see her pasha once again. She made her way back to Çankaya, but this time she was met at the gate by an aide she had never seen before, who coldly insisted that it was impossible to see Mustafa Kemal without an appointment. Driven away, in effect, from the place she had once considered her own home, she engaged a horse-drawn carriage to take her back to the center of the city. As the carriage made its way down the hill through vineyards and clusters of buildings, the driver heard the report of a gun. Fikriye had shot herself. Quickly, she was taken to a hospital, where she died shortly after arrival. Mustafa Kemal personally called the hospital for news of her, only to learn that she had died. Now, a dead woman stood between Mustafa Kemal and Lâtife.[7]

Persons with a narcissistic personality organization lack the capacity for grief as we know it. They are incapable of having appropriate feelings of sadness and regret, for in their attempts to maintain their grandiose selves they keep up the illusion that they have no need of the representation (preserved memory) of the person lost through death. At the time of his mother's death Mustafa Kemal had continued to concern himself with national affairs. In his speech at her graveside he spoke of his mother in terms of the nation's struggle rather than mentioning any personal feel-

[6]Oranlı 1967, p. 145. Bozdağ (1975*a*, p. 200) states that this slip of the tongue occurred after Fikriye's death.

[7]It is possible that Fikriye's death increased Mustafa Kemal's identification of Lâtife with his grieving/engulfing mother image, for his dead siblings stood between his mother and himself.

ings of loss he might have had. Now, he could not grieve for Fikriye, and Lâtife's presence further obstructed his response to the woman's suicide.

Narcissistic people behave as though they were entirely capable of doing without the lost other, but under their grandiosity they hide considerable paradoxical dependence. They need to keep the representation of the dead person "alive" in order to continue to depend upon the representation. At the same time, they are unable to obliterate the dead individual, as is necessary if the course of grieving is to move toward resolution. This inability absorbs a vast amount of the bereaved's energy. Fikriye's death was an appreciable drain on Mustafa Kemal's energy, despite his outward appearance of taking it lightly, and as a result he had a diminished reserve for relating to his wife. He and Lâtife drew further apart.

Personal tragedies such as Fikriye's suicide and his increasing alienation from Lâtife were kept from overwhelming Mustafa Kemal by his capacity to engage in splitting. Like Muhammad in the example he himself had cited, Mustafa Kemal separated his personal business from the affairs of state, putting each preoccupation in its proper place. Despite what had occurred, he continued to be a shrewd administrator and strategist. Among other advances, the second Grand National Assembly declared Ankara to be the capital city of the new Turkey. That arid little town upon which the "sun" of Mustafa Kemal's presence had shone on 27 December 1919 had come a long way.

On the political front Mustafa Kemal was sailing into stormy waters. There was no officially organized opposition party, but opposition to Mustafa Kemal and his policies continued within his own party. What he later described in his "Great Speech" as "a secret opposition faction" (Atatürk 1927, p. 645) formed around Rauf. In response, Mustafa Kemal maneuvered the resignation of his cabinet, knowing full well that the secret group lacked the support necessary to have their men elected to a new cabinet. While Mustafa Kemal was putting his new cabinet together, Rauf was in Istanbul. Kâzım was there, too, in command of the First Army. Refet and Halide had been there for some time, together with Halide's husband, Dr. Adnan. It began to seem that those people whom Mustafa Kemal had considered friends were in favor of maintaining the sultanate, and their open support of the caliph created anxiety in Ankara. Accustomed early on to making drastic decisions, Mustafa Kemal gathered a group that included İsmet for dinner in the house at Çankaya to tell them, "Tomorrow we shall proclaim the Republic" (Atatürk 1927, p. 648). He asked İsmet to stay after dinner, and the two men worked on a draft of the proclamation, although a story persists that Mustafa Kemal had begun working on such a statement three months earlier.

On the following day, 29 October 1923, he attended the session of the assembly, allowing a delegate first to express himself on some issues. Then he announced that the question of the establishment of the republic would be voted upon. Within fifteen minutes the republic was approved, and Mustafa Kemal was elected its first president. More than a hundred delegates abstained from voting, but 159 votes were cast for him. İsmet was then hailed as the new republic's first prime minister, and Fethi was elected president of the assembly.

Next on Mustafa Kemal's agenda was the abolition of the caliphate. Throughout the struggle for independence, he had been cautious about offending the deep religious beliefs of the people, in spite of his profound distaste for the prevailing practice of religion which he viewed as an obstruction to his country's progress. It seemed necessary to reduce the influence of religion if he were to move the new Turkey out of the Middle Ages into modern times. His opportunity came when the Aga Khan, the hereditary head of the Ismaelis,[8] and Ameer Ali, a noted Indian Muslim intellectual and author of several books on Muhammad and Islam, wrote to İsmet to request that the "political situation" of the caliphate be protected. The day before this letter was delivered to İsmet, it was published in *Tanin*, an Istanbul newspaper owned by a man who had been sympathetic to the old Committee of Union and Progress. In Ankara it was felt that those advocating the retention of the caliphate were ready to use their influence. Clearly, the time had come to abolish the caliphate before the opposition could rally its forces into an organized movement. The bill to do so was passed by the Grand National Assembly with little debate on 3 March 1924. On the following day the caliph of all the Muslims was forced to leave Turkey, vacating his title. The Ottoman dynasty was truly at an end.

[8]The Aga Khan is the spiritual leader of the Nizari Ismaelis, who are Shi'ite Muslims. Their leader was Sultan Sir Mohammed Shah (1877–1957), who was the third holder of the title Aga Khan. At this time the center of the sect was in India. Today they are found in India, Pakistan, Iran, Syria, and East Africa. The Ismaelis originated in the eighth century in a dispute over succession in Islam, and the split of the movement into Nizaris and Mustalis occurred in the eleventh century. Hasan ibn al-Sabbah was the Nizari leader who established the assassins at Alamut (1090). In 1840 the leader migrated to India, where the sect flourished.

21
Personality Splitting Paralleled by Splits in the Real World

HABITS OF MIND ARE KNOWN TO AFFECT THE BODY, AND HISTORY INDICATES they are reflected in politics as well. The splitting mechanism that characterized Mustafa Kemal's personality organization was influential in creating splits in Turkey's body politic. In the fall of 1924 there was a generally acknowledged alignment of Kâzım, Rauf, Halide and her husband Dr. Adnan, and Refet in opposition to a second group of which İsmet and Fevzi were the most prominent members. With Turkey's external enemies put to rout, Mustafa Kemal saw the first group of prominent people as a new enemy. In reading his perception of the situation in 1924 as expressed in his "Great Speech" (Atatürk 1927, pp. 620–721), one can observe his tendency to be "paranoid" about that group.[1] He saw them as plotting against him and planning his downfall. The narcissistic person, like Mustafa Kemal, typically exhibits this sort of reaction: assessing his valued objects, he repairs them when necessary in order to make them idealized extensions of himself (so that they can then minister to his needs). If he senses that they are separated from him, he can still use them as adorers. In addition, he transfers devalued aspects of his own self to a target of which he is always aware and about which he develops a tendency toward paranoid ideation.[2]

[1]For example, note his statement, "Now, Gentlemen, with your permission, I will tell you something about a *great plot*" (italics added; Atatürk 1927, p. 686). The plot had to be "great" to suit his personality, but obviously it also had a basis in reality.

[2]Volkan (1980) suggested that narcissistic leaders can be divided into "reparative" and "destructive" ones. He stated: "The reparative narcissistic national leader strengthens the cohesiveness and stability of his grandiose self by idealizing a group of others whom he then includes in an idealized extension of himself. Even when such idealized external objects are not fused with his grandiose self, the narcissistic person feels elevated because those who adore him are themselves so superior. In marked contrast, the destructive narcissistic national leader attacks a group of people who represent his own devalued aspects and thus supports the defensive gap of primitive splitting between his grandiose self and the devaluated self- and object-representations.

"In some respects the distinction between the reparative and destructive types of narcissistic leader is artificial, since not only may one turn into the other in certain circumstances, but both induce collective regression among their followers. His followers see a leader of the reparative type as a true savior; they regress in the service of the ego (Kris 1952) in order to reorganize on a higher level. However, as the reparative narcissistic leader moves from that type of leadership to a destructive one, the collective regression of his

Mustafa Kemal was convinced that he was facing a plot against himself from the first group of prominent leaders. On 30 August 1924, he traveled to the site of the Battle of the Commanders in Chief at Dumlupınar, near Afyon, on the second anniversary of the great offensive to celebrate his grand victory there. That trip, and the speech he gave there, are of special importance in view of the fact that he had never revisited the sites of his earlier victories at Gallipoli or the eastern front.

In this speech he speaks of the sun once more, identifying himself with it and emphasizing his role as savior. In the space of one setting and rising of the sun, the Greeks were thoroughly defeated:

> As the sun began to sink in the west there was a feeling in everyone's soul that a fiery, bloody, deadly hell was about to break loose. Within a moment a terrible destruction would be let loose in the world. And, in order for the savior-sun, whose arising we awaited, to be born, that destruction was necessary. This destruction had to take place in the pitch darkness. Truly, in a moment decreed by the heavens, Turkish bayonets assaulted those ridges jammed with the enemy. Opposite us no army or force remained any longer. There was just a completely defeated and ruined remnant spared from the sword, as they themselves described it, a formless mass full of fright and terror, seeking an opportunity for flight. Then, the deepening darkness of night required us to wait until the sun rose again in the east in order to see the results with our own eyes. [Atatürk 1952, vol. 2, p. 178]

Asserting that the foundations of the new Turkey were laid on that battlefield and that the aim of the victory gained there was to enable the Turkish nation to take charge of its full and complete sovereignty, Mustafa Kemal went on to depict what the new Turkey would be. It would be civilized in all its aspects. Sovereignty was a pure light that dissolved chains and completely consumed crowns and thrones. He then went on to exhort the nation's young people: "Youth! You are the ones who strengthen and perpetuate our resolve. Oh rising generation! The future is yours. We have created the republic. You are the ones who will exalt it and cause it to prosper" (Atatürk 1952, vol. 2, p. 184). After that journey to the scene of his greatest victory, Mustafa Kemal spent the next month and a half traveling about the countryside trying to repair the nation.

---

followers in the service of the ego may in the long run be decompensated" (p. 139). Atatürk could remain as a reparative leader, for "the 'fit' between him and the national group he led was so great that not only did he easily maintain his grandiose self, but his followers in turn maintained their perception of him as a superman" (p. 140).

Reporting some time later about his return to Ankara, he noted ominously that although many deputies and friends met him at the station, "Rauf Bey and Adnan Bey, who were at Angora, were not among them. I did not expect such conduct, which could very easily have been taken as a sign of resentment. I did not hesitate for a moment to tell myself that I was face to face with a plot" (Atatürk 1952, vol. 2, p. 688).

Mustafa Kemal's psychological need to split apart his followers, adorers, and enemies and to influence the immediate environment to fit his psychological makeup did indeed effect a split in the real world. Some of Mustafa Kemal's original followers had cogent reasons for caution about the Ghazi. No doubt, most of the more traditional-minded among them wanted to keep the sultanate or caliphate or both, although they appeared willing enough to go along with the proclamation that established the republic. Later, when their growing antagonism became more blatant, they began to form a more coherent opposition. The two groups into which the prominent followers split, pro- and anti-Ghazi, fought each other psychologically and politically, echoing in the real world the schismatic aspects of Mustafa Kemal's personality. With the polarity now externalized in the real world, inwardly the Ghazi could feel more comfortable because the struggle (between "good" objects and "bad" objects) was taking place outside of himself between two opposing groups of men, rather than within his own psyche.

Ali Fuat had been one of the original followers and supporters of Mustafa Kemal. When Şevket Süreyya Aydemir was researching his biography of Atatürk he spoke with Ali Fuat, who explained that he had had no need to take a position opposing Mustafa Kemal (Aydemir, 1974), but he had been forced into it. Mustafa Kemal himself related the incident leading to the rift in his "Great Speech" of 1927, hearing that Ali Fuat had arrived in Ankara from Konya, he invited him to dinner at Çankaya, but when Ali Fuat did not appear, he concluded that the missing guest had become an enemy.[3] Ali Fuat told Aydemir that he would have gone to the dinner gladly, but he never received the invitation. İsmet had intercepted it. In any case, the alignment of opponents within the same party, which symbolically represented the inner splitting of its leader, was confirmed on 9 November 1924, when the former friends of the Ghazi who now opposed him organized an opposition faction under the name of the Progressive party. It was headed by Kâzım, with Rauf and Dr. Adnan sharing the office of vice-president, and Ali Fuat serving as secretary-general.

[3]Mustafa Kemal (Atatürk 1927, pp. 687–88) later recalled this incident:

"I was told, on the other hand, on the 30 October that Ali Fuad Pasha, Inspector of the Second Army, had arrived from Konia. I invited him to dine with me at Ishan Kaya. I waited till late at night, but he did not arrive. When I sent for him, I learned that on his arrival at

A closer look at the way in which Mustafa Kemal's splitting mechanism was reflected in party politics suggests the existence of an even further split—the division of his "good" followers into two groups. One group was composed of İsmet and others who seriously addressed themselves to state affairs and with whom Mustafa Kemal behaved as a shrewd revolutionary politician bent on transforming the Turkish nation in accordance with the highest principles. The other group was made up of uncritical personal friends (many of whom he had known in Salonika), cronies with whom he could find easy gratification, act out his regressed wishes, and defend himself against his intense object need—that is, his search for substitutes for the ever gratifying, good mother.

Narcissistic people often find another person they can regard as a virtual twin, over whom they exert influence or control in such a manner as to support their illusion of omnipotence. In effect, they use the "twin" as an extension of the self.[4] Although Mustafa Kemal had at one time used Arif as his "twin" (see chap. 15), the two men had been drifting apart. Arif's own personality had made him a useful "twin" during the period of war and destruction, when he became a depository for Mustafa Kemal's own aggressive feelings and a shield against aggression from the outside world. Now, however, a different kind of "twin" was needed, one with whom he could regress to the (defensive) adaptation of his early days in Salonika and in whom he could find the idealized nurturing mother.

With such cronies, his "twins," he would display great nostalgia for the old days, singing the songs of their common childhood, eating the foods he had enjoyed in Salonika. Such regression permitted him to get in touch with, or "visit" unconsciously, the idealized mother. This behavior was

---

Angora he was received by Rauf Bey who had met him at the railway station, that he was afterwards at the War Ministry, and had had some short interviews with his comrades, had then gone to the Chief of the General Staff and had a conversation with Fewsi [Fevzi] Pasha. Leaving the latter, he left the following letter with Fewsi Pasha's aide-de-camp.

> To the Chief of the General Staff.
>
> As I have to exercise my legislative functions as deputy, I have the honour of submitting my resignation as Inspector of the Second Army.
>
> [Signed] Ali Fuad,
>
> Deputy for Angora

[4]Kohut (1971) describes twinship transference in psychoanalysis as a variant of narcissistic transferences in general. The other "is experienced as being like the grandiose self or being very similar to it" (p. 115).

Brody (1952) studied dreams in which twin personalities appeared. He concluded that in each instance they represented the dreamer and his mother. Twins refer to a pregenital union with the mother and one twin draws sustenance from the other twin (mother) at the latter's expense.

Coen and Bradlow (1981) suggested that twin transference, together with all twin fantasies, serves multiple functions, of which they highlighted gratification and defense against dangers of intense object need.

performed in the service of gathering strength from his fusion with the idealized mother so that he could be strong enough to perform his national responsibilities as an idealized father. His activity with these cronies repeated his first memory of life, of the time when he had tried to console his mother for her broken heart, stemming in part from his leaving the religious school for the modern, westernized school, and to turn her away from her grief toward his nurture. In addition, it also served to enable him to move away from her in the direction of becoming an idealized father, after he performed his duties toward her.

Among those in his group of intimates whom he used for his own psychological purposes as "twins" were Salih, his chief aide-de-camp, Kılıç Ali, and perhaps most of all, Nuri. His need to have these "twins" around him at all times was also in the service of bringing his dead siblings to life in them so that his mother's grieving would be erased. His need to have them always present overrode his more conscious recognition of having become an adult and a family man. By then, indeed, his self-concept as a family man had been damaged by the alienation that had set in between himself and Lâtife as a result of Fikriye's suicide.

Nuri he had known since they were children rolling hoops together through the streets of Salonika and later when they attended military school together. He had shared with Nuri his early grandiose ideas about saving the country, and they had both served at Gallipoli. Nuri later commemorated his experience there near a place called Conk by taking the surname of Conker.

Long before Mustafa Kemal went to Samsun to initiate the war of independence, Nuri had gone to Germany with his wife and children, three boys and a daughter named Kıymet. The daughter spent her first seven years in Germany, where her father acted as a representative of sorts for the Kemalist Nationalists, keeping in touch with Mustafa Kemal. In an interview fifty years later Kıymet (Tesal), a graduate of a Turkish law school, recalled going to nursery school in Berlin, hearing at home constant mention of her father's friend back in the homeland (Tesal 1975). She never saw the Ghazi when she was a small child, but grew up feeling as though—in her own rather interesting expression—he was "in our dough." After the war of independence was won, her father received a telegram from Ankara asking him to return with his family. On their third day in Ankara her father told her that they were going to visit the pasha. Riding in a horse-drawn carriage on the dusty road to Çankaya, Kıymet saw her hero for the first time. She recalled that she found her eyes "blinded with a burst of sunlight" (once again the sun symbolism), so handsome and compelling was he. Her memory of that meeting many years earlier was so keen that she could recall many details of his garb and the appearance of his brown hunting dog.

Her hero married before Kıymet saw him for the second time. Her family was not impressed with Lâtife and spoke of her as an ill-mannered woman, much too short in stature. Kıymet's adult recollection of Lâtife was of a woman whose manner was nervous and aggressive rather than gentle and loving. She claimed that Lâtife had no skill in caressing and soothing a child or a pet, but handled them roughly. Kıymet saw Mustafa Kemal for the second time when he sent word to Nuri's household to expect a visit. He made a grand entrance dressed in the uniform of a field marshal, to which he had added a long blue cape. He explained to Nuri that this elaborate costume had been chosen deliberately: "I wanted your children to see me like this at least once. From now on I will always be a civilian and will not wear my uniform any more" (Tesal 1975). The children kissed the savior's hand as he made this exhibitionistic farewell to his military persona, relishing the impression he was making on the children and basking in their adoration.

Nuri had an uncanny perception of his friend's inner needs and allowed himself to be used to shore up the Ghazi's grandiosity. It is reported that sometimes Mustafa Kemal would make a great show of modesty when he received any elaborate compliment, saying to the person who tendered the compliment, "Me? Why don't you ask Nuri about me. He really knows me!" Nuri would then rise to the occasion, exclaiming, "How is it possible that Mustafa Kemal is a great man? His job used to be to run about in the bean fields and scare the crows" (Tesal 1975). The reference, of course, was to his boyhood on a relative's farm after his father's death. On the surface this story seems to point to Mustafa Kemal's modesty, but it also emphasizes the enormous distance he had traveled from the bean fields to his position as the country's savior. It was a tremendous gratification for his grandiosity. Nuri was perhaps the only person who could sit next to Mustafa Kemal "with knees touching," which is the Turkish expression for intimate friendship.

Mustafa Kemal's demeanor in the company of Nuri, Kılıç Ali, and other intimates was altogether different from his bearing among those who dealt seriously with the affairs of state. With the former he would sit in a relaxed fashion, with one leg tucked under him, and talk about acquiring the Balkans, especially Salonika. With statesmen and politicians not in his most intimate circle he would sit rather haughtily, maintaining an austere and reserved sense of decorum.

It was at about this time that he crystallized his daily habit of entertaining at dinner a motley group of men with whom he could play out the demands of his psychological makeup, often regressing in boisterous companionship with them, but never losing sight of his creative opportunities. Psychoanalysts know, especially from the work of D. W. Winnicott (1971) and Erik Erikson (1977), of the interplay between play and creativity. The accounts that İsmet Bozdağ (1975*b*) published in a series of articles in the Istanbul daily newspaper, *Günaydın*, in 1975 indicate that Mustafa Kemal's dinner parties were both spirited and fruitful. The guests sometimes included political figures and scholars, but almost invariably included men with whom the Ghazi could regress as they drank. He could easily separate serious people from cronies.

Lâtife appears to have had deep resentment about being set aside as hostess in her own home and considered those stag dinners an offense. She wanted her husband to be a civilized, westernized man who would eat his evening meal in proper fashion, with his guests accompanied by their wives and with waiters offering food and drink with formal courtesy. In her husband's presence, Lâtife once warned Nuri never to come to the presidential palace again without his wife. She threatened that if he failed to comply, he would be sent away. Nuri's answer was, "As you wish, Madame, but if you send me out the front door, I will re-enter through the back" (Tesal 1975). Nuri reported that conversation to his family, claiming that Mustafa Kemal had laughed heartily at his rejoinder. Nuri, among others of the Ghazi's friends, often stayed the night at the house in Çankaya, and sometimes he would accompany his host at early dawn, hunting rabbits from horseback. Because of these activities, he kept riding gear at Çankaya. Often the two men would hunt at Anıt Tepe, the memorial hill where Atatürk now lies buried. No other companion was acceptable on those rides, which often concluded with a breakfast of *tahin* and *pekmez* (sesame and molasses) at Nuri's house. Mustafa Kemal would say with satisfaction, "I have loved *tahin* and *pekmez* since my childhood in Salonica" (Tesal 1975), and he would talk affectionately with Nuri's children. He was readily affectionate toward children and animals and had a special fondness for horses and dogs. Children and animals did not threaten his grandiosity. Mrs. Tesal remembered that when a dog, whose name she recalled as Joli, bit Mustafa Kemal, he permitted it to be killed, but grieved over it and never forgot it.

Entirely at home at Nuri's, Mustafa Kemal treated his friend's wife with utmost courtesy. He once apologized to her, saying, "I don't think you like me because I keep your husband away from you all the time." He is reported to have phrased this in Turkish as *kocanızı zaptettim*, which means literally, "I have taken possession of your husband" (Tesal 1975). While in Nuri's home, he was not too proud to explain his refusal of a dish of strawberries as due to the fact that he wore false teeth that made eating berries uncomfortable for him. With these friends he was able to admit such an imperfection. This candid relationship allowed him to divulge to Nuri that while married he had remained faithful to Lâtife.

Mustafa Kemal's gentle side was evident in his interest in flowers and in his insistence on introducing their culture to dry and dusty Ankara with its extremes of seasonal temperature. Only in the spring did the region have wild mountain flowers in fields that stood empty the rest of the year. When Mustafa Kemal declared that as a civilized person he wanted flowers on his table, he was told that the cultivation of flowers was impossible in Ankara. He objected, saying that Ankara, like every place else, had soil. "If I bring water to you would you raise flowers?" he asked (Tesal 1975). Soon, not only were flowers being grown in Ankara, but he established his model farm at the beginning of a forest that would in later years be known as Atatürk's forest. One can only speculate about whether the establishment of his own forest might have been undertaken partly to repair the representation of his father whose downfall came after bandits destroyed the forest from which he made his living. One thing is certain, however; he enjoyed seeing anything, a child or a tree, grow. He had about him something of a motherly quality.

Motherliness was not the trait Lâtife was becoming most aware of in her hero. Considerable competition had entered the relationship between the Ghazi and his wife, who was determined to change his habits, particularly his drinking. Sometimes he complied with her wishes, but more often he did not. She would go so far as to leave the dining table with its male guests and make her disapproval known by banging on the floor of the room above. A respite from their struggle came when, two weeks after the proclamation of the republic, he felt pain in his chest while out walking with Kılıç Ali, Salih, and another man and began to sweat profusely. Some authorities suggest that this was a mild heart attack, but it seems more likely that it was a cardiac spasm. It is apparent from the evidence we have that he had occasional spells of hypochondriacal preoccupation, a "typical" symptom of persons with narcissistic personality organization. In any case, the episode led him to stop competing with Lâtife for awhile, and in turn she seemed to be deeply concerned about him, taking care of him as long as he was "ill." They took a trip to Izmir, where he arranged some war games. Lâtife was heard to say that since he had been ill she had achieved some kind of inner comfort. İsmet Bozdağ strongly suggests that on the way back to Ankara she herself simulated an illness to test his concern for her (Bozdağ 1975*a*, p. 234). He did indeed show concern, but Lâtife took exception at his failure to send ahead to arrange for a physician. The harmony they had managed to achieve lasted only for a brief time.

Storms at home were matched for Mustafa Kemal by difficulties on the international scene and by a serious internal revolt. The Mosul question was still pending, and the Kurds, under their charismatic leader Sheikh Said, rose in rebellion in the name of religion. Both these problems demanded the Ghazi's attention.

After the Lausanne Conference Mustafa Kemal had sought to effect a rapprochement with the British. The test of that policy would be the settlement of the Mosul question. On 19 May the first Anglo-Turkish conference on the subject opened in Istanbul. The talks lasted until 5 June 1924, but not much progress was made on establishing the border between Turkey and Iraq, which had become a British mandate. Mustafa Kemal had hoped that the friendlier relations he had established with the British in Ankara would have some effect on the Istanbul conference. He was on especially good terms with a young second secretary named Knox Helm in the British embassy (still located in Istanbul at the time). Helm was attracted to the young Turks running the government, and he became a friend of the Ghazi's. Eventually he located at a beautiful site near Çankaya, halfway between today's Botanical Gardens and the presidential mansion, where the British would one day build their embassy compound. Knox Helm became one of Mustafa Kemal's circle of poker players. The Ghazi enjoyed playing poker, often straight through the night into the early hours of the morning. They met frequently at the Anatolian Club in Ankara to play, but such personal, congenial associations with a British diplomat did little to promote a mutually satisfactory settlement on the Mosul question. It was agreed to refer the matter to the League of Nations.

Visits to the Mosul region were made by representatives of the league. They quickly determined that the area was largely populated by Kurds, who appeared content with the autonomous arrangement they had worked out with the British in Iraq. Moreover, the Turkish contention that the Kurds were Turks was dispelled. In September 1925 the league commission on Mosul presented its report. A plebiscite for the area was ruled out as impractical, since sentiment was clearly in favor of inclusion in Iraq. They proposed the incorporation of the Mosul province into Iraq under a twenty-five year mandate from the league. The British had already agreed to be bound by what the commission recommended, but the Turks turned surly and refused to accept the report. They pulled their delegation out of Geneva, leaving the council of the league no alternative but to grant the mandate without Turkish approval. It was not until June 1926 that Turkey, Britain, and Iraq signed an agreement that recognized the transfer of Mosul to Iraq. Oil does not appear to have played much of a role in the entire matter. Britain did not wish to present herself as playing oil politics, and the Turks viewed the problem as a territorial rather than an economic issue. In fact, the Turks ultimately settled for a lump sum payment of £500,000 in lieu of oil royalties. Needless to say, in the light of present-day concerns, revisionist historians in Turkey see this settlement in a less favorable light.

Another factor that must have influenced Mustafa Kemal to seek a quick end to the Mosul question was the Kurdish rebellion, which broke out during the Mosul negotiations and which was more threatening to Kemalist Turkey. In February 1925 a Kurdish revolt was initiated in the Dersim region on the upper Euphrates River. Led by Sheikh Said, a crafty, rich overlord who regarded Mustafa Kemal as godless, the Kurds sought to revoke the abolition of the sultanate and the caliphate and to restore the religious law of Islam. Separatism also played a role in the rebellion, but its rhetoric was couched mostly in religious terms. Responsibility for dealing with the revolt was left to Prime Minister Fethi. He had recently succeeded İsmet, who had resigned the office ostensibly on account of illness, but who had in fact been urged to do so by Mustafa Kemal. The Ghazi was seeking to appease the newly formed Progressive party whose leaders were unhappy with İsmet. Mustafa Kemal suspected the Progressive party leaders of plotting against him and held them responsible for the Kurdish revolt. Fethi tried to contain the problem and keep the focus on the Kurds rather than on the Progressive party. He asked its leaders to dissolve their party and to support the government's attempts to deal with the Kurds. They refused to dissolve the party, but did agree to support the government's measures to suppress the revolt.

Compromise, however, did not quell the revolt, nor did it ease Mustafa Kemal's suspicions. İsmet rushed back to Ankara to lead the forces in the assembly seeking to impose harsher measures that would have the effect of stifling the Progressive party as well as the Kurds. Their demands included the institution of press censorship and the resurrection of Independence Tribunals, courts responsible to the assembly that could dispense justice quickly and efficiently on the scene. Matters came to a standstill in the assembly, forcing Mustafa Kemal to lecture the delegates. He warned them that it was necessary to take the nation by the hand and that those who started the nationalist revolution would complete it. His keen power of persuasion prevailed once again, and a vote of no confidence in the restrained measures of Fethi's cabinet was passed. Thereupon, he and his government resigned, and İsmet was returned to the office of prime minister in which he would serve until 1937.

Spreading to a dozen provinces in the southeast of Turkey, the Kurdish revolt took on a serious aspect. A bill was passed in the assembly permitting censorship and the reestablishment of the Independence Tribunals. As soon as the weather permitted, the regular Turkish army began to move against the Kurds. Within two months of its inception the Kurdish revolt was put down. Sheikh Said himself was captured. He was tried by an Independence Tribunal and found guilty of treason. Having unfurled the green banner of revolt in the name of Islam against the red and white flag of Mustafa Kemal's new Turkey and lost, Sheikh Said paid for his audacity with his life. At the end of June 1925, he was publicly hanged in front of the main mosque of Diyarbekir.

Only four and a half months had elapsed since the outbreak of the Kurdish revolt. Using the unrest created by Sheikh Said as a screen, Mustafa Kemal had extracted extraordinary powers from the Grand National Assembly which he exploited to rid himself of the opposition movement that had found form and expression in the establishment of the Progressive party. Sensitive to criticism in the press, the government invoked its new powers and shut down a number of newspapers in Istanbul. Leading editors were harassed, and one was even sent off in "exile" to the town of Çorum, northeast of Ankara. A journal that had exhibited Marxist leanings was closed, and a number of its writers were sentenced to prison terms. Among those sentenced was Şevket Süreyya Aydemir, who would eventually come to write an outstanding biography of the Ghazi. The culminating act in this drive against the opposition was the termination of the Progressive party on 3 June 1925.

While Mustafa Kemal was able to find solutions to his political problems, his relationship with Lâtife was relentlessly unraveling. She had accompanied him to Dumlupınar near Afyon at the end of August 1924, for his speech on the anniversary of that battle. The couple then went to Bursa, apparently in a happy mood. Making their way to Istanbul by ship, Mustafa Kemal decided to have the ship sail through the Bosporus and on to the Black Sea without putting in at Istanbul. This was a reprise of his trip in the *Bandırma* when he had gone from Istanbul to Samsun in that old tramp steamer to initiate the Turkish struggle for independence. Now, however, he was his country's savior, sailing in a Turkish naval vessel with his wife.

Their trip took them past Samsun all the way to Trabzon. They called at several ports where Mustafa Kemal enjoyed himself by mingling with the people. Lâtife became jealous whenever the women demonstrated their adoration of the Ghazi. More destructive to their pleasure, however, was the news of an earthquake that had hit the city of Erzurum. Breaking their journey, they returned to Samsun by ship and then went to the disaster area by automobile. The trip from Samsun was disagreeable. As they started out, Mustafa Kemal insisted that Salih and Kılıç Ali accompany him in the same car with Lâtife. Whenever she felt left out of the conversation, she would sulk. They were all tired by the time they reached Tokat and went immediately to dinner. In addition to Salih and Kılıç Ali, the dinner party included the governor of Tokat. No alcoholic beverages were served at dinner, Mustafa Kemal having stopped drinking when he received word of the earthquake. Such abstention was perhaps an indication of his respect for the victims of the quake, but it was usual for the Ghazi, whenever he felt that the welfare of his country depended upon his alertness and ability to remedy some difficult situation, to refrain from drinking.

Tokat was well behind Ankara in amenities, but on any scale the surroundings would have to be considered primitive. The entire group was rather fatigued, but when Lâtife at last suggested that she and her husband retire for the night, he refused. Lâtife stalked out of the room and went upstairs, soon venting her displeasure by banging on the floor with her shoe (Bozdağ 1975*a*, p. 253). Those who were left in the dining room were aghast at her behavior. They were further embarrassed when Mustafa Kemal found it necessary to say that perhaps it had been a mistake for him to marry. On the following day the couple was still sulking as they traveled toward Erzincan, which was also damaged by the quake. Another contretemps took place at dinner when Mustafa Kemal complimented a general's wife on her beauty. Lâtife made it clear to all present that the Ghazi's behavior had upset her greatly. In the morning Mustafa Kemal invited the general's wife to join him in his car and left Lâtife obliged to accept a seat in someone else's car.

Although their personal feud was upsetting, its intensity faded in the face of the devastation that had struck Erzurum. As Lâtife and Mustafa Kemal walked about the city, they were stunned. Buildings had been destroyed and the people were living in tents. The death toll was high. While in the quake-torn city Mustafa Kemal, his patience exhausted, asked his wife to return to Ankara. As she departed, accompanied by Salih and Kılıç Ali, he managed to wish her a safe trip. The two men, aware of the couple's intermittent differences, were conspiring to effect a reconciliation. With that in mind, Kılıç Ali returned to Erzurum to ascertain the Ghazi's attitude toward his wife. It was planned that Salih would send a telegram to Kılıç Ali, who would reply, "The patient is well" if Mustafa Kemal had recovered from his anger, but "The patient has a high fever" if he were still full of rage (Bozdağ 1975*a*, p. 261). The first telegram elicited the response that the patient was still feverish, but a second one was answered with the news that the patient was well. In the meantime, Salih and Lâtife tarried on the road to Ankara, going no farther than Kayseri, halfway between Ankara and Erzurum. When Lâtife learned that Mustafa Kemal would be willing to have her back with him again, they met for a second honeymoon at an inn in Kayseri. From there they went on to the Mediterranean resort area of southern Turkey around Adana and Mersin. It soon became obvious, however, that Lâtife's envy would continue to flare up, and by the summer of 1925 no improvement in their relationship seemed possible.

Like many husbands unhappy at home, Mustafa Kemal began to stay away more and more from the house in Çankaya, spending an increasing amount of time with his cronies, either playing poker or devoting himself to serious political matters. He was in the habit of talking familiarly with the soldiers who guarded the house, joking with them and watching them wrestle as though he were himself a soldier among them in the barracks. One night as he was engaged in his usual raillery with them, the scolding voice of Lâtife was heard. She addressed him as Kemal and told him to come in at once and to stop demeaning himself by being familiar with his men. That episode was the last straw for him. He demanded that Salih and Kılıç Ali make ready to leave with him the following day. Mustafa Kemal then spoke with İsmet by phone and told him that he was divorcing his wife. He asked that a public announcement of the divorce be prepared, and in the morning Mustafa Kemal and his boon companions left on a trip. Kılıç Ali was left behind to ensure that Lâtife made her departure for her family home in Izmir. The Ghazi was able to divorce Lâtife under the old Islamic law, which gave the husband the unilateral right to set aside his wife, for Turkey's new civil code would not be adopted until 17 February 1926. His marriage had lasted for two years, six months, and four days when it was dissolved on 5 August 1925.

22

The Man in the Panama Hat Adopts Daughters

When Mustafa Kemal asked Lâtife to marry him after his first visit to Zübeyde's grave, she seemed on one level to be the opposite of the representation of his grieving mother who had depended upon him for solace. That dependence was experienced by Mustafa Kemal as threatened engulfment. With her European education and Western viewpoint, Lâtife seemed triumphantly sophisticated rather than victimized and grieving. There is, however, an old saying that opposites are the same, and, paradoxically, Lâtife became an engulfing woman for her husband. As he had done in his youth, Mustafa Kemal now turned away from female engulfment. By divorcing he sought liberation for himself, even as he sought release from the tyranny of the past for the nation that represented his grieving mother. With the nation's liberation he could hope to return to a repaired mother. His divorce thus set in motion the psychological wheels that would enable him to act boldly. He would modernize his Turkish nation.

Inconsequential as some of the steps he took may appear to Westerners, they were revolutionary in the context of his time and place, and they proved to his people his ability to do the impossible. One of those steps was the elimination of the fez as the standard headgear and its replacement by the ordinary hat worn by Westerners.

Near Eastern society, prior to the forced-draft modernization of the twentieth century, was a corporate society in which one's identity was closely tied to one's religious affiliation. Dress and type of headgear were the primary outward manifestations of religious affiliation and were often as much a mark of social status as accent is in England. Traditionally, the Muslim headgear was the turban. It facilitated touching the forehead to the ground during prayer and offered protection from the sun. Hadith, that is, traditions originating in statements attributed to Muhammad, bolstered the unique position of the turban among the Muslims. Sayings such as "God and the angels give their blessing at the Friday prayer to those who wear the turban" and "The turban is the barrier separating belief and nonbelief" are two that affirm the sanctity of that particular headgear. As much as Muslims were admonished to adhere to their distinctive apparel, non-Muslims were prohibited by sumptuary laws from appropriating the dress of Muslims.

Political changes, especially the replacement of one dynasty by another, or even a new ruler's succession to the throne within a dynasty, were often signaled by a change in headgear. The adoption of red headgear by the Turkoman tribesmen, who provided the military power upon which the Safavid dynasty rested, is only one of the more famous cases in point.[1] They took their name, the *kızılbaş*, the "red heads," from their headgear. Within the Ottoman context a significant change in headgear had taken place in 1826, when Sultan Mahmud II moved against the recalcitrant Janissaries, who, from the late sixteenth century on, had become a focal point of discontent.[2] They disliked campaigning far from the comforts of Istanbul, gouged the government with their incessant demands for special gifts and favors, and initiated a number of revolts that sapped their military power. Forging a coalition of bureaucrats, religious dignitaries, and military leaders, Mahmud II abolished the Janissaries on 15 June 1826. They put up a modicum of resistance, but troops loyal to the sultan fired upon the holdouts, and the abolition of the Janissary corps was carried through.

Faced with the necessity of organizing a new military establishment along Western lines, Sultan Mahmud II introduced a new headgear for his army, the fez. Worn previously in North Africa and by the Greek Christians who inhabited Ottoman-held islands in the Mediterranean, the fez was taken up first by the military, and then in 1829 a decree made it compulsory headgear for other classes of Ottoman officials. Reluctantly, Muslims accepted the fez despite its European connotations, and it soon became the universal symbol of Islam.

After a century of its assimilation into Islamic culture, Mustafa Kemal proposed to extirpate the fez from Turkish society. He wanted to make his countrymen look properly westernized by giving up their characteristic dress for that of the Europeans. Despite the fact that great suffering had been inflicted upon the Ottoman Empire by the Western world, Mustafa Kemal fervently believed that "there is only one civilization"—that of the West. He held the practices of Islam in Ottoman times responsible for obstructing civilization's advance among the Turks. When he set about to crush the ways of Islam, he was, in effect attacking the culture of the people from whom he had sprung and whom he had saved. There had to be a connection in his mind between the "bad" parts of his mother, which he held responsible for her continued grieving and

[1]The Safavid dynasty, founded by Shah Ismail, ruled Iran from 1500 to 1722. They were militantly Shi'ite in outlook.

[2]The Janissaries were the elite Ottoman infantry corps who had been the scrouge of Europe and of Ottoman enemies in the East as well. Organized under Murad I (1362–89), the Janissaries were Christians levied as a tax on the Greek Orthodox subjects of the empire, converted to Islam, and trained for service.

for her inability to give him adequate mothering, and certain Islamic practices. Ridding Turkish society of those "bad" practices would serve to heal the nation (always identified with his mother in need of repair) and prepare Turkey to assume her rightful place and role in the family of nations.

Determined to change the way Turks dressed, Mustafa Kemal set out from Ankara early on 25 August 1925, accompanied by Nuri, another friend, his two aides-de-camp, and a secretary. He was bound for Kastamonu, north of Ankara, which had been described to him as one of the most conservative districts in Turkey. He was going there to introduce the Turks to the hat and convince them of the need to adopt Western dress. The impact would be equal to that of an American president arriving in New York City dressed as a desert nomad, demanding that everyone follow his example.

Just as he had attacked the strongest Greek position when he launched the great offensive, Mustafa Kemal chose to intiate his program for dress reform in a place notably identified with extreme, conservative Islamic loyalty. He had not previously visited the region, but he knew that his journey would take him past the site of the great battle fought on 27 July 1402, between Sultan Bayezid I and Tamerlane. On the plain of Esenboğa, Tamerlane had defeated the Ottoman army and taken Bayezid prisoner. He then dismantled the fledging Ottoman Empire. It took the Ottomans almost three decades to recover from that disaster. Mustafa Kemal admired Tamerlane and liked to read about the man whom he considered one of the outstanding military commanders in world history, a man the Turks claimed as being of their own stock. As the Ghazi went into what was to prove to be a challenging, although nonmilitary, engagement of his own, he talked to his companions about the old conqueror and his strategies. Traveling the desolate road, Mustafa Kemal could not fail to recall that in Tamerlane's time central Anatolia had been heavily forested, but the absence of any governmental policy on forest conservation had allowed the land to fall into a state of denuded aridity. Mustafa Kemal dreamed of the greening of his Anatolian motherland.

At Çankırı, south of Kastamonu, the same day, the crowd that greeted the party must have been taken aback to see the Ghazi in European dress. His suit was of grey linen, but its cut was decidedly Western. He wore a shirt and tie, and in his hand he carried a white Panama hat (without a hatband). Since he was bareheaded, the people in the crowd removed their own headgear—fez, kalpak, or turban—out of respect, and cheered him to the heavens. All along the road the people had set up victory arches, and as the Ghazi passed under them, sheep were ritually slaughtered as a mark of respect and honor and as an offering for continued good fortune. The contrast between the old Islamic practice of sacrifice carried out before the national hero who was dressed in a distinctly Western fashion could not have been more striking. In a situation ideal for his posture as a narcissistic, charismatic leader, Mustafa Kemal wasted no time. As he shook hands with the people in the crowd, he asked them, "Where are your hats?" (Aydemir 1969, vol. 3, p. 237).

Kastamonu had been made ready for the Ghazi's arrival. The local dignitaries had commandeered practically every automobile in the area, some twenty, and had come out some distance from the city to honor Mustafa Kemal. The excitement was at its peak when the savior came into view—in his linen suit and carrying his Panama hat in his hand. As though on signal, everyone shed his Muslim headgear as Mustafa Kemal began walking among the crowd. After the first shock of seeing the Ghazi bareheaded, everyone was compliant and joined in the festivities. A few people, wanting to be emphatic about their acceptance of the new mode, had quickly constructed makeshift hats to wear for the occasion.

As a charismatic leader Mustafa Kemal was able to alter his style from gentle persuasion (a mother image) to that of a strong father. On his second day in Kastamonu, dressed in the uniform of a field marshal, he went to visit a military garrison. Emerging from the barracks he had just inspected, he saw a placard that read, "One Turk is equal to ten of the enemy." He called for the officer on duty and asked him if that were true. The officer replied, "Yes, my Pasha!" The Ghazi, replying as the hot-blooded, narcissistic, charismatic leader, cried out, "Not according to me. One Turk is the equal of the world!" (İmece 1959, p. 4).

Tarrying in Kastamonu on 26 August, Mustafa Kemal spoke to a group at the municipal offices. He was fired by his hopes of taking Turkey into the modern world and further separating her from the "bad" parts of Islam. After ridiculing the fez and the skullcap worn under it, which also served as the foundation for the turban, he gave some insight into his thoughts:

> We must become civilized people from every point of view. We have suffered much. This is because we have failed to understand the world. Our thoughts and our mentality will become civilized from head to toe. . . . Look at the Turkish and Islamic worlds. What great calamity and distress they are in because they have not been able to transform and elevate their thoughts as civilization commands. That is the reason why we have remained backward up to now and [why we] sank into the mud of this last calamity. If we have rescued ourselves in the past five or six years, it is because of the alterations in our conceptions. Now we can not stand still. Come what may, we shall go forward, because we must. The nation must certainly know that civilization is such a forceful fire that it burns and destroys those who are heedless of it. We shall take our

> rightful place in the family of nations in which we find ourselves, and we shall defend it. [İmece 1959, pp. 17–18]

Later that day the Ghazi and his party left Kastamonu for İnebolu, on the Black Sea coast. There he continued to lecture his people, always appearing in Western dress with his Panama hat in his hand. He spoke of civilization and of the need to advance. Illiteracy was another aspect of Turkish society that needed to be eradicated. It is, of course, interesting to remember that his mother was illiterate. Recordings of Mustafa Kemal's voice do not reveal him as having an especially effective speaking voice, but he managed nevertheless, to whip crowds into a kind of antiphonal fervor. "Is it possible for a nation to be civilized without dressing in a civilized manner?" he would cry out, and the crowd would answer, "Never! Never!" Then he would persist, "Are you ready to be described as uncivilized?" And again the answer would ring out with even more vigor, "Never! Never!" The Ghazi then compared the people to jewels—but jewels covered with mud. "In order to see the jewel shine, one must get rid of the mud," he told his audience. Getting rid of the mud, he insisted, involved "shoes on the feet, trousers over the legs, shirts with neckties under the collar, jackets, and naturally, to complement all of this, a headcovering to protect you from the sun." Then came his most celebrated comment on the revolution in dress. Pointing to his Panama hat, he told the onlookers, "The name of this is 'hat' [*şapka*]." He then pressed his point home: "There are those who say this is not permissible by religious law. Let me say to them, you are very ignorant and heedless, and I want to ask them, if wearing the fez, which is the headgear of the Greeks, is permitted by religious law, why isn't it so with wearing a hat?" (İmece 1959, p. 46).

Shocking as this speech was, there was still more provocative material to come. The Ghazi went on to say that women had been downtrodden long enough in Turkey, and civilized society demanded their liberation:

> During my trip I have seen our women comrades' eyes and faces covered rather carefully and elaborately, not just in the villages, but in the towns and cities as well. I am sure that this fashion, especially in this hot time of year, undoubtedly is a source of pain and suffering to them.
>
> My male comrades, this is a bit the product of our selfishness. . . . But, my dear friends, our women are sensible and thinking people like ourselves. After having inspired their sacred morality, explaining our national ethics to them, and furnishing their minds with enlightenment and purity, there will be no more need for selfishness. Let them show their faces to the world, and let them be able to view the world carefully. There is nothing to fear in this. [İmece 1959, p. 47]

Equal status for women, a worthwhile goal in its own right, was associated for Mustafa Kemal with the uneasy relationship he had had with his engulfing mother. Freeing the Turkish woman to stand on her own feet before the world would render her, in a sense, less dangerous. The enemy is far less threatening when out in the open.

His visit on the Black Sea coast with its memories of the initiation of his struggles gave Mustafa Kemal an exhilarating three days. He mingled with the sailors and fishermen and joined in their revelries. The Ghazi always stood out in any crowd, and the people of İnebolu fed his narcissistic need for recognition. They showered him with love and affection, which he repaid through several speeches. They hung on his every word, as though each were a drop of milk given by a caring mother. He possessed that extraordinary ability to appear simultaneously as mother/father, male/female, thus offering something to everyone in his audience.

Leaving İnebolu with his spirits buoyed, Mustafa Kemal stopped again in Kastamonu. There he found the men now wearing hats, some in fact having modified women's hats to their purposes when they could find no other Western headgear. This trip coincided with the third anniversary of his great military triumph over the Greeks. He paid it no attention, however, being swept up in another kind of campaign that necessitated putting his military struggles behind him. He was now on an unrelenting war against illiteracy and backwardness, a war conducted with lectures and speeches. His goal of liberating his countrymen seemed irrevocably intertwined with his own wish to be liberated himself from the engulfing influences of his childhood. One of his targets was the religious establishment as represented by the brotherhoods centered in the *tekke*s, or dervish lodges. In Ottoman Turkey there were several dervish orders that were empirewide in organization, with branches in many cities and towns. Each great order centered on the life and works of a significant person. The Mevlevi Order of Whirling Dervishes, with their center in Konya, was focused on the life of Celâleddin Rumi (1207–73) and his body of mystical poetry. That order was highly urbanized and influential in governmental circles. The Bektaşi order, drawing its inspiration from the life of Hacı Bektaş, a legendary Muslim saint of Anatolia, had been intimately associated with the Janissaries and more rural in its orientation. In the rural areas there was a great deal of superstitious worship of saints. The people sought to appease the saint's spirit to win favor for themselves and to avoid punishment. Certain tombs, often so old that no one knew any longer whose body they contained, had become invested with enormous religious significance. It was customary to pray at these tombs and to tie strips of green cloth to them.

These practices of folk Islam, which Mustafa Kemal could not help but associate with his mother's superstitious behavior, outraged him. In a speech at Kastamonu he launched his attack upon the folkways of Islam. "To seek help from *the dead*," he chided the people of Kastamonu, "is a disgrace to a civilized community" (Atatürk 1952, vol. 2, p. 214; italics added). As a child, of course, he himself had been influenced by the awareness of dead siblings through his interaction with his mother, and, by being a link to them, he could be considered immortal. He wanted to shake off that influence just as he had wanted to be liberated from his mother's focused all-embracingness in order to separate from her and to be able to individuate.

It took nine days for Mustafa Kemal to complete his circuit from Ankara to İnebolu and back to the capital, but in that short span of time he destroyed many of the traditional ways in which Turks had interacted with their world. When he reentered Ankara, the welcoming crowds had a surprise for him—they were all wearing Panama hats. A photograph taken of the people shows that many of the hats were ill-fitting, some being too large, others too small. In Ankara hats now outnumbered fezzes. The Ghazi followed up his speaking tour with legislation to consolidate his attack on the external manifestations of Islamic backwardness. On 2 September the wearing of religious vestments by those not holding religious office was banned, and on 25 November the fez was formally banned. The hat was to become the headdress of the Turks. November also saw legislation that dissolved the dervish brotherhoods. They were banned and their capital assets were taken over by the government. Their colorful ceremonies were also prohibited.[3] Enforced closure of the dervish monasteries and convents aroused much reaction, especially in the more conservative regions of eastern Turkey, but the government moved swiftly and managed to contain the discontent. With the enactment of this legislation Mustafa Kemal achieved an acceptable degree of success in his crusade, which was both personal and national, against superstition and the legacy of the past.

There was one item from that past he neglected to legislate against. Perhaps he shied away from it because of the popular reaction that the measures against the religious orders had aroused, but the wearing of the veil was not prohibited by law. Instead, the Ghazi continued to speak out against it and sought by persuasion to eradicate it from Turkish life.

More intimately associated with the old fabric of life, but much less apparent than hats or veils, was the system of law. In Ottoman Turkey there were two main bodies of law, the administrative law that governed one's relation with the state, especially if one were an officeholder, and the religious law that regulated man's relationships with his neighbors

[3]Today, only at a special time of the year, usually in December, the whirling dervishes are allowed to perform in the city of Konya.

and God. The traditional stronghold of religious law was personal status law, concerning such matters as marriage, divorce, and inheritance. In 1917 the Ottoman parliament had enacted a rather liberal law pertaining to families, and now Mustafa Kemal set out to eradicate completely the impact of the religious law on Turkish society. He had initiated his attack at the end of August, 1924 during the ceremonies commemorating the second anniversary of the victory over the Greeks. In a speech he declared:

> the basis of civilization, the foundation of progress and power, are in family life. A bad family life inevitably leads to social, economic, and political enfeeblement. The male and female elements constituting the family must be in full possession of their natural rights and must be in a position to discharge their family obligations. [Atatürk 1952, vol. 2, p. 183]

Here can be heard an echo of the difficulties his own family experienced as his father's fortunes declined and he himself fell more under his mother's sway.

Mustafa Kemal entrusted the development of legal reform to a commission that went to work in September 1924. He spurred on their year-old labors with a speech given on 5 November 1925 at the opening of the new law school in Ankara. After a short synopsis of how jurists had for centuries prevented the introduction of printing into the Ottoman Empire, he said, "All these events show that the greatest, and at the same time the most insidious, enemies of the revolutionaries are rotten laws and their decrepit upholders" (Atatürk 1952, vol. 2, p. 243). On 17 February 1926, a completed civil code modeled on that of the Swiss was adopted by the assembly. The code precluded such unilateral divorces as that by which Mustafa Kemal had set Lâtife aside. Other legal reforms included the adoption of a penal code taken from Italy and a new code of business law drawn from Germany.

Mustafa Kemal's divorce from Lâtife was not prompted by the anticipated change in family law that would soon have made his divorce both more public and difficult to obtain. With the divorce out of the way, however, the Ghazi was free fully to support the new, westernized civil code. After their divorce both Mustafa Kemal and Lâtife were dignified in their attitude and behavior toward each other. Lâtife lived a private life until her death in Istanbul in 1975, refusing to be interviewed and declining to lend her name to anything sensational. In turn, Mustafa Kemal treated her and the members of her family with respect. They never publicly vented the resentment they felt toward him. When Mustafa Kemal would say, as he sometimes did among his friends at his dinner table, that Lâtife had been the queen when they were married, he seemed ambivalent—mocking her even as he praised her idealized image. When H. C. Armstrong's sensationalistic book *Grey Wolf* appeared in 1932, one of the Ghazi's secretaries who knew English well read it to him, expecting him to be angry at its depiction of him as a lecherous drunk. Armstrong's description was, of course, not unfounded, but it took a rather simplistic view of a man who, whatever his habits, had achieved so much. Mustafa Kemal was not offended and launched into a discussion of how often we compare people to animals, speaking of a lion's courage, and the like, concluding that the comparison of him to an animal did not upset him. He is known, however, to have entertained the suspicion that Armstrong may have been in touch with Lâtife to learn details of their intimate life together.

After divorcing Lâtife, the Ghazi never married again, but he did not lack feminine companionship in his home, for he proceeded to adopt a number of daughters.[4] Abdürrahim, adopted during Zübeyde's lifetime, was the only male child to be taken into the household in this way, but Mustafa Kemal also brought home to Zübeyde a six-year-old girl, an orphan named Afife, who lived in Istanbul with his family until she married. Then, in the early years of his presidency, he adopted one young girl after another. Among the first was Sabiha, who in time became a successful military pilot. She was interviewed by Dr. Volkan in December 1974 at her home. Sabiha (Gökçen) recalled the occasion of her adoption and the details of her life in Mustafa Kemal's household.

Born in Bursa, she was a twelve-year-old orphan living with her brother's family in that city when she first met Mustafa Kemal. The war had interrupted her schooling, and when her brother was away with the army, she and her mother lived in a household without a male head. Then, her mother died and her brother returned. He was well disposed toward her, but she felt she was a burden and longed to go to a boarding school. When Mustafa Kemal visited Bursa in 1925, he stayed in a house near Sabiha's brother's. She ventured into the garden to catch a glimpse of the great man, and when he did appear, she ran toward him in excitement, only to be stopped by his guard. The Ghazi had seen her, however, and motioned for her to be allowed to approach. At first she was speechless, but he could always put people at ease, especially the young. The little girl relaxed almost at once and began talking as though she were addressing someone no more formidable than another child. He asked her who she was and why she sought him out. She told him about her family circumstances and her desire to go to school. Since she was a pubertal child in search of new parents, the psychological and circumstantial elements of the situation were in agreement.

[4]We will examine the psychological motivation of his adopting daughters later.

Responding to her charm, the Ghazi asked if she would like to come and live with him as a daughter and let him send her to school. She replied that she would have to ask her brother, who was promptly summoned. In her conversations with Dr. Volkan so many years later, Ms. Gökçen emphasized that Mustafa Kemal's interest in shaping her future, with his own hands, as she put it, was present from their first meeting—evidence of a creative, almost maternal feeling toward someone just starting out in life. The child's family assured her that she would continue to be welcome in their house, but that it would be an honor, one which they would share, for her to become the great man's daughter. Her Cinderella story began on the following day when she became a member of Mustafa Kemal's entourage on her first trip away from home. When the party arrived in Izmir after a long journey, he had her outfitted in the shops of Izmir, and in little more than a month she was enrolled in the Çankaya elementary school,[5] in the garden of the presidential mansion. The approximately twenty students, who were the children of the city's elite, including Mustafa Kemal's other adopted daughters, were under the care of one teacher.

Ms. Gökçen remembered their first teacher as a young woman who often played games with her students even though they were already over age for elementary school. One day when Mustafa Kemal quizzed them on what they were learning, they were at a loss to reply. He quickly replaced the young woman with a middle-aged teacher. In short order the girls rebelled. Sabiha and Zehra, another adopted daughter, were expelled and went weeping to Mustafa Kemal. After talking with their new teacher, he told them in "a sweet, firm way" to honor and obey her. Ms. Gökçen spoke of her realization that the Ghazi had been both mother and father to his daughters and had always substituted his "sweet firmness" for the harshness he might have expressed in view of his determination that they reach their potential. Like many a parent, he told the girls that he himself had always honored his teachers, choosing to forget how rebellious he had actually been, especially toward his religious teachers, and how severely he had once been punished.

Another adopted daughter was Rukiye, whom he found on a trip to Konya. He had her educated, and she later married a gendarme officer. In the same year that he adopted Sabiha, he adopted another "daughter," Afet, a young woman about eighteen who replaced Lâtife. An elementary school teacher, she was not only a surrogate wife, but in time she would become his intellectual extension and eventually a university professor of history. She not only attended many of the meetings around

[5]This school was designed to accommodate his adopted daughters as well as the children of those people who worked at the presidential palace or who lived nearby.

Mustafa Kemal's dinner table, but also took notes on what went on there, making her writings an important source for reconstructing the Ghazi's activities and patterns of thought.[6]

In June 1927 Mustafa Kemal returned to Istanbul for the first time since the end of the national struggle. There he was visited by three students from a teachers' college. One of them was an eighteen-year-old blue-eyed blonde named Nebile, whom he offered to adopt. After some hesitation, she accepted and went to Çankaya. Another young girl, Sabriye, was added when Afet went off to school in Europe. In turn, Sabriye went to law school and ultimately became a judge. Later, the household was joined by Bülent, who was the sister of the captain of a yacht on which Mustafa Kemal used to go sailing. Toward the end of the Ghazi's life, he adopted a little girl named Ülkü, who became the center of his attention.

It has never been established how many of these women had a sexual relationship with the Ghazi. It is interesting that he was willing to let Afet, whose relationship with him appears to have been sexual, go off to improve her education. He was intensely interested in changing all these women—westernizing them—but his interest in doing that extended to all Turkish women. He not only legalized the emancipation of women from the bonds of an old restrictive society, but he also sought drastic alterations in their social roles. Progress on that front, however, was not without its snags. Aydemir (1969, vol. 3, pp. 261–62) tells a story of the first ball given in Ankara. Since only three Turkish women appeared, it was necessary to enlist the participation of some bar girls. Their presence offended the three, who decided to leave. Before they could exit, however, the bar girls were sent away. Mustafa Kemal was still determined to show the nation that men and women could dance together in public. He asked one of the women to dance with him and thus got the dancing under way. The floor was so highly polished that one of the first couples to set forth on it fell down, giving a comical touch to the Ghazi's earnest attempt at social change. Nonetheless, the ball was another first successfully launched by Mustafa Kemal.

Breathing life into Ankara's social scene took only a small part of the Ghazi's time. He continued to be concerned about the countryside, promoting forest management and establishing his own model experimental farm on the outskirts of the city. Soon he was spending as much time at the farm as at the mansion in Çankaya. Photographs of him in a Panama hat operating a tractor appeared everywhere. It demonstrated that he could and would wear the infidel's hat and use the infidel's machinery in his fight to transform the nation.

[6]Besides writing about her many memories of Atatürk, Afet Afetinan wrote extensively on other topics as well; see a list of her writings from 1930 to 1956 in Afetinan 1958, pp. 176–80. In 1968 she wrote the history of the women's rights movement in Turkey.

He traveled incessantly and continued to mingle with the people to preach his reforms. One such trip, beginning on 7 May 1927 took him all the way to Silifke on the Mediterranean coast, where he inspected an experiment in farming. Wherever he went, he was met by adoring followers who, by now, appeared in hats or anything that resembled them. Women appeared alongside men. School children turned out to meet him, and some were chosen to go forward to the podium and read poetry on civilization and its advance, westernization, and reform. His homeward trip from Silifke took him back toward Bursa en route to Izmir. Before he reached Izmir a telegram brought him the news of a plot to assassinate him and of the capture of his would-be assassins.

23

The Izmir Assassination Plot: Immortality Threatened

Along the route Mustafa Kemal would travel from the Izmir train station to his hotel there was a point where three narrow streets converged. This was the spot chosen for the assassination attempt. Traffic moved so slowly there that the three hired assassins—a Laz, a Georgian, and a man identified only as "the pockmarked one," all with police records—could attack the Ghazi with revolvers or hand grenades and make their escape in the confusion. Their plan called for them to be driven to a landing point on the shore where they would board a boat operated by a man from Crete who had agreed to take them to a nearby island.

Pangs of conscience may have afflicted the Cretan conspirator, or perhaps when Mustafa Kemal's arrival in Izmir was delayed for a day, he may have suspected that the police had discovered the plot. He was already uneasy because two of his co-conspirators had taken a trip to Istanbul in order to establish alibis for themselves. Whatever the reasons, he revealed the plot to the authorities who promptly arrested not only the hired assassins, but the man who contracted for their services as well. He was a handsome young naval officer named Ziya Hurşid. A stubborn extrovert with a flaming temper, he had been elected a deputy to the first Grand National Assembly from the Laz country but had not been reelected to the second. He also seems to have harbored a grudge against Mustafa Kemal for the death of Ali Şükrü at the hands of the chief of Mustafa Kemal's Laz bodyguard. Seeking to avenge Ali Şükrü's death and festering with disappointment over the setback in his political career, Ziya Hurşid had strong personal reasons for conspiracy against the life of Mustafa Kemal.

Others who believed that they had suffered injury at the Ghazi's hands had willingly joined with Ziya Hurşid's plot. One with compelling psychological reasons was Colonel Arif, Mustafa Kemal's virtual "twin" during the war of independence. Not only had the Ghazi lost interest in Arif and discarded him, finding other men to serve as "twins" in his stead, but also Arif had never received the promotion to general, which he coveted greatly and anticipated as a reward for his services to the Ghazi. Neither Arif nor Mustafa Kemal understood the unconscious mechanism of "twinship." Arif mistook his being cast aside, which was a function of

Mustafa Kemal's narcissistic personality, as a personal affront. Having been one of Mustafa Kemal's cronies, a member of the inner circle with whom the leader relaxed, Arif expected to become a pasha. Such a promotion would have confused the boundaries Mustafa Kemal maintained between his cronies and his collaborators on national affairs. Thus, Arif's elevation to general was a psychological impossibility, and Arif was cast into the growing crowd of people who held grievances against the Ghazi. Despite the fact that he had become a deputy from Eşkisehir, Arif was still an aggrieved party.

Another conspirator was a deputy from Izmir also named Şükrü. He had belonged to the Committee of Union and Progress and had served as minister of education when the Young Turks had come to power. Exiled to Malta by the British after the Greek landings in May 1919, he returned to Turkey when the Ankara government prevailed over the British on the issue of political prisoners. He served for a while as the governor of Trabzon. Joining Mustafa Kemal's political party did not prevent him from maintaining contacts with the proponents of the old Union and Progress notions.

When Ziya Hurşid was arrested, he made no attempt to resist the police, who apprehended him at midnight in his hotel. Nor did he deny participating in the assassination plan, which had in fact grown out of an early conversation in which Ziya, Şükrü, and Arif had taken part. One night while drunk, Şükrü made a cryptic remark about the proposed assassination to a member of the Progressive party, the new opposition party. Rauf, Ali Fuat, and Refet apparently did not take the matter seriously when they were told of it. Mustafa Kemal's old friends who had formed the Progressive party were, nevertheless, "contaminated" with the plan to destroy him.

Suspicious moods often overtook Mustafa Kemal, and this happened now. He declined to treat the assassination plot as an act of personal animosity, choosing instead to view it as a major political conspiracy that needed to be dealt with by the Independence Tribunals. At this time the tribunals were headed by "Bald" Ali (Çetinkaya), who had earned the sobriquet the "hanging judge" after ordering the execution of the leaders of the Kurdish revolt. The Independence Tribunals struck terror in the hearts of many Turks, and the era resembled the reign of the guillotine during the French Revolution. It was a period in the life of the new Turkey that reflected the intertwining of Mustafa Kemal's personal psychological state (his suspiciousness), his conscious political need to rid himself of the opposition, the historical reality of the assassination plot, and the animosity of a certain few toward him. Many deputies, Şükrü and Arif among them, were arrested in spite of their parliamentary immunity. Also taken into custody were many people high up in the Progressive party, including Kâzım, Refet, Ali Fuat, and other pashas who had been the Ghazi's close friends during the war. Rauf, together with Dr. Adnan and Halide Edib, all of whom were out of the country, were also charged with conspiracy. Cavid, an important economist who had been Turkey's finance minister under Enver and who was obviously tainted by his connection with the Committee of Union and Progress, was also arrested as a conspirator.

In 1919, Kâzım had declined to arrest Mustafa Kemal on the sultan's orders and had declared his loyalty to him instead. Mustafa Kemal had depended on him more than on any other to launch the national struggle. Now he was behind bars. İsmet tried without success to extricate him from the tribunal, but Mustafa Kemal was determined to teach the opposition a lesson.

When Mustafa Kemal entered Izmir a day later than originally scheduled, his would-be assassins, along with Ziya Hurşid, were already in prison. He was greeted enthusiastically by the people of Izmir, who seemed embarrassed that their city had been chosen as the site of an assassination plot. They called for the blood of the conspirators. Mustafa Kemal responded to them with moving words, telling them that even had he died, the nation would not forsake the road he had charted for it. A statement released to the entire country acknowledged that his insignificant body was sure to return to dust one day, but the Turkish republic would live forever. The real implication of such "humble" rhetoric was that he would prove to be immortal in his spiritual oneness with the nation and that his ultimate corporeal oblivion would affect this not at all.

It would appear that the asassination plot led the Ghazi to a preoccupation with life and death, and his concept of immortality derived from his interaction with the grieving mother of his childhood. He seems to have been fascinated with his would-be assassins and the man who was the moving spirit behind the plot. He had Ziya Hurşid brought before him. During that confrontation he reminded Ziya of their former association in a common struggle and asked why he wanted his death. When Ziya admitted having planned the assassination attempt, Mustafa Kemal said that he would not have expected such treachery from him. Ziya is supposed to have replied, "The world is full of unexpected things, my Pasha" (Aydemir 1969, vol. 3, p. 273). Throughout the exchange Mustafa Kemal seemed calm and understanding of Ziya's motivation. Moved by the Ghazi's gentleness, Ziya asked to see him on the following day, perhaps in the hope of being forgiven. Again the Ghazi's posture was mild-mannered, as Ziya expressed his appreciation for the way he had been received on the previous day. Mustafa Kemal maintained that he himself was not a vengeful man, but the matter was one for the courts. Both men knew the presiding judge would be Bald Ali, the hanging judge. Here again Mustafa Kemal demonstrated his basic pattern of splitting: he was gentle and understanding with his would-be assassin, but his extension—the Independence Tribunal—in whose hands he would place the prisoner's fate, could be counted on to treat him with extreme prejudice.

Far more fascinating than his confrontation with Ziya was his meeting with one of the hired killers. Here the drama enacted seems to have been in the service of recrystallizing Mustafa Kemal's feelings of immortality. When the hireling was brought before the Ghazi, a man he had never seen before and whom he did not recognize, the gunman explained that he had been hired to murder Mustafa Kemal because the Ghazi was bad. When asked how he could have accepted the assignment to kill a man he had never seen and whom he could, therefore, easily confuse with someone else, he explained that his target was to have been pointed out to him as he made ready to fire his revolver. Mustafa Kemal then dramatically handed his own revolver to the man and announced, "Well, I am Mustafa Kemal. Come on, take this revolver and shoot me now" (Kinross 1965, p. 486). Those who witnessed that scene recalled later the surprise on the face of the would-be killer, who sank to his knees and started to cry. Mustafa Kemal's psychological notion that no one could kill him was thus dramatized in a way that echoed his having proven invulnerable at the battle of Gallipoli. His behavior toward his would-be killer served opposing ends: it gave him an opportunity to test his immortality, and it provided a counterphobic exercise for dealing with his intense fear of death.[1] His mother must have expected him to die as her other children had died, and she probably conveyed this anxiety to him. Mustafa Kemal's feeling of immortality was a defensive adaptation to this anxiety of being harmed.

With this byplay finished, the Independence Tribunal was summoned to Izmir from Ankara and was convened quickly by Bald Ali on 27 June. Kılıç Ali, a close associate of the Ghazi's, was a member of the tribunal panel. The list of the accused included not only those directly involved in the assassination conspiracy, but also some less directly part of the plot, but known to be sympathetic to the old Committee of Union and Progress. The ghost of Mustafa Kemal's rivalry with Enver Pasha stalked the proceedings of the tribunal. Also among the accused were members of

[1]This counterphobic exercise, exposing one's self to danger, was in the service of reducing his anxiety over his hidden fear of death. We think that although Mustafa Kemal's mother saw him as a savior, she also believed that he, too, would die, as his siblings had. Immortality was not only due to the dead siblings, it also had defensive qualities against his fear of death (separation from his mother) which obviously was condensed, at the oedipal age, with fear of castration at the hands of his father, whose image (due to his death) could not easily be tested against reality.

the now-defunct Progressive party who had at one time been among Mustafa Kemal's closest friends, advisers, and supporters. Once the trials started, negative feelings about the arrest and treatment of the latter were rather widely voiced. When Kâzım, Refet, and Ali Fuat were led into the courtroom, those present would rise and salute them. The pashas remained calm throughout their trial, but one must believe that there was a good deal of anxiety among them as they heard Bald Ali read the verdict regarding the men directly involved in planning the plot. For this group, including Şükrü, Arif, and Ziya, the verdict was guilty, and the sentence was death by hanging.

Ziya Hurşid went to his doom appearing nonchalant. He joked and conversed sarcastically with the hangman. Much has been written about Arif's fate (Froembgen 1937, pp. 253–55). During the ordeal he remained certain that he would be pardoned by the man whose twin he had been. When the time came for Mustafa Kemal to sign Arif's death warrant, along with all the others, he simply set aside his cigarette and put his signature to it without the slightest show of emotion. The thirteen condemned men went to the gallows as a ghostly crew in white shrouds, one no different from the others. It was a terrible death for Arif, who had been faithful to Mustafa Kemal throughout all the hazards of the struggle against the Greeks and who had shared intimately in the Ghazi's life. After Arif's execution, Mustafa Kemal never again mentioned his name. Arif had become a "bad object" for the Ghazi, and quite simply he was no more, even in the memory of the man he had served.

One of the most important results of the Izmir trials was the establishment of the innocence of Kâzım, Refet, Ali Fuat, and a number of others. News of this spread swiftly across the country. It was greeted by the people with cries of "Long live justice! Long live our pashas!" Nevertheless, the trial definitely separated Mustafa Kemal from his old friends, none of whom, save Ali Fuat, returned to the army or to political life as long as the Ghazi lived. Only Ali Fuat was again invited (in 1927) to Mustafa Kemal's dinner table. In 1933 he was elected to the Grand National Assembly as an independent deputy representing the district of Konya. In his memoirs (Cebesoy 1967) he wrote that when he once again sat at the Ghazi's dinner table, he was told that it was on his account that Mustafa Kemal had forgiven the other pashas. The implication was that Mustafa Kemal had influenced Bald Ali to free those men.

Thirteen hangings did not bring down the curtain on the Izmir assassination plot. On 1 August the Independence Tribunal reconvened in Ankara. It continued in session for twenty-six days, becoming in effect a jury before which the defendants, the old Committee of Union and Progress, the Young Turks, and even, posthumously, Enver Pasha, passed in review. Some executions were ordered, and Rauf and Adnan, who were already living abroad, were sentenced to exile from Turkey for twelve years. Some intellectuals viewed Rauf's sentence of exile with disbelief and sadness, but as time went on the people came to agree with Mustafa Kemal's desire to purge the country of what he considered to be bad influences. The Ankara trials turned out to be a critical review of Turkish history in the time of Enver Pasha. Thirty-seven of the accused were acquitted, Rauf and a few others were exiled, and three were sentenced to death. Çavid, the economist who had once worked with Enver, was among the latter. Some historians suggest that with the loss of Cavid Turkey deprived itself of a man badly needed to deal with its economy. When his sentence became known in Europe, many Western governments appealed for his release, as did a number of Jewish organizations since Cavid was considered to have had Jewish origins. He was, in fact, a *dönme*[2] but whatever his ethnic origins, there was no hope for his rescue.

After the Ankara trials the Independence Tribunals lost their importance as a political weapon in the hands of the Ghazi. Throughout 1925 and 1926 they had served as a government within a government. It was not until 7 March 1927 that they were officially removed from the scene. It is said that İsmet was influential in their termination. One night at dinner at Çankaya Mustafa Kemal told Bald Ali that he wanted the tribunals abolished. He was, as usual, operating in a grand manner when he suddenly set a limit on his aggression. Bald Ali tried to buy time for their continuation by telling Mustafa Kemal that he would prepare a report on them for his consideration. Having none of this, the Ghazi told Bald Ali that he had already studied the situation in detail and had arrived at a firm decision to abolish them. On the following day his decision was confirmed by a party caucus, and the tribunals ceased to exist. Mustafa Kemal was then free to engage in another act of splitting, externalized this time to the city of Istanbul.

[2]The *dönmes* are members of a Muslim sect formed by the Jewish followers of Shabbetai Sevi. He was considered by them to be the messiah. They converted to Islam in Salonika in 1683, following the conversion of their leader. The word comes from the verb *dönmek*, "to turn," and the verbal noun *dönme* means "convert." The *dönmes* are still active today.

24

Istanbul, Not Byzantium

MUSTAFA KEMAL HAD NOT STAYED IN ISTANBUL SINCE HIS DEPARTURE FOR Samsun on 16 May 1919 over eight years before. He had, however, passed through the city with Lâtife in 1924, a year after the Allies had evacuated it. On that trip, as the couple sailed through the Bosporus, the crowds waiting on shore in the hope that the Ghazi might disembark numbered in the thousands. At that time he did not oblige them. On the contrary, he had rather pointedly refrained from including Istanbul in his wide-ranging itinerary, which had been arranged to celebrate the signing of the Treaty of Lausanne. It would appear that his inability to visit Istanbul for so long had a certain psychological basis, having something to do with the city's psychogeography—its symbolic impact for him.[1]

Istanbul's topography makes it a city on which psychological processes can be externalized readily. A city of legend and history, it is the meeting place, in a psychological as well as a geographical sense, for the opposites of East and West, although the union was more metaphorical than real until 1972, when a bridge was built across the Bosporus linking Europe and Asia. In addition to the physical splitting effected by the Bosporus, a body of water called the Golden Horn cuts through the European part of Istanbul. In a sense the topography of the city echoed the splitting in Mustafa Kemal's psychological makeup. Moreover, the city had undergone several name changes. Its origins are lost in the shadows of the seventh century B.C., but it is said to have been founded by Megarians, who named it Byzantium after their commander Byzans. In 196 B.C., during the reign of Septimius Severus, the city was rebuilt and called Antoninia. When Constantine moved the capital of the Roman Empire there in 330 A.D., he renamed the city New Rome, but later it was

[1]William Niederland, a psychoanalyst, has studied geographic symbolism, introducing the term "psychogeography" to reflect the way a given environment may symbolically represent externalized images, wishes, or conflicts of an individual or group (1977). Niederland was interested, for example, in the naming of America (Niederland 1971), maintaining that the people of that period of discovery fantasized America as an island paradise, one promising eternal bliss. Early descriptions of the new land were fanciful and extremely euphoric. The name America is derived from the given name of Amerigo Vespucci, but in the feminine form. This may account for America's having been regarded by countless immigrants as a good mother who would nurture them.

changed to Constantinople. Under the Turks the city had many names and sobriquets. It was variously referred to as the Abode of Felicity, the City of Islam (Islambol), Stanbul, and Istanbul, which is a corruption of the Greek expression *eis tin polin*, "in the city." In 1926 the Turkish government officially adopted Istanbul as the city's name.

Istanbul may have had at least two significant representations for Mustafa Kemal. As a female entity the city embodied the oedipal mother for whom he had incestuous strivings. In approaching the city he faced confrontation with the bad oedipal father, but Istanbul also represented both the good mother and the bad, as well as the conflict this split induced in him. His narcissistic personality led him unconsciously to externalize onto Istanbul his inner conflictual psychological processes. He could not, therefore, visit the city until he was psychologically ready to deal with them. Two sources validate this conclusion. One is a poem called *Sis* ("Fog"), written by the renowned Turkish poet Tevfik Fikret and said to have been Mustafa Kemal's favorite poem.[2] Fascinated by it even before leaving Istanbul in 1919, he recited it or referred to it whenever he reminisced about his youth and his days spent at the War College in Istanbul. The other is in an odd letter he dictated in 1924, an indirect communication with the journalist Yakup Kadri (Karaosmanoğlu), who had written about the postwar situation in Istanbul (Aydemir 1969, vol. 3, pp. 293–96).

In the poem "Fog" the poet speaks of Istanbul as "the eternal queen of the East" who has been deserted by a thousand husbands. Fikret's perception of this "queen" follows what psychoanalysts call the Madonna/prostitute split in which women are seen as either altogether pure or ready to prostitute themselves. The establishment of such polarity obviously serves an oedipal theme—the mother/woman image is split on behalf of the oedipal son who can feel close to her in the absence of any possibility of sexual interaction, since he then need not anticipate being punished by the father. Sexual potency is possible for him only with a prostitute whom neither the son nor the father could confuse on a conscious level with the image of the mother. This relieves him of the guilt of incestuous strivings. In many cases, however, the Madonna/prostitute view of women reflects the inability of the child—or of the adult with a persistent childhood intolerance of ambiguity—to abandon his earliest perception of those around him as either "all good" or "all bad" (Volkan 1976, pp. 307–15). Persons with a narcissistic personality organization fall into this category, and, indeed, Mustafa Kemal retained

[2]We are grateful to Professor Fuat Göksel (1975) for bringing Mustafa Kemal's preoccupation with the poem to our attention.

a double image of his mother—one being highly idealized and the other seen as smothering. He was never able to remain loyal to any one woman, since his orientation led him to an expectation of disappointment. Riza Nur (1968, vol. 3, p. 643), at one time a close friend of Mustafa Kemal's, noticed this behavior pattern. After falling out with the Ghazi, he wrote his memoirs in which he observed, "Our respected leader has one habit. He loves women, but he does not love one woman. He has to change them rapidly. He must be the chief court taster." What Riza Nur failed to comprehend, however, was that Mustafa Kemal clung to the illusion that one day he would possess the idealized woman (the Turkish nation).

Tevfik Fikret's poem clearly expressed the dilemma of dealing with a fascinating woman/city one fears will be engulfing. The poet notes that the city seen from afar looks so gentle, but closer acquaintance discloses her lack of compassion and her indifference to the tears of those who love her. In fact, she contains within her boundaries "millions of *corpses*" (italics added). Mustafa Kemal may very well have (unconsciously) associated this image of the city of the dead with the image of his mother grieving over his dead siblings and their father. The poet indicated that among the city's numerous dead were many with "clean foreheads"—the Turkish equivalent of "clean hands"—in short, guiltless victims.

One line in the poem refers to the city's being a means of "transferring the past to the future." That concept was close to Mustafa Kemal's heart, for unconsciously he must have perceived that his mother had transferred her "past grief" into the future, through her last son. When the poet calls Istanbul "the incestuous figure of the era," he touches on Mustafa Kemal's unrepressed incestuous strivings. While drinking at his dinner table, Mustafa Kemal would say, almost nightly, "I am in love with my mother" (Gökçen 1974), continuing to use the present tense in a way that demonstrated that he kept her image alive while expressing his love for her in a sexual rather than filial way.

While the poem "Fog" fascinated Mustafa Kemal, it was not his own personal expression. He did, however, dictate a letter that gives a clear idea of how he had transferred to the city of Istanbul his perception of his early, preoedipal as well as his oedipal mother. A parliamentary deputy from the Siirt district named Mahmud, who was visiting Mustafa Kemal on 26 June 1924, had received a letter from Yakup Kadri (Karaosmanoğlu) describing the deplorable conditions in Istanbul. Mahmud shared this letter with the Ghazi, who dictated a reply for him to send to Yakup Kadri. The journalist kept the letter and ultimately permitted Şevket Süreyya Aydemir to include long passages from it in his biography of Mustafa Kemal.

These passages translated below were dictated by Mustafa Kemal himself:

> Istanbul, Byzantium, always preserves its heterogeneous nature and character as if it were its lot in life. From time to time, from one era to another, however, the nature of its miscellany changes. Today, therefore, one must never despair of seeing the real face of Istanbul manifest itself. If one remains in Istanbul, despair is natural. But, for those who know to go to a high point that overlooks the city from a distance and can take a good look at it, there is no need for despair. [Aydemir 1969, vol. 3, p. 294]

We know that Mustafa Kemal kept such a distance from his mother even while he was preoccupied with her real or fantasied images. One senses the personification of Istanbul in this passage, its designation as an entity in which opposites persist without ever melding, and an entity one should guard against losing oneself in. One gets the feeling that Mustafa Kemal was describing Istanbul as a woman, the mother of his early childhood, who grieved but also smiled with pleasure upon him. He fears being engulfed by her and needs to keep a safe distance away from her. The letter continues with other suggestions that his early (preoedipal) perceptions of the mother were transferred to the city. He suspects the presence of those bent on secret aims of their own "in an environment surrounded by dark white horizons" (Aydemir 1969, vol. 3, p. 294). His ambivalence in this phrase is marked, and his splitting is certainly suggested. He speaks of the city as Byzantium and describes it as a place where even the press is capable of carrying out an assassination.

Another passage from this letter gives further indications of his inner world having dictated his perception of the city. He seems to identify himself with Yakup Kadri and describes the atmosphere of Byzantium as that of the bad mother. He tells "Dear good-hearted Brother Yakup Kadri" that:

> You are having difficulty breathing the air of Byzantium in which you find yourself. This is rather natural. While it should be the most pure, clean, and exhilirating air because of its *geographical location and its topography*, it is exactly the opposite, and you are having trouble breathing it. Had it kept its original oxygen and hydrogen it would give strength instead of sorrow to those who breath it. [Aydemir 1969, vol. 3, p. 294; italics added]

He then comments on the dust of centuries weighting the air, referring no doubt to the past as it represented his own currently regressed state. Noting that the new Turkish republic was less than a year old, he speaks of the difficulties involved in changing the nature of Byzantium. One catches in such a remark an echo of his attempt to change the grieving mother into a gratifying one. It is he himself who is not yet one year old, but he will soon grow up and rid himself of the badness belonging either to the early perception of the bad mother or to the bad father. Certain oedipal elements, however, can also be seen here. On another level, he wants to remove all trace of the dirty Byzantium father in the good Istanbul mother. He continues:

> The republic will make a man out of Byzantium. The republic decidedly, come what may, will make a man out of Byzantium, which, by becoming habituated to filth, duplicity, lies, and immorality, has lost its natural state, its original beauty, and its immeasurable value. It will turn it back to its natural state and purity. [Aydemir 1969, vol. 3, p. 295]

Oedipal issues are symbolically involved in the passages that speak of how he proposes to cleanse Byzantium (the bad) and transform it into Istanbul (the good). It is the little boy who will sweep a typhoon into Istanbul and rid it of the Byzantine father's dirtiness. It is in the Bosporus—which suggests the female genitalia in shape—that the boy's power will confront the dirt of Byzantium and prevail over it.

> The following operation will take place, an operation that will cleanse what is dirty, dig out the dirt, and explode into the air; and in order to clear the water, perhaps the whole Black Sea with its waves will enter the Bosporus to flood everything.
>
> Yes, this will happen, but while this typhoonlike high and low tide [the expression in Turkish refers to the rhythmic movement of tidal water symbolic of sexual intercourse] is cleansing Istanbul, would it be only with the aim of cleansing soil and stones, or would the living but unthinking creatures there be washed also?

Here Mustafa Kemal symbolically refers to his incestuous strivings, but he also seems to identify with the tides that washed out his brother's corpse—the cause of his mother's grief.

Following the dictates of his own personality organization, Mustafa Kemal continues by pointing out that this typhoonlike phenomenon (clearly himself and his ejaculatory power) will effect its cleansing operation without asking advice or taking suggestions from anyone.

His notion of being immortal had been reconfirmed by news of the failed assassination plot and the drama that followed. He was, therefore, emboldened to confront Byzantium/Constantinople/Istanbul (the split image of the mother), to tame or mend it and have his oedipal triumph over it. Indeed, when he arrived in the city for the first time in eight years on 1 July 1927, it looked as though the city were being hit by a typhoon. The crowds pressed forward wave after wave to greet their hero. Istanbul had never seen anything like it. One of the city's newspapers made an effort to calm the hysteria by arguing that Mustafa Kemal was not after all an immortal. The writer was, however, conveying his own ambivalence about the matter. "The Ghazi is a person like other persons. He is not a prophet or a superman, but the appearance of such a person occurs very seldom in history. Such perform miracles" (Aydemir 1969, vol. 3, p. 301). The Turkish people had found a new god to believe in. The charismatic, narcissistic leader and his followers had coalesced.

On the previous day the send-off given him in Ankara had been enormously gratifying. The trip to Istanbul had been widely publicized, and the railroad station in Ankara was hung with flags and lined with soldiers in military formation. Crowds of spectators cheered him on as he began his return to the city where he had gone to military school, formulated grandiose ideas, and been depressed while searching for something to support his narcissistic needs. He was now adored and accompanied by a devoted coterie that included Kılıç Ali, Nuri, Salih, several of his adopted daughters, and his personal physician Refik—the man who had stood by him since he had left Istanbul on 16 May 1919 and who had responded to his physical, and probably hypochondriacal, needs.

After traveling by rail to the coast of the Sea of Marmara, the party boarded the former royal Ottoman yacht, the *Ertuğrul*, named for the father of Osman, the eponymous founder of the Ottoman dynasty. Entering the Bosporus, the yacht zigzagged between the European and Asian shores prior to dropping anchor before the Dolmabahçe Palace, which had been erected in Istanbul in 1853 on orders from Sultan Abdülmecid I.

Dolmabahçe is an ornate palace built in the European style; several such palaces were constructed in Istanbul in the nineteenth century as residences for the royal family. Now an immortal man risen from the common people was entering it to the cheers of his fellow citizens. Cries of joyous excitement could be heard from both shores of the Bosporus, and the naval vessels in the harbor gave booming salutes. As Mustafa Kemal entered the grand salon of the palace where sultans had engaged in imperial ceremonies, he looked majestic in the glitter of the elaborate chandeliers. Welcomed by the mayor of Istanbul, he responded with a speech that clearly included psychological references as well as historical considerations. Once again the city was seen as the grieving mother, one in which opposites could join together. History, geography, and psychology were intertwined:

> My Dear Countrymen:
>
> Eight years ago I left the sorrowful, weeping Istanbul with pain in my heart. There was no one to bid me farewell. Eight

> years later, with a comforted heart, I have come to a smiling and flourishing Istanbul. Istanbul, located at the piont where *two great worlds are united*, the ornament of the Turkish nation, the treasure of Turkish history, the dearest object of the Turkish nation, is a city that has a place in the hearts of all countrymen. [Atatürk 1952, p. 249; italics added]

He then referred to the palace in which he was speaking as a place where until eight years earlier, the Turkish people had been asked to believe "a phantom with the power of seven dragons lived" (Aydemir 1969, vol. 3, p. 301). He had heard that expression from his mother. When he had been "plotting" with his friends against the sultan, he was overheard by his mother. She took him to task for opposing the sultan, who "had the power of seven dragons."[3] His speech indicates that Mustafa Kemal was now engaged in conquering the bad phantom-sultan-father image and experiencing oedipal triumph. What is more important in our view, however, is that he was finding a "solution" that would enable him to individuate and remove himself from his mother's influence. It is important to remember here that his mother had remarried during Mustafa Kemal's adolescence, the period when the oedipal struggle is reawakened in what has been termed the second individuation (Blos 1967) process. Partly in response to her marriage he went off to military school. After becoming an officer, he returned to his mother and achieved an oedipal triumph when her new husband stood up to greet him. Now, after eight years of absence, he was returning "home" to reclaim his mother and to sieze a second chance to relate to her as an oedipal child would, in the hope of individuating from her successfully.

Mustafa Kemal's return to Istanbul in triumph after winning the war and silencing his opposition during the trying birth of the new nation was in the service of a psychological step that would enable him to be a true reformer who believed at long last that he could change the mother/nation as he saw fit. Such attempts had obviously been made over and over again, both in fantasy and in reality throughout his life, but this was the moment of his highest psychological readiness. His golden years as a reformer would come later, but first he had to put in order all the struggles he had undergone up to his time. In a sense he needed to "package" all the struggle, to make it his new product, a creation of his own. It was at this point that he began composing his "Great Speech," in which he would present, that is, package, his external struggles in his fight to save the nation.

Among those who welcomed Mustafa Kemal to Istanbul was his sister Makbule. She had expected him to stay in her home, but he made it clear

[3]See Mustafa Kemal's interview with Falih Rıfkı and Mahmud (Saydam) in *Milliyet*, 13 March 1926. Also see Baydar 1967, p. 104.

that the palace would be more suitable since it now belonged to the nation and no longer, as he put it, "to those who considered themselves God's shadow on earth." "I am here," he said, "as an individual belonging to the nation, a guest" (Aydemir 1969, vol. 3, p. 301). He seemed fond of his sister, but as president he kept her at a distance. He once asked his men to keep an eye on her new husband, lest he capitalize on their relationship with him. He was always watchful about giving favors to anyone related to him, although he honored long-lasting connections with faithful friends from his Salonika days such as Nuri.

When he went into the dining room of the palace on the morning after his arrival in Istanbul, he was accompanied by Makbule and his adopted daughters Rukiye, Sabiha, and Zehra. He ordered the heavy draperies to be pulled aside to admit the sunshine. There were still excited crowds gathered outside the palace. On the second night of his stay he watched a parade of ships ablaze with lanterns pass by the palace. Everyone wanted to share in this marine spectacle, and so many people rented boats. Boatloads of schoolgirls came in rather close to the palace. One of those girls was Lütfiye (Gürsoy), who was to play a very small part in Mustafa Kemal's life, although his memory remained like a shining monument in hers (Gürsoy 1974). When interviewed by Dr. Volkan, Mrs. Gürsoy, then a retired history teacher in her mid-sixties, recalled that night with glowing eyes. "The earth shook," she said, "when Mustafa Kemal visited Istanbul." The very fact that a crowd of girls attended the celebration was evidence of considerable social change in the country in which women had traditionally been homebound after dark. Lütfiye, in her crowded boat, was thrilled to catch a glimpse of her hero, waving his hands at the multitude and silhouetted against the sky. Even after all those years she recalled how her heart had jumped at that sight and that the girls had spontaneously begun to sing his favorite song, beginning, "The mist has fallen on top of the mountain."

25

No Time to Relax!

ISTANBUL WAS GOOD FOR MUSTAFA KEMAL. HE NOW FELT COMFORTABLE walking through the nineteenth-century marble halls of Dolmabahçe Palace. A high wall hides the palace from the city itself, but its many marble balconies overlook the Bosporus and from almost any one of them he could look across the water and see the passing ships. The colors playing on the waters of the Bosporus pulsate differently at various times of day, and the hearts of the people of Istanbul appeared to be beating in harmony as long as he remained in residence. He came to have a love for the water and took long boat rides on the Bosporus and the Marmara. His sudden appearance at some pastry or coffee shop along his route quickened heartbeats. In the days of the Young Turks, women of Istanbul, hiding in their homes behind drawn curtains, had entertained fantasies about Enver Pasha, but now Turkish women who were learning the freedom of no longer being confined thought constantly of Mustafa Kemal. He was once again a bachelor with the kind of charisma that suggested the enormous virility longed for in a leader.

During his stay in Istanbul the Ghazi adopted another daughter, Nebile, one of three girls who had been brought to the palace from Çapa Teachers' College to welcome Mustafa Kemal to Istanbul. The other two left, but Nebile stayed. She was an eighteen-year-old of medium height with blue eyes and blonde hair. All who reminisced about her later spoke of her having been rather beautiful. She followed Mustafa Kemal to Ankara and took her place among his adopted daughters, alongside Rukiye, Sabiha, and Zehra. Afet, however, was becoming the most important woman in his life, not only being a surrogate wife, but also gradually, and at his urging, his extension in intellectual matters.

Nonetheless, the Ghazi's life at that point was not given over to pleasure. He could not stop, even for a day, turning over in his mind projects he felt would benefit the Turkish nation. All sorts of plans for reform, all sorts of images of the new Turkey engaged his attention. Even during the war of independence he had talked with Halibe Edib and her husband about substituting the Latin alphabet for the Arabic script, which Ottoman Turkish was written in. He felt that if the Turkish people were to become westernized, they must become literate and have an alphabet in common with the West. It was probably not clear to him yet how he would go about the reforms he thought would be good for the new Turkey, for at that time he was totally absorbed in the writing of what would become known as his "Great Speech" (Atatürk 1927). This was to be his personal documentation of the events that had taken place between 1919 and 1927—his own history of the Turkish national struggle. Psychologically, he needed to complete this task of saving the mother/country (with this summary to the nation) before he could divert his energies to reform. His speech was a symbolic rendition of his own personal struggle to be free from the bonds of the unfinished business of his childhood. The struggle for inner freedom, which he perceived could be won only by rescuing his mother from grief, was identical with the national struggle for freedom. The nation represented the grieving mother for whom he was a combination of the savior son and the idealized father. Obviously, in the historical events he described, his own viewpoint, in which he was the star and the central figure, prevailed.

Composition of the "Great Speech" required three months. Its delivery took six days, 15–20 October 1927. The Ghazi actually stood on the podium before the congress of the People's party in Ankara for a total of thirty-six hours over the course of the six-day delivery. The writing of the speech was completed in Ankara. Ms. Gökçen recalled later that the Ghazi would work without stopping sometimes for as long as twenty-four hours at a stretch, subsisting mostly on coffee and cigarettes. When absorbed in an important task, Mustafa Kemal never touched alcohol. He kept three sets of secretaries busy on the speech. When one tired, another would be summoned, and a third might be required to work through the night. Ms. Gökçen still cherishes the image of the Ghazi lying on a huge white bearskin rug in his library, smoking a cigarette, sipping his Turkish coffee, and going over dozens of documents while he dictated or put his thoughts down on paper himself (Gökçen 1974).

Opening dramatically with the declaration, "Gentlemen, I landed at Samsoon [Samsun] on the 19th of May, 1919" (Atatürk 1927, p. 9), the speech is a great tour de force. It can be read as an historical document and as a magnificent piece of self-justification, as well as for insight into Mustafa Kemal's unconscious. For example, an early passage contains a cynical reference to "some women,"[1] levelled at Halide Edib, but also unconsciously evoking the image of his smothering mother from his early childhood. The speech includes an account of Turkey's conquest by the enemy when the sultan, the bad father image, was weak and a report on how the nation was being smothered until he, by himself, assumed the

[1]"Certain prominent personalities—amongst them some women—in Constantinople were convinced that the real salvation of the country lay in securing an American protectorate over it. They stubbornly persisted in this idea and tried to prove that acceptance of their point of view was the only thing possible"; see Atatürk 1927, pp. 13–14.

burden of saving it. Rauf, Ali Fuat, and Kâzım, among others, had started out on the same road, he recalls, but they had limited vision and failed to stand by him. His description of events and the dissolution of allegiances is a symbolic depiction of the salvation of the grieving mother and the mending of her wounds, as well as the rejection of the weak, bad father. What interests us the most in all of this is his powerful peroration addressed to the youth of Turkey, in which he charges them with the protection of the Turkish republic forever. At the time he had an inner feeling of having repaired the grieving mother, and at last being able to separate himself from her because he had integrated the split images he had had of her. He is himself "the Turkish youth." He had not only made effective historical moves, but he had achieved the resolution of inner conflicts and developmental issues,[2] doing this *all by himself* in the lonely fashion of one who is narcissistic. His remarks to the Turkish youth constituted a declaration of the triumph of his narcissistic personality, a triumph he had accomplished on the basis of his inner strength and power, proving that one need not depend on others in order to succeed:

> Turkish Youth! Your primary duty is ever to preserve and defend the National independence, the Turkish Republic.
>
> That is the only basis of your existence and your future. This basis contains your most precious treasure. In the future, too, there will be ill-will, both in the country itself and abroad, which will try to tear this treasure from you. If one day you are compelled to defend your independence and the Republic, then, in order to fulfill your duty, you will have to look beyond the possibilities and conditions in which you might find yourself. It may be that these conditions and possibilties are altogether unfavourable. It is possible that the enemies who desire to destroy your independence and your Republic represent the strongest force that the earth has ever seen; that they have, through craft and force, taken possession of all the fortresses and arsenals of the Motherland; that all its armies are scattered and the country actually and completely occupied.
>
> Assuming, in order to look still darker possibilities in the face, that those who hold the power of Government within the country have fallen into error, that they are fools or traitors, yes, even that these leading persons identify their personal interests with the enemy's political goals, it might happen that the nation came into complete privation, into the most extreme distress; that it found itself in a condition of ruin and complete exhaustion.

[2]This is correct to some extent and it was illusionary to some extent. Therefore, he kept continuing his attempts to repair the nation/mother until he died.

> Even under those circumstances, O Turkish child of future generations! It is your duty to save the independence, the Turkish Republic.
>
> *The strength that you will need for this is mighty in the noble blood which flows in your veins.* [Atatürk 1927, pp. 723–24; italics added][3]

Defenders of the Turkish future would have a modern Ankara from which to do it. Mustafa Kemal wanted to split Ankara off from the decrepitude of its Ottoman past and give it an entirely new and westernized face, but he wanted the development to be orderly. City planners from Germany and Austria were called in as consultants. Among the chief architects of the new Ankara was Hermann Jensen, a German. The city took on a Germanic character, with wide boulevards and avenues, all tree-lined, and, of course, an opera house. A marsh in the midst of the dusty city was drained and replaced by a large park called Youth Park, with a man-made pond at its center. Whenever the water supply in Ankara permits, fountains play there and an artificial waterfall spills into the pond. Boating is a great attraction during the hot summer months. Several piazzas were created and adorned with statues of Mustafa Kemal, making him seem truly omnipotent and omnipresent. Such physical representation of a human being was a significant departure from traditional Islamic culture and another triumph for Mustafa Kemal, as well as a gratification associated with seeing himself immortalized in marble and bronze while still living. Unfortunately, no one at that time realized that Ankara's population would number over two million within half a century. Much that was planned turned out to be more appropriate for a small city than for a sprawling metropolis.

Physical change was accompanied by far-ranging linguistic reform. Early in their history in Central Asia, the Turks had used a thirty-eight character alphabet known as the Altay alphabet, similar to Chinese ideographs. When the Turks subsequently came under the influence of Islam, they adopted the Arabic alphabet, with the addition of some letters from Persian. The Arabic writing system is not the best vehicle for the presentation of the complex vowel system of Turkish, since it can represent but three vowel sounds and their elongation, and Turkish has eight vowels. This meant, in effect, that when one saw a word, one had to know its meaning in order to pronounce it, and many words had more than one pronunciation and meaning. Written (and spoken) Ottoman Turkish differed from the everyday Turkish of the people, called *öz Türkçe* in that it was originally a court language and was composed of

[3]The last sentence again clearly reflects the direction of his personality organization. The Turkish youth, like himself, can save the country alone, without dependence on others.

many Arabic and Persian, as well as Turkish, elements. In fact, much of the vocabulary consisted of Arabic and Persian words. Through the ages this had made it difficult to learn and its acquisition was a sign of social status. By and large, Ottoman Turkish was a monopoly of the Ottoman ruling elite. The simpler folk Turkish existed alongside Ottoman Turkish.

Father of the Turks teaches his children. The Ghazi explains the new alphabet to the nation in a famous photograph.

In the nineteenth century, during the reign of Sultan Abdülaziz (r. 1861–76), there was some interest in reforming the alphabet in order to reduce illiteracy. Later, Enver Pasha toyed for a while with the idea of language reform, but his efforts were largely unsuccessful. Mustafa Kemal was impressed with the fact that in western countries the people's sharing of a common language was a vital factor in their nationalism. One of his compelling preoccupations after the delivery of his "Great Speech" was the introduction of the Latin alphabet. He was careful to call the new alphabet Turkish rather than Latin and worked with his alphabet commission to create some new characters so that each sound in the Turkish language would be represented by only one character. For example, the sound of *ch*, as in the English word "church" would be represented by a new character *ç*.

Although Mustafa Kemal was conscious of the need to spread literacy in Turkey, he was unconscious of his motivation in sponsoring the language reform. The alphabet and the Ottoman language, with its Arabic-Islamic overtones, were connected in Mustafa Kemal's mind with his mother's religious and superstitious mentality. Language, in the form of incantations and magical formulas scribbled on scraps of paper,[4] were part of his mother's world that had served to solidify his view of her as a powerful (magical) but damaged person. One can only surmise that her care of him as an infant and young child, which was already impaired by grief, was permeated with her religious and superstitious behavior. Ridding the Turkish language of its Arabic script with its religious implications would be a contribution to the process of healing his damaged and grieving mother.

One might have expected sharp and outraged resistance to such language reform where the adoption of the new letters could easily have been seen as an alignment with the infidel world. Even those whose feelings and desire for change matched Mustafa Kemal's cautioned him against so rash a step. İsmet, among the most cautious, felt that it would require at least seven years to change the alphabet. Mustafa Kemal held that the alphabet should be changed within three months (Atay 1980, p. 440) if it were to change at all. He was right once again. Mustafa Kemal succeeded in getting the people to share in his unconscious and accept his desire for change.

The first important step in the language reform was taken on 24 May 1928, when the numbering system was changed to conform to that of the West. Two months later Mustafa Kemal organized a special commission

[4]For example, a piece of folded paper on which a magical semireligious statement is written is pinned to the clothing that one wears and is called a *muska*. It protects the person from the evil eye or other dangerous influences.

to devise the new alphabet, and he took an active interest in the commission's work. That alphabet was unveiled by the Ghazi in dramatic fashion at a fête given by the People's party in the park at Seraglio Point in Istanbul on the evening of 9 August. The affair boasted two orchestras, one playing modern jazz and the other playing the traditional Turkish music known as *alaturka* music.[5] Egyptian entertainers sang songs in Arabic. At times he would ask both orchestras to play, and he would ask his entourage to compare the two musical styles and state their preference. They were all well aware that he wanted them to favor European music, in spite of his private fondness for *alaturka* music, which he disclaimed publicly as monotonous and a poor standard for the new Turkey.[6] On this issue he was once again struggling with a split (both internal and external) which, through him, led to mending between the two musical camps since some Turkish composers began composing their works in the Western mode for Western musical instruments.[7]

On that August evening in Istanbul, after duly complimenting the Egyptian singers, Mustafa Kemal commented that such music no longer made much of an impression on him. While everyone watched his star performance, he rose with a piece of paper in his hand and asked for someone to come forward and read it. One young man offered, but he was nonplussed to see Latin characters on the paper. The Ghazi then handed the paper to Falih Rıfkı (Atay), his journalist friend and a member of the alphabet commission. Falih Rıfkı read the new letters to the gathering. It was a message to the Turkish nation from their savior, indicating that:

[5]Turkish musical tradition during Ottoman times may be classified as follows: (*a*) secular music (or Turkish classical "art" music), (*b*) religious music including the music of the mystical order, (*c*) folk music. Both classical music and religious music adhere strictly to the *makam* (modal) system, which is monophonic, with the octave divided into smaller intervals than that of Western music (Gökçen 1975).

Religious music lost its importance when the state adopted secularism. The classical "art" music was associated with the Ottoman past and was considered backward. In spite of Mustafa Kemal's statement that the classical Turkish music was insufficient to satisfy his own feelings and soul (Karal 1956, Cunbur 1973, Gökçen 1975), he liked to sing some classical songs. The Turkish music known as *alaturka*, which was played at Seraglio Point on the evening of 9 August, was classical "art" music. It should be remembered, however, that Atatürk treated folk music differently, considering it purely Turkish.

[6]For a brief period in 1934 traditional Turkish art music was banned from the radios. Earlier, in 1926, the traditional Turkish art music conservatory (Darülelhan) in Istanbul was closed.

[7]Some composers used Turkish classical "art" music in their compositions. For instance, Ferid Alnar wrote a *kanun* (dulcimer) concerto, and Adnan Saygun used Turkish classical motives in his Yunus Emre oratorio, based on the life of the thirteenth-century mystic poet (Hoffman 1965). Many folk tunes or melodies also have been harmonized (Réchid 1927, Egüz 1969).

> our rich and harmonious language will now be able to display itself with new Turkish letters. We must free ourselves from these incomprehensible signs that for centuries had held our minds in an iron vise. You must learn the new Turkish letters quickly. Teach them to your compatriots, to women and to men, to porters and to boatmen. Regard it as a patriotic and national duty . . . and when you perform that duty, bear in mind that for a nation to consist of ten or twenty percent of literates and eighty or ninety percent of illiterates is shameful. . . . The fault is not ours; it is of those who failed to understand the character of the Turk and bound his mind in chains. *Now is the time to eradicate the errors of the past. We shall repair these errors.* [Atatürk 1952, pp. 254–56; italics added]

This staged drama was followed by cheers, and in an additional flourish the Ghazi rose to his feet and lifted his glass full of rakı in a toast, saying, "In the past, those two-faced impostors [the Ottoman elite] in their dunghills used to drink this secretly a thousand times more. I am not an impostor. I drink to the honor of my nation" (Atatürk 1952, p. 256). Such behavior dealt yet another blow to Muslim tradition, for the consumption of alcohol is forbidden in Islam. Most of his audience followed suit as their hero drank openly.

Leaving the park, Mustafa Kemal encountered an attractive woman wearing the traditional *çarşaf* over her head (Kinross 1965, p. 504). He stopped and asked her to remove it. Without hesitation, she revealed her face in public and even went so far as to embrace Mustafa Kemal. As usual, when mingling with the people in this way, he was at the peak of his charisma, influencing others to follow him with enthusiasm and excitement on the road to reform.

Now he became his nation's headmaster, teaching the country the new letters. He had blackboards set up around the Dolmabahçe Palace, where he gave lessons in the new script to visitors. Parliamentary deputies were required to learn the new alphabet and were then sent to various parts of the country to teach their countrymen. A famous photograph of Mustafa Kemal shows him standing before a blackboard under a tree engaged in teaching the new script. By then, the slender, tanned, handsome man that he had been just after the war when he met Lâtife was gone, now replaced by a man considerably thicker in body, with a receding hairline. It is not difficult to imagine him as a schoolteacher.

Deputies were not the only ones who went out into the countryside in the service of the alphabet reform. The Ghazi himself started to travel in his role as schoolmaster. The first place he visited was Tekirdağ, between Istanbul and the Dardanelles. His famous Nineteenth Division had been organized at Tekirdağ before moving to Gallipoli (see chap. 8). He was returning in a sense to Gallipoli, the scene of his military triumph, to initiate his career as an educator with, he hoped, the same prospect of success. He arrived at Tekirdağ by yacht from Istanbul on 23 August 1928 (Yücebaş 1973, pp. 15–20). The landing dock was covered with beautiful rugs and a crowd awaited him. On his arrival he wore a dark suit with a vest, a watch chain, and a large handkerchief tucked into the breast pocket. Perhaps this sartorial display was an unconscious reminder of the incident during the battle of Gallipoli in which a watch in his breast pocket had taken the shrapnel that would have killed him. This time, however, he was not facing enemy fire, but rather the exaggerated love of his people.

At the town's administration building he used a huge blackboard to give a two-hour lecture on the new alphabet. He then questioned many in the audience to see if they had absorbed his teaching. When some did not do too well, he seemed rather upset. The leader of the local teachers' association then told the Ghazi apologetically that they were not yet ready to read and write in the new script, but they would do so as quickly as possible.

After Tekirdağ, Mustafa Kemal visited other places. In one of them he had an encounter with a religious man wearing the traditional coat and turban. The Ghazi called the man in front of him and, writing a sentence in the Arabic script, asked the man to read it. The man did so, and then Mustafa Kemal read the same sentence in an alternate way with a different meaning. He then lectured the religious man, telling him that one could not be sure what the sentence meant when it was written in the Arabic script, but with the new alphabet there could be no doubt about its meaning.

Whether through the medium of a religious man or his own lectures at the blackboard, Mustafa Kemal used every means to promote the new alphabet and speed its adoption by the Turks. He even considered using a rhyming march composed around the new alphabet as a teaching device in the hope that people would learn it more quickly by singing it. He ordered some musicians to compose such a march but was dissatisfied with their efforts and abandoned the project. A cabinet regulation passed on 11 November transformed the entire nation into a school for the purpose of teaching the new alphabet. Articles 3 and 4 of that regulation organized the School of the Nation, in which "every male and female Turkish citizen is a member" and "The chief instructor of the School of the Nation is His Excellency the President of the Republic, Ghazi Mustafa Kemal." Children naturally learned the new letters faster than adults. It was not unusual, therefore, to see children instructing their parents. It was particularly gratifying to a man of Mustafa Kemal's personality to see children repairing their mothers and fathers and relying upon their own inner strength as they became superior to their parents. He himself was the brightest child of them all!

Even children, however, have to face reality sooner or later. Within a few years Mustafa Kemal found that the closeness he had enjoyed with his followers was not to be taken for granted. There are always those who blindly follow a charismatic leader, but there are also those who hate him just as tenaciously. As Mustafa Kemal vigorously went about trying to westernize a country for whose people westernization meant the rejection of longstanding traditions, especially religious ones, some began to view him as the devil incarnate. These were mostly hocas, mollas, and dervishes, who had commanded a certain status in Ottoman times and to whom mystical powers had often been attributed. After having enjoyed veneration for so long, they found it difficult to accept rejection and discredit. Mustafa Kemal's new alphabet, officially in place as of 1 January 1929, further undermined their special status as teachers of the Arabic writing system. Although they continued to have devotees, the Ghazi's tight control over a one-party parliament shut them out from political power and any effective demand for a return to the old religion. Clearly the day belonged to those who were young, at least in attitude if not in age—or so it seemed until religious fanaticism erupted in the small town of Menemen, near Izmir in December 1930. Its eruption took Mustafa Kemal and the nation by surprise, and it must be viewed against a panorama of events and developments in Turkey.

As Mustafa Kemal basked in the adoration of his followers, he may have been aware of having detractors, but his personality organization made it possible for him to hold them in such contempt that they ceased to exist for him. We can safely assume that he kept the illusion—which was justified to a considerable extent by reality—that he was loved and venerated by everyone of importance. Therefore, he did not consciously feel threatened by the hatred of religious nobodies. From 1928 on he enjoyed the roles of teacher, iconoclast, and playboy. Greatly preoccupied with galas and other entertainments at which he was the center of attention, he was transforming his grief-stricken mother/nation into a convivial and fun-loving being. Sabiha (Gökçen 1974) recalled that Mustafa Kemal had once told his adopted daughters that they were to smile as much as possible and not to trust anyone who did not smile.

Constantly surrounded by an adoring circle of cronies, he was gradually separated from the general populace, the kind of people with whom he had been in the habit of mingling on his many trips through the country. To an increasing extent he was becoming an adored prisoner in such places as Çankaya and Dolmabahçe. He knew little about economics and left the day-to-day management of the government to İsmet, who was equally unschooled in financial matters. They were the leaders of a new country that was virtually penniless in spite of its triumphs. Cavid, Turkey's only internationally known economist, had been hanged. A new specialist in economic matters was found, Mahmud Celâl, who, as Celâl Bayar, would later become Turkey's third president. He proved highly capable in opening up new lands to agriculture and in the formulation of economic policy. Mustafa Kemal's expectations of him, however, were unrealistic, a reflection of his own narcissism. The Ghazi felt that Celâl could perform miracles, saying comfortably, "I gave him a bag of gold and he gave me a bank" (Kinross 1965, p. 519).

Meanwhile, as Mustafa Kemal became more and more dependent on his cronies, Turkey's strategic geographic position compelled her to take a more active interest in the international scene. A changed Europe had emerged from World War I, and there was now a new Russia, a communist country. Although Russia had been helpful to the Turkish nationalists during their struggle for independence, Mustafa Kemal resisted the temptation to join the Communist movement. Despite his reticence, Russia remained friendly toward Turkey during the 1920s, and a treaty of friendship between the two states was signed in 1925. Russia did not object to renewed German economic interest in Turkey as long as Turkey did not fall into the orbit of any power hostile to Russia.

Relations between the Turks and the Greeks were cold, but "normalized." The first Turkish ambassador to Athens was appointed in 1925 and a treaty of friendship was signed in 1930. France lost its status as a most favored nation in Turkey and withdrew its interests. Muslim countries generally looked askance at a Turkey governed by a man who had refused to declare himself caliph and who opposed the traditional religious establishment. The Arabs in particular blamed the Turks for having impeded their development since their conquest of the Arab heartland in 1517. Germany and Italy began to loom large on the world scene, and the names of Hitler and Mussolini were beginning to resound in Turkey as elsewhere.

The American stock market crash in October 1929 sent out shock waves that reached even Turkey and caused a worldwide depression in which the new country found itself in need of some economic miracle. Failure of the harvests in Anatolia worsened matters. The peasants of Turkey quickly sobered, forgetting their euphoria over Mustafa Kemal's military victories. Were they being punished for having turned away from God? Was the man they followed Satan? The old religious ways now offered solace, and so did banditry, which had virtually died out after the national struggle. It resurfaced again during these hard times, especially on the Black Sea coast and in Anatolia.

Faced with such unrest, Mustafa Kemal launched another political experiment. He had been criticized by Europeans for insisting on only one political party in Turkey and for being a dictator. His genuine interest in doing what was best for Turkey led him to ponder the advantages of a two-party system. Earlier, he had speedily put down the ill-fated Progressive party organized by Kâzım, Rauf, Ali Fuat, and Dr. Adnan. Perhaps now, two parties, *over both of which he would prevail and from both of which he would receive loyal support*, would be beneficial. A two-party system might even be able to deal better with matters of the economy, especially since İsmet's management of the economy was being harshly criticized.

During the summer of 1930 Mustafa Kemal spent some time at Yalova, the hot springs resort near Bursa that he enjoyed so much. There he had as his guest his old friend from the days in Macedonia—Fethi. They had always been on good terms, and Fethi had even served as Mustafa Kemal's prime minister. Now, the Ghazi instructed him to form a second political party. Fethi was known to be an admirer of the British parliamentary system and knew how it functioned. After a show of polite resistance, Fethi agreed to form a new party to be called the Free Republican party, in contrast to the original and continuing Republican People's party. In order to give the new party appropriate prestige, Mustafa Kemal asked his close friend Nuri to serve as its general secretary. The Ghazi's sister, Makbule, was also among the founders, as was Ahmet Ağaoğlu, the driving force and theoretician of the new party movement.

Despite the sanguine expectations of narcissistic leaders, assimilation of radical ideas takes time. Mustafa Kemal had depended in good part on inspiration when he began to stifle religion in Turkey. His antireligious attitudes did win him many followers, but his radical ideas were far from being assimilated. Dissent within Turkey was on the rise because of economic conditions and Mustafa Kemal's remoteness from the people. Formation of this new party gave the dissenters a base for their opposition to him, although he himself had carefully chosen its leaders.

There was a good deal of bickering on how the new party should organize. Some feared that the people would not accept it and urged caution. Others, the Ghazi among them, encouraged Fethi to get on with his task. No one had anticipated the tumultuous reception that awaited Fethi when he arrived at Izmir by ship on 4 September 1930 to make some speeches and to open the party's first branch office. Fifty thousand people crowded the dockside and instead of jeering him, as some had predicted, they welcomed him enthusiastically. Concerned over this outpouring of emotion, the local Republican People's party representatives decided to hold their own rally and used the local newspaper to discredit Fethi and his adherents as unsavory men seeking a return to the days of the Ottoman constitution. Sensing the mounting tension, Fethi feared the consequences of the speech he was going to make. He offered to postpone it, but Mustafa Kemal sent Fethi a telegram, imploring him to give it. The supporters of both parties faced one another in a street fight, and a young boy was killed by a stray police bullet. The father took the body to Fethi's hotel, and the crowd importuned Fethi to save the people. Local officials sought to contain the incident by a postponement, but the Ghazi's telegram to Fethi said, "I understand that they are trying in Izmir to stop you from giving your speech. You will give it immediately, and inform me of any obstacle that you may encounter" (Aydemir 1969, vol. 3, p. 398; Weiker 1973, p. 91). Fethi gave his speech without further incident and then moved on to nearby cities for other rallies. Wherever he spoke, people appeared waving the green flag of Islam and demanding a return of the fez and the Arabic script, among other things. Fethi naturally expressed his disapproval of such regressive sentiments, but it was clear that the organization of a second political party provided a forum for opposition to Mustafa Kemal's reforms.

Fethi's party entered the mayoral elections on a nationwide basis. They were important because increased powers had been given to local officials to ensure proper management and were hotly contested with many cries of irregularities. The Republican People's party scored a smashing victory, which was somewhat tainted by widespread bullying and manipulations. Ironically, Fethi's party won in Samsun, the city that had come to symbolize Mustafa Kemal's independence struggle. A country without experience in democracy had been able to accept orders from above but encountered difficulty in sharing power in the electoral process.

On 15 November 1930, Fethi launched an attack on İsmet's government in the assembly because of the way his party had been discriminated against in the mayoral elections. The struggle now became personal. Mustafa Kemal, sitting solemnly in the presidential box in the assembly hall, saw his illusion of being the father of Turkish democracy (which to him meant being loved by both parties) shattered. He refrained, at least in public, from interfering with the democratic experiment as he watched Fethi go down in defeat 225 to 10 after contesting the fraudulent practices of İsmet's minister of the interior in the elections. There was no effective way to deal with İsmet's political power. Fethi, no longer willing to be a figurehead, had his party dissolved on 17 November 1930.

Many historians have written on this experiment in democracy, pointing out that perhaps Fethi lacked the characteristics necessary for success and that under different leadership the party might have succeeded. The major flaw, however, lies elsewhere. The entire experiment was based on the grandiose thinking of one narcissistic individual. It failed because it was not the outgrowth of a natural process. Out of the turmoil of those few short months came Mustafa Kemal's realization that all was not well in the country. Once again, as he had done in the past, he managed to reorganize himself and to redefine what he could realistically accomplish; that is, he set new boundaries. He went once again to the people, quitting the glorious cocoon in which he had been so comfortably surrounded by sycophants. Once again he was determined to feel the pulse of the nation himself and make his own diagnosis. Gathering around him a number of sober followers and some cronies as well, he set out on a three-month tour of the nation and ordered his handpicked deputies to undertake serious study of the economy and other areas of popular discontent.

On his tour he spent much time with children and young people, as he had on previous trips. It would appear that he wanted young Turkish people to grow up to be like himself, serving the country/mother, but depending upon their own resources in the protection of the new Turkey, a viewpoint he had already articulated in his "Great Speech." He visited schoolrooms, sitting among the students and listening to the teachers give their lessons. No doubt he terrified the teachers, especially when he gave them impromptu oral examinations in front of their students. He did that often, beaming with pleasure at a clever reply and sulking ominously at any failure, rejecting that teacher, male or female, out of hand. The psychodynamics of such "oral examinations" will be taken up later.

These events, national and international, culminated on 23 December 1930 in an ugly incident in the town of Menemen near Izmir. Curiously, we know something about this incident from the girl Lütfiye (Gürsoy 1974), one of the young schoolgirls who had serenaded Mustafa Kemal from a boat on the Bosporus near Dolmabahçe. She had come on a holiday to Menemen with a number of other young women, all of them in their girl scout uniforms, from Izmir, where they attended a teachers' school. They were the products of Mustafa Kemal's Turkey—idealistic, free, young women. In Menemen the girls met some young Turkish military officers whose pro-Ghazi ideals matched their own. Among them was a young man named Mustafa Fehmi Kubilay, a name that recalled the memory of Kublai Khan, the great Mongol conqueror with whom the Turks have connected themselves over the centuries. The modern Kubilay was bent on being a conqueror in his own right, quelling the religious notions the Ghazi considered bad. The young people amused themselves by taking photographs, but life became brutal and brief when, on the day after Lütfiye and her friends left Menemen, Kubilay ran into a disturbance in the course of his duty.

On 23 December several men of the Nakshibendi order of dervishes, the same group that had initiated the Kurdish revolt in 1925, came to the main square of Menemen and started to berate the people there who were engaged in the morning prayer. One in the group was a certain Sheikh Mehmed who considered himself a prophet. The dervishes may have been on drugs or affected by fasting.[8] Sheikh Mehmed took the green flag from the mosque and asked the people to follow him in demanding a return of the veil, the fez, and the Arabic script. He wanted the downfall of the godless republic.

Kubilay was passing through the square with some of his men when he saw the crowd and heard the sheikh. Annoyed with their anti-Ghazi religious sentiment, he ordered the dervishes to disperse. When the fanatics refused, he ordered his men to fire a few rounds of *blank* ammunition to scatter them. When no one fell as a result of the firing, the dervish leader declared that he and his fellow dervishes could not be killed because they were holy men. The riot escalated to murderous insanity, and Kubilay was caught and decapitated. His head was put on the pole of the green flag and paraded about while dervishes chanted their incantations. Order was restored when experienced troops arrived on the scene and their officers shot the dervish leader. A number of arrests were made over a wide area and, as a result of later trials, several people were hanged.

Mustafa Kemal went into a rage when he heard the news of Menemen. He ordered the town burned and then rebuilt, speaking out of his intense anger. The order was not executed, but he used the events at Menemen to galvanize the country against religious fanaticism.

After Mustafa Kemal's return to Istanbul and after he had composed and delivered his "Great Speech," he might have had the illusion that his inner world was completely integrated. He readily used externalization (the placing of one's own images of oneself and others, as well as one's conflicts, onto the outside world) and tried to change the world to meet his inner demands. Unlike the average man, he did this in the arena of history. If he anticipated that after the "Great Speech" his internal and external worlds would be congruent, he was due to be disillusioned, for changes continued in the external world which demanded accommodation from him. This required that he take action again by reinvesting himself in external events and try once again to change them and make them good, according to the dictates of his inner world. There was, indeed, no time for him to relax!

[8]Dervishes traditionally used drugs and other substances as well as fasting in their quest for a more perfect union with the deity. See Gibb and Bowen 1957, vol. 1, chap. 13.

26
From Ghazi M. Kemal to Kamal Atatürk

Spurred on by Mustafa Kemal's relentless drive to transform Ankara into a modern capital, the city was humming with activity in the early 1930s. Among some groups dancing became the rage. More and more Turkish women began to attend the increasing number of gala events at which the Ghazi was the main attraction. He derived enormous pleasure and satisfaction from seeing Turks dance and display "civilized" manners. Now in his early fifties, he was enjoying his golden years, reigning as the glittering golden sun shining over Ankara.

Witnesses who were youngsters in those days describe the scene in surrealistic terms. Professor Göksel (1975) recalls a number of occasions when he stood on the steps of the building in which the Grand National Assembly met and saw the Ghazi emerge at the head of his entourage. Though not a tall man, Mustafa Kemal seemed to tower over ordinary people, like an image from a dream. To be in the same city with him was to know ecstatic psychological intoxication. The citizens of Ankara were united in a kind of worshipful brotherhood.

Flattering himself that Ankara was now a European city, the Ghazi took pleasure in the gaiety he saw there. Everyone adopted the new plaything popular in the West at the time—the yo-yo—and tossed them in the streets while whistling the latest hit tunes. Ankara still left much to be desired as a facsimile of a European city, but German planners were busy at work. A handsome avenue, now called Atatürk Boulevard, was built to connect the slopes of Çankaya with those of the old citadel at the other end of the city. Donkeys and camels, once common in the streets of Ankara, were increasingly relegated to the back lanes as buildings sprang up along the main arteries.

In 1931 Turkey drew closer to Europe by adopting the metric system. A small number of emigrant Europeans had a great impact on the emerging nation. Mustafa Kemal came to offer a home to these European intellectuals by a curious route. He had considerable trouble with his teeth and went often to a Jewish dentist named Sami Günzberg, who spoke to him at great length about Hitler's anti-Semitism and the plight of Jews in Germany. That information led him to consider the advantage to Turkey of giving asylum to some of Germany's gifted Jews who might help develop the new Turkey. Many German Jews and other refugees from Hitler's madness did migrate to Turkey in the 1930s, scholars and artists among them. In 1936 the State Conservatory was founded in Ankara under the direction of Paul Hindemith to introduce Western music to the country. Archaeology and medicine benefited enormously from the arrival of European intellectuals.[1] Eventually many of these academicians were disappointed with the lack of opportunity available in Turkey and left, some going to the United States, but a number remained permanently. In the early 1950s some of the departments in the medical schools in Istanbul and Ankara were still chaired by physicians who were German Jews.

Another European import of the time was Freudian theory, introduced by a German analyst, Edith Weigert. Although not Jewish herself, she was married to a Jew, Professor Oskar Weigert, who had represented Germany in the office of the International Labor Organization in Geneva. Her husband went to Turkey to work with the Ghazi to bring labor out of its feudal state. In Anatolia labor had been a family affair centered around a common loom located in the home. In Ottoman times work and family life had been interwoven in that form of cottage industry. Changes wrought in Turkey by the First World War necessitated a change in the attitude of Turkish men toward labor. It had to be seen as dignified and worthy of their best efforts. Professor Weigert brought with him from Germany such ideas as the eight-hour day, regular vacations for workers, and workmen's compensation as well as other forms of insurance. His travels took him to every corner of Turkey, but he and his wife made their home in Ankara. From their cottage they could see Mustafa Kemal's house and the lights that burned there far into the early morning hours. Professor Weigert considered Mustafa Kemal a genius and a serious and altogether dedicated patriot.

When interviewed in Washington, D.C., in 1974, Edith Weigert had a more realistic view of Ankara during that period than has come down in the enchanted recollections of some Turks. She spoke of the lack of social contact between the ordinary people of the city and the foreigners, most of whom lived on the slopes of Çankaya. During her days in Ankara she sensed a cultural revolution coming from above and was particularly

[1]Ruth W. Lidz, now professor of psychiatry at Yale University, arrived in Istanbul in the fall of 1935 at the age of twenty-five. Having been graduated from medical school in Basel, Switzerland, in the spring of that year, she then spent a year in Gurabe Hospital in Istanbul as a research assistant in the Department of Otolaryngology. Her recollections of her year in Istanbul depict the reactions of a young, educated, European woman to the customs and the ways of life of a different culture.

Dr. Lidz states that Professor Phillip Schwartz, who had been professor of pathology at the University of Frankfurt, was instrumental in bringing many German Jewish doctors to Istanbul and Ankara. He, for some reason, had influence at the ministry of health in Ankara and presented himself as a friend of the minister (Lidz 1981).

interested in its effects upon the women. Without their veils, which had provided a peculiar safety for them, they were, paradoxically, unhappy with the anxiety that stemmed from being exposed. Mustafa Kemal must have felt the unique power exercised by a woman who is covered and thus mysterious, and no doubt one of the psychological reasons he wanted to liberate women was his unconscious need to rob his mother and all women of their power. One German woman married to a Turkish military officer and accustomed to wearing a veil told Edith Weigert that she was unhappy over losing its protection. The analyst observed that suicide among Turkish women had never been as common as in the 1930s, and although there are no data to support or negate that statement, it seems valid.

Given special permission by the government to practice psychoanalysis in Turkey, Edith Weigert worked mostly with Jews who had fled Europe's anti-Semitism. Dr. İzzeddin, a Turkish physician, translated the more important works of Freud into Turkish, and although they were of no interest to the general population, they did come to the attention of Turkish intellectuals who would become the leaders of Turkey. Along with the yo-yo, the tango, and the Charleston, Freudian theory entered the stream of ideas and things Western that would have a far-ranging effect on the new Turkey.[2]

At the same time, the Ghazi worked feverishly to establish a kind of scientific theory of his own, much of which can only be labeled pseudoscience. It is clear that unconscious motivation lay behind his conscious dedication to patriotic activity. He was successful in requiring that everything published in Turkey, including religious writings, be printed in the new alphabet. Early in 1932 a version of the Koran was prepared in Turkish (the Koran, Islam holds, is an Arabic book and cannot be translated). Previously, the Koran could not be read by the overwhelming majority of Turks, many of whom managed to memorize it. Now the average Turk could read and understand the holy book of Islam. No longer would the call to prayer come from the minarets in the traditional Arabic, *Allahu ekber*, "God is great." The muezzins would now chant the same call in Turkish, *Tanrı uludur.* That change can be compared to the profound effect of the introduction of the vernacular mass in churches

[2]Another European, Professor Wolfram Eberhard, a sociologist at the University of California at Berkeley, lived in Ankara during 1938. His diary notes of 15 January of that year reflect the Turks' wish and reluctance to be involved in the European custom of ballroom dancing. On that day, as part of a celebration at the University of Ankara, there were speeches, and the orchestra played samples of both European and Turkish music. Professor Eberhard wrote, "I could sense the students' reluctance to dance; only some of them danced. Since among the professors only a few joined the dancing, the atmosphere was heavy. But, all in all, it was a successful gathering" (Eberhard 1981).

that had heretofore offered it only in Latin. Such changes served Mustafa Kemal's unconscious wish to excise the bad parts of his mother.

Change in the alphabet led to changes in the Turkish language itself. It was felt that the language should be purged of its Arabic and Persian influences. Those existed both in the realm of vocabulary and grammar. On 12 July 1932, the Turkish Linguistic Society was founded by a directive from Mustafa Kemal, building on a scholarly apparatus that had been organized back in 1926 as the Turkish Linguistic Academy. Its task was "to make it easier for people to learn to read" and "to cut young Turks off from their Ottoman heritage" (Shaw and Shaw 1977, p. 376). A concerted effort was made to rid the Turkish language of all its Arabic and Persian elements of grammar and vocabulary and to replace them with Turkish grammatical and syntactical forms. Items of vocabulary were sought in Turkish, its dialects, and related Turkic languages. For example, the word for assembly, *meclis*, is originally Arabic. It was replaced by *kurultay*, a word used in Mongol to describe a meeting of tribal notables. This movement is still active today, with new words being coined constantly, based on old roots and forms.

Work on language reform went hand in hand with Mustafa Kemal's passion for Turkish history. He sought some unified theory that might serve to restore pride to his countrymen. His experience of seeing Turks held in contempt by Europeans certainly stirred him to action, as did a slur brought to his attention by Afet in 1930. She was reading a French work on geography that maintained that the Turks belonged to the "yellow" race and were inferior in comparison with Europeans. Afet showed the statement to Mustafa Kemal and asked if it was true. He replied, "No, definitely not, but let's look into it" (Aydemir 1969, vol. 3, p. 433).

Look into it he did. His investigations produced such a bizarre string of events and discussions that one can only surmise that his own unconscious reasons underlay his wish to avenge slights to Turkish people. Mustafa Kemal came up with two concepts, the first the sun-language theory and the other the national history thesis. In his language theory he drew upon the work of a Viennese philologist who postulated the idea that the first sounds made by primitive man were evoked by awe of the sun. Other theories at the time fixed on the moon in the same vein, but, given the Ghazi's personal associations with the sun, it is not surprising that he found this sun-language theory congenial. The sun-language theory put forward in Turkey held, in short, that pure Turkish, purged of its Arabic and Persian influences, was the orginal language of primordial mankind. Such a conclusion would make Turkish the mother and father of all other languages. It is, in effect, a creation story stemming from Mustafa Kemal's own grandiosity emanating from his narcissism.

Closely related to the sun-language theory was the national history thesis. It postulated that since all humans began as Turks, basically all human achievement was Turkish. Furthermore, there was an unbroken line of development from the earliest Turk to modern Ankara in which could be found the true meaning of world history. Certainly an attempt to buoy the spirits of the Turks was involved, but the lengths to which the Ghazi pushed this theory and the manner in which he pursued it (and the difficulties encountered by those in Turkey who refused to accept it) require consideration of the unconscious elements involved. This, too, is a creation myth with the Ghazi's own grandiosity intimately associated with it.

Much of the work on the new Turkish language and historical theory took place at the Ghazi's dinner table. A committed educator, Mustafa Kemal used the blackboard set up in his dining room (Afetinan 1971, pp. 25–26) to record for discussion the views of his dinner guests. A motley group of scholars, pseudo-scholars, and sycophants gathered each evening for these discussions. Topics other than history and language were sometimes introduced. There was even philosophical and pseudo-philosophical speculation about such issues as whether human speech somehow persisted in space, where the voices of the past might be heard if only one had the means (Afetinan 1971, pp. 48–49). Such inferential considerations of immortality are not surprising at the Ghazi's dinner table.

Afet functioned in her role as his intellectual extension, even to the point of becoming an historian. She would sit at his side, sometimes the only woman at the table, just as she was often the sole woman in the retinue when they dined out. Devoted to Mustafa Kemal, Afet kept a record of his ideas and of some of the rituals practiced at his nightly gatherings.[3] Without her recollections the more colorful aspects of life at the Ghazi's table would be lost, along with information on his emotional state at the time. Exhibitionistic and sexualized behavior was common, along with boasts of what seemed to be oedipal triumphs, but it was at his dining table that Mustafa Kemal's creative urges first found expression. Regression and reorganization alternated under his absolute control. He was like a child *at play*. He reviewed issues from different psychosexual levels, moving toward the oral and then back to the phallic, attempting to create a new Turkey, one uncontaminated by Arabic-Persian (religious) influences. We are reminded of Winnicott's (1971, p. 53) statement that "in playing, and perhaps only in playing, the child or adult is free to be creative."

[3]See Afetinan 1971. For another collection of memories by many who attended Mustafa Kemal's dining room gatherings see Yücebaş 1973, pp. 187–219. See also Bozdağ 1975*b*.

Mustafa Kemal's dining room activities were repetitive, and he was "addicted" to them. Without engaging in them, he could not sleep, as some children cannot sleep until they have played with a teddy bear or some such treasured plaything, called in psychoanalysis a "transitional object." Psychoanalysts regard such objects as the matrix of creativity.[4]

Of special interest is Mustafa Kemal's devising new words and letters. He would spend hours on the creation of a new word. Beginning, usually, with a "pure" Turkish word, perhaps an archaic one, he would play with it until a new Turkish word emerged. The new word might have a link to some known word "out there," but have a different configuration, and make a locus in which the stimulus from within merged with that from without, as happens in a transitional object. After writing the newly created word in a sentence he would summon a youngster to the dining room and ask the child to read it aloud so that he could listen to the way it sounded.[5]

[4]The transitional object is something chosen by the small child himself, usually during the first year of life and from among those things that he can see, touch, and smell—perhaps a teddy bear, blanket, or something similar. Linus's blanket, in the famous cartoon *Peanuts*, is a transitional object. Winnicott (1953) pointed out the importance of such an object to the child, who may regard it as more necessary to him than his own mother. He stated:

"I have introduced the terms 'transitional object' and 'transitional phenomena' for designation of the intermediate area of experience, between the thumb and the teddy bear, between the oral erotism and true object-relationship, between primary creative activity and projection of what has already been introjected, between primary unawareness of indebtedness and the acknowledgment of indebtedness ('say: ta!').

"By this definition an infant's babbling or the way an older child goes over a repertory of songs and tunes while preparing for sleep come within the intermediate area as transitional phenomena, along with the use made of objects that are not part of the infant's body yet are not fully recognized as belonging to external reality" (p. 89).

The main function of this inanimate object (or phenomenon) is to allow the infant to develop, in response to the ministrations of the "good enough" mother, "the *illusion* that there is an external reality that corresponds to [his] own capacity to create" (Winnicott 1973, p. 95). A first "not-me" possession is created.

Atatürk's nightly activity at the dining table can perhaps be called "transitional activity," a term that parallels the term "transitional fantasies," which Volkan used in telling of the analysis of a narcissistic man. That patient used his specific fantasies as intangible representations of transitional objects; they remained under his control and permitted him the illusion that he had like control over the environment and was wholly self-sufficient. Volkan's explanation is that "some patients select specific fantasies from all those they have and resort to them over and over. The ones they select to use and reuse include aspects of wishes for and defenses against issues from different psychosexual phases. Appropriate interpretation of these aspects does not cause them to disappear, and soon the analyst and his patient become aware that the latter is addicted to them as a child is addicted to his transitional object" (Volkan 1973, p. 235).

[5]Tesal 1975. Atatürk's creative use of language can be considered to parallel a child's creation of neologisms, the developmental aspects of which are examined by Weich (1978) from the viewpoint of the transitional phenomenon.

Life had settled into some sort of routine for the Ghazi. He usually rose between two and four in the afternoon. He would sip his first Turkish coffee of the day dressed in his long gown. After shaving, bathing, and having a body massage, he took his standard breakfast—one slice of white bread (from an Italian-style loaf) with a glass of *ayran* (yogurt mixed with water) or regular yogurt (Granda 1973, p. 30). Then he would work in his study on political and cultural issues. He read a great deal, underlining in pencil whatever he considered important. Having had no training as a scholar, his reading was not altogether disciplined or systematic. It was, however, far-reaching, and most eagerly pursued when it seemed to offer validation of his own ideas.

When in Ankara, Mustafa Kemal enjoyed visits to his nearby farm, where in the late afternoon he would again have some *ayran* or yogurt along with a Turkish coffee to which he might add a few drops of milk. In the early evening his chief aide would ask him to designate the guests he would have at his dinner table later that evening (Afetinan 1971, p. 22). Ten or more people were usually invited. Only İsmet and the minister of foreign affairs or the minister of the interior could attend without invitation. A few men, such as Nuri and Kılıç Ali, were in regular attendance. The soirées continued until the early morning, and it was not unusual for someone whose knowledge of a certain subject was fancied to be summoned in the middle of the night.

Fastidious in character, the Ghazi could often be seen smoothing the tablecloth before his guests arrived in his anxiety to have everything arranged perfectly. Such observations come from Professor Perihan Çambel, who knew Afet. Like most of Afet's female contemporaries, Professor Çambel had mixed feelings about her. She recalled, in an interview with Dr. Volkan in 1975 going to visit Afet at Yalova, which was one of the Ghazi's favorite spots for relaxation. Professor Çambel found Afet wearing slippers, but when Mustafa Kemal joined the two women, he demanded that Afet put on proper shoes and never forget that shoes were de rigeur when receiving visitors in a presidential residence.

His meticulousness was evident also in the way his evening dinner meetings were stylized. Guests first entered the billiard room, a game that the Ghazi loved to play. Often he would not appear until the drinking was well underway. Rakı was the drink usually served, accompanied by hors d'oeuvres (*meze*), often roasted chickpeas, olives, humus, and feta cheese. The drinking would go on for at least an hour before dinner was served. Not particular about the menu, Mustafa Kemal was content with simple meals.

He was a "night person," who could outdrink and outlast everyone else. Apparently he handled his liquor well. Oskar Weigert, who was sometimes summoned in the middle of the night for a discussion of labor issues, found him serious and alert, even at those hours. It would, however, be impossible for a man to drink more than a liter of rakı every night without incurring some injury. Some of his behavior at the dining table suggests intoxication accompanied by regression. He disliked having anyone come to his table drunk or having anyone drink enough during the meal to become foolish, but he did enjoy joking and raillery as long as he himself was not the butt of it. He demanded that gossip or personal criticism be openly expressed rather than hinted at, though it was generally understood that his tolerance of any negative remarks about himself was extremely limited.

Regressing with drink at his dinner table, Mustafa Kemal sometimes led his company in the songs of his Macedonian childhood. Once when he ordered scrambled eggs made with cheese, a dish his mother had prepared for him when he was a child, he petulantly returned it twice to the kitchen, complaining that it was not like his mother used to make. Extremely upset, he summoned the chef and demanded in a scream, "Do you know what an egg is?" Nuri had to calm him down. He, too, was a Macedonian and was able to help the chef prepare the desired dish as the Ghazi's mother would have made it. Nuri described that event to his daughter Kıymet (Tesal 1975), explaining to her also Mustafa Kemal's intense longing for his birthplace—the European part of the Ottoman Empire called Rumeli—its food, and its songs, likening it to his mother's longing for Salonika until the day of her death.

Mustafa Kemal's rather pedantic conduct at the dining table seems to indicate that he was repeating, in a ritualistic and practical manner, aspects of his childhood conflicts and their attempted solutions. His first memory of life, it will be recalled, dealt with his education and the conflict between his mother and father on the subject. It referred to paying homage to the religious, grieving mother and mending her broken heart before leaving her (or her influence) for his westernized father. The push toward the West that his father gave him prior to his death was his last gift to his son. In reality, his father had been drinking and was depressed when he made little Mustafa this gift, but he succeeded in taking him to see Şemsi Efendi, the headmaster of the westernized school in Salonika. Şemsi Efendi himself was being harassed by Salonika's religious elements, but stubbornly refused to give in to them.

After his mother's death, Mustafa Kemal would be in touch with her symbolically at the dinner table before casting off her influence (the religious, Arabic, and Persian elements of his country) and joining the idealized father by turning toward the West. He stood in his own "classroom," like Şemsi Efendi, and gave oral examinations to his guests.[6] He

[6] "There was always someone in front of him (Mustafa Kemal) to be examined by him"; Afetinan 1971, p. 30.

seemed to go to excess at times in his preoccupation with grandiose theories about the language and the history of Turkey, but what made him a genius was his ability to put limits (borders) to his grandiose expansion. Somehow, it appears to us, the functions of the father as a customs official patrolling the border were included in the idealized image of the father. Mustafa Kemal must have been fascinated as a child to hear his father tell stories of the border and to explain that one could go just so far before having to acknowledge a limit, beyond which one could not realistically pass.

Afet recorded the following statement made by Mustafa Kemal, indicating his respect for "borders," or limits beyond which one does not go:

> Naturally, everyone wants to have within his society the happiest, easiest, and sweetest aspects of life, but the strong think little of the weak. As a result, it is impossible to live in harmony, tranquility, security, and order. Thus, the principles of law . . . make it possible for people to be helpful to one another, and to respect one another, to bring order instead of fighting. No one can demand a right *outside the established border*. [Afetinan 1971, pp. 29–30; italics added]

His character was such that he had a tendency to feel contempt for the weak. At the same time he felt obliged to respect the borders beyond which he could not expand his power at the expense of other people. He never hesitated to go as far as he could, at every opportunity, only to test reality and halt when halting seemed indicated. This discrimination made him different from a contemporary like Hitler, who did not know where to stop in his efforts to "purify" his country.

Mustafa Kemal knew enough to withdraw from endorsing the sun-language theory and other grandiose historical notions when they began to seem too bizarre. He dropped the sun-language theory altogether but remained interested and active in purifying and simplifying the Turkish language in a more realistic way, and continued to study his country's history. He never advocated pan-Turanic ideals, which called for uniting Turks all over the world, including those millions living outside the borders of the Turkish state. "Peace at home, peace abroad" became his motto.

His transformation into an educator brought his self-concept to a new level. He now felt that he had become the idealized father. Thus, not only was the final separation from his mother completed, but the oedipal triumph was also achieved. Accordingly, in 1934 he changed his name once again. Turks had had no surnames until that year. That eastern tradition had led to some confusion, often making it difficult to tell one

The hero ages. Atatürk, late in life, gazes from the window of a train.

Mustafa or Mehmed from another. Following the Western style, he decided that surnames should be adopted. At the same time, titles such as pasha, ghazi, and efendi, as well as names indicating noble lineage, would no longer be used. A man would simply be addressed as *Bay* ("Mr.") and a woman, whether married or not, as *Bayan* ("Ms."). A law requiring everyone to take a surname within two years was passed. On 24 November 1934 a special law gave Ghazi M. Kemal a surname, that of Atatürk, "Father Turk." A slip of the tongue made over Radio Ankara betrayed the fact that he was regarded charismatically as having both motherly and fatherly characteristics by his people: he was mistakenly called Anatürk ("Mother Turk") over the air when his surname was announced (Granda 1973, p. 38). On 17 December 1934 another law forbade the use of Atatürk, or any modification of it, by anyone else. Thus, he became the *one and only* Father Turk. His sister Makbule was given the name of Atadan, meaning "related to the father." Atatürk gave İsmet the surname İnönü, honoring him for his success at the Battles of İnönü. He also suggested certain surnames for other people as well. Dr. Adnan refused to take a surname, maintaining that everyone knew who he was, but under pressure he finally took the name Adıvar, meaning "he has a name."

Most people simply called Mustafa Kemal, Ata ("father") or Atam ("my father"), although he himself preferred Atatürk. There is no record, however, of his ever having rebuked anyone for addressing him as Atam. Later, he considered altering his name Kemal to Kamal (perhaps again giving birth to himself in the same manner that he gave himself the birthdate of 19 May). There is an inscription on the wall of the Faculty of Political Sciences in Ankara that gives his name as Kamal. He even had a calling card printed with this name (Granda 1973, p. 35). Kemal was Arabic in origin, and if he were to be the purified Father Turk, his name should be pure Turkish, too. Finally, he decided to remain Kemal Atatürk, though he usually signed his name simply as K. Atatürk.

27
Oral Examinations

ÇANKAYA WAS NOT THE ONLY PLACE FOR ALL-NIGHT DISCUSSIONS AT THE presidential table. When Mustafa Kemal was in residence in Istanbul, they took place at Dolmabahçe Palace. In truth, the entire nation was his presidential table. Even before taking the name of Atatürk, Mustafa Kemal behaved as though all the citizens of his nation were his children, and at times he plunged into intense involvement with their personal lives.

It is revealing to observe Atatürk's impact on those whom he knew well and on those whose contact with him was only marginal. An appreciation of that impact elucidates not only the character of this fascinating man but the ways in which people change in the presence of a charismatic leader of significant stature.

Mrs. Lütfiye Gürsoy (Gürsoy 1974) is a case in point. Her involvement in the Menemen incident has already been noted. Perhaps because she knew young Kubilay, who was slain, she felt so drawn into the history of the time that her recollection of meeting Mustafa Kemal in the early 1930s remained especially vivid. The Ghazi visited Izmir soon after the Menemen incident in order to respond to the religious fanatics, as well as to send a signal to Mussolini, who seemed to be interested in extending Italian conquest into Turkish territory along the Aegean. When Lütfiye heard that her hero was coming to Izmir, she camped out all night with another female teacher at the railroad station, in anticipation of his arrival. The two women found themselves completely lost among the hundreds and hundreds of people who crowded into the station. They were excited, therefore, to learn that the Ghazi planned to visit schools on the following day and that their school was included in his itinerary. After the alphabet reform, Mustafa Kemal made a habit of visiting schools on his travels, sitting among the students, and giving them and their teachers oral examinations on the innovations.[1] Lütfiye was delighted with the prospect of seeing the Ghazi at close range, but at the

[1]Stories of Mustafa Kemal giving oral examinations to teachers, as well as to others, are numerous. See Granda 1973, pp. 128–30, for the story of his examining his butler. See Kinross 1975, p. 516, for Mustafa Kemal's giving an oral examination to Hasan Ali Yücel, who later became minister of education. See also Afetinan 1971, p. 20.

same time she was frightened of being asked questions she might not be able to answer.

When Mustafa Kemal arrived at her school she was introduced to him. He took her hand and looked into her face. She trembled. When she was interviewed by Dr. Volkan, Mrs. Gürsoy, then in her mid-sixties, was still a lively and attractive woman, but she insisted that at the time she first met Mustafa Kemal she was "unattractive." One must conclude that, like many other educated young women of her day, she found an idealized father in her hero, and her modest claim of "unattractiveness" was useful in the service of denying any sexual implications in the encounter. She thought his eyes were sweet and warm. Although a father transference was evident in her account of her reactions to the meeting, a mother transference was also suggested by her speaking of "the warm feeling state that flowed into my being from his warm blue eyes." The presence of Afet introduced a triangular (oedipal) situation for most young women who met Atatürk in circumstances such as those of Lütfiye's encounter with him.

Arrangements for the Ghazi to observe the class of one notably beautiful female teacher in that school had been made by the principal. They all went to her classroom and sat at the students' desks. Their distinguished visitor chose for discussion the topic, "Is it possible for a woman to be a soldier?" The teacher, it is reported, passed the examination by responding in the affirmative, but adding that women had a more important duty, that of motherhood. The discussion continued after the class was dismissed. Over tea, the Ghazi, Afet, and the minister of education, Vasıf (Çınar), met with the teachers. Lütfiye was able to observe Mustafa Kemal's gentle, almost feminine, manner as he daintily dipped part of his sweet biscuit into the Turkish tea and ate it. Such a gesture was more commonly seen among "sophisticated" Turkish gentlewomen. From Lütfiye's recollection of that day, it would appear that he was preoccupied on this occasion with a comparision between aggressive/phallic and "pure"/gentle women.

An hour after he took his leave, the teachers' telephone rang with an invitation from Mustafa Kemal to attend a ball that evening. They were met at the ball by Vasıf. At about ten o'clock Mustafa Kemal appeared and went directly to their table, even before he officially greeted the assembled guests. When the orchestra struck up, the Ghazi asked one of the teachers to tango with him. In recalling the events of that evening, Lütfiye beamed as she remembered how gracefully her hero had danced and how dashing he had been. Soon, however, even the ball was turned into a classroom, with Mustafa Kemal holding forth to those at his table, recounting stories and historical anecdotes. He told them how his watch had saved his life at Gallipoli, that he had given the shattered watch to

General Liman von Sanders, and that the German general had given him his watch in turn. As other historical topics arose, Mustafa Kemal asked one of the history teachers to settle a point. Lütfiye was afraid of being called upon, for she knew that this would involve one of the Ghazi's "examinations." She felt fortunate when his attention to her was limited to asking a young man to dance with her.

Mustafa Kemal was taken with the beautiful teacher whose classroom he had visited. He tried to arrange a marriage between her and Vasıf, who was a bachelor. This suddenly conceived project demonstrated another aspect of his personality—the impulsiveness that coexisted with painstaking patience. He had demanded that Lâtife marry him immediately, and now he was impulsively trying to arrange the lives of Vasıf and this teacher. Lütfiye recalled that nothing came of the suggestion, for the young woman's father disapproved of Vasıf.

This attempt at matchmaking was not an isolated incident. Lütfiye reported that Mustafa Kemal had a lively interest in young women and often tried to be a matchmaker. He later found husbands for some of his adopted daughters as well. Despite his eye for women, Mustafa Kemal could not tolerate having someone else bring a particular woman to his attention, and he disliked women wearing provocative makeup. His personality was such that he preferred to take the initiative with women. Once, at a ball in Istanbul, a middle-aged man tried to curry favor with him by openly offering him a young woman. Any such undignified behavior in public angered him, in spite of his sometimes indiscreet behavior while among his cronies. He railed against the heavy makeup the young woman was wearing and proceeded to give her one of his famous "examinations," demanding in front of the entire gathering that she name the cosmetic preparations on her cheeks and lips. The poor girl fainted, and Mustafa Kemal then dismissed her and her sponsor.

That incident was witnessed by Adile (Ayda) (1975), the daughter of the law professor and deputy to the Grand National Assembly, Sadri Maksudi (Arsal). Her father was a guest at Mustafa Kemal's dinner table on numerous occasions. Dr. Volkan's interview with her, along with articles (Dilacar 1974, Granda 1973, p. 211–12) about her father's interaction with Mustafa Kemal, shed considerable light both on the Ghazi's character and on the way his people perceived him.

As an unmarried man in his fifties, Mustafa Kemal had a tremendous reputation for aggressive virility. It is difficult to know where reality ends and myth begins, but one thing is certain—he was intimate with a number of women. Yet, here too he was able to establish borders or limits. Nuri always insisted to his wife and children that the Ghazi never took advantage of any woman, nor broke up any family with his amorous adventures (Tesal 1974). At social gatherings he was, as a rule, surrounded by men, except for Afet when she was present. His celebrated answer to the question about what he liked best in women—"availability"—does not tell the entire story of his complicated relationship to them.

Adile first saw Mustafa Kemal in 1929, when she was seventeen years old. The occasion was a visit by Mustafa Kemal to the school she attended. Still extremely beautiful in her sixties when interviewed, she must have been a startingly lovely young girl. She entered law school in 1930 and became one of the exceedingly few young, unmarried girls of good family to appear in party-going circles of Ankara, frequently accompanying her father to cocktail parties and balls. Adile was acquainted with Afet and had ambivalent feelings toward her, as did many other women of her age. While they acknowledged Afet's importance since she was Mustafa Kemal's adopted "daughter," they implied that she was not intelligent enough to have such an honor.

Commenting upon Mustafa Kemal's physical magnetism, Mrs. Ayda noted that even in an adjoining room his presence could be felt, and when he entered a room, he was too awesome to look at directly.[2] Mustafa Kemal must have been taken with her. He asked Afet to introduce them, and when the two women chatted at a ball shortly thereafter, he broke in to ask Afet to invite her friend to Çankaya.

On the surface, such an invitation might seem harmless, but Mrs. Ayda recalled that it gave great anxiety to her and her family. Her father was almost a regular at Mustafa Kemal's table. He thought the gatherings there "highly academic" from eight o'clock until midnight, but he suspected that after midnight there would be much drinking and regressed behavior of the sort that a family man would find distasteful both in reality and in fantasy. He was also convinced that Mustafa Kemal was a womanizer. It was a terrible dilemma to have his daughter receive such an invitation, which, considering the source, amounted to an order.

In the end, the family decided that Adile should go. One afternoon, at about 4:30 as arranged, she went to Çankaya. There she was met by Afet, who took her into the study. Adile recalled that she felt nervous, and the fact that the study adjoined Mustafa Kemal's bedroom made her apprehensive. Soon, the Ghazi appeared wearing a robe. From the tousled look of his hair it was obvious that he had just gotten out of bed. He apologized to Adile for his appearance. Then, he asked her age and "other routine questions that a man asks a young girl." "My worries were groundless," she confessed. One can only speculate about the Ghazi's original intentions in inviting Adile to the presidential quarters.

Mrs. Ayda's recollections show how reality and myth were intermin-

[2]Once more the shining sun symbolism associated with Mustafa Kemal can be seen in Mrs. Ayda's statement.

gled in the way people envisioned Mustafa Kemal's private life. She continucd to see him at cotillions and other events, and she was present at the famous ball held in the Ankara Palace Hotel in 1933 in celebration of the republic's tenth anniversary. It was there that she underwent her "examination." Mustafa Kemal was standing with a Russian diplomat when Adile came up to him and kissed his hand in the traditional manner. Holding her hand firmly, he said to her, "You have kissed my hand. What will you do with my friend's?" She then shook hands with the Russian as the Ghazi nodded approvingly. Adile had passed her "examination."

Completing her education, Adile went on to become a lawyer and later a wife and mother. She was the first woman to hold a ranking position, second only to the ambassador, in the Turkish embassy in Italy. But Mustafa Kemal had made an indelible impression upon her. While in Italy she became interested in the highly evolved, ancient Etruscan culture and pondered such questions as where the Etruscans had come from and who they really were. Her father had been involved in the presidential dinner discussions of grandiose, historical theories citing Turkey as the center of world civilization. She heard about those discussions, and after her tour of duty in Italy, she wrote a book that sought to prove that the Etruscans were really Turks (Ayda 1975). When Dr. Volkan interviewed her he sensed that in spite of her many achievements she was engaged in an unconscious competition with Afet. The same seems to be true of Professor Perihan Çambel (Çambel 1975), whose father, like Adile's, was a close associate of the Ghazi's. Adile gave Dr. Volkan the impression of having been "abandoned" by important men in her life and reported that two years after Atatürk's death she saw him in a memorable dream in which she worried that he would find fault with her, despite her wanting to please him. In the dream he turned into her father and then assumed his own identity once more.

Mrs. Ayda was not the only woman to have a dream in which the manifest content involved the interchangeability of the father and Atatürk, representing the dilemma of having to choose which was the father figure to whom she should be loyal.[3] Kıymet (Tesal), Nuri's daughter, also had such a dream (Tesal 1975). Nuri died in 1937 at the age of fifty-five, twenty months before Atatürk's death. Kıymet was in school in London at the time of her father's heart attack, and Atatürk was in the city of Konya. She was told that until her father lost consciousness he kept asking, "Has the Ghazi come yet?" Atatürk did rush to Ankara, hoping

[3]In dealing with dreams, psychoanalysts consider their manifest content—the content that is recalled and reported by the patient—as well as their latent content. The latent content of the dream refers to the deeper meanings of it and can be best understood through the patient's free associations.

to see his old friend, but the doctors refused to admit him to Nuri's bedroom. Two years after Atatürk's death, Kıymet had a dream on the night of 26 October, the eve of her birthday. In her dream it was her birthday, and she stood at the side of a grave which began to erupt from the ground. Although it remained covered on top, its interior could be seen from the sides. The grave contained two corpses, or so it seemed, since from one side the contents appeared to be Atatürk's body and from the other side King Solomon's. Obviously, it would be impossible to understand this dream in any depth simply from its manifest content, and any attempt on our part to interpret it would be wild analysis at best. The manifest content and Mrs. Tesal's awareness of the King Solomon story about a mother's loyalty tested by threats to cut her child in two, suggest, however, that the dreamer was torn between loyalty to her father Nuri and to Atatürk. In her daily life Kıymet had no difficulty in remaining loyal both to her father and to her idealized father whom she saw on a continuum. Adile, on the other hand, appears to have had a conflict about remaining loyal to both her father and Atatürk.

It was only possible for Mrs. Ayda to remain loyal to both by means of symptom formation. That symptom was related to a disagreement her father had with Atatürk. Despite abandonment of his belief in the sun-language theory, Atatürk remained interested in the creation of a new and purified Turkish tongue. His difference with Sadri Maksudi grew out of the name Atatürk wanted to bestow on a new bank being established to assist in the funding of Turkey's new maritime undertakings. Atatürk proposed the name "Denizbank" (Seabank). Others wanted to call it "Denizcilik Bankası" (Maritime Bank) or "Denizci Bankası" (Seaman's Bank). In the draft of the law establishing the bank, which was read in the Grand National Assembly, it was named "Denizbank," as Mustafa Kemal had suggested. Sadri Maksudi objected, arguing that the name "Denizbank" was inappropriate because, it violated the rules of Turkish grammar. In Turkish, when a noun modifies another in construct, the first noun is the possessor and the second is the thing possessed. The second noun takes a suffix, called the *izafet* suffix, to indicate the special relationship it bears to the first member of the construct. Sadri Maksudi's criticism constituted a narcissistic injury to Mustafa Kemal who never took kindly to intellectual criticism, as his early years in school indicate. Sadri Maksudi was never again invited to the presidential table, but Atatürk did not let the matter drop—further evidence that he had indeed sustained a narcissistic injury.

The way in which Atatürk went about repairing his self-esteem is instructive. That evening, 27 December 1937, the topic for discussion at his dinner table was the issue of the name "Denizbank." His guests agreed with his choice, offering a wide range of examples in which the type of construction he had employed was already in use. As a matter of fact, two banks had been organized in 1935 and given names with the same type of construction, Sümerbank and Etibank, respectively, the Sumerian Bank and the Hittite Bank, the former being heavily involved in the textile industry and the latter in mining. During a lull in the conversation, Atatürk became aware that the radio station was still on the air. Immediately, he ordered that Radio Ankara not sign off as usual at 10:30 P.M. but continue broadcasting as he would be sending down some people to talk about the term "Denizbank" and its relationship to pure Turkish (Dilacar 1974). He then sent several of his guests in relays to the station, ending with Falih Rıfkı Atay. On the following day *Ulus*, Ankara's daily newspaper and the official organ of Atatürk's political party, ran a long article on the front page under the headline "Denizbank Is Pure Turkish."

Out of this steamroller attack on her father, Adile developed her symptom, which was a phobia, at times rather exaggerated, to radio. When she was interviewed in 1975, Mrs. Ayda pointed out that not only was there no radio in her apartment, but she took great care to see that radio sounds did not enter her home, taking pains to keep the windows tightly shut. The exaggeration of her phobia made this intelligent and lovely lady a virtual prisoner in her own apartment. Apparently there were periods in her life when her symptom was in remission. Whenever she visited her married children, she would summon a taxi known by her not to have a radio. We have no way of knowing the psychodynamics of her personal life, or their origins in her childhood, but it seems safe to assume that by "denying," in a sense, the existence of the radio, which had been the instrument of Atatürk's aggression toward her father, she could remain psychologically loyal to her father and to Atatürk at the same time.

Narcissistic injuries were, perhaps, unavoidable at Atatürk's dinner table, where the guests drank a great deal and challenges were offered to the leader in ways that easily attacked his sense of self-esteem. Nuri was ever ready to save the day with quips and mollifying remarks but was not always successful in blunting the impact of some remarks. Many anecdotes of these evenings have appeared in memoirs published in the Turkish press.[4]

One of the most widely reported incidents that took place at Mustafa Kemal's table has become known as the Reşid Galip incident. It provides insight into one of the ways in which the Ghazi would repair a narcissistic

[4]In the summer of 1975, İsmet Bozdağ serialized a collection of stories about what took place at the presidential table in Ankara, Istanbul, and Bursa in the Istanbul newspaper *Günaydın*. They have since been issued in book form; see Bozdağ 1975*b*.

injury—playfully. Reşid Galip was a physician by training, but he was immensely interested in linguistics, history, and literature. He was, at the time (1931), in charge of the Halkevi (People's House) movement. People's Houses were opened all over the country to bring Kemalist cultural ideas to all strata of society. Reşid Galip was in favor of developing theaters in the People's Houses, feeling that theater was an effective means for the presentation of new ideas. He needed, as an expression of westernization, to involve women in this work, and he wanted to encourage young women teachers to take part. Opposition to that idea came from Esad Mehmed, the elderly minister of education and one of Mustafa Kemal's former teachers, who recommended caution in view of small-town attitudes.

Over dinner at Mustafa Kemal's table one evening, Reşid Galip attacked the leader, claiming that, in taking sides against the theater project, Mustafa Kemal was protecting his old teacher. Reşid Galip maintained that Esad Mehmed was out of date and that Mustafa Kemal was at fault in championing him. Nettled, Mustafa Kemal cautioned him to be more careful in what he said on that issue, but the man did not know when to stop. The leader suggested that perhaps Reşid Galip had had too much to drink and that he should leave the table. Undaunted, Reşid Galip replied that the table did not belong to Mustafa Kemal, but rather to the nation, and since they were discussing the affairs of the nation, he had as much right to be there as Mustafa Kemal did. Thereupon, Mustafa Kemal stood up, threw his napkin on the table, and strode out of the room.

Reşid Galip was not invited to sit at Mustafa Kemal's table again for some time, although Mustafa Kemal did confide to his general secretary that he admired the man's courage. One evening, about a month after the incident, Mustafa Kemal heard Reşid Galip speak on Radio Ankara with passionate enthusiasm on the subject of the People's Houses. Impressed with the man's intense commitment to Kemalism, he decided to forgive him. Reşid Galip was back on the persona grata list, and about two weeks after his radio lecture, he reappeared at the leader's table. Mustafa Kemal greeted him and, out of the hearing of others, told him that he would be appointed minister of education. During the meal, Mustafa Kemal ordered two strapping soldiers to have some fun with Reşid Galip in a children's game in which they took hold of him and tossed him about, catching him before he hit the floor. Putting an end to the game after a bit, Mustafa Kemal remarked that he wished he could have taken part in it. The message was clear to all—Mustafa Kemal was still in charge, and he raised up those whom he would, and he could just as easily lay them low. Having given that message, he no longer saw Reşid Galip as sufficiently his equal to challenge his indisputable superiority. What Mustafa Kemal admired in Reşid Galip was his audacity, again admiring a part of himself in another person. That evening Mustafa Kemal had a long conversation with his old teacher, whom he urged to relinquish his post as minister of education for reasons of health. Shortly thereafter Reşid Galip was named in his place.

Dramatic gestures, such as asking the soldiers to toss Reşid Galip about or giving his revolver to his would-be assassin, were part of Mustafa Kemal's repertoire, whether sober or not. They seem designed to reestablish the cohesiveness of his narcissistic personality organization following an injury. Examples of this behavior are legion, and one more episode, concerning music, typifies the entire category.

In spite of Atatürk's insistence that the new Turks should learn and come to love European music and his temporary ban on the broadcasting of Turkish music, he himself continued to love it, singing Turkish music and dancing to Turkish tunes. The two outstanding popular Turkish singers of the day were Safiye Ayla, a woman, and Münir Nureddin Selçuk, a man. They were often summoned to the presidential table to entertain Atatürk. Since Safiye's voice was considerably more beautiful than her countenance, it is reported that at times Atatürk demanded that she sing from a dark corner. It was with Münir Nureddin, however, that Atatürk had a contretemps.

One evening Münir Nureddin was singing at a party. Atatürk sang along with him, spoiling the professional singer's rendition of the song. Münir Nureddin could tolerate it no longer and told Atatürk to stop his singing. Atatürk was hurt to the quick. After the incident, Atatürk was relaxing in the parlor car during a train trip and asked his waiter to play a record on the gramophone. Unwittingly, the man put on a record by Münir Nureddin. As soon as Atatürk heard the man's voice, he shouted for his waiter to change the record. Knowing nothing about the falling out between the two, he put on a different record by the same singer. Atatürk became enraged and made the waiter throw the records out the window.

Repair of his self-esteem damaged in the incident with Münir Nureddin was not achieved until one day when a reception was being held in Bursa's main hotel at which Atatürk would be present. Münir Nureddin was there, an indication that Atatürk was amenable to a possible rapprochement. Everyone was drinking rakı when Atatürk arrived. He drew a pistol from his back pocket and motioned the singer to place his glass of rakı on top of his head. When the singer obeyed, Atatürk took aim at it. Was he going to be another William Tell? The audience thought he was joking, but he pulled the trigger, putting a bullet in the wall behind the singer, having shifted his aim slightly just before shooting. That bullet hole can still be seen today.[5]

[5]See General Fahrettin Altay 1973, for this version of the bullet hole at the Çelik Palas Hotel in Bursa. However, another version of how this hole came to exist is given by Bozdağ

After the shooting, Münir Nureddin raised his glass of rakı and draining it of its contents, bowed then to Atatürk. Responding to this gesture, Atatürk said, "You have proved that your courage is as wonderful as your voice." When he had opposed Atatürk, the singer was a "bad" object, but he was now reestablished as a "good" object by one dramatic gesture. Identifying with the courageousness of the act, Atatürk could regard the singer as an extension of himself. Reconciled, Münir Nureddin was permitted to sing before Atatürk. He sang a song that begins, "Your most wonderful eyes," a clear reference to the Ghazi's remarkable feature. This time Atatürk refrained from singing along with him. His idealized extension could carry on by himself, without presenting a challenge.

Alongside this process of making good any narcissistic injuries, Atatürk continued to discriminate between those who were "good," and therefore worthy of his attention, and those who were not, by means of his "examination." He used this approach with the consulting dentist called in by his personal dentist, Dr. Günzberg, who needed advice regarding a difficult extraction during the summer of 1935. A tooth that appeared beyond saving was causing Atatürk extreme discomfort. Having felt the pain of the extraction, Atatürk gave the new dentist an "examination" to ascertain whether he was good enough to take care of him in the future. Afet (Afetinan 1971, p. 21), who was present, wrote about this later, as did the dentist's assistant (Kızıldağlı 1979). Between visits to his illustrious patient, the dentist studied everything he could find on the history of dentistry. He so impressed Atatürk that he was designated professor of the subject at the University of Istanbul and in 1936 represented Turkey at an international meeting of dentists held in Vienna.

Atatürk's need to "examine" others was overdetermined; that is, there was more than one psychological factor at work in producing this particular behavior pattern. He not only had to decide, according to the dictates of his personality organization, whom to ignore and whom to accept as a

---

1975*b*, pp. 175–76. He describes the following story: In 1930 Mustafa Kemal arrived in Bursa and attended a ball at Çelik Palas given to honor him. He seemed in a happy mood. He became even happier when a young woman read a poem praising him. Upon this, he gave a speech to those who were present and told them that he could see they loved him. He asked them to love him after they believed in him and trusted him. In order to make a point, he asked if there was anyone among them who would step in front of him with a glass on top of his or her head. He stated that he would try to shoot down the glass.

A pregnant woman, the wife of Dr. Talat Şahin, a physician, stepped forward and stated that she trusted him. A glass was put on her head. First, Mustafa Kemal aimed his revolver at the glass, but, before pulling the trigger, he turned the weapon toward the place where now the bullet hole still exists.

disciple, but he also wanted, unconsciously to identify with Şemsi Efendi, his first European-style schoolmaster. In that way he could become the idealized teacher, and thus, in a peculiar manner, he would have the illusion of winning his oedipal struggle through identification with the idealized father. At times, however, the examiner and the examinee changed places, as in the scene he described from his student days when another student questioned him and then he, in turn, became the questioner (see p. 36).

On the tenth anniversary of the founding of the Turkish republic, at a celebration held in the Ankara Palace Hotel, Atatürk stood on a chair in the middle of the ballroom and invited those present to ask him questions. He was confident that he had all the answers, and he would thus seem perfect (Kemal) to those who would, for the moment, be his "teachers" and examiners.[6] We also see in his examinations an element of his separation from the mother of his childhood, as when he gained admission to the military school by taking and passing an examination, presenting her with a fait accompli and his departure from home.

Those examinations could be awesome affairs, but Atatürk was always gentle in giving them to villagers and children, for they were no threat to his self-esteem and he could afford to treat them tenderly. They represented himself as a child. He took delight in seeing them gain hope and given intimations of future blossoming. He often asked shepherd boys if they knew who the Ghazi was, and he was delighted when they recognized him. Bent on keeping intact his concept of his own uniqueness and superiority, he would try to patch any wound inflicted on this image, no matter how trivial. One evening his virility came into question at a dinner given in Dolmabahçe Palace. He ordered the guests to gather in the early morning hours at the house of Madam Katrina, a brothel keeper, so that the aging madam could certify to those present that he had always been the most virile among her customers (Aydemir 1974).

One of his most remarkable encounters with a shepherd boy took place in the summer of 1930 when he was riding with a party of some twenty other horsemen near Yalova. They came upon a youngster tending his flock. They asked him the way, and then Mustafa Kemal asked his name. The boy said that his name was Mustafa. Mustafa Kemal said that his name was Mustafa as well and asked if the boy knew who the Ghazi was. The boy obviously did not know that he was speaking to the Ghazi himself, which amused Mustafa Kemal. He asked the boy how much he earned and whether he would come to work for him if he matched the

[6]Elsewhere, in 1937, referring to the Turkish youth (as an extension of himself) and their involvement in sports, he indicated that they were always ready "to be examined" (Afetinan 1971, p. 56), as, indeed, the whole Turkish nation was.

sum. The boy replied that if his employer and his mother approved (he, like Mustafa Kemal, had no father), he would. The lad further impressed the Ghazi by refusing to accept money that was offered to him. He agreed to take it only if Mustafa Kemal took in return some of the walnuts the boy had with him. On the following day Mustafa Kemal summoned the youth into his presence to show him that he was indeed the Ghazi. Later when Mustafa Kemal learned that the boy had malaria he made arrangements for his treatment in Istanbul. The Ghazi and his cronies later visited the child in the hospital, and Mustafa Kemal began to talk about having him sent to school. Some of his crowd opposed this notion, maintaining that he was just a poor peasant without any schooling at all. The Ghazi countered those objections, recalling that he himself used to chase the crows from his uncle's fields and herd his sheep. His uncle recognized that he was intelligent and had him educated. "Look what has become of me," he added (Granda 1973, pp. 96–100). In the end, the boy was sent to military school, was eventually commissioned, and achieved the rank of major.

Such examples of Atatürk's involvement in the lives of others, sometimes in eccentric ways, and no doubt at times under the influence of alcohol, should not blind us to the fact that, generally, he was serious and responsible in the conduct of governmental affairs. He was able to handle contradictions in his life by splitting off what was eccentric and personal from the serious business of the day. He received far more evidence of his unique superiority than of challenge or scorn. His narcissistic personality structure was largely reinforced by the adoration of the public. His belief in his mission as savior and purifier of his country was never shaken. Continuing to have an unquestioning faith in the benefits of Western civilization, he constantly urged his people to westernize. He told Afet, "We are importing Western civilization not because we want to imitate it, but because we have found its benefits suitable to our nature" (Afetinan 1971, pp. 23–24).

Afet was firmly installed as his female companion at the time. With her he worked out his notions of Turkish history and Turkish identity. While she was in one sense his adoring "slave," she was also, of necessity, free in the political sense, in the mold of a westernized woman. He asked her to study women's rights and to lecture and write about the theories behind the women's rights movement (Afetinan, pp. 23–24). She was also to familiarize herself with the way Western women voted. Such issues were discussed in her presence at the presidential table. Turkish women received international attention when one of them, Keriman Halis, became the beauty queen of Europe. On 8 December 1934, Turkish women were acclaimed in their own country and given the right to vote in parliamentary elections.

Atatürk's other adopted daughters were also growing up. Rukiye and Nebile were married off in weddings that took place at the Ankara Palace Hotel. Rukiye, who had been educated at a French school in Istanbul, married an army lieutenant. Nebile's husband was chief secretary of the Turkish embassy in Vienna. This marriage failed and after her divorce she married an engineer and returned to Turkey, but apparently she was never a happy woman. Bülent was removed from Çankaya, where she was rumored to have had a Christian lover. Zehra and Sabiha were sent to the American College in Istanbul after finishing their preliminary schooling in Ankara. Sabiha, second only to Afet in the Ghazi's esteem, fell ill. Tuberculosis was suspected. She was sent to a sanatorium, first in Vienna and then to one in the mountains of Switzerland. Upon her return to Turkey she studied with special teachers at Çankaya, which she still called her home many years later in her interview with Dr. Volkan. The Ghazi bought her an Arabian horse named Sülün, and her fondest memories of those days were of their riding and practicing target shooting together.

In her sitting room Ms. Sabiha Gökçen keeps a scrap of Atatürk's handwriting preserved in a silver frame. It testifies in Turkish that her name is Sabiha Gökçen (her surname is a reference to the sky). It is dated 1934 and is mute evidence of his desire that Sabiha excel greatly. It is no surprise that she became one of the most celebrated women pilots in the world. Not until a decade after the founding of the Turkish Airlines Association in 1925 did Mustafa Kemal decide that Turkey should have an aviation school. Both Sabiha and Zehra attended its opening, watching foreign pilots dazzle the crowd with their exhibitions of gliding and parachute jumping.

Responding to unconscious pressure from the Ghazi, Sabiha showed an interest in learning to parachute. Once she spoke of it to him he quickly summoned foreign experts to teach her. Perhaps they both thought that she could learn at once, for Atatürk had always followed his own decisions to undertake a task with immediate action. Quickly, however, Sabiha discovered that she would need formal schooling, especially if she were to advance from parachuting to flying, and she enrolled in the Türk Kuşu (Turkish Bird), the aviation school. Later, she was sent with seven Turkish men to Russia for six months of specialized training and returned to Turkey as a glider teacher. How far Turkish women had come from the days of the veil and the harem!

"At first I started the whole business because it was fun," Ms. Gökçen explained to Dr. Volkan. "But Atatürk never stopped showing interest. I realized that he was trying to develop me as a pilot. Now it was serious business, and the sky became my career." At that time military schools did not accept women, but Sabiha was permitted, through a request from

Atatürk, to enter the Turkish Military Air Academy from which she graduated. Later, she became the head instructor at the Türk Kuşu and remained in that position for eighteen years. Perhaps more than any other of Atatürk's adopted daughters, she had an appreciation of his wish to mold his daughters in the Western image, one quite different from that of his grieving mother's. She responded affirmatively to the pressure he put on his "daughters," but Zehra, on the other hand, was not able to stand up to it.

Zehra was sent to London to complete her education, but the psychological difficulties of living in a foreign country were too much for her. She knew that any failure on her part would disappoint the Ghazi greatly. Sabiha had guessed at her adopted sister's vulnerability, but she could do little about the situation. Zehra failed in London and while en route home to Turkey she committed suicide in France by jumping off the train into a lake where she drowned.

We know nothing of Atatürk's reaction to this tragic event. According to Ms. Gökçen, however, both she and Zehra had developed warm sympathy for Fikriye, who had committed suicide earlier. Zehra had never known her, but she knew her story. It is not unlikely that Fikriye's fate played some role in Zehra's tragic end.

28
Internal Processes and Real World Engagements

ASSUMPTION OF THE NAME ATATÜRK, WHICH DECLARED HIS NEWLY WON identity, did not mean that the play of the psychological forces which led to that name change had come to a complete halt. Nor can we believe that the "Atatürk" identity brought Mustafa Kemal any ultimate comfort. Afet recorded his answer to the question, "Are you happy?" to which he replied, "I am, for I have succeeded" (Afetinan 1971, p. 105).[1] Yet, his need always to follow one success with another meant that he could never rest. His drive to mold his environment in response to his inner needs seems to have been never ending. It was only an illusion that by becoming Atatürk he had finally separated from the representation of his mother, integrated his self-concept, and resolved his oedipal struggle. He was compelled to keep working on these issues, which, because of who he was, unfolded in the arena of history as he went about working out those inner processes in his own grandiose, but creative, style. Prey to an inexorable internal push to do more, to follow one impressive achievement with another, Atatürk was certainly not happy, or, more precisely, never happy for very long.[2]

Inner tensions could not be hidden from some of his more astute observers. Yakup Kadri Karaosmanoğlu was one of the worshipful admirers who penetrated to the essence of the man. He recorded that "the depths of his psyche were turbulent with typhoons, storms, and silent revolutions" (Karaosmanoğlu 1971, p. 123). Observation of the great leader led Yakup Kadri to speculate whether Atatürk had "*A terrible secret or grief that he had never spoken about to others*" (italics added). Perhaps drawing more upon his talents as a writer than a diplomat, Yakup Kadri demonstrated his acute perception of Atatürk's unconscious when he wrote:

[1]Mustafa Kemal had given this answer on 21 June 1935 to a question put to him by a newspaperman.

[2]Falih Rıfkı Atay stated that it was during the tenth anniversary of the establishment of the Turkish republic that he noted Atatürk's inability to be happy. There was excitement among the people who were close to Atatürk as the celebration neared. One night at his dining table Atatürk confessed, "When it comes to me, I can't feel anything"; Atay 1980, p. 483.

> neither the bloody commotion of battle, nor the deafening roar of the victorious cannons, nor his ability to recreate a nation, nor the attainment of honor and glory beyond the dreams of any mortal, nor the celebrations of love could comfort him. This unassuaged soul, this roaring will, this stream of energy always wanted the excitement of some new victory, and the creation of something new.

What that something was Yakup Kadri could not discern. We have seen, however, that from childhood on, Mustafa Kemal had depended on his own inner resources, defensively feeling that he was unique. As a youth he generated grandiose ideas geared to saving the Ottoman Empire and as a young man he became a war hero. As an adult he was the charismatic savior of his country, and in his mature years leader of the nation, its schoolmaster, and purifier. All this he accomplished as a lonely soul. Demanding loyalty from his followers, he gave none in return, but alternated between being gentle and shy, and aggressive and abrupt.

Penetrating to the core of the conflict in the mature Atatürk, Yakup Kadri wrote, "In his soul the unending struggle between 'reality' and 'fantasy,' between the 'will' and the 'possibility' continued strong." (Karaosmanoğlu 1971, p. 123). Atatürk devoted all his energy, Yakup Kadri maintained, to the realization of his one burning ambition, "that the Turkish nation should with one blow be put ahead of all others" (Karaosmanoğlu 1971, p. 123). In hundreds of speeches Atatürk outlined his hopes for the country. In hundreds of acts he led the way. The term "Kemalism" came to be applied to Mustafa Kemal's vision of the future Turkey. Representing both his philosophy and his actions, Kemalism began to be studied on an intellectual level and articulated in a schematic way. The doctrine of Kemalism was summarized under six ideological principles enunciated by Mustafa Kemal in a manifesto published on 20 April 1931. The first article of the manifesto, which set forth the ethos of the Republican People's party, stated that the party was "republican, nationalist, populist, etatist, secularist, and revolutionary" (Lewis 1961, p. 280). These six principles were later enshrined in the constitution and in the emblem of the party, which consists of six white arrows on a field of red, each arrow representing a principle. All six points of the Kemalist program became part of Article 2 of the Turkish Constitution adopted in February 1937.

Republicanism was the natural result of Mustafa Kemal's elimination of the Ottoman dynasty as the embodiment of sovereignty in Turkey. His sense of borders is reflected in his slogan "Sovereignty belongs to the nation" and in his rejection of any royal role for himself. As Mustafa Kemal and his supporters struggled in Anatolia to save that remnant of the Ottoman Empire from the Allies and the Greeks, the basis of that endeavor evolved to a new idea, a nation-state with defined territorial borders based on the Turkish population residing there. While the document known as the National Pact, which served to state the principles of his movement and rally the people to his banner, spoke of Ottoman Muslims, Mustafa Kemal soon indicated that his concept of the new Turkey was really a nation demarcated in its boundaries by the Turks living on their land. Again, the notion of borders loomed large in his mind and served to energize him and his movement.

Nationalism was an essential element in the war of independence and in the formation of the republic. Territorial losses and the inability of the Ottoman minorities to renounce their national aspirations turned Ottomanism into Turkish nationalism. Furthermore, in the Turkish republic of 1927, 97.3 percent of the people were Muslim. Thus, the new Turkish republic was for the most part ethnically and culturally homogeneous.

Populism as a concept was enunciated by Mustafa Kemal as early as July 1920, when he told the Grand National Assembly in Ankara, "I think that the fundamental reality of our present-day existence is demonstrated by the general tendency of the nation, and that is populism and people's government. It means the passing of government into the hands of the people" (Lewis 1961, p. 251). The same principle led to the extension of equal rights to all citizens, regardless of creed, to practice their own religion and the constitutional guarantee that "The People of Turkey, regardless of religion and race, are Turks as regards citizenship."[3] This was, in effect, the demise of the *millet* system[4] that had been one of the main elements in the long history of confrontation between the Ottoman Empire and Europe. There would no longer be any pretext for the intervention of any foreign state in the internal affairs of Turkey based on the interests of coreligionists within Turkey. Possibly, populism, which sought to prevent the splitting off of any segment of the population from any other, reflected Mustafa Kemal's own efforts to mend the many splits within himself.

Etatism as a means of managing the economy spoke to the paucity of Turkey's natural and human resources (Hershlag 1960, part 3). The state would have to assist private enterprise to develop Turkey's economic future.

[3]This is Article 88 of the constitution. Here it is quoted from Shaw and Shaw, vol. 2, 1977, p. 378.

[4]The Ottoman world was divided into Muslims, who constituted the *umma* (the community of believers), and non-Muslims, who were organized into corporate religious bodies, each known as a *millet*. Each *millet* was responsible for the dispensation of justice concerning its own members, in accordance with its own religious law. The main *millet*s in Ottoman times were the Greek Orthodox, the Armenian Christians, and the Jews. In the nineteenth century the *millet* system became enmeshed in the Eastern Question, as the foreign powers championed the cause of one or another *millet*. See Itzkowitz 1972, p. 59.

Secularism echoed much in Mustafa Kemal's personal makeup. Islam would be disestablished in Turkey, and each Turk would be free to seek his own path to salvation. He would root out superstition and backwardness for the nation as he had done for himself.

Revolutionism was an attempt to institutionalize Mustafa Kemal's will to create a new Turkey free of the influence of the past. He had shown the way by fighting one battle after another and gaining one success after another, and he exhorted the Turks to adopt a life-style that would continue the pattern.

Kemalism was peculiarly Turkish and unlike any system espoused by any other contemporary world leader. What was appropriate for Turkey in that particular period of her history was not easily adoptable by any other nation, although many developing nations, especially in the East, regarded Atatürk's Turkey with awe and wished to emulate his example. Kemalism required nothing from any other nation except peaceful coexistence and was, accordingly, perfectly congruent with Atatürk's lonely psychological makeup. Thus, in the 1930s Turkey lived in what was, in a sense, self-imposed isolation from the rest of the world. Reflecting her leader's personality makeup, Turkey was overly self-centered. There were, of course, some limits to such isolation, for Turkey had to live with her neighbors and exist in the world in which such leaders as Hitler, Stalin, and Mussolini had come to power.

Atatürk wanted his country to have the "merry widow" image, in a peaceful environment which would be the reverse of the anxiety-ridden atmosphere of his childhood. In such circumstances he would be at the center of the universe as the idealized child/mother, father/lover. It took great energy to support such a self-concept. His words on a bronze plaque in the main square of downtown Ankara, offer an admonition to his countrymen that was his own guiding principle: "Turk! Be Proud! Work and Trust!"

Setting borders or limits to their activity and choosing not to be expansionist must have been frustrating to the romantic and adventurous among the new Turks. Hitler had at his disposal Germany's great natural resources and military potential, while Atatürk had inherited a nation born amidst the ruins of a once-great agricultural empire. Even had he possessed military power, it seems unlikely that Atatürk would have made much mischief on the world scene. The psychological forces that dominated him were reparative in nature, despite his failure to attain peace as an individual. Although he was a Macedonian and remained one at heart all his life, longing always for Salonika (Tesal 1975), he never spoke publicly of a desire to bring Salonika back again within Turkish borders. He wanted peace in the Balkans. As soon as the war of independence was over he behaved as though he were above feeling hostility toward the Greeks. Military success precluded any attempt to convey to a new generation of Turks the historical hurt that had been suffered at Greek hands. It is likely that most Turks were not as successful as Mustafa Kemal in forgetting the wrongs done to them. Certainly, the Greeks clung to their belief that they had been victimized.[5] Atatürk's inflated self-concept, which made him seem to rise above all injuries in general, was useful in bringing Greece and Turkey together in the post-war years. He and the Greek premier, Venizelos, understood each other. At a time when Bulgaria's desire to gain access to the Aegean Sea might have strained the "friendship" between Greece and Turkey, Venizelos traveled on a diplomatic mission to Ankara in October 1930. He received a well-orchestrated welcome. Greatly taken with Atatürk, he even proposed some kind of union between their two nations, in what was, at best, an unworkable fantasy.

Returning the Greek premier's visit, İsmet İnönü set out for Athens in early October 1931. Worried over the possibility of assassination in Greece, İsmet entrusted his children to Atatürk, who understood İsmet's anxiety and assured him that he need have no fear for his family, that he would indeed care for them.

Peace in the Balkans was seen by Atatürk as a defensive measure against the growing imperialism of Germany and Italy. Turkey's reconciliation with Greece, symbolized by the signing of a treaty of friendship and neutrality on 30 October 1930, was also directed against the rising prospect of Bulgarian aggression. That understanding was extended in 1934 to include Yugoslavia and Rumania in the Balkan Pact, which called for the signatories to hold consultations with each other if their security were threatened.

While Turkey's Balkan neighbors were primarily preoccupied with Bulgaria's pretensions, Atatürk's concern was with Mussolini, who was several years his junior and whom he disliked intensely. Two things made Atatürk uneasy—Mussolini's dream of recreating the glories of ancient Rome and the covetous glances he directed toward the Mediterranean coast of Turkey. Atatürk considered Il Duce a caricature of a soldier, a wicked man parading in uniform, and predicted that one day he would be hanged by his own people (Yücebaş 1963, p. 60).

On one occasion Atatürk was able to show his dislike for the Italian dictator in a dramatic fashion and in a way that only he could have managed. Mussolini's ambassador came to Çankaya to renew Italy's

[5]Dr. John E. Mack (1980) and Dr. Rita Rogers (1980), in personal communications, proposed the idea that historical hurts are transmitted from generation to generation and are thus kept alive to generate new situations of continued rancor. Dr. Mack uses the phrase "the egoism of victimization" (see Introduction, Volkan 1979) to describe how little empathy is felt by a national group for the suffering of a traditional enemy.

claim to the Antalya region of southern Turkey. During the ambassador's presentation Atatürk excused himself and obliged the man to wait for his return. When he did return, he was in full-dress military uniform of a field marshal, wearing it for the first time since the proclamation of the republic (Kinross 1965, p. 522). Whip in hand, he sat before the Italian ambassador, making sure that one of his military boots was in clear sight. As he encouraged the ambassador to continue talking about Mussolini's claims to Turkish soil, he deliberately whipped at his boot, which symbolically represented Italy's boot-shaped peninsula to both men. The confrontation came to an end with the message that Mussolini should curb his ambitions with respect to Turkish territory.

While Atatürk's contempt for Mussolini was quite blatant, he seems to have had less emotional response in the early 1930s to Hitler as a person. As the creator of a new Reich, the grandiose Hitler, unlike Atatürk, was destructive. After reading *Mein Kampf*, Atatürk described Hitler as a "tin peddler" and expressed horror at "the madness of his thoughts" (Kinross 1965, p. 522). Hitler's most diabolical deed, the extermination of the Jews, came after Atatürk's death. He would not have been able to comprehend such an act. Atatürk's mission was to assuage grief, not to cause it. Unlike Hitler, Atatürk was able to contain his own aggressive impulses.

Mussolini and Hitler were seen by Atatürk as destructive toy soldiers, but he viewed Stalin in a more realistic light. Incredible changes, both social and political, had been taking place in Russia, Turkey's eternal enemy, since the 1920s, and Atatürk was aware of them. His eyes, however, were turned to the West. He remained opposed to communism, despite the friendly pressure that had been brought to bear upon him since his days in Samsun. "It should be smashed whenever it is seen," he would say (Kabaklı 1973, Yücebaş 1963, p. 187.)

Changing winds in world politics had brought Turkey closer to her Balkan associates. In October 1933, King Alexander of Yugoslavia and his queen paid a visit to Istanbul. The king called upon Atatürk at Dolmabahçe Palace wearing an admiral's uniform, but was received by the Turkish leader dressed in frock coat, striped pants, and top hat (Graham 1939, p. 205). Uniforms were for fighting men, and Mustafa Kemal had long since given up his role as pasha; this helps to explain his distaste for posturers like Mussolini. He entertained his royal guests at an elaborate banquet that featured the finest French cuisine and the latest in hot jazz. He dazzled King Alexander to the point of hero worship. One of their exchanges during the visit offers a glimpse of Atatürk's ready wit. The king confided in him that had he believed the promises of territorial conquests the Allies had made to him, it would have been the Yugoslavian army rather than the Greeks who landed in Anatolia. Atatürk's response was "Geçmiş olsun!" a Turkish expression said to one who has just had a narrow escape from some disease, accident, or other disaster (Granda 1973, p. 344).

Another Balkan king, Carol II of Rumania, visited Atatürk in June 1938, in what would be the last year of Atatürk's life, and he came unexpectedly. Cruising on a yacht in the Black Sea, he had sailed down the Bosporus to anchor opposite the Dolmabahçe Palace. Atatürk was out on his own yacht at the time. When King Carol's desire to call was communicated to him, Atatürk consented to receive the king, despite being rather ill. When the king came aboard he found Atatürk impeccably dressed in a light grey suit with a silk shirt and green tie. His doctor was at his side. The two heads of state discussed European affairs over a meal. A story about that meeting reveals Atatürk's tragic condition at the time. He insisted that his royal guest be offered alcoholic drinks and argued with his doctor that as the host he should have something to drink as well, although for medical reasons such indulgence was forbidden. The doctor compromised by agreeing that his patient might have one finger of liquor. What the good doctor had in mind was an amount measured by the breadth of one finger. When the waiter poured the drink, Atatürk held his finger upright as a measure and said that he was simply following his physician's orders when he asked for a finger's *length* (Yücebaş 1963, pp. 117–18).

Adoring eyes looked upon Atatürk from countries to the east of Turkey as well. While his secularism caused frustration in the Muslim world, he offered that world a new vision. The Muslims of India had supported him during the Turkish war of independence, and later the Indian Sinha (1972) compared him favorably with Gandhi.

On 20 May 1928 the ruler of Afghanistan, Amanullah Khan, and his wife arrived in Ankara for a visit with Mustafa Kemal. They were received with unusual cordiality. That evening a great banquet was held in Amanullah's honor at the Ankara Palace Hotel. In his welcoming speech, Mustafa Kemal had recourse to one of his favorite metaphors: "The sun which is dawning on the high horizon of the future is the talisman of nations who have suffered for centuries. This talisman's never again being enveloped in dark clouds is dependent upon the scrupulous solicitude and self-sacrifice of those nations and their leaders" (Kocatürk 1973, p. 310). Remaining in Ankara for a week, Amanullah became another worshipper of that hero/sun. He would never see Atatürk again, but when he was no longer a sovereign, he attended his funeral, and witnesses saw tears in his eyes.

An Eastern visitor of greater importance arrived in 1934. He was the shah of Iran, who had sought a meeting with Atatürk. By then the new and stable Turkey had been in existence for more than a decade. Atatürk was eager to show the shah what westernization had accomplished and what benefits it had brought to Turkey. Reza Khan, the shah, had no more royal blood than his host, but, having come to power and established a dynasty, he wanted to embark upon a reform process in his own land. A hot-tempered colonel in the Persian Cossack Brigade who had risen from the ranks, Reza had led a coup against the government in 1921, become prime minister in 1923, and two years later forced the Iranian parliament to dissolve the reigning Qajar dynasty in his favor. As shah he took the dynastic family name of Pahlevi. His son, Mohammed Reza Pahlevi, would later attempt to westernize Iran more thoroughly, but would be overthrown by the Ayatollah Ruhollah Khomeini, a Muslim fundamentalist of the sort that would have thrown Atatürk into a blind rage.

Officially welcomed at the Black Sea port of Trabzon, Reza Shah was taken on board the Turkish warship, the *Yavuz*, one of the two ships Enver had acquired from the Germans and sent to the Black Sea to bombard Russian ports, thus bringing the Ottoman Empire into World War I. From Trabzon the *Yavuz* steamed to Samsun. There the shah disembarked just where Mustafa Kemal had set foot on that fateful, misty morning of 19 May 1919. Reza Shah's arrival was marked by an official welcome, and beautiful Turkish rugs were spread on the ground. In Ankara, Atatürk greeted him as "My Brother" (Kinross 1965, p. 524). The Turks had constructed a special bed for the shah, who was unusually tall, and two weeks of hectic travel and sight-seeing were scheduled.

Fully aware that he was a model for the shah, Atatürk took great pains to dazzle his guest with the results of westernization in Turkey. Atatürk had never forgotten the impression made on him as a young man when he saw King Ferdinand of Bulgaria preside over a glittering reception and masked ball and on another occasion appear at the opera house in lavish style. He determined to show the shah that Turkey, too, had opera in all its splendor.

Much of what we know about the presentation of the opera, composed especially for this occasion, comes from Mrs. Kıymet Tesal's vivid memories of those days (Tesal 1975). Atatürk was the guiding genius behind that first Turkish operatic production, offering determination and his ability to organize the talents of others to compensate for his ignorance of that musical art. The opera *Özsoy* was developed around the theme that Iranians and Turks were cultural brothers separated only by sectarian differences, the Iranians being Shi'ites and the Turks Sunnis. A young Turkish musician, Ahmed Adnan Saygun, just returned from Paris, was commissioned to compose the music. Composition, casting, direction, and production had all to be accomplished in twenty days. The orchestra was rather poor and lacked an adequate number of musicians.

Music teachers and high school students with musical talent were pressed into service. Rehearsals took place in Ankara's People's House. Mrs. Tesal, then in her mid-teens, was chosen to lead the girls' chorus. She remembers that Atatürk appeared at the People's House almost daily and that he was involved in every aspect of the production. Infatuated with the composer, Ahmed Adnan Saygun, Kıymet felt that he would be a much better conductor than the one chosen, who was more administrator than musician. Forgetting her shyness, she approached Atatürk with her suggestion. Although he protested at first, he promised to think about the matter. At the table that night he brought up the proposal Nuri's daughter had made. Finally, after consultation with the two men on the following day, he gave Ahmed Adnan Saygun the honor of conducting the first Turkish opera before the visiting Eastern potentate. This young man, who never forgot his gratitude toward Kıymet, became in time one of Turkey's foremost composers.

From Ankara Atatürk took the shah to see other parts of the country and to observe the Turkish army on maneuvers. In Istanbul, Atatürk ordered a gala Eastern Night featuring belly dancers, some naked, and the event no doubt rivaled the Arabian Nights. Reza Shah tried to emulate Atatürk's success in a number of areas, most especially in secularization. He took many ideas on westernization back to Iran, but his results were far less impressive than those of his mentor.[6]

Other Near Eastern leaders visited, including King Faisal of Iraq and Emir Abdullah of Jordan. As the uncertainty in world affairs deepened, collective security seemed one means of ensuring a nation's survival. In July 1937, the Saadabad Pact was entered into by Turkey, Iraq, Iran, and Afghanistan, establishing an Eastern Entente that balanced the Balkan understandings of 1934. The pact called for nonaggression, consultation among the signatory states in case of a threat, and cooperation in stopping subversive activity. Turkey was now the stable link between East and West as the pivotal member of both the Balkan and Eastern agreements. Atatürk was achieving results from yet another "mending" process.

Psychological factors were also at work in the ultimate settlement of the Hatay problem. Hatay was the Turkish name of the province of Alexandretta, which had been placed under a special administrative regime by an agreement with France in 1921. Alexandretta's population was at least 40 percent Turkish, and the Turkish government in Ankara hoped to recover full sovereignty over the province. In September 1938,

[6]Reza Shah was impressed with Atatürk's opera, and after he returned to Iran, he ordered the building of an opera hall. Later, when he abdicated his throne in favor of his son, the opera house still stood, but it had never been used up until that time; Ramazani 1981.

the French, as the mandate power, reached an agreement with Syria that promised independence and included Alexandretta within Syria. Turkey protested, and unrest in the province escalated.

The Hatay had personal significance for Atatürk. It was there that he had stood with his men facing the enemy until the Turks evacuated the area. Perceiving the Turks who lived in the disputed province as grieving persons, Atatürk took action. Using his influence with the French ambassador at social gatherings and flexing his muscle by sending Turkish troops on military maneuvers near the Hatay border, he applied pressure on France. The French sent a military mission to Ankara for discussions that resulted in an agreement on 3 July 1938, calling for a French-Turkish condominium in the province. A general election was to be held to determine the final disposition of the case. Turkish troops entered the province, and in September an election produced a Turkish majority in the assembly, which, on 2 September 1938, declared the province autonomous under the name of the Republic of Hatay. A delegation was then sent to Ankara to seek union with Turkey. When that step was taken, on 30 June 1939, Atatürk was already dead, but his actions, based in part on his personality makeup, had laid the groundwork for the incorporation of the Hatay within the borders he had established as legitimate.

Two visitors to Turkey in the 1930s merit special mention, King Edward VIII and General Douglas MacArthur. In the summer of 1936, Edward VIII decided to spend some time outside of England in relaxation. At the same time his connection with Wallis Simpson was being gossiped about openly, and he wanted to get away for awhile with her and some close friends. He chartered the beautiful yacht *Nahlin* in order to cruise along the Dalmatian coast. The cruise was planned as a holiday, but the Foreign Office was concerned about the king's activities, and the holiday soon took on a semiofficial character. On the way out to the coast, Edward VIII met with King George II of Greece on an island in the Mediterranean where the Greek king was summering. George II had only recently returned to his throne after more than a decade in exile which he spent at Brown's Hotel in London, one of the more discreet and fashionable hotels in the British capital. Edward VIII asked him how he was getting on. George replied that he was not getting on at all well, was having a difficult time with his prime minister, and might just as well be back at Brown's Hotel (The Duke of Windsor 1951, p. 310). After honoring the British dead who had fallen in the battles for the Dardanelles, Edward VIII sailed on to Istanbul. There on 4 September he was met by Atatürk. The Turkish leader was on his best behavior. When the small craft that brought the king ashore swayed at the dock, causing Edward to touch the ground to keep his balance, Atatürk quipped, as Edward tried to clean his hands before greeting him, "Do not worry,

Your Majesty. My country's soil is clean. It will not dirty your hands" (Granda 1973, p. 362; Yücebaş 1963, p. 31). Such a remark surely seems to echo his concern with the purification of the Turkish nation. Years earlier, for example, he had spoken of himself as a surging wave that would cleanse the shores of Byzantium.

Edward VIII spent three days in Istanbul and had several meetings with Atatürk. One of them took place at dinner at the Dolmabahçe Palace. During the meal one of the Turkish waiters dropped a plate with a crash. Atatürk excused the incident, saying, "I have taught the people of this nation to do most things, but I have been unable to teach them to be servants, or to wait on other people!" (Granda 1973, p. 363). His mind was constantly preoccupied with the defense of pure Turkish excellence. On the following day the *Ertuğrul*, Atatürk's yacht, was anchored alongside the *Nahlin*, and the two men and their parties watched a sailboat race organized to honor the king, who was a sailing enthusiast. Later, the king and Mrs. Simpson went aboard the *Ertuğrul* to take Turkish coffee with Atatürk. Observing how enslaved Edward was by Mrs. Simpson, Atatürk is reported to have confided to friends that he felt Edward would lose his throne because of his devotion to her (Yücebaş 1963, pp. 97–98).

At the conclusion of the stay in Istanbul the British party was scheduled to return through Europe by land. Atatürk put his own presidential train at Edward VIII's disposal, and on 6 September he left for Vienna. In his memoirs, Edward VIII remarks that Atatürk's eyes "were the most piercing I have ever looked into." He also notes in an ironic tone that as Atatürk spoke to him of his reforms, "the melancholy echo of George of Greece bemoaning his fate provided a counterpoint in my mind to a theme on the realities and illusions of power in the modern world" (The Duke of Windsor 1951, p 310).

General Douglas MacArthur was chief of staff of the United States Army in 1932. In that capacity he traveled to many countries to observe military maneuvers and to meet with foreign leaders. He arrived in Istanbul by ship from Constanza, Rumania, on 25 September. He held several discussions with his host on world affairs two days later. The nature of their conversations, including Mustafa Kemal's uncanny perception of the shape of the future, was not made public until August 1951, when it was reported that he had told the general:

> The Versailles treaty has not removed a single one of the reasons which caused the First World War. On the contrary, it has deepened the chasm between the main rivals of yesterday. The victors, steeped in hostile feelings, dictated to the vanquished conditions of peace without taking into account either the ethnical, geopolitical, or economical peculiarities of the defeated countries. Hence the peace we have today is better

> described as an armistice. If you, American gentlemen, had not withdrawn from European affairs and had insisted on the execution of Wilson's programme, we could today have had a lasting peace.
>
> It seems to me that the future of Europe depends today, as it did yesterday, on the situation of Germany. [*The Caucasus*, no. 1 (August 1951) p. 16]

He further predicted that 70 million Germans, whom he considered "extremely dynamic," would prepare an army capable of conquering all of Europe except for Britain and Russia and that the war would likely be fought between 1940 and 1945. France's defeat in such a war was also predicted by Atatürk. He told MacArthur that Mussolini was pretending to be a Caesar, and therefore Italy could not play a role in any peaceful solutions. "The European problem," he said, "has long passed the stage when it was caused by differences between England, France, and Germany," and he spoke of Russia as "a new power which threatens civilization, and even the whole of mankind." MacArthur was warned that the Russians were using their material and psychological strength for world revolution and that they were utilizing political methods unfamiliar to Americans and Europeans. Warming to his topic, Atatürk continued:

> In the war, which will break out in Europe, the first victor will not be either England, France, or Germany, but bolshevik Russia. As close neighbours to Russia and as a nation which has fought Russia oftenest, we Turks are better placed to watch the events occurring in that country, and see the danger which it is preparing in all its nakedness. The bolsheviks, who are exploiting the feelings of the awakening peoples of the East and are conniving in their national passions and feelings and who know how to excite their hatred, have become a power, which threatens not only Europe, but also Asia. [*The Caucasus*, no. 1 (August 1951) p. 16]

Atatürk was capable of thinking in uncanny ways, but in the 1930s there was no mighty Ottoman Empire to manipulate the balance of power in world affairs. He was the leader of a new Turkey, which was like a tender plant. He nurtured his new nation as tenderly as he cared for the real trees and flowers on his farm. The world around him interested him less and less. In his last years the new Turkey came to be symbolized for him in the person of a little girl named Ülkü. Hers was one of the new Turkish names he had created. Ülkü means a grand wish to which one aspires, and Ülkücü means idealist, someone who wants to create something better.

As Atatürk's health began to fail, he preferred Ülkü's company to that of kings or shahs. As a flesh and blood symbol of his creation, she was the center of his world. He took such pleasure in her presence, in letting her pull his hair, sit on his lap, and play with his watch chain, that it appeared he could approach real happiness only with her. At times he would dress her up as a tiny Carmen (recalling the first opera he had seen when he was in Sofia), and she would dance for him and any guests he might have (Aydemir 1974).

Ülkü was the daughter of a woman named Vasfiye, who had been a member of Zübeyde's household as a maid. She had taken care of Atatürk's mother on her journey to Istanbul, then in Istanbul, and later in Ankara. At the time of Zübeyde's death, Atatürk's sister "inherited" her. One day the woman left without any word to Makbule, got married, and disappeared. Her whereabouts were unknown until she appeared at Dolmabahçe one day in 1930 and told Mustafa Kemal's aides of her unhappy life (Granda 1973, p. 317). The man she had married already had one wife, and she had to share him with another woman. When Mustafa Kemal heard that she had returned, he had her taken in as a maid on the staff of the presidential palace. Thus, she worked for Atatürk and became part of the mixed team that gave him a body massage each day after he had awakened and bathed. Soon, she married the man who managed the railroad station on Atatürk's farm. When Atatürk learned that she had given birth to a daughter, he ordered that the child be named Ülkü, although he had not yet seen her. When he did see her for the first time—she was two months old—he was completely taken with her. The man and the child soon developed a special relationship. On one of his visits to Istanbul when Ülkü was about a year and a half old, he asked that she be brought to him. From then on he began to take her everywhere with him. In the past he had adopted adolescent girls and had shown no interest at all in very small children, but Ülkü swiftly became the center of his emotional investment, as well as the most popular and widely known child in all of Turkey.

Ülkü was not particularly pretty. Her face was rather large and round, with prominent cheekbones, and her coal black hair was cut short in a Buster Brown bob. Previously, only Ayla, Afet's younger sister, had seemed to fill the role of a young daughter, but toward the end of his life he took Ülkü as a child of his own. "Children are our extension into the future," he would say (Granda 1973, p. 317). He talked about how to raise children and about how he was molding Ülkü into a modern Turkish woman with his own hands. His system of raising her was one of extreme permissiveness. Through her mother, Ülkü was connected with his own mother. He created a home for her in which she could have such pleasure and so many gratifications that it contrasted sharply with the one in which his mother had failed him because of her grief.

Motion pictures taken of Ülkü and Atatürk in 1937 show him an aging man with a paunch, doting over the little girl as any parent might.[7] In 1937 the film was shown to President Franklin D. Roosevelt, who wrote a letter to Atatürk telling him that he had seen the movie and that he was especially pleased to see him playing with Ülkü. Roosevelt also remarked how impressed he was with the changes Atatürk had wrought in his nation and expressed a wish that one day they might meet. Apparently Atatürk was sending Roosevelt Turkish postage stamps for his famous collection, and Roosevelt thanked him for that as well (Borak 1970, p. 184).

In a reply, Atatürk wrote, "I would like to take this opportunity to express my admiration for the United States of America. Our two countries have the same ideals for general peace and the happiness of humanity" (Borak 1970, p. 184). He added that he, too, would welcome a meeting and looked forward to being able to greet Roosevelt in Turkey. The two men never got the opportunity to satisfy their wish, and when Atatürk died, Roosevelt expressed his sorrow on two counts: a great man was lost to the world and now his wish to meet him would not be fulfilled (Borak 1970, p. 185).

Ülkü was bereft of more than a protector with Atatürk's death. Unfortunately, his child-rearing practices seem to have had unfavorable psychological consequences. She was only five when he died, but she was to pay the price later for having been his indulged favorite, the symbol of his great passion for freedom and westernization. He left her a monthly allowance, just as he did his other "daughters." She grew up to marry a lieutenant who later became a senator in the Grand National Assembly. She was unhappy in the marriage, however, and divorced the man to marry a Jew. That marriage received bad publicity in the Turkish press. She tried a third marriage, this time to a farmer (Granda 1973, p. 323). It is not unlikely that in her marriages Ülkü was in search of her "creator," the man who had been a soldier, transformer of an Islamic empire into a secular state, and husbandman of the soil of his land.

[7]The motion pictures were taken by Julian Bryan. They are part of a film about Turkey for foreign service officers and their spouses about to take up posts in that country.

29
The Last Battle

FOLLOWERS OF ANY CHARISMATIC, NARCISSISTIC LEADER MAY BE SO enthralled by his presence that they dismiss any untoward act he performs as irrelevant or perceive it as not connected with him at all. Similarly, they are blind to any physical impairment the leader may have, as though he were beyond any illness or suffering experienced by the rest of mankind. It may be that Atatürk infected others with his own belief in his immortality, or they may simply have conceived of him as being incapable of falling ill or dying, but in fact his health was so poor that he needed a personal physician to supervise his life from the day he stepped ashore at Samsun on 19 May 1919.[1]

When Atatürk began the struggle for independence, he suffered periodically from kidney trouble and was subject to attacks of malaria. There is also the possibility of hypochondriacal attacks during his depressive moods. It seems likely that the "cardiac difficulty" he experienced in 1924 while he was still married to Lâtife was not genuine. It may have been simply a spasm of the coronary arteries, although there is a report of cardiac symptoms appearing (reappearing?) in 1927 (Arar 1958, pp. 19–20; Atay 1980, p. 484). It seems likely, however, that he reached his mid-fifties without any serious heart trouble.

From 1919 to 1923 he was attended by Dr. Refik (Saydam), who became the minister of health in the republic. After 1923 his principal doctor was Neşet Ömer İrdelp. He was assisted by several others, one of whom was assigned to the presidential palace at Çankaya to supervise the health of all who worked there.

Atatürk's death on 10 November 1938 was due to cirrhosis of the liver. Interviews with some who knew him well in his later years convey the impression that liver problems had appeared as early as 1936, but his physical symptoms and his emotional state were so interdependent that one cannot be certain whether he was physically ill at any particular stage or merely depressed, sulky, and suspicious. In any event, he had that demonstrated capacity to shake off any physical or emotional vapor and to come to center stage, roaring like a lion, denying any impairment.

[1]When Mustafa Kemal landed, he was not feeling well. He required a hot bath every five or six hours in order to feel comfortable, more than likely for his recurrent kidney ailment; Atay 1980, p. 483.

One psychological blow that thoroughly upset his equilibrium and could not be shaken off was Nuri's death. That event, condensed with Zehra's suicide, which may in turn, have reactivated Atatürk's response to Fikriye's self-destruction years earlier, were psychological toxins that affected his behavior. Dr. İrdelp had not been able to save Nuri, and his was one death Atatürk could not ignore. Nuri had stood by him from childhood, at Gallipoli, on the Russian front, and, most important, during his presidency. Nuri was one of his "twins," but with a critical difference. Atatürk had discarded several "twins" when they no longer served their purpose, but he was both unmotivated and unable to do this with Nuri, whose very mission in life seemed to be to bind Atatürk's wounds. He was made of sterner stuff than the other "twins" who had come and gone. He could absorb the raillery, the aggression, and the cynicism and still continue to adore Atatürk. While they were drinking together, Mustafa Kemal once suggested half in jest to Nuri that they were indeed half-brothers. He pointed to the fact that the man known as Nuri's father had often visited Zübeyde (Aydemir 1974). Whether the story is true or not, it underlines how close Atatürk felt they were.

Nuri's death on 10 January 1937 was a crucial event, for it removed the cornerstone of the support for Atatürk's cohesive self. Because Nuri was in fact an extension of Atatürk, his death resulted in Atatürk's loss of self-esteem—as though part of him had died. A less-than-cohesive self is more vulnerable to external dangers, real or fancied. Once more Atatürk grew suspicious and subject to depressive moods because of his lowered self-esteem.[2] In addition, Atatürk was growing old, and aging brings with it many losses, such as the diminution of physical attractiveness and the reduction of sexual prowess that further attack self-esteem. Many people can tolerate this process by turning to other satisfactions—parenthood, inner respect, and the like—but it is terrifying for the person with a grandiose self to have to watch the approach of old age. The narcissistic individual depends on his beauty, creativity, and the adoration of others. To be threatened by their loss is to stare death in the face. Nuri had been the chief adoring acolyte; now he was dead.

While his people continued to perceive Atatürk in his last years as a vital, even virile individual, in reality his sexual prowess was impaired by age and heavy drinking. It is said that although he continued to prowl after women, his encounters with those who consented to be alone with him were more often no more than a ceremony in which he bathed them

[2]Falih Rıfkı Atay (1980, p. 487) recalled his perception of changes in Atatürk's psychological condition: "Especially after 1937 we could see that he had difficulty regarding his nervous balance. He had become very touchy. We felt that he had difficulty controlling his nervous tension which needed to be discharged constantly. Especially at the later part of his dining room activities we began to behave carefully."

and then fell asleep. The women would be left to find their own way out of the palace, sometimes with the help of the staff. A connection may be seen between this bathing ritual and his passion for "cleansing" the country/women of "badness."

One perceptive person interviewed by Dr. Volkan considered Atatürk's heavier drinking in his final years a sign of suicidal intent. On one level he may have contemplated meeting death bravely inasmuch as he was proudly immortal in the eyes of his adoring people. The losses of his later years did not, however, lead to a total surrender to death, and he continued to manipulate those in his environment just as he had always done, for the sake of feeling superior. Nuri's death changed the pieces on the chessboard of his life, and he forged new relationships to replace the old. His investment in Ülkü was intensified. In turn, she gave him the adoration one would expect from any child whose every wish was being gratified. İsmet İnönü, ever the realist, was perceived now by Atatürk as a threat, one that had to be put at a distance after so many years of close association. There was another complication in their relationship that had some effect on events. It is known that Atatürk had a number of romantic liaisons after Afet's departure for Geneva. One of his amours was a mistress of İsmet's brother. That connection may have contaminated İsmet in Atatürk's mind, making him a member of the "competition." There were other reasons, some politically realistic, for the replacement of İsmet as prime minister. He was being increasingly criticized for his failure to set the nation's economy on a solid footing more rapidly.

Moreover, Atatürk felt that he was being left out of government affairs, while his long-term, thoroughly entrenched prime minister had tight reins on the government and spoke of "my budget," and "my government," and the like. Prior to 1937 Atatürk had always expressed contentment in having İsmet head the government, but now he began to resent his primacy. In an unguarded moment he confessed to his secretary-general how bored he was. "I am living here like a prisoner," he is reported to have said. "During the daytime I am almost always alone. Everyone else is at work. Everyone has his job, but most days I have nothing to keep me occupied for even an hour. Oh, I can fall asleep. I can sleep. If I don't do that, I can read, or write something." Speaking of the evening gatherings, he sighed, "I wish there were some variety there, but where is my luck? I keep seeing the same old people—the same faces—and I hear the same words over and over. I am bored—bored! Well, never mind. What kind of news do you have?" (Selek 1974–75). He was quick to conceal his lamentations, but he felt that İsmet had something precious that he himself lacked. İsmet was the top man, and Atatürk wanted to be the top man once again.

The final straw that led to Atatürk's falling out with İsmet was a trivial thing, but this triviality represented a significant inner drama. Atatürk had a heavy emotional investment in his farm. The farm was not operating at a sufficient profit, although it also included a brewery. Atatürk put pressure on İsmet to get the government to underwrite some of the farm's expenses. İsmet's counterproposal was that Atatürk give the farm to the nation as a gift. In the long run he did just that, but initially the suggestion was not palatable to him. When he did present the farm to the nation, Atatürk received a telegram from İsmet thanking him for his generosity, pointing to its future use as a model for the peasantry as well as a symbol for agriculture. Atatürk replied, "You will remember that I have always said that the Turkish peasant is Turkey's master. I rejoice in serving the Turkish peasant in this small way." He could not deny his narcissistic personality the last word and added, "This gift is valueless in comparison with my real gift to the Turkish nation—that of my life—should that become necessary" (Selek 1974–75).

The farm issue continued to be a sore point between Atatürk and İsmet, and it became entangled with their differences on international affairs. During the Spanish civil war, after the breakdown of the naval blockade instituted to protect ships bringing noncontraband goods to Spain, submarines began to attack ships from any nation destined for Loyalist ports. A conference was convened at Nyon, Switzerland, by France and England in September 1937 to discuss these attacks, which were being branded as acts of piracy (Black and Helmreich 1959, p. 505). Turkey was represented at the conference by her foreign minister, Tevfik Rüştü Aras. He informed both Atatürk and İsmet of developments at the conference, and the two disagreed on the course that Turkey should follow.

At the time, Atatürk was in Istanbul, where he had just received a distinguished visiting French intellectual at his seaside resort in Florya. On 16 September he left for Ankara. As the train approached Ankara the following day, İsmet joined him. While passing the farm on the way into the city, their differences about it came to the surface to add to their lack of agreement on the Nyon conference (Atay 1980, p. 495; Selek 1974–75).

At Nyon a decision had been made to authorize an Anglo-French naval patrol to attack any submarine, surface vessel, or aircraft that attacked any non-Spanish vessel. On the next evening a meeting of ministers was held to prepare the government's position on this decision to be voted on the next day by the Grand National Assembly. (Turkey would endorse the decision.) Atatürk and İsmet exchanged harsh words in front of the ministers. İsmet would later explain that although he and Atatürk had had many disagreements in the past about government policy, it was especially upsetting on that occasion because he had been attacked in the presence of the cabinet (Selek 1974–75).

Those who attended that meeting have recalled a number of details, some of which might have constituted an injury to a narcissistic person. For example, Atatürk's farm came under discussion once again. It was said to be run down and dirty; one of the swimming pools was polluted. Atatürk viewed such talk as a personal attack upon himself. He became enraged when İsmet promised to assign new people to manage the farm who would also clean it up. Apparently, the staff of the farm had been handpicked by Atatürk. İsmet is reported to have told Atatürk at one point in the discussion, "I understand that when the Shah of Iran is angry he spanks his minister. Do you want to be like that?" (Selek 1974–75).

Following the favorable vote for the Nyon decision in the Grand National Assembly, Atatürk returned by train to Istanbul to attend the opening of the Second Congress of the Turkish Historical Society on 20 September. He arranged to have a private conversation with İsmet on the train. Atatürk asked, "What are you going to do?" and İsmet replied, "Whatever you think best."[3] They decided that İsmet should resign as prime minister, but first, in order to keep up appearances, he would step down temporarily for a month and a half for reasons of health. Atatürk suggested Celâl Bayar as acting prime minister. On 20 October the announcement was made, and on 25 October, İsmet resigned fully.

After their falling out in September, the two men did not meet again until 6 November, although they must have had glimpses of each other at the military maneuvers held along the Aegean coast in early October. Celâl Bayar, who became prime minister in his own right after İsmet's resignation, was present at their November meeting, which took place at Çankaya. İsmet is said to have angered Atatürk greatly by speaking of a government crisis that the new prime minister had handled skillfully. "The government is in my hands, my hands," Atatürk objected (Selek 1974–75). The two men did not meet again for several weeks, and then they had infrequent confrontations until the time of Atatürk's death, the last in April 1938. Atatürk found it difficult to depend on Celâl Bayar, for he had been accustomed for so long to place absolute trust in İsmet, and Celâl Bayar's views on economics differed from İsmet's. Atatürk was sarcastic toward his former prime minister at their meeting, but they managed to stay on fairly friendly terms. From some of the comments Atatürk made to friends, it appears that he missed having his old comrade at the head of the government.

[3]Selek 1974–75. Atay (1980, p. 497) states that he was with Atatürk on the train that day. Atatürk, according to Atay, told İsmet, "Our working relationship is ended. But our friendship will continue," whereupon İnönü covered his face with both his hands. Atatürk told him, "You should rest!"

One of the most important moves in the chess game that Atatürk was playing in the organization of his immediate world was the reestablishment of Ali Fuat Cebesoy in a position of significance. In spite of all that had taken place, Ali Fuat had remained loyal in his heart to Atatürk. He had an easygoing nature and soon began to appear in public with Atatürk and to accompany him on his travels. Refet, and even Rauf, both of whom had once been "good" objects but had then been discarded as "bad," were reinstated in Atatürk's regard after Nuri's death tipped the balance of his support system. As a gesture of friendship, Atatürk even invited Kâzım Karabekir to the meeting of the Turkish Historical Society in Istanbul. That attempt at reconciliation was abortive, for Kâzım did not attend the meeting. The two men did meet later, but whether by accident or design is unclear.

By 1937 Atatürk and those around him must have found it difficult to deny the physical changes he was undergoing. He was feeling increasingly tired and weak. He was pale, had headaches and fever, and was irritable. His manly physique had given way to one with a pronounced paunch. Falih Rıfkı Atay recalls an incident that occurred one evening at Atatürk's table during that period. When Falih Rıfkı left the gathering for a few minutes to smoke his pipe in an adjoining room, he was summoned back by Atatürk, who was in a fury at his departure. Falih Rıfkı noticed how jaundiced Atatürk looked and realized that he had become afraid of having others leave him (Atay 1980, p. 487). No one really dared to tell the great man that he was ill. The yellowness of his skin might, after all, be attributable to the darkening of his face in anger.

Other symptoms of illness began to appear. At a time when he insisted on closely following the activities of Hitler, continuing his obsession with Turkish history and language, and giving great thought to the Hatay problem, Atatürk became tormented by itching. His physician prescribed various ointments for him to put on his legs, which were cross-hatched with fingernail marks. In the fall of 1937 his secretary wrote to the ministry of health, complaining of a plague of ants in the Çankaya palace. Atatürk's itchiness was being blamed on the ants (Aydemir 1969, vol. 3, p. 549). Indeed, there were ants in the palace, and they were found to be of a variety that had recently migrated to Europe from China. Extermination experts were summoned. Atatürk left the palace while the exterminators did their work, but that did not put an end to his itching. He looked ill and began to have nosebleeds that were difficult to stanch and required frequent packing with cotton.

Given these individual symptoms, it is difficult to understand why no serious diagnostic workup was attempted. Presumably, he was given some medication, but nothing was done about the cause of his symptoms. No doubt he was denying his condition, as were those around him. He could rationalize that if he were known to be ill, the news would jeopardize his efforts to resolve the Hatay issue by incorporating the province into Turkey. It would also influence other political problems as well. The official record of his activities between 1 and 16 September in Istanbul indicates from his habits that he was sad and lonely there. He slept every day until three in the afternoon. Around 5:30 or 6:00 he would take a boat to the Princes' Islands in the Sea of Marmara just off Istanbul, where he would spend some time in a casino, returning to Dolmabahçe Palace around two or three in the morning, sometimes as late as five o'clock, to go to bed. When he left Istanbul on 16 September 1937 for Ankara, it seems to have been in an effort to improve his world, now so disturbed by his illness. He succeeded only in effecting a break with İsmet. Upon his return to Istanbul for the opening of the Second Congress of the Turkish Historical Society, he was too weak to walk the 150 meters between his private quarters in Dolmabahçe and the hall in which the meeting was being held. With the worsening of his condition, an elevator was installed in Dolmabahçe to enable him to go from floor to floor. The presidential palace at Çankaya already had one.

His illness was finally diagnosed in January 1938 at the Yalova hot springs near Bursa. The spa was under the direction of Dr. Nihat Reşat Belger, who had been active at one time in the Young Turk movement. Atatürk had asked Dr. Belger to examine him. He was told that his liver was enlarged and dysfunctional and that this accounted for his symptoms. Atatürk took the news calmly and asked, "What do we do now?" (Ünaydın 1957, p. 11). His personal physician was called from Ankara and permitted to make a searching examination. The two physicians agreed on the diagnosis. It is a pity that cirrhosis was not diagnosed at least within the year after the first symptoms appeared, for had this been done he might have lived several years longer with proper management. This fatal oversight indicates something of the peculiar interaction that prevails between a powerful, charismatic, narcissistic leader and his followers.

Falih Rıfkı Atay has described the scene at Çankaya on the evening the diagnosis was confirmed and the denial of Atatürk's illness overcome:

> Atatürk, pale and jaundiced, was presiding at the table. . . . The evening went on silent and joyless. . . . He was calm in an exhausted way, as the sea is calm after a storm.
>
> His lips moved with difficulty. Mirth was overtaken by the season of falling leaves. The sweet and warming smile of his thin lips had disappeared like a fading fragrance.[4]

[4]Falih Rıfkı Atay was invited along with his wife to Atatürk's dining table that evening, the last such occasion to be held at Çankaya. He noted that only a handful of people were present that night; Atay 1980, p. 489.

Before long, however, denial prevailed again, after a rest ordered by his doctors. He appeared at the head of the huge presidential table at the Çelik Palace Hotel in Bursa. He and his party went on to a ball, where, despite mild protests, he ordered the orchestra leader to play the music of the region's folk dance, the energetic *zeybek*. In this dance the dancers go around and around, arms raised, kneeling down to the floor on one knee from time to time. And there was Atatürk, prancing through this strenuous dance like a young warrior. It was to be his last ball. The next day he fell ill with pneumonia (Aydemir 1969, vol. 3, p. 534). *Intellectually*, he knew that he would soon die. He had looked up cirrhosis in a French dictionary.

Ordinary Turks were spared knowledge of this drama. They still saw their hero as a god. On 16 March 1938, Atatürk was examined again, this time in the presence of İsmet. A report on his condition was prepared and signed. He asked that it be read to him aloud. One of its recommendations was the prohibition of alcohol. Celâl Bayar then consulted appropriate people to learn the name of the best medical authority in Europe to treat Atatürk. He was given the name of a French physician, Dr. Fissinger, whom Atatürk finally consented to have summoned to Turkey. After examining his patient at Çankaya in March 1938, Dr. Fissinger told him, "You have been through great battles, and you have won them. But now I am the commander-in-chief, and you will obey me. You will help me."[5] Atatürk approved of this approach. No Turkish physician would have dared to speak to him in such a fashion, and he followed the orders of this firm old man. When Celâl Bayar spoke privately with Dr. Fissinger, asking for his candid opinion, the physician was optimistic, estimating that with proper care Atatürk could live for seven years. Bayar was greatly relieved.

Dr. Fissinger had not reckoned with the "grieving mother" in the form of the Hatay that had to be saved. In the summer of 1938 Atatürk headed south. In a number of cities near the Hatay he stood up in the intense heat of the summer day to observe several military parades. He was so weak he could hardly stand. Salih and Kılıç Ali were by his side and tried to help by suggesting that he lean on them but he refused. It was imperative that he give the appearance of strength in order to influence the French on the Hatay issue.

After his tour of the south Atatürk went to Istanbul by way of Ankara and settled in on his yacht, the *Savarona*. It was his new toy, but he could enjoy it only listlessly, as a sick child enjoys his favorite plaything. The yacht was originally built for an American millionairess. Hitler put a bid

[5]Celâl Bayar's extensive interview with Abdi İpekçi regarding the last days of Atatürk appeared in the Turkish press; see İpekçi 1974. İpekçi was one of Turkey's leading journalists and was slain on 1 February 1979.

in for it, which he withdrew when he learned that the Turks had made an earlier bid. Now, over a year after the commencement of negotiations, the yacht was Atatürk's, but he feared that it would become his grave.

His mind continued to function well, and he continued to demonstrate his usual concern about his inner circle. He sent Dr. Fissinger to examine İsmet, who was a diabetic. The Frenchman counseled against an operation that had been suggested for the former prime minister. Conditions in Ankara were relayed to Atatürk by Celâl Bayar, who left Ankara each Thursday for Istanbul to be with the ailing president, returning to the capital on Mondays. He remembers that Atatürk was irritable and nervous during this depressing time of his life but also that he managed to focus on political matters with his old brilliance. Atatürk came to believe that the Maginot Line would not stop Hitler,[6] and he told Bayar that if Hitler were successful, he would prevent any attempt at industrialization on the part of any underdeveloped country such as Turkey (İpekçi 1974).

On 14 June, Atatürk wrote to Afet, who was in Geneva. In his letter he blamed his doctors: "I am of the opinion that because of the doctors' mistakes and erroneous decisions, the illness [he refrains from saying "*my* illness"] has not stopped, it has progressed. . . . The government, with my consent, brought Fissinger here. Once more we[7] were investigated and went through a physical examination" (Borak 1970, pp. 78–79). As though he were the physician writing an objective report, he described to her the physical findings. One can see the affective denial of his illness by his cold treatment of his illness in this letter. Such denial served a purpose, perhaps helping him cope with potential anxiety while allowing him to maintain intellectual oversight of Turkey's affairs. "They found the liver not changed from its previous condition, the abdomen filled with a few kilos of liquid and gas, and therefore, swollen and disfigured" (Borak 1970, p. 79). Again, speaking as though someone else was the patient, he indicated the orders given—lying on a couch and absolute rest. Then, he tried to comfort Afet, writing "My general condition is good. The hope and promise of my returning to health is strong. You must not worry. I wish you success in your examinations, which you must go through calmly, and I kiss your eyes" (Borak 1970, p. 79). He closed by saying that the *Savarona* was anchored directly in front

[6]The Maginot Line, named for its principal creator, André Maginot, was a line of fortifications in northeast France designed to prevent a German attack. The line was a series of strong points connected by rail and protected by heavy concrete. It gave the French a false sense of security and contributed to French complacency in the face of Germany's renewed militarism. With the blitzkrieg and a flanking movement through Belgium, the Germans rendered the line worthless.

[7]Atatürk used the phrase *muayene yapıldık*, "we were examined," instead of *muayene yapıldım*, "I was examined."

of Dolmabahçe and that he continued to receive the prime minister and other ministers on the yacht itself.

Afet might be far away but close at hand were Sabiha and Ülkü. In May, Atatürk was visited by some Ankara delegates of a number of Balkan nations. He asked Sabiha to wear her air force uniform for the occasion. His real reason for this request was that he wanted Ülkü to see her in uniform. Ms. Gökçen told Dr. Volkan that she had been scheduled to tour the Balkans in a new type of American bomber. She did not want to leave Atatürk and lied to him for the first and only time, telling him she was not ready. Her instructor, an American test pilot whose name she recalled only as Jack, told Atatürk that she was prepared. Atatürk then spoke to her, telling her, "My child, I know that you don't want to go because I am ill. But you made a promise. You must go" (Gökçen 1974). It was to be a solo flight, and she departed for Athens on 16 June, returning to Istanbul from Bucharest on 21 June.

Immediately upon her return, Sabiha went to the *Savarona*. The yacht was becoming a veritable hospital, with the patient becoming more and more disturbed. Cirrhosis of the liver is a terrible illness. Difficult to classify, its etiology is sometimes clear and at other times exceedingly obscure. It is a chronic illness inasmuch as it is characterized by significant loss of liver cells, with collapse of the supporting connective tissue and subsequent scarring. The architecture of the liver becomes distorted, and its functions are impaired. Malnutrition is thought to be a contributing etiologic factor. Laennec's cirrhosis is also known to the lay public as alcoholic cirrhosis, although the role of alcohol in this disease is not clearly established. It may exert a direct toxic effect upon the liver, or it may promote malnutrition by providing calories without essential nutrients. Not only did Atatürk drink regularly, but his eating habits failed to provide him with a balanced diet. He had had the initial symptoms of the disorder for some years—weakness, low-grade fever, yellow skin, and itching. Signs of portal hypertension became evident, a result of the extensive scarring around the blood vessels of the liver. The veins of his abdomen were distended, and other varices developed, accompanied by bleeding. Spidery vascular lesions had appeared on his body. By the summer of 1938 his condition was decompensated. The abnormalities of his circulation resulted in the collection of fluid in the abdomen and in the extremities, scrotum, and penis. The sight of a person with decompensated cirrhosis is not a pleasant one. Atatürk's belly was swollen, he had marked muscular wasting, especially in the trunk, and he was developing the so-called hepatic facies—a pinched subicteric face with dilated capillaries. He complained of being unable to breathe. Blocks of ice were brought to his cabin on the yacht to cool it and make it easier for him to breathe, but the summer was even then too hot for comfort. He could barely walk. One day while he cruised on the Sea of Marmara in a motor launch, the people saw him and cheered, most not being aware of his personal suffering.

Grasping at straws for relief, Atatürk asked Kılıç Ali[8] to send for his mother's home remedies. She forwarded them, providing him with at least a symbolic touch of motherly care. Finally, everyone realized that he could no longer stay on the yacht. One night they carried him into Dolmabahçe Palace in an armchair. He had refused to use a stretcher. He was removed from the *Savarona* at night so that only those immediately involved would know of his tragic condition. Once inside the palace, he walked with bravado to his bedroom, brushing aside all offers of help (Kinross 1965, p. 563). His bedroom, with its beautifully carved walnut bed, would literally be his home for the rest of his life. In his bed he would listen to his secretary read the news of the world to him, just as years earlier he had listened to the adoring Lâtife, who acted as his "talking newspaper."

Final arrangements had to be made. A notary went to his bedside on 5 September 1938, for the signing of his will (Kılıç, 1955). He left his estate, including Çankaya, to the People's party. Five of his adopted daughters and his sister each received a specified sum of money. Sabiha was given an extra amount to buy a house in the Çankaya area close to Makbule. The remainder went to the Turkish Historical Society and the Turkish Language Society. Some money was left for the education of İsmet's children, possibly because Atatürk believed İsmet was ill or even supposed he was dead (Selek 1974–75).

His discomfort increased, and his belly was tapped to give some relief. The procedure left him looking shrunken; yet he continued to sign state papers, and he and Ali Fuat talked about politics and the future of the world. Soon, on 29 October, it would be the fifteenth anniversary of the founding of the Turkish republic, and Atatürk wanted to go to Ankara for the occasion. When Ali Fuat offered encouragement about his health, he stopped him, saying, "you're trying to soothe, and in vain. One has to see the truth exactly as it is" (Kinross 1965, p. 564). That was the last time the two men were together, for his physicians soon cut back the number of people he could see.

On 26 September, Atatürk went into a coma that lasted for forty-eight hours. He longed more and more to return to Ankara, the city he had created, but the doctors thought a train ride would be fatal. When the fifteenth anniversary arrived he was still in his bedroom in Dolmabahçe and could share in the celebration only by hearing the clamor from the

[8]Kinross 1965, p. 562. Kılıç Ali also wrote his recollections of the last days of Atatürk; see Kılıç 1955

street outside his window. On 9 November he went into a second coma, following another tap of his belly, and he remained comatose for thirty-six hours. The coma ended with his death. His last words before he lapsed into coma were, "What time is it?" (Aydemir 1969, vol. 3, p. 565). His life ended at 9:05 A.M. on November 10, 1938.

A few days earlier, Ülkü had been sent to Ankara,[9] perhaps to spare her from these final grim days. Afet, who had returned from Geneva, Sabiha, and Rukiye, who was now married, were at his deathbed. Dr. Fissinger was not there, but Dr. İrdelp and some other physicians attended.

As soon as he died the palace fell into a deep silence broken only by the report of a pistol. Salih, his faithful aide, thinking that life without Atatürk was meaningless, tried to kill himself in a nearby waiting room.[10] His attempt failed, but he died a year later.

İsmet İnönü became the second president of Turkey on 11 November. The succession had been arranged when Atatürk's condition made it necessary to plan for the immediate future without him. Fevzi Çakmak, who had been the only chief of the general staff of the Turkish republic since 1923, did not want the office, and Celâl Bayar had been persuaded to endorse İnönü's presidency. Just before he lapsed into his final coma, Atatürk had wanted İsmet at his beside, but he was told that İsmet was too ill to travel. At one point somewhat earlier Atatürk had convinced himself that İsmet had died and that the news was being kept from him because of his condition; he sent his dentist to Ankara to see İsmet and report back on his condition. İsmet's remaining in Ankara facilitated a smoother transition to the presidency.[11]

Turkey went into shock at the news of Atatürk's death.[12] It was unbe-

[9]Gökçen told Dr. Volkan this in a personal interview (1974). She had read somewhere that Ülkü had remembered being in Istanbul on the day Atatürk died. Gökçen insisted that Ülkü's recollection was not correct.

[10]At this time, Salih Bozok was a deputy to the Turkish parliament from the province of Bilecik.

[11]Why Atatürk had a fantasy that İsmet was dead is not clear. He thought that İsmet was a victim of an assassination attempt. Atatürk had fallen away from his long-term "good object," and it is possible that İsmet was now invested with Atatürk's aggressive drive, i.e., had become a "bad object." İsmet, the realist, by staying in Ankara apparently wished to ensure that there would be a smooth transition of the presidency.

[12]Professor Eberhard (1981), who was in Turkey on 10 November 1938, wrote the following in his diary: "The news of Atatürk's death is everywhere by half past noon. While it was expected, its shock is impressive. The flags are being lowered and schools are being closed. [Masses] of people are in the streets and silence is ruling the day. Everyone seems to be going home or to the monument at Taşhan. It is not only the children who are crying, also women and even men. All the stores are closed. The grief is real and genuine and nothing like it has been seen by another nation. Atatürk was really loved by the people who never saw him as a dictator."

lievable. Films and photographs taken at that time in Turkey show exhibitions of initial horrified grief expressed in blank, numb, staring faces, and uncontrollable sobbing. His body was embalmed and placed in the throne room of the Dolmabahçe Palace in an ebony coffin draped with the Turkish flag surrounded by six torches. Four officers with swords kept vigil over him for nine days and nine nights as he lay in state. Hundreds of thousands filed past the coffin with tears in their eyes and the cry of "Atam, Atam" (My father, My father) on their lips. After the nine days there was a prayer service requested by Makbule, followed by the funeral procession in which his coffin was placed on a gun carriage drawn by soldiers. An officer marched behind the coffin carrying a velvet cushion on which rested his medal of the War of Independence. The funeral procession marched to the strains of Chopin's Funeral March, and the coffin was carried through the crowds of mourners to Seraglio Point, where it was placed on board the torpedo boat *Zafer* (Victory). The coffin was then transferred to the warship *Yavuz*. As his body rested on the *Yavuz* on the afternoon of 19 November, a one hundred and one gun salute echoed across Istanbul. The British warship *Malaya*, which had carried the last Ottoman sultan into exile, returned to pass before the *Yavuz* in salute, and other foreign ships paid their respects.

Atatürk's travels were not yet over. The *Yavuz* sailed through the Sea of Marmara to the port of Izmit, where the coffin was put aboard a train for Ankara. He would at last have his wish to return to his city. Thousands of people—peasants, city dwellers, men, women, children, the young, and the aged—crowded by the tracks to bid farewell to their hero. When the coffin arrived in Ankara it was displayed in front of the Grand National Assembly building. On 21 November in a second funeral procession in which visiting dignitaries and diplomats took part, the coffin was transferred to a *temporary* grave site in the Ethnography Museum in Ankara near the People's House.

Atatürk had never liked domes on buildings. Although we do not have any evidence as to the psychological reason for his dislike, clinical experience leads us to speculate that domes probably represented religion (as on mosques) and dependency (the breast) to him, as well as his dread of dependency that stemmed from childhood conflicts. Atatürk could not even escape his mother in death, for his temporary grave in the museum was under a dome! Fifteen years later, in 1953, the coffin was finally removed from under the dome and permanently placed in a sepulchre in a special memorial complex built on a hill in Ankara.

30

The Transformation into Immortal Atatürk

After a grievous loss, such as the death of someone enormously esteemed, the bereaved must go through mourning, one phase after another, until the force of the love invested in the deceased is diminished sufficiently to allow another object to receive attention and perhaps eventually love. Initially, a loss creates in its wake shock and pain. A totally unexpected death can induce intense shock. With the passage of time, the mourner reassesses memories in piecemeal fashion, slowly withdrawing emotional investment from the representation of the deceased. It is normal for memories to persist and for the mourner to continue to identify with aspects of the dead person's personality, but without being thereby cut off from the possibility of making new emotional commitments. This entire process is called the work of mourning (Freud 1917), and its conclusion brings the resolution of grief.

When the mourner has what in psychological terms amounts to unfinished business with the deceased (Volkan 1982*a*), it becomes difficult to bring mourning to its resolution. An inordinate emotional investment in the mental representation of the dead may persist, along with an unquestioning identification with it. In such cases, passage through the serial steps of the mourning process remains incomplete.

Mourners may develop symptoms that betray a pathological incapacity to grieve. Or they may create links with the deceased, either internally or externally. Those links, when they exist in the external world in the form of an object or objects having strong connection with the deceased, are known as "linking objects" (Volkan 1972, 1982*a*). For example, the watch of the dead father becomes a linking object for the surviving son. The latter cannot use the watch in the usual way since it now becomes magical. It has to be kept in a special place and induces an eerie feeling in the son, who may develop the illusion that through the manipulation of the watch he can bring the dead father back to life or really "kill" him in a psychological sense. "Killing" would mean an end to the mourning, but meanwhile the mourner who uses a linking object stays in limbo regarding the fate of the representation of the dead. The linking object absorbs the ambivalence previously felt toward the dead person when he was alive.

As a child, Atatürk had been a *living* linking object for his mother that served to keep alive her connection with the several children she had lost prior to his birth. Perhaps he never consciously recognized his fantasies of resurrecting the dead and rescuing the grieving mother, but he might well have been aware of his creative urges. In a speech on 17 March 1937, he spoke of the pleasure of a gardener who cultivates flowers, in an obvious reference to himself, and compared such a gardener with one who likes to "cultivate men."[1] He saw himself as the creator of men, someone able to bring them to life and cause them to bloom. In this musing he might have been saying that if he could raise men in an omnipotent way, he could undo the death of his siblings and thus rescue his mother from her grief. He indicated that the man who cultivates men should act with the mentality of the flower gardener, who expects no tangible return for his efforts. When he saw himself as thus anticipating no reward, his position had, of course, altruistic elements. Hidden underneath his altruism, however, was the wish to rescue himself from knowing his oral aggression which would ruin any hope for a good relationship.

As a national leader Atatürk became a necessary, idealized object for his countrymen, one essential for the maintenance of Turkish pride. At the time of his death, unfinished psychological business involving that special relationship was left behind. He was too greatly idealized to be dispensed with, that is, to be "killed" in psychological terms. Muslim tradition requires that a dead body be ritually washed, wrapped in white linen, and placed in a coffin from which it is removed for interment before the next sunset.[2] As in life, Atatürk broke with tradition in death. His body was embalmed, and his mourners, the Turkish people, postponed the final burial of his body for a decade and a half. The apotheosis of the man, his transformation into the immortal Atatürk, came about through the inability of his countrymen to complete their process of mourning, which coincided with his own personal longing for immortality.

Mourners gratify their unconscious wish to bring the dead back to life by maintaining links with them. Atatürk has continued to live as a symbol and a concept. His picture continues to be reverenced alongside the national flag and is displayed beside it on days of national celebration or

[1]Melzig 1944. E. F. Sharpe (1937) wrote about the last dream of a woman of eighty-one years of age three days before her death: "I saw all my sickness gathered together; as I looked they were no longer sicknesses but roses and I knew the roses would be planted and that they would grow" (p. 200). Atatürk's metaphor of a gardener who cultivates flowers, like this woman's dream, refers to his unfailing hope, which sustained him in life. There is a wish for immortality.

[2]For details of Muslim Turkish ceremonies surrounding death, see R. Lewis, 1971, pp. 105–6.

remembrance. He is omnipresent. He is on postage stamps and money, both bills and coins. Statues of Atatürk are everywhere, and his words are chiseled on the stone facades of buildings. His photograph is found in government offices and in the corner grocery store. His name has been bestowed on boulevards, parks, stadiums, concert halls, bridges, and forests. When the Turks seized the northern sector of Cyprus in 1974, busts of Atatürk were brought ashore with the troops and erected in every liberated Turkish village. Mental and physical representations of Atatürk have fused with and are symbolic of the Turkish spirit, and thus he has indeed become immortal.

Dr. Robert Jay Lifton (1968, p. xiii), a prominent psychiatrist, speaks of the sense of immortality as the "individual's connection with man's general past and future." Obviously, Atatürk is not the only leader to have perceived himself as immortal in the sense of having such bonds. For example, Lifton points to Mao Tse-tung's attempts to ensure the immortality of the fruits of his revolution, and Hitler believed in a thousand-year reich. The psychoanalyst George Pollock, who has studied immortality from a psychoanalytic perspective, states:

> The belief in immortality conventionally refers to personal survival in some form after death. However, one can extend this idea to include the survival of a particular social, economic, political organization in perpetuity . . . there is . . . personal and historic continuity as well as a transcending of individual death via eternal life within the continuing social revolution. . . . Immortality can thus be seen as a personal union with the broader idealized social system—utopia, which lives on ideologically after the individual's physiological demise. [Pollock 1975, pp. 347–48]

As Turkey's second president İsmet İnönü was a most loyal perpetuator of Atatürk's ideals. He was referred to as *Milli Şef*, "National Leader." The title *Ebedi Şef*, "Eternal Leader," was reserved for Atatürk, who, in that role, became a brooding presence watching over and guarding his nation.

The conviction that Atatürk would never die, which was sounded in the writings of Turkey's poets and philosophers, was echoed among the common people. It helped to ease the initial reaction of grief and shock that swept Turkey when his life came to an end. In spite of the intellectual awareness that he was no longer among them, Turks continued to behave as though he were. The first indication that the Turks were unable to separate themselves from him was the initial interment of Atatürk in a temporary grave. This permitted the illusion that he was not really dead and buried. His temporary marble tomb in the Ethnographic Museum in Ankara was above ground, suggesting that he was not lost in the earth.

No grave in clay was good enough for him, and a commission was established to determine his final resting place. After seven months' deliberation, the commission announced on 7 June 1939 that a hill in Ankara known as Rasat-tepe (Observation Hill), soon to be spoken of as Anıt-tepe (Mausoleum Hill), had been selected as the site for Atatürk's entombment. An international competition for the mausoleum's design was announced, and by March 1942 forty-nine designs had been submitted. In the end, the rather grand architectural plans submitted by two Turks, Emin Onat and Orhan Arda, were chosen by the commission as a fitting tribute/memorial for the revered leader. Its selection was announced two days before the fifth anniversary of his death.

Interest in the construction of Atatürk's mausoleum continued during the early years of World War II. Turkey's delicate international situation, as she maintained her position of neutrality despite pressure, now from the Axis and then from the Allies, to side with them, and her deteriorating economic condition served to delay progress on the mausoleum project until the end of 1944, when ground was finally broken. Construction dragged on for years, years that witnessed important political developments. Among those developments was Turkey's transformation into a multiparty state from the one-party politics it had known under Atatürk. That transformation was aided by Turkey's entry into World War II on the Allied side[3] and her signing of the United Nations Charter. That document called for the observance of civil and political rights through free voting procedures in the political process of member nations. Politicians who had become disenchanted with İsmet İnönü's leadership of the nation used Turkey's commitment to the United Nations Charter to step up their pressure for a multiparty political system. Their efforts were crowned with success when the National Resurgence party was formed in July 1945, followed shortly by the organization of the Democratic party under the leadership of Celâl Bayar in January 1946 and later the Nation party, to which Field Marshal Fevzi Çakmak lent his distinguished name and support. Taking part in the elections of 1946, the Democrats won sixty-four seats, other independents garnered six, and İnönü's party came away with three hundred ninety-five. Turning its efforts to organization at the local level, the Democrats surprised everyone, including themselves, in the elections of May 1950, winning 53.3 percent of the vote and gaining control of the government. Celâl Bayar succeeded to the presidency. It was during his term in office that the Atatürk Mausoleum was completed.

[3]Turkey entered the war against Germany on 23 February 1945 in order to become a charter member of the United Nations and be eligible to attend the founding session of the United Nations at San Francisco on 25 April 1945. No engagements were fought on Turkish soil.

In an arrangement that would have pleased the dead leader, the hillside of Anıt-tepe was planted with trees sent to Ankara from numerous foreign countries. At the tomb site a long walk flanked by statues of Hittite lions points the way to a huge courtyard that is the parade ground for ceremonial occasions. The lions were chosen to honor Atatürk's consuming interest in Turkey's past. (Historical research encouraged by Atatürk had "established" a connection between the Hittites and the Turks.) The main mausoleum is entered by steps rising from the courtyard. Anyone looking past its columns gets a majestic view of Atatürk's growing city of Ankara.

On 10 November 1953, Atatürk's body was transferred to the mausoleum that stands on the hill where he and Nuri so often rode at dawn (Tesal 1975), seeking a moment of solace. The transfer took place the day after a committee of prominent figures had witnessed the opening of his coffin in the Ethnographic Museum and attested to the good state of his embalmed corpse. Exactly fifteen years to the minute after his death, his coffin was placed on the same gun carriage that had transported it from Dolmabahçe to the quay at Seraglio Point in Istanbul. As the procession made its way to Anıt-tepe with the coffin flanked by six generals, one of whom carried Atatürk's Independence Medal, cannons boomed throughout the city and units of the Air Force flew formations overhead.

As a medical student in Ankara at the time, Dr. Volkan witnessed the transfer of the body to its new resting place. The day was fine, with a bit of a breeze. Celâl Bayar and his prime minister Adnan Menderes walked behind the coffin, as did İsmet İnönü and other dignitaries. The crowds that lined the route showed no evidence of grief, for the immortal Atatürk now pervaded Turkey, and the mummified body was irrelevant as something to prompt tears. The symbol was larger than the body, which could now be allowed to return to the earth.

Today's visitor to the mausoleum will see a splendid block of beautiful pink Turkish marble weighing forty-four tons. Atatürk's body is not contained within the marble, which is shaped like a huge coffin. Indeed, the marble does not even press upon the ground in which his remains do repose. The marble is on the upper floor of the mausoleum which is used for ceremonies, and the body itself is interred below it on a lower floor.

Psychoanalysts believe that the use of tombstones grew out of an unconscious dread that the dead might return. A tombstone obstructs any such escape by pressing real or symbolic weight upon the ground covering the body. Atatürk's burial place is represented by a stone of great size and weight, but it does not press down upon him. In spite of that great piece of marble he can rise out of the tomb!

While the process of ensuring the immortality of Atatürk continued on

The nation enshrines its founder. Atatürk's mausoleum in Ankara.

its inexorable path, the mere mortals who had been associated with him in the national struggle for independence and who had survived him began to die. Ali Fethi (Okyar), Atatürk's senior by a year, who had been his superior in Sofia, his first prime minister, and the man he had picked to organize the first opposition party, died on 10 May 1943. He was followed on 26 January 1948 by Kâzım Karabekir. After Atatürk's death, Kâzım had rejoined the People's Republic party and was the president of the Grand National Assembly when he died. His funeral created quite a stir in Istanbul as thousands turned out to accompany his coffin to the cemetery. Some young people in the crowd who observed the shabby condition of the Turkish flag that covered his coffin set up an outcry, demanding that such a hero have a better flag. They were quieted when told that this was the very flag he had raised over the citadel of Kars when he had liberated the city.

Field Marshal Fevzi Çakmak died on 10 April 1950, at the age of seventy-four. He had left the military in 1944 and entered politics, serving as a deputy and then as the titular head of the Nation party. In 1955, another distinguished career came to an end with the death of Adnan Adıvar. He and his wife had been driven into exile by Atatürk and returned to Turkey only in 1939, after Atatürk's death. The trusted "twin," Refet Bele, died in 1963, and in the following year two of the more significant figures of the era departed the scene. On 15 January 1964, Halide Edib Adıvar died in Istanbul at the age of seventy-nine. The first Turkish woman to graduate from the American Girls College in Üsküdar, she had married Adnan Adıvar in 1917, having already been married and divorced, and she accompanied Adnan Adıvar into exile and spent many years with him in England and France. In 1931–32 she served as a visiting professor at Columbia University in New York City. Her command of English was excellent, and she wrote in it with great style. One of her novels was written originally in English under the title *The Clown and His Daughter* (Adıvar 1935, 1959). Six months after her death, Rauf Orbay died in Istanbul on 16 July 1964. He too had lived abroad. Upon his return, he had lived quietly until World War II, when he served with great success as Turkish ambassador to London. Incessantly importuned to write his memoirs, he refused, not wishing to tread on any toes. Ali Fuat Cebesoy felt no such compunction, and his memoirs constitute an important legacy of first-hand recollections of the early, exciting, tragic, and glorious days of Atatürk and his struggle to bring Turkey into existence (Cebesoy 1953). Ali Fuat died in 1968.

Perhaps fittingly, the last survivor of the innermost circle was İsmet İnönü. After losing the presidency to the Democratic party in 1950, İsmet İnönü led the opposition for ten years. Following a military coup in 1960, he became prime minister once again on 20 November 1961 and served in that capacity until 21 February 1965. During his last years he was a special senator in the Turkish parliament. İsmet İnönü always stirred deep feelings among the people.[4] Until his death, on 23 December 1973 at the age of eighty-nine he remained the most prominent living link to Atatürk. Known in his later years because of his longevity as "Ölmez," the man who would not die, İnönü was buried at the mausoleum built for Atatürk, the man who cannot die. His body lies at the far side of the courtyard, directly opposite the massive marble block.

With both Atatürk and İnönü dead, life went on vigorously in Turkey—the population rising from more than 10 million inhabitants in 1923 to 46 million in 1981. Prime ministers and other leading lights have come and gone, none, one supposes, finding it easy to withstand unconscious comparison with Atatürk, although most have felt a kinship with him. It seems likely, indeed, that failure to replicate his leadership may be a

[4]Dr. Volkan recalls how he felt ecstatic and almost merged with everyone else when he first saw and touched İsmet İnönü while İnönü was visiting Ankara University where Volkan was a medical student. Later, during his last year of medical school, he saw İnönü by chance standing alone at a street corner in Ankara. Approaching him, Volkan kissed İnönü's hand. İnönü inquired about Volkan, who told the ex-president that he was a Cypriot Turk planning to be a psychiatrist after his graduation. İnönü wanted to know more about psychiatry and psychoanalysis. Soon his driver came and İnönü left. This incident made a big impression on young Volkan, who felt that his career choice was blessed by İnönü, and, by extension, by Atatürk himself.

psychological factor in the political instability that has afflicted the Turkish democracy in recent times. Bülent Ecevit became a new national hero during the summer of 1974, when Turkish troops occupied northern Cyprus during his tenure as prime minister. Books with such titles as *Yesterday Atatürk, Today Ecevit* (Yurdanur, 1974) began to appear, but Ecevit publicly stated that he should not be compared with Atatürk. He belied the comparison by failing to unite Turkey behind him after the first wave of enthusiasm over Cyprus subsided, despite his high intelligence and oratorical powers, which Atatürk himself might have envied.[5]

Atatürk entrusted the safety of Turkey's future to her youth, but in effect it has been the military, linking themselves directly with Atatürk and his tradition, who have taken control of state affairs whenever it appeared that the revolution he wrought was in danger, for example, in 1960, 1971, and most recently in 1980, with the expressed intention of

[5]That recent and current Turkish leaders feel a special relationship toward the representation of Atatürk can be illustrated by the following story told to Dr. Volkan by Rauf Raif Denktaş, president of the Turkish Republic of Northern Cyprus.

In the summer of 1974 an attempt was made by a group of Greeks on the island of Cyprus to kill Makarios, the official president of the Cyprus Republic, but Makarios was able to flee the island. This development might possibly have led to the annexation of the island by Greece, and this would have meant death for the island's Turkish minority. Eventually, Turkish troops landed in Northern Cyprus to protect the Cypriot Turks, and this led to the island's being divided into northern Turkish and southern Greek sections; see Volkan 1979, for further details.

Two-and-a-half months before the mainland Turkish troops arrived on the island, the island's Turkish leader, Mr. Denktaş, had a dream about Atatürk. The immortal leader was dressed in civilian clothes, but he had his boots on. Denktaş himself appeared in the dream and he went to Atatürk and said to him, "Save us, save us!" Atatürk responded by saying, "Konjektür is important. Pay attention to konjektür." Then he passed Denktaş and turned a corner. Denktaş wanted to follow him, but Atatürk told him not to follow. Denktaş thought that Atatürk was going to a Turkish bath.

Mr. Denktaş was very impressed by his dream, and he wrote it down in his diary. Two-and-a-half months later the new developments mentioned above took place, and Denktaş knew that the time had come for the mainland Turks to interfere physically. He sent a message to Bülent Ecevit, the Turkish prime minister, urging him to send Turkish troops to the island. Soon he was asked by the Turkish ambassador to Cyprus for consultation. At the embassy there was a message to Denktaş from Ecevit: "Tell Mr. Denktaş not to worry. We are in the process of preparing *konjektür.*"

Mr. Denktaş thought then that he had had a telepathic dream and was satisfied in feeling that, after all, Atatürk himself played the leading role in saving the Cypriot Turks. President Denktaş told Dr. Volkan that prior to the Turkish intervention on the island, he and other Cypriot Turkish leaders had developed a shared wish to be saved by Atatürk. There is a statue of Atatürk, holding his hands in front of his chest, in the Turkish section of Nicosia, and most of the ceremonies on national holidays take place in front of this statue. During such ceremonies, Denktaş and other leaders would whisper to each other, "If Atatürk opens his hands, he will take us into his bosom, strike the enemy and save us" (Denktaş 1980).

setting the nation back on the road indicated for it by Atatürk. Just what that road is requires some examination. What did Atatürk really envision for Turkey? What is "westernization"? Turkish and non-Turkish scholars have looked critically and soberly at that phenomenon. Sociologist Niyazi Berkes, a Cypriot Turk, talks about the "loneliness" of the new Turkey in respect to its economy, politics, and culture. In 1975 he wrote:

> Today's Turkey is neither a western nor a Moslem nation; it does not belong to a Christian, socialist, or capitalist community. It is neither Asian nor European. It is in fact, however, that throughout its history, in respect to its economy and politics, it has been more western than eastern. The dominant direction of Ottoman history has tilted more toward the west than toward the east. But its adherence to an eastern cultural reference has prevented Turkey's inclusion in the western world. . . . Europe has never considered itself as including Turkey, and if we think the contrary, no one but ourselves believes it. [Berkes 1975, p. 167]

The "loneliness" Berkes refers to may well be a reflection of Atatürk's personality. He was grandly lonely, desiring peace for himself, as well as for his country and the world. Serenity, that is, the notion of an individual, nation, or world without "grief," is an unattainable illusion, since human beings, whether as individuals or as groups, have a propensity for aggression. Atatürk's legacy included his omnipotence, with which his people were quick to identify, but that identification is not entirely consistent with Turkey's present position in world affairs in which she is not a major power. Atatürk, however, left another and more useful and adaptive track for Turks to follow. In 1977 Arnold Hottinger, the distinguished Swiss foreign correspondent, examined the special course "westernization" has taken because of Atatürk's personality and found it quite different from that followed by other Muslims of the Middle East more recently:

> Atatürk opened a wedge-shaped path of *bon sens* and even cool reason through the thick forest of Turkish politics. In the time of the Father of Modern Turkey, the end of the wedge was so wide that it seemed at first to be clearing the whole of the thicket. In the course of the decades that followed his death the broad path narrowed, and trees and undergrowth grew tall on both sides. But the general direction of the path remains, and one can advance along it. [Hottinger 1977, p. 81]

He holds that other Muslim states, "having entered the wood by chance paths" (Hottinger 1977, p. 81), do not possess the historic sense of direction with which Turkey was provided by Atatürk, following upon victory in war and the accompanying tremendous resurgence of national pride.

Atatürk's pathway was put to the test once again in 1980 in the midst of national planning for the centennial of his birth in 1981. Strong effective government in Turkey had given way to weak coalitions because no major party was able to gain a clear mandate at the polls. Bülent Ecevit, İnönü's successor, and Süleyman Demirel, the head of the Justice party, which was the heir of Celâl Bayar's Democratic party after 1960, vied for dominance. Those two leaders displayed increasing personal animosity toward each other,[6] and national aims became more and more contaminated with the desire for political gain. Religious influences of the kind that had enraged Atatürk began to insinuate themselves into the political arena. Atatürk's cultural revolution had come from the top down, and now it appeared that the gap between Turks who were educated, cosmopolitan, and fully westernized and those who were not was widening. Lacking oil resources, Turkey also began a flirtation with the oil-rich Muslim countries of the Middle East.

Turkey's economy went from bad to worse, a situation that was not helped by the embargoes imposed by the United States, partly through the influence of the pro-Greek lobby. An undeclared civil war was smoldering in Turkey which the government was helpless to stop. Reluctantly, the Turkish army intervened for the third time in September 1980. When the generals took over, they did so, in a sense, in the name of Atatürk. Overnight, the Turkish people felt a surge of relief because their faith in the principles and heirs of Atatürk was restored. Some of the military figures had been small children when the Turkish republic was established in 1923 and some had not yet been born at the time of that momentous event, but they were perceived as Atatürk's "children," the last military group whose lives overlapped that of the great leader. General Kenan Evren, who headed the new military regime, was born in 1918, a year before Mustafa Kemal's arrival in Samsun. After the successful military coup he went on national television to say, "Measures will be taken to keep our youth—the protectors of our future—from deviating from Atatürk's ideal and so accepting foreign ideologies as to become anarchists." He then gave the toll of terrorism in the country for the past two years—5,241 lives taken and 14,152 people wounded. Those statistics are close to the number of dead and wounded for the Battle of the Sakarya. Disavowing any interest in the attainment of personal power by

[6]In September 1975, when Volkan interviewed Süleyman Demirel, at that time the prime minister of Turkey, as part of preparing a book on Cyprus (see Volkan 1979), he noted Demirel's personal dislike of Ecevit. Demirel called Ecevit a poet who could not understand politics and who could not be a leader (Demirel 1975).

means of the coup, the generals declared that they had effected it in order to save Turkish democracy by overcoming the prevailing disorder.

One of the generals' first official acts after taking power on 12 September was to visit with the spirit of Atatürk by placing a wreath before the pink marble slab in his mausoleum. After observing a reverential moment of silence, General Evren wrote in a special visitors' book what was, in effect, a letter to Atatürk, as though he were still alive. It began, "Great Leader Atatürk," and explained that the Turkish army, as guardian of his ideals, had had to halt those who were pushing Turkey toward "darkness and helplessness."[7] The letter ended, "We remember you once again with gratitude and a sense of obligation, and bow before you in respect." The highest authority in the nation acknowledged that Atatürk still lived. Such is, in truth, the legacy of immortality.

[7]Eventually General Evren was elected president of Turkey. (So he did stay in power.) Turkey returned to a civilian government in December 1983.

31
Postscript

WE HAVE ATTEMPTED TO TELL THE STORY, WITHOUT UNNECESSARILY INTERrupting the flow of the narative to focus on the clinical aspects as they unfolded, of Mustafa Kemal Atatürk's personal development from the infant Mustafa into the immortal Atatürk and the interaction between his inner domain and the real world as he founded and then transformed Turkey into a modern nation. It might be useful here to present in one place a short overview of our understanding of Atatürk's personality and the major influences on its development.

One of our main themes is that the infant Mustafa was born into a house of death to a "grieving mother" who perceived him as both a replacement child and a new hope. He was special—a savior—for his grieving mother and a link to his dead siblings. It was around this specialness that he developed what is known technically as a "grandiose self," a subjective experience of being self-sufficient, above the need for others, and preeminent in the world. His grandiose self inflated his own self-regard as a defensive adaptation toward the lack of good and consistent mothering he experienced. Because of her fear that he too might die and add to her grief, we believe, she maintained aloofness from her infant son, an aloofness that was underscored by the insufficiency in her own milk, which necessitated his placement with a wet nurse. In addition, she may have been overintrusive and perhaps overseductive, both of which would have contributed to his growing sense of specialness.

Little Mustafa's grandiose self was his basic character trait. To it was added a premature oedipal triumph when his father died while Mustafa was in the oedipal age. Another central theme is Mustafa's receipt of a "gift" from his father who, despite his illness and devaluation, directed his son away from his mother's Muslim ways toward a more modern, westernized education. This meant to the young Mustafa that a gift-giving father could help him separate himself psychologically from an overwhelming relationship with his mother.

His father's death deprived Mustafa of enough real interaction with a "good enough" father. By his presence and through such interactions that father would have helped Mustafa tame his inflated self-regard and his natural incestuous desires. Mustafa kept an idealized image of a strong father with whom he could have an experience in order to attempt to resolve his oedipal conflicts. The idealized image of his father was a supplement to his own idealized grandiose self, and he tried to combine the two within himself. Early in his adulthood the idealized image of his father was projected onto others regardless of whether they merited such treatment. Mustafa Kemal kept another image of his father, that of the weak, bad father. It was, however, disassociated from the idealized good father image. Later, Mustafa Kemal would project the bad father image onto some people in his environment, such as the sultans, and would enjoy the repetition of oedipal triumph over them.

During the pubertal years there is a second chance to reconsolidate the self-system as one "obligatorily" revisits and reexamines childhood images of one's self and the important others in one's life. Mustafa Kemal suffered a harsh blow in those crucial years through his mother's remarriage. He consolidated his character traits that existed as his main character without benefitting much from the useful modification that can take place during adolescence. Included in those traits was a reserving for himself of all idealized and good self and object images (or the projection of such images onto others as long as he could be an extension of those idealized others).

From the psychological perspective, when Mustafa Kemal survived a shrapnel wound above the heart received at Gallipoli while in his thirties, his childhood unconscious fantasy of specialness, that is, immortality, which he shared with his mother, passed the test of reality. He began more and more to keep the idealized father image contained within himself rather than search for an idealized father in others. His landing at Samsun on 19 May 1919 was inwardly significant for Mustafa Kemal as well. It was like a rebirth—a reconsolidation and recrystallization of his grandiose self, which included his idealized father image. He began to act in a more bold, brave, and decisive fashion.

The existence of a "grieving nation" provided him with an external reality upon which to project that inner image of his grieving mother. It gave him his lifelong mission to save and repair the Turkish nation. When he became Atatürk—the idealized father Turk—the grieving nation was repaired. In other words, he had changed the environment of his sad childhood into a happy and grand one. He wanted the Turks, especially the young Turks, who represented himself as a child, to have a happy and idealized environment. As soon as possible he used the historical arena as the setting for his own internal drama. There appeared to be a "fit" between the basic demands of his inner world and the external world in which he lived. When there was no such "fit," he constantly attempted to change the external world to make it respond to his internal needs in order to insure the cohesiveness of his grandiose self-concept. Atatürk's career provides rich material on the ways in which a leader can adapt to the external world and shape it to meet the requirements of his inner world. While not all of Atatürk's creative works in the military and in modernization were the direct result of his personality organization, many of them took form according to the demands of it. Psychological factors cannot be disregarded by historians in the assessment of historical causation.

Physical, or constitutional, factors are outside the expertise of psychoanalysis, but in Atatürk's case there seems to have been a "fit" also between his narcissistic grandiose personality and his actual physical, or constitutional, makeup. This made his personality an asset for him as a leader rather than a liability, as it usually is in many simple cases of narcissistic personalities who cannot live up to their grand inner expectations but are driven at the same time to maintain an illusion of greatness. Atatürk felt that he knew everything better than anyone else and that he could be a better savior than anyone. This became an asset and enabled him to act decisively.

In truth, Atatürk was a highly intelligent and handsome man. From childhood on he was preoccupied with his personal appearance and with beauty and power. He paid great attention to how he dressed and to his collection of adorers. Self-centered, he was at the same time object-related with respect to the Turkish nation. While the origin of this most intense relation to the Turkish nation may have been selfish—to repair the grieving mother in order to have her nurture him better—in his adult life he sublimated his original motivation and behaved as a true patriot, devoted to the good of his people. He was blindly loyal to the Turkish nation while in his daily activities and in his one-to-one relationships he was cutting and scornful and never loyal to anyone who did not adore him uncritically. Inviting opposition in debate, he was secure in the knowledge that in the end his views would prevail.

Atatürk's specialness, which he actualized from a fantasy into a reality attested to by the entire Turkish nation, was only one of the dominant themes in his personality. Another was his oral dependency which was also related to the lack of constancy in the early mothering he had experienced. His dominant grand self overshadowed his dependent self, which paradoxically provided fuel for his dominant side so he could remain defensively and adaptively cohesive and ward off becoming aware of his dependent side. We can say that to a great extent he never integrated his grandiose and dependent sides. The resulting contradictions within himself made him a most complicated person. In order to deal with his opposing aspects, Atatürk worked hard to maintain the cohesiveness of his dominant grandiose self, to be really number one and to be accepted as such by other people and by history. On occasion he would strengthen the gap between his contradictory images in order to escape the tension that resulted from attempts to integrate them. Thus, he often tended to see matters as black or white, that is, in terms of things being "all good" or "all bad."

The love Atatürk had for the Turkish nation was related to the sublimated original love feelings for his mother. It is interesting to observe that in adulthood Atatürk maintained a ritualistic distance from his real mother while seeking to heal the "grieving mother"/Turkish nation. Sporadically, aggression appeared in Atatürk, but he was able to place a "border" around it, having absorbed a respect for limits from his father. His aggression had an oral quality to it, not surprising since many oral character traits stayed with him, but were sublimated—such as his majestic ability as an orator. Another expression of his orality was the subjugation of others to "oral examinations." Only those who could pass the exams were considered worthy of his attention and available to become "valued" followers. The Turkish nation as a whole was the most valued follower.

Narcissistic leaders can be divided into two general categories. One is the destructive leader who attempts to protect the cohesion of his grandiose self chiefly by devaluing others in order to feel superior. The destructive narcissistic leader poses a considerable danger. History shows that an excessive need to devalue a group often leads to the destruction of that group. For the destructive leader the devalued persons or groups become targets for the externalization of his split and devalued self and object images, and those people and groups have to be suppressed.

The other type of narcissistic leader is reparative, and Atatürk is representative of this category. The reparative leader wants adoration from his "valued" followers and may attempt to uplift them in order to build his support on as impressively high a level as possible. The followers are idealized so that their mental representations can be fused into the grandiose self of the leader, making the cohesiveness of his inner world more stable.

In some respects the distinction between the reparative and destructive grandiose leaders is artificial, since one may turn into the other under certain circumstances. Atatürk, however, maintained his role as a reparative leader because of the great "fit" between him and his people. That "fit" enabled him to hold on to his grandiose self and allowed the Turkish people to perceive him as a superman. More than forty years after his death his image is still used to foster a sense of national unity in Turkey. In this sense Atatürk is like a prophet whose mystical image exists as a powerful unifier forever and ever. No other modern leader has achieved the degree of immortality Atatürk enjoys among the Turks.

In the process of repairing the Turkish nation, Atatürk instituted his nightly ritual of the president's table around which he would gather a host of people for discussion of his many projects. He had an uncanny ability to regress in the service of the ego in that environment and psychologically review issues of the psychosexual scale of development. During those nightly rituals he was in a sense a child and an artist at play, experimenting and creating. His medium was Turkey. His need to make it better forced him to impose his will upon the nation, attempting to have an idealized product. He emptied himself in a lifelong labor for Turkey and his life ended in a regressive surrender to his oral conflicts—as they manifested themselves in his drinking and cirrhosis. One almost feels a need to romanticize things and say that his life ended in a kind of altruistic suicide after he had given all he could to Turkey in a tour de force of creative synthesis. Who knows, perhaps that is closer to the truth.

References

Abse, D. W., and Jessner, L. 1961. "The Psychodynamic Aspects of Leadership." In S. Graubard and G. Holton, eds., *Excellence and Leadership in a Democracy*, pp. 693–710. New York: Columbia University Press.

Abse, D. W., and Ulman, R. B. 1977. "Charismatic Political Leadership and Collective Regression." In R. S. Robins, ed., *Psychopathology and Political Leadership*, pp. 35–52. New Orleans: Tulane University Press.

Adıvar, H. E. 1926. *Memoirs of Halide Edib*. New York: Century Co.

———. 1928. *The Turkish Ordeal*. New York: Century Co.

———. 1935. *The Clown and His Daughter*. London: George Allen & Unwin. Turkish ed. *Sinekli Bakkal* [*The fly-ridden grocery shop*]. Istanbul: Ahmet Halit Kitabevi, 1949.

Afetinan, A. 1958. *Herkesin bir dünyası var* [Everyone has his own world]. Ankara: Türk Tarih Kurumu Basımevi.

———. 1959. *Atatürk hakkında Hatıralar ve Belgeler* [Memories and documents concerning Atatürk]. Ankara: İş Bankası Yayını.

———. 1968. *Atatürk ve Türk kadın haklarının kazanılması* [Atatürk and the achievement of Turkish women's rights]. Istanbul: Milli Eğitim Basımevi.

———. 1971. *M. Kemal Atatürk 'ten yazdıklarım* [My notations from M. Kemal Atatürk]. Istanbul: Milli Eğitim Basımevi.

Altay, F. 1973. *Atatürk ve Münir Nureddin* [Atatürk and Münir Nureddin]. In H. Yücebaş, ed., *Atatürk'ün Nükteleri-Fıkraları-Hatıraları* (2d ed.), pp. 181–83. Istanbul: Kültür Kitabevi.

Anderson, M. S. 1966. *The Eastern Question*. London: Macmillan.

Apak, R. 1957. *Yetmişlik bir Subayın Hatıraları* [The recollections of an officer in his seventies]. Ankara: E. U. Basımevi.

Arar, A. 1958. *Son günlerinde Atatürk* [Atatürk during his last days]. Ankara: Selek Yayınları.

Armstrong, H. C. 1932. *Grey Wolf—Mustafa Kemal: An Intimate Story of a Dictator*. London: Arthur Barker, Ltd.

Atatürk, M. K. 1952. *Atatürk'ün Söylev ve Demeçleri* [Speeches and statements by Atatürk]. 2 vols. Istanbul: Türk Inkilâp Tarihi Enstitüsü.

———. 1964. *Atatürk'ün Tamim, Telegraf ve Beyannemeleri* [Atatürk's circular letters, telegrams, and other declarations]. Ankara: Ankara Üniversitesi Basımevi.

———. 1927. *A Speech Delivered by Ghazi Mustafa Kemal, Oct. 1927.* Leipzig: K. F. Koehler, 1929.

Atay, F. R. 1965. *Atatürk'ün Hatıraları 1914–1919* [Atatürk's recollections, 1914–1919]. Ankara: Türkiye İş Bankası Kültür Yayınları.

———. 1980. *Çankaya.* Istanbul: Bateş.

Aybars, E. 1975. *İstiklâl Mahkemeleri* [Independence tribunals]. Ankara: Bilgi Yayınevi.

Ayda, A. 1975. Interview with V. D. Volkan, 1 April, Ankara.

Aydemir, Ş. S. 1969. *Tek Adam* [The singular man]. 3 vols. Istanbul: Remzi Kitabevi.

———. 1974. Interviews with V. D. Volkan, 20 November and 13 December, Ankara.

Bach, S. 1977. "On the Narcissistic Stage of Consciousness." *International Journal of Psychoanalysis* 58:209–33.

Bateson, M. C. 1972. *Our Own Metaphor.* New York: Alfred A. Knopf.

Baydar, M. 1967. *Atatürk'le Konuşmalar* [Conversations with Atatürk]. 3d ed. Istanbul: Varlık Yayınları.

Bayur, Y. H. 1963. *Atatürk, Hayatı ve Eseri* [Atatürk, his life and his work]. Ankara: Güven Basımevi.

Beres, D. 1959. "The Contributions of Psychoanalysis to the Biography of the Artist: A Commentary on Methodology." *International Journal of Psychoanalysis* 40: 26–37.

Bergmann, M. S. 1973. "Limitations of Method in Psychoanalytic Biography: A Historical Inquiry." *Journal of the American Psychoanalytic Association* 21:833–50.

Berkes, N. 1975. *Türk Düşününde Batı Sorunu* [The western question in Turkish thought]. Ankara: Bilgi Yayınevi.

Berlin, I. 1979. "Nationalism: Past Neglect and Present Power." *Partisan Review* 46:337–58.

Black, C. E., and Helmreich, E. C. 1959. *Twentieth-Century Europe: A History.* New York: Alfred A. Knopf.

Blos, P. 1967. "The Second Individuation Process of Adolescence." *The Psychoanalytic Study of the Child* 22: 162–86.

———. 1979. *The Adolescent Passage.* New York: International Universities Press.

Borak, S. 1970. *Atatürk'ün özel mektupları* [Atatürk's private letters]. 2d ed. Istanbul: Varlık Yayınevi.

Bozdağ, İ. 1975*a*. *Atatürk ve eşi Lâtife Hanım* [Atatürk and his wife Lâtife]. Istanbul: Kervan Yayınları.

———. 1975*b*. *Atatürk'ün Sofrası* [Atatürk's dining table]. Istanbul: Kervan Yayınları.

Brock, R. 1954. *Ghost on Horseback: The Incredible Atatürk.* New York: Duell, Sloan & Pearce.

Brody, M. W. 1952. "The Symbolic Significance of Twins in Dreams." *Psychoanalytic Quarterly* 31:172–80.

Brown, L. C., and Itzkowitz, N. 1977. *Psychological Dimensions of Near Eastern Studies.* Princeton, N.J.: Darwin Press.

Busch, B. C. 1976. *Mudros to Lausanne: Britain's Frontiers in West Asia, 1918–1923.* Albany, N.Y.: State University of New York Press.

Çambel, P. 1975. Interview with V. D. Volkan, 5 January, Ankara.

Cebesoy, A. F. 1953. *Milli Mücadele Hatıraları* [Recollections of the national struggle]. 2 vols. Istanbul: Vatan Neşriyatı.

———. 1967. *Sınıf arkadaşım Atatürk* [My classmate Atatürk]. Istanbul: İnkilâp ve Aka Kitabevleri.

Çetiner, Y. 1964. Article on Emine H. *Cumhuriyet*, 10 Nov.

Cocks, F. S. 1918. *The Secret Treaties*. London: Union of Democratic Control.

Coen, S. J., and Bradlow, P. A. 1982. "Twin Transference as a Compromise Formation." *Journal of the American Psychoanalytic Association* 30:599–620.

Cumming, H. H. 1938. *Franco-British Rivalry in the Post-War Near East*. London: Oxford University Press.

Cunbur, M. 1973. "Atatürk'ün musiki üzerine düşünceleri" [Atatürk's thoughts on music]. In *Cumhuriyetin 50. Yılına Armağan* [Honoring the 50th anniversary of the republic], 41:A3 Ankara: Türk Kültür Araştırma Enstitüsü Yayınları.

Davison, R. H. 1953. "Turkish Diplomacy from Mudros to Lausanne." In G. A. Craig and F. Gilbert, eds., *The Diplomats*. Princeton, N.J.: Princeton University Press.

Demirel, S. 1975. Interview with V. D. Volkan, 11 September, Ankara.

Denktaş, R. R. 1980. Interview with V. D. Volkan, 18 October, Nicosia.

Dilacar, A. 1974. " 'Denizbank' olayı" [The "Denizbank" incident] *Türk Dili* 30:872–75.

Dwight, H. G. 1915. "Saloniki." *National Geographic Magazine* 30:203–32.

Eberhard, W. 1981. Written communication to V. D. Volkan.

Ellison, G. 1923. *An Englishwoman in Angora*. London: Hutchinson.

Egüz, S. 1969. *Koro için halk türküleri* [Folksongs for choir]. Ankara: Ayyıldız Matbaası.

Ergin, O. 1939–43. *Türkiye maarif tarihi* [The history of education in Turkey]. 5 vols. Istanbul: Osman Bey Matbaası.

Erikson, E. H. 1958. *Young Man Luther*. New York: Norton.

———. 1969. *Ghandi's Truth*. New York: Norton.

———. 1977. *Toys and Reason*. New York: Norton.

Etheredge, L. 1979. "Hardball Politics: A Model." *Political Psychology* 1:3–26.

Freud, A. 1936. *The Ego and the Mechanisms of Defense*. Vol. 2 of *The Writings of Anna Freud*. New York: International Universities Press, 1966.

Freud, S. 1900. *Interpretation of dreams*. In *The Standard Edition of the Complete Psychological Works of Sigmund Freud*, vols. 4 and 5. London: Hogarth Press, 1953.

———. 1917. "Mourning and Melancholia." In *The Standard Edition of the Complete Psychological Works of Sigmund Freud*, vol. 14, pp. 247–58. London: Hogarth Press, 1957.

———. 1910. "Leonardo da Vinci." In *The Standard Edition of the Complete Psychological Works of Sigmund Freud*, vol. 11, pp. 57–137. London: Hogarth Press, 1957.

———. 1921. "Group Psychology and the Analysis of the Ego." In *The Standard Edition of the Complete Psychological Works of Sigmund Freud*, vol. 18, pp. 54–143. London: Hogarth Press, 1955.

Froembgen, H. 1937. *Kemal Atatürk*. Trans. K. Kirkness. New York: Hillman-Curl.
Georges Gaulis, B. 1921. *Le nationalisme Turque*. Paris: Librairie Plon.
———. 1922. *Angora, Constantinople, London, Moustáfa Kémal et la politique anglaise en Orient*. Paris: Librairie Armond Colin.
———. 1924. *La nouvelle Turquie*. Paris: Librairie Plon.
Gibb, H. A. R., and Bowen, H. 1957. "The Dervishes." In *Islamic Society and the West*, vol. 1, part 2, pp. 179–206. London: Oxford University Press.
Gökçen, M. I. 1975. "Kemalist Turkey and Music." Paper read at the annual meeting of the Society for Ethnomusicology, 16–19 October 1975, Wesleyan University, Middletown, Connecticut.
Gökçen, S. 1974. Interviews with V. D. Volkan, 2 and 5 December, Ankara.
Graham, S. 1939. *Alexander of Yugoslavia*. New Haven, Conn.: Yale University Press.
Granda, C. 1973. *Atatürk'ün uşağı idim* [I was Atatürk's butler]. Istanbul: Hürriyet Yayınları.
Greenacre, P. 1955. *Swift and Carroll: A Psychoanalytic Study of Two Lives*. New York: International Universities Press.
Grey, E. 1925. *Twenty-Five Years, 1892–1916*. 2 vols. New York: Frederick A. Stokes Co.
Güntekin, R. N. 1949. *The Autobiography of a Turkish Girl*. Trans. W. Seedes. London: Allen & Unwin.
Gürsoy, L. 1974. Interview with V. D. Volkan, 16 October, Ankara.
Hamilton, Sir Ian. 1920. *Gallipoli Diary*. New York: G. H. Doran.
Henderson, G. B. 1947. *Crimean War Diplomacy and Other Historical Essays*. Glasgow: Jackson, Son & Co.
Hershlag, Z. Y. 1958. *Turkey: An Economy in Transition*. The Hague: Von Keulen.
Hoffman, D. S. 1965. "An Introduction to Music in Modern Turkey." *Consort* 22: 54–61.
Hottinger, A. 1977. "Turkey's Search for Identity: Kemal Atatürk's Heritage." *Encounter* 48:75–81.
İğdemir, U. 1962. *Mustafa Kemal Atatürk, Anafartalar muharebatına ait tarihçe* [A short history of the battles of Anafartalar]. Ankara: Türk Tarih Kurumu Basımevi.
İmece, M. S. 1959. *Atatürk'ün şapka devriminde Kastamonu ve İnebolu Seyahatları, 1925* [Atatürk's visits to Kastamonu and İnebolu during the hat revolution, 1925]. Ankara: Türk Tarih Kurumu Basımevi.
İpekçi, A. 1974. "Konuğumuz Celâl Bayar" [Our guest, Celâl Bayar]. *Milliyet*, 11 and 12 November.
Itzkowitz, N. 1972. *Ottoman Empire and Islamic Tradition*. New York: Alfred A. Knopf.
Jacobson, E. 1964. *The Self and the Object World*. New York: International Universities Press.
Kabaklı, A. 1973. "Atatürk'e sormuşlar" [They asked Atatürk]. *Tercüman*, 17 August.

Karal, E. Z. 1956. *Atatürk'ten Düşünceler* [Atatürk's thoughts]. Ankara: Türk Tarih Kurumu Basımevi.

Karaosmanoğlu, Y. K. 1966. *Sodom ve Gomore* [Sodom and Gomorrah]. Ankara: Belgi Kitabevi.

———. 1971. *Atatürk*. 4th ed. Istanbul: Remzi Kitabevi.

Kernberg, O. F. 1966. "Structural Derivatives of Object Relationships." *International Journal of Psychoanalysis* 47:236–53.

———. 1975. *Borderline Conditions and Pathological Narcissism*. New York: Jason Aronson.

———. 1980. *Internal World and External Reality*. New York: Jason Aronson.

Kılıç, A. 1955. *Kılıç Ali hatıralarını anlatıyor* [Kılıç Ali relates his recollections]. Istanbul: Hisar Matbaası.

Kinross, Lord. 1965. *Atatürk: A Biography of Mustafa Kemal, Father of Modern Turkey*. New York: William Morrow & Co.

Kızıldağlı, E. 1979. "Atatürk'ün bir dişi" [Atatürk's tooth]. *Dirim* 54:182–83.

Klauber, J. 1968. "On the Dual Use of Historical and Scientific Method in Psychoanalysis." *International Journal of Psychoanalysis* 69: 80–87.

Kocatürk, U. 1973. *Atatürk ve Türk devrimi kronolojisi* [A chronology of Atatürk and the Turkish revolution]. Ankara: Ankara Üniversitesi Basımevi.

Kohut, H. 1960. "Beyond the Bounds of the Basic Rule." *Journal of the American Psychoanalytic Association* 8:567–86.

———. 1971. *The Analysis of the Self: A Systematic Approach to the Psychoanalytic Treatment of Narcissistic Personality Disorders*. New York: International Universities Press.

———. 1977. *The Restoration of the Self*. New York: International Universities Press.

Kris, E. 1952. *Psychoanalytic Explorations in Art*. New York: International Universities Press.

Levy, M. J., Jr. 1966. *Modernization and the Structure of Societies: A Setting for International Affairs*. 2 vols. Princeton, N.J.: Princeton University Press.

———. 1972. *Modernization: Latecomers and Survivors*. New York: Basic Books.

Lewis, B. 1968. *The Emergence of Modern Turkey*. 2d ed. London: Oxford University Press.

Lewis, R. 1971. *Everyday Life in Ottoman Turkey*. London: B. T. Batsford; New York: G. P. Putnam's Sons.

Lidz, R. W. 1981. Written communication to V. D. Volkan.

Lifton, R. J. 1968. *Revolutionary Immortality*. New York: Random House.

———. 1972. "On Psychohistory." In R. R. Holt and E. Petertreund, eds., *Psychoanalysis and Contemporary Science*, 1:355–72. New York: Macmillan Co.

Liman von Sanders, Otto. 1927. *Five Years in Turkey*. (Reprinted from the August Scherl edition, Berlin, 1920.) Annapolis, Md.: United States Naval Institute.

Mack, J. E. 1971. "Psychoanalysis and Historical Biography." *Journal of the American Psychoanalytic Association* 19:143–79.

———. 1978. "Psychoanalysis and Biography: A Narrowing Gap." *Journal of the Philadelphia Association for Psychoanalysis* 5:97–109.

———. 1979. Foreword. In V. D. Volkan, *Cyprus—War and Adaptation: A Psychoanalytic History of Two Ethnic Groups in Conflict.* Charlottesville: University Press of Virginia.

———. 1980. Personal communication with V. D. Volkan

Markides, K. C. 1977. *The Rise and Fall of the Cyprus Republic.* New Haven and London: Yale University Press.

McCarthy, J. 1980. "Greek Statistics on Ottoman Greek Population." *International Journal of Turkish Studies* 1:66–76.

Melzig, H. 1944. *İnönü Diyorki* [İnönü says]. Istanbul: Ülkü Basımevi.

Modell, A. H. 1976. "The 'Holding Environment' and the Therapeutic Action of Psychoanalysis." *Journal of the American Psychoanalytic Association* 24:285–307.

Moore, F. 1906. "The Coveted City of Salonica." *Harper's Weekly*, 27 October, pp. 1537–39.

Niederland, W. G. 1965. "An Analytic Inquiry into the Life and Work of Heinrich Schliemann." In M. Schur, ed., *Drives, Affects, Behaviour*, vol. 2. New York: International Universities Press.

———. 1971. "The Naming of America." In M. Kanzer, ed., *The Unconscious Today: Essays in Honor of Max Schur.* New York: International Universities Press.

———. 1977. Written communication to V. D. Volkan

Nur, R. 1968. *Hayat ve hatıralarım* [My life and memoirs]. 3 vols. Istanbul: Altındağ Yayınları.

Oranlı, Z. 1967. *Atatürk'ün şimdiye kadar yayınlanmamış anıları: anlatan Ali Metin, Atatürk'ün emir çavuşu* [Hitherto unpublished recollections of Atatürk by Ali Metin, his orderly]. Ankara: Alkan Matbaası.

Orbay, R. 1962–63. Rauf Orbay'ın hatıraları [Recollections of Rauf Orbay]. *Yakın Tarihimiz*, March 1962–January 1963.

Orga, İ. 1958. *Phoenix Ascendant: The Rise of Modern Turkey.* London: Robert Hale.

Özbek, A., and Volkan, V. D. 1976. "Psychiatric Problems within the Satellite Extended Families of Turkey." *American Journal of Psychotherapy* 30:576–82.

Öztürk, O. M. 1963. "Psychological Effects of Circumcision as Practiced in Turkey." *Turkish Journal of Pediatrics* 7:126–30.

———. 1973. "Ritual Circumcision and Castration Anxiety." *Psychiatry* 36:49–60.

Öztürk, O. M., and Volkan, V. D. 1971. "The Theory and Practice of Psychiatry in Turkey." *American Journal of Psychotherapy* 25:240–71.

Parushev, P. 1973. *Atatürk, "demokrat diktator"* [Atatürk, "democratic dictator"]. Trans. N. Yılmaer. Istanbul: Güryay Matbaası.

Pasinler, G. 1938. Memoirs. *Akşam*, 13 December.

Pollock, G. 1975. "On Mourning, Immortality, and Utopia." *Journal of the American Psychoanalytic Association* 23:334–62.

Ramazani, R. K. 1981. Personal communication with V. D. Volkan

Rechid, D. [Reşit, D.] 1927. *Douze chants d'Anatolie.* Paris: Heugel.

Rochlin, G. 1973. *Man's Aggression: The Defense of the Self.* Boston: Gambit.

Rogers, R. 1980. Personal communication with V. D. Volkan
Rustow, D. A. 1965. "Enver Pasha." In *The Encylopaedia of Islam*, ed. B. Lewis, C. Pellat, and J. Schecht. Leiden and London: E. J. Brill and Luzac & Co.
———. 1970. "Atatürk as Founder of a State." In D. A. Rustow, ed., *Philosophers and Kings: Studies in Leadership*. New York; George Braziller.
El-Sadat, A. 1979. *In Search of Identity: An Autobiography*. New York: Harper Colophon Books.
Şapolyo, E. B. 1959. *Kemal Atatürk ve Milli Mücadele Tarihi* [Kemal Atatürk and the history of the national struggle]. Ankara: Refet Zaimler Yayınevi.
Saydam, M., and Atay, F. R. 1926. "Büyük Gazinin hatıralarından Sahifeler" [Some pages from the memoirs of the great Ghazi]. *Hakimiyet-i Milliye*, 19 March–12 April.
Schiller, J. C. F. von. 1798–99. *Wallenstein*. Trans. S. T. Coleridge. In D. Coleridge, ed., *The Dramatic Works of Samuel Taylor Coleridge*. London: Edward Noxon, 1852.
Schur, M. 1972. *Freud, Living and Dying*. New York: International Universities Press.
Selek, S. 1974–75. "Ölümünün birinci yılında İnönü—İnönü-Atatürk ayrılığı" [İnönü, on the first anniversary of his death—İnönü's estrangement from Atatürk]. *Milliyet*, December 1974–January 1975.
Shah, Sirdar Ikbal Ali. 1934. *Kamal: Maker of Modern Turkey*. London: Herbert Joseph.
Sharpe, E. F. 1937. *Dream Analysis*. New York: Brunner/Mazel, 1978.
Shaw, S. J. 1976. *History of the Ottoman Empire and Modern Turkey*, vol. 1. Cambridge: Cambridge Unversity Press.
Shaw, S. J., and Shaw, E. K. 1977. *History of the Ottoman Empire and Modern Turkey*, vol. 2. Cambridge: Cambridge University Press.
Sinha, R. K. 1972. *Mustafa Kemal ve Mahatma Gandi (1919–1928)*. Istanbul: Milliyet Yayınları.
Stratton, A. 1972. *Sinan*. New York: Charles Scribner's Sons.
Sümer, E. A. 1970. "Changing Dynamic Aspects of the Turkish Culture and Its Significance for Child Training." In E. J. Anthony and C. Koupernik, eds., *The Child and His Family*, pp. 413–28. New York: Wiley Interscience.
Terzioğlu, S. A. 1964. *İnsancıl Atatürk* [The humanitarian Atatürk]. Istanbul: Ak Kitabevi.
Tesal, K. 1975. Interview with V. D. Volkan, 13 May, Ankara.
Tevetoğlu, F. 1971. *Atatürk'le Samsun'a çıkanlar* [Those who landed at Samsun with Atatürk]. Ankara: Ayyıldız Matbaası.
Trumpener, U. 1968. *Germany and the Ottoman Empire, 1914–1918*. Princeton, N.J.: Princeton University Press.
Tuncak, A. 1974. Interview with V. D. Volkan, 5 December, Ankara.
Turkish National Commission for UNESCO. 1963. *Atatürk*. Trans. A. J. Mango. Ankara: University of Ankara Press.
Uğur, D. 1975. Interview with V. D. Volkan, 29 April, Ankara.
Ünaydın, R. E. 1930. *Anafartalar kumandanı Mustafa Kemal ile mülâkat.* [Interview with Mustafa Kemal, Commander at Anafartalar]. Istanbul: Hamit Matbaası.

———. 1957. *Atatürk'ü özleyiş* [Longing for Atatürk]. Ankara: Türk Tarih Kurumu Basımevi.

Volkan, V. D. 1972. "The Linking Objects of Pathological Mourners." *Archives of General Psychiatry* 27:215–21.

———. 1973. "Transitional Fantasies in the Analysis of a Narcissistic Personality." *Journal of the American Psychoanalytic Association* 21:351–76.

———. 1976. *Primitive Internalized Object Relations*. New York: International Universities Press.

———. 1979. *Cyprus—War and Adaptation: A Psychoanalytic History of Two Ethnic Groups in Conflict*. Charlottesville: University Press of Virginia.

———. 1980. "Narcissistic Personality Organization and 'Reparative' Leadership." *International Journal of Group Psychotherapy* 30:131–52.

———. 1981. "Immortal Atatürk: Narcissism and Creativity in a Revolutionary Leader." In W. Muensterberger and L. B. Boyer, eds., *Psychoanalytic Study of Society*, vol. 9, pp. 221–55. New York: Psychohistory Press.

———. 1982*a*. *Linking Objects and Linking Phenomena: A Study of Forms, Symptoms, Metapsychology, and Therapy of Complicated Mourning*. New York: International Universities Press.

———. 1982*b*. "Narcissistic Personality Disorder." In J. O. Cavenar and H. K. H. Brodie, eds., *Critical Problems in Psychiatry*, pp. 332–50. Philadelphia: J. B. Lippincott & Co.

Von Mikusch, D. 1931. *Mustafa Kemal: Between Europe and Asia*. Trans. J. Linton. London: William Heinemann.

Weich, M. H. 1978. "Transitional Language." In S. Grolnick, L. Barkin, and W. Meunsterberger, eds., *Between Reality and Fantasy*, pp. 411–23. New York: Jason Aronson.

Weigert, E. 1974. Interview with N. Itzkowitz and V. D. Volkan, 29 May, Washington, D.C.

Weiker, W. F. 1973. *Political Tutelage and Democracy in Turkey: The Free Party and Its Aftermath*. Leiden: E. J. Brill.

Windsor, Edward, Duke of. [Edward VIII]. 1951. *A King's Story: The Memoirs of the Duke of Windsor*. New York: G. P. Putnam's Sons.

Winnicott, D. W. 1965. *The Maturational Process and the Facilitating Environment*. New York: International Universities Press.

———. 1971. *Playing and Reality*. New York: Basic Books.

———. 1953. "Transitional Objects and Transitional Phenomena." *International Journal of Psychoanalysis* 34:89–97.

Wortham, H. E. 1931. *Mustafa Kemal of Turkey*. Boston: Little, Brown & Co.

Xydis, S. G. 1971. "Modern Greek Nationalism." In P. F. Sugar and I. J. Lederer, eds., *Nationalism in Eastern Europe*, pp. 207–58. Seattle: University of Washington Press.

Yalman, A. E. 1922. "Büyük Millet Meclisi Reisi Başkumandan Mustafa Kemal Paşa ile bir mülâkat" [An interview with Mustafa Kemal Pasha, President of the Grand National Assembly and Commmander-in-Chief]. *Vakit*, 10 January.

Yücebaş, H. 1963. *Atatürk'ün nükteleri-fıkraları-hatıraları* [Atatürk's witty sayings, stories and memories]. 2d ed. Istanbul: Kültür Kitabevi.

Yurdanur, S. M. 1974. *Dün Atatürk, bu gün Ecevit* [Yesterday Atatürk, today Ecevit]. Istanbul: Gül Yayınları.

Index